The Pius War

The Pius War

Responses to the Critics of Pius XII

Edited by
Joseph Bottum and
David G. Dalin

LEXINGTON BOOKS
Lanham • Boulder • New York • Toronto • Oxford

LEXINGTON BOOKS

Published in the United States of America
by Lexington Books
An imprint of The Rowman & Littlefield Publishing Group, Inc.
4501 Forbes Boulevard, Suite 200, Lanham, Maryland 20706

PO Box 317
Oxford
OX2 9RU, UK

British Library Cataloguing in Publication Information Available

Library of Congress Cataloging-in-Publication Data

The Pius war : responses to the critics of Pius XII / edited by Joseph Bottum
and David G. Dalin.
        p. cm.
    Includes bibliographical references.
    ISBN 0-7391-0906-5 (alk. paper)
        1. Pius XII, Pope, 1876–1958. 2. Holocaust, Jewish (1939–1945) 3. World War,
1939–1945—Religious aspects—Catholic Church. I. Bottum, J. II. Dalin, David G.

    BX1378.P595 2004
    282'.092—dc22   2004006988

Printed in the United States of America

⊗™ The paper used in this publication meets the minimum requirements of
American National Standard for Information Sciences—Permanence of Paper for
Printed Library Materials, ANSI/NISO Z39.48–1992.

Contents

Introduction

Joseph Bottum

The Pius War is over, more or less. There will still be a few additional volumes published here and there, another article or two from writers too slow off the mark to catch their moment. But, basically, in the great argument that has raged over the last few years about the role of Pope Pius XII during World War II, the books have all been written, the reviews have all been printed, and the exchanges have all simmered down. It was a long and arduous struggle, vituperative and cruel, but, in the end, the defenders of Pius XII won every major battle. Along the way, they also lost the war.

Who, even among scholars in the field, could keep up with the flood of attacks on Pius XII that began in the late 1990s? John Cornwell gave us *Hitler's Pope*, and Michael Phayer followed with *The Catholic Church and the Holocaust*. David Kertzer ended his accusations with Pius XII in *The Popes Against the Jews*, and Susan Zuccotti reversed her previous scholarship to pen *Under His Very Windows: The Vatican and the Holocaust in Italy*. Garry Wills used Pius as the centerpiece for his reformist *Papal Sin*, as did James Carroll in *Constantine's Sword*. So, for that matter, did Daniel Goldhagen when he wrote what proved to be the most extended and straightforward assault on Catholicism in decades: *A Moral Reckoning: The Role of the Catholic Church in the Holocaust and Its Unfulfilled Duty of Repair*.

Meanwhile, the essays and occasional pieces were collected in such volumes as *Holocaust Scholars Write to the Vatican*, and *The Holocaust and the Christian World*, and *The Vatican and the Holocaust*, and *Pope Pius XII and the Holocaust*, and *Christian Responses to the Holocaust*—and on, and on, until we seemed to be facing what the exasperated reviewer John Pawlikowski called "a virtual book-of-the-month club on institutional Catholicism, anti-Semitism, and the Holocaust."

1

The champions of Pius had their share of book-length innings, as well—although, one might note, never from the same level of popular publisher as the attackers managed to find. In 1999 Pierre Blet produced *Pius XII and the Second World War According to the Archives of the Vatican* and got Paulist Press, a respectable but small Catholic house, to publish it in America. Ronald Rychlak finished his first-rate *Hitler, the War, and the Pope*, and the hardback was brought out by a press in Columbia, Missouri, known mostly for printing romance novels. For the paperback edition, Rychlak's work was picked up by the book-publishing arm of the Catholic newspaper *Our Sunday Visitor*.

Those are both fine presses in their way, and Rychlak has done well for them. But one can reasonably point out that *Our Sunday Visitor* is not quite at the level of distribution, advertising, and influence enjoyed by Doubleday, Houghton Mifflin, Knopf, and Viking—the large houses that issued the books against Pius. The religious commentator Philip Jenkins recently suggested this disparity in publisher sends a message that the mainstream view is the guilt of Pius XII, while praise for the pope belongs only to the cranks, nuts, and sectarians.

Jenkins's suggestion is worth considering. Still, no one can say Pius's supporters were squashed or censored. In just six years, Margherita Marchione managed five books in praise of the pope. The Thomistic philosopher and novelist Ralph McInerny, aggravated by the wave of slurs, issued a splenetic volume called *The Defamation of Pope Pius XII*, while Justus George Lawler (a writer best known in Catholic circles for his liberalism) penned a witty evisceration of Pius's critics called *Popes and Politics: Reform, Resentment, and the Holocaust*. José Sánchez added *Pope Pius XII and the Holocaust*, and a slew of German and Italian books might be mentioned as well, prompted, for the most part, by the popular visibility of the English-language criticisms even in Europe.

But it was primarily in book reviews and responses that the defenders of Pius XII fought out the war—which is the reason that David Dalin and I decided to edit this book, *The Pius War*, a collection of reviews, deliberately chosen from both the scholarly and popular press.

Every pope precipitates biographies, hagiographies, and maledictions, like the dropping of the rain; it is part of the job to be much written about, and the works on Eugenio Pacelli that began to appear when he became pope in 1939 seem innumerable. (Well, actually, it turns out not: In the extraordinary, eighty-thousand-word annotated bibliography that concludes this volume, William Doino Jr. has actually attempted to enumerate them. It is a task for which he may be remitted years in Purgatory.) But no supporter has yet produced a book-length biography in the wake of the recent years of extended blame. Even Rychlak's *Hitler, the War, and the Pope* was essentially reactive, devoting a thirty-page epilogue to a catalogue of the errors in Cornwell's book.

We have seen this pattern before. Rolf Hochhuth's play *The Deputy* premiered on the German stage in Berlin in 1963, and its picture of a greedy pope, concerned only about Vatican finances and silent about the Holocaust, immediately caused a firestorm of comment from the world of public intellectuals. Everyone who was anyone—the literary critic Alfred Kazin and the philosopher Karl Jaspers, to take just two examples—felt compelled to weigh in.

Hochhuth himself faded away when he tried to extend his censure to Winston Churchill, penning a play in 1967 that claimed Churchill had ordered the murder of the Polish General Wladyslaw Sikorski and, later, the murder of the pilot who had crashed Sikorski's plane. Unbeknownst to Hochhuth, the pilot was, in fact, still alive, and he won a libel judgment that badly damaged the London theater that had staged the play. Thereafter, Hochhuth found it harder to get a hearing—although, interestingly, the current notoriety of Pius XII seems to have resurrected the playwright to some degree, and in 2002 the Greek filmmaker Constantin Costa-Gravas released a movie version of *The Deputy* with the English title *Amen* (or *Eyewitness*, in other copies).

But even in Hochhuth's absence, the wide discussion about Pius XII *The Deputy* initiated in 1963 went on for several years. It produced some overheated journalistic attempts to cash in on the public interest, like Robert Katz's *Black Sabbath* and *Death in Rome* (also the target of a successful libel suit, this time brought by Pius XII's niece, Countess Elena Pacelli Rossignani against the movie version of the book). But the era brought forth as well three more serious and scholarly—indeed, by today's standards, quite moderate and thoughtful—attacks: Guenter Lewy's 1964 *The Catholic Church and Nazi Germany*, Carlo Falconi's 1965 *The Silence of Pius XII*, and Saul Friedlander's 1966 *Pius XII and the Third Reich: A Documentation*.

The brouhaha also prompted the Vatican to begin releasing material from Pius's pontificate, which slowly appeared as the eleven-volume series *Actes et Documents*. In part by relying on these new documents, but, more, simply by gathering their forces and investigating each of the incidents taken as the core of the indictment, the defenders gradually tamped down *The Deputy*'s claims about Pius XII and the Holocaust. Pope John Paul II was a consistent advocate for his predecessor, and even once-popular notions about Pius—that he was, for instance, the great reactionary opponent against whom Vatican II turned—gradually seemed to lose steam by the late 1970s and early 1980s. It took more than a decade, but the reactive reviewers appeared to carry the day, and the popular magazine press and major book publishers lost interest.

A few commentators noted that the whole thing hadn't entirely died. The historian Michael Tagliacozzo said he kept an open file labeled "Calumnies Against Pius XII." But most were unprepared when the criticism began again in the late 1990s. To journalists and cultural commentators, *Hitler's Pope* seemed almost to come out of nowhere in 1999, and it received almost entirely ecstatic reviews when it first appeared. A few skeptical journalists who remembered the Hochhuth battles—*Newsweek*'s Kenneth Woodward and the *New York Times*' Peter Steinfels, notably—doubted Cornwell's conclusions, but it had been years since they had investigated the topic, and they were unprepared to provide details about the book's errors.

Time was necessary for scholars to gin up the machine again, check the claims in *Hitler's Pope*, and publish the reviews. Some of the results proved deeply embarrassing for Cornwell, particularly the falsity of his boast that he had spent "months on end" in the archives, when he visited the Vatican for only three weeks and didn't go to the archives every day of that. The Italian letter he placed at the center of his book was, he claimed, waiting secretly "like a time bomb" until he did his research. In fact, it had been published in 1992 in a book by Emma Fattorini, who—an actual Italian, not working on a partisan translation—thought it meant very little. By the time all this came out, however, *Hitler's Pope* had ridden out its time on the best-seller list.

Pius's supporters were better prepared for Susan Zuccotti, and still better prepared for Garry Wills, and David Kertzer, and James Carroll, and, particularly, Daniel Goldhagen, who was especially harried in late 2002. By then, the whole thing had turned into a giant game of "Whack the Mole," with dozens of reviewers ready to smash their mallets down on the next author to stick up his head. Poor Peter Godman, for instance, has recently written *Hitler and the Vatican: Inside the Secret Archives that Reveal the New Story of the Nazis and the Church*, and before the book was even out of galleys, the scholars had ready a list of Godman's factual errors, missed documents, and wrongheaded translations.

As it happens, Godman appears not to have done a terrible job with *Hitler and the Vatican*. Despite its tendentious opening—how could the Vatican "not raise its voice against the cruelties of racism, the brutality of totalitarianism [and] the repression of liberties in the Third Reich?" Godman asks, although his own book goes on to prove the Vatican to some degree did exactly that—*Hitler and the Vatican* seems, on the whole, slightly more a defense than an assault, blaming mostly the Austrian bishop Alois Hudal for what other authors have charged against Eugenio Pacelli while he was nuncio in Germany and secretary of state in Rome. Just as *The Deputy* moved the archivists in Rome to release *Actes et Documents* over the next fifteen years, so the current Pius War has prompted an accelerated—by glacial Vatican norms—opening of a few new archives from the pontificate of Pius XI (1922 to 1939), whom Pacelli served as the Vatican's secretary of state. Along with an Italian Jesuit named Giovanni Sale (who has been writing a torrent of articles for the Roman Jesuit journal *La Civiltà Cattolica*), Godman is among the first scholars to use the new documents. And although he looked at only a handful—the title of his book is considerably overblown—he seems to have done so in a relatively reasonable and balanced way, particularly given the standard set by Cornwell and Goldhagen.

Unfortunately, you would never guess it from the publicity material his publisher, Free Press, issued to reviewers. Godman is carefully identified as "an atheist," lest anyone think he has a personal stake in exonerating Catholicism—but the press release begins by denying that he is, in fact, doing anything other than denouncing the Church. "Finally," it opens (and, oh, that telling, breathless "finally": *Yes, finally!*), "the full story of the Catholic Church and its connection to the Nazis can be told—thanks to the historic opening of the Vatican's most secret and controversial archives. Ever since 1542, the Catholic Church's secretive office known as the Roman Inquisition has been its most feared, and of its most powerful as the organization responsible for all matters concerning Catholic faith and morals. It was this committee of cardinals that was charged with formulating church policy toward the Nazis in the 1930s. Records of the Inquisition concerning the Nazis have been kept at the highest grade of papal secrecy, breach of which entails excommunication, until now."

Until now, you understand. *Until now!* It would be funny—in fact, it *is* funny, although one feels a little guilty quoting a publisher's press release against an author, just as one tries not to blame professors for the notes their students take in class—but the publicists at Free Press are not responding to nothing. They're trying to sell a book, and they have correctly grasped the public consensus that has been formed over the last few years.

There was a curious moment during the exchanges about *A Moral Reckoning* in which Daniel Goldhagen appeared to admit that he had gotten the details wrong, but the point remained untouched. At one level, that makes no sense: He was writing an argumentative essay, after all, and if his evidence fails, so must his conclusion. But at another level, it makes perfect sense. However successfully the reviewers refuted the pope's detractors, the sum of all those well-publicized swipes, from Cornwell on, has had a tremendous impact on what people think—the tropes they use, the pictures they form, the things journalists think they can get away with saying, the images pundits believe will prove useful when they wish to strafe a particular target.

In the public mind, at the present moment, there's almost nothing bad you can't say about Pius XII. The Vatican may end up declaring him a saint—the slow process of canonization has been winding its way through the Roman curia since the mid-1960s—but the general American public has gradually been persuaded that Pius ranks somewhere among the greatest villains ever to walk the earth. Nearly every crime of the twentieth century seems to be laid at this man's feet. Disapprove of the war in Vietnam? Well, according to the Ft. Lauderdale newspaper, Pius XII was "the main inspirer and prosecutor" of that war, despite his death in 1958. Hate racism? An article in 2002 painted him as a slavering racist who mocked the Moroccan soldiers fighting for the Free French. Another had the young Pacelli denouncing black soldiers for "routinely raping German women and children" after World War I.

Worse, he signed for the Vatican a hitherto unknown "secret pact" with Nazi Germany in the 1930s. The Catholic hierarchy has suppressed all copies, so nobody knows what it said, but it must have been bad—although it scarcely seems necessary, since (a French author assured us in 1996) the Vatican and Germany began secretly working together all the way back in 1914 to bring about a German domination of Europe. Perhaps it doesn't matter that this contradicts other theories floating around these days: that Pius XII was secretly working with Mussolini to achieve an Italian domination of Europe, for instance, or that he was secretly plotting with hardline anti-Soviets to make the Protestant United States and Great Britain the world's great powers. The point is that there is simply no depravity one can put past the man. He suppressed the anti-Nazi encyclical that Pius XI on his deathbed begged him to release. He was utterly implicated in the German's massacre of 335 Italians in the Ardeatine Caves. He expressly permitted, even encouraged, the S.S. to round up Rome's Jews in 1943.

At the root of all this lies the fact that Pius XII was, fundamentally, a follower of Hitler, a genocidal hater of the Jews in his heart and in his mind, and once we recognize him as a Nazi who somehow escaped punishment at the Nuremberg trials, we can see the origin of all the rest. He was *Hitler's Pope*, in the title of John Cornwell's book. The Holocaust happened *Under His Very Windows*, in the title of Susan Zuccotti's. Pius XII represents the highest pitch of *Papal Sin*, in Garry Wills's title. Modern times are defined by *The Popes Against the Jews*, in David Kertzer's—and just so nobody misses the point, the drawing on Michael Phayer's dust jacket features a Nazi with whip and a Catholic priest standing on the body of a Holocaust victim.

Meanwhile, the *Times* of London named him "a war criminal" in 1999. The television program *60 Minutes* insisted there was "absolutely" no difference between the writings of Pius and the writings of Hitler in 2000. Daniel Goldhagen called him a "Nazi collaborator" who "tacitly and sometimes materially aided in mass murder"—which was relatively mild compared to Goldhagen's other description of the pope as a willing servant of "the closest human analogue to the Antichrist" and a man's whose Church's two-thousand-year history is nothing but preparation for the Holocaust's slaughter of the Jews.

Forget the often-denounced "silence of Pius XII" about the Holocaust. Pacelli didn't just accept Hitler; he *loved* the Nazi leader and agreed with him about everything. Did you know that shortly after World War I he gave the starving Adolf Hitler money because he so much approved the young man's ideas? (This, by the way, is from a book that also reveals how Pius XII was merely the puppet of his Vatican housekeeper, Sister Pascalina.) Perhaps avarice to increase Vatican finances is what made him force reluctant Swiss banks to confiscate Jewish accounts. But only enduring belief in Nazi ideas can explain why Pius was the chief funder and organizer of the ratline that helped hunted Gestapo agents escape to South America after Hitler's defeat.

Regardless, the pope was manifestly an anti-Semite of the first water—John Cornwell declared his views "of the kind that Julius Streicher would soon offer the German public in every issue of his notorious Nazi newspaper *Der Stürmer*"—except when Pius is said to have merely allowed Hitler free rein, accepting the murder of the Jews as the price to be paid for getting Germany to war against the greater menace of the godless Communists in Soviet Russia. These notions are not necessarily contradictory. In a 1997 essay, the widely published Richard L. Rubenstein concluded: "during World War II Pope Pius XII and the vast majority of European Christian leaders regarded the elimination of the Jews as no less beneficial than the destruction of Bolshevism."

All of these claims are mistaken, of course—and more than mistaken: demonstrably and obviously untrue, outrages upon history and fellow feeling for the humanity of previous generations. But none of them is merely the lurid fantasy of conspiracy mongers huddled together in paranoia on their Internet lists. Every one of these assertions has been made in recent years by books and articles published by mainstream and popular American publishers.

And when we draw from them their general conclusion—when we reach the point at which Rubenstein, for example, has arrived—then discourse is over. Research into primary sources, argument about interpretation, the scholar's task of weighing historical circumstance: All of this is *quibbling*, an attempt to be fair to monstrosity, and by such fairness to condone, excuse, and participate in it. After printing the opening salvo of Goldhagen's offensive against Catholicism, the publisher of the *New Republic* announced that Pius XII was, simply and purely, "a wicked man." And once one has said that, one has said all that needs to be known.

It was here that the Pius War was lost—and lost for what I believe will prove at least a generation—despite the victories of the reviewers. The question of "why now?" is an interesting one. Philip Jenkins understands it as not particular to Pius XII at all, but merely a convenient trope by which American commentators express what he calls an entirely new form of anti-Catholicism. Others see it in a continuum of more old-fashioned American distaste for the Whore of Babylon that dwells in Rome, spinning Jesuitical plots. Ralph McInerny linked it darkly to contemporary hatred of the Church's stand against abortion. Noting the predominance of a certain sort of Catholic author in these debates, Justus George Lawler suggested the root lay in a "papaphobia" that has turned against the entire idea of authority. David Dalin argued that it was finally about John Paul II, not Pius XII: an intra-Catholic fight over the future of the papacy, with the Holocaust merely the biggest club around for opponents of the current pope to use against his supporters.

All of these are quite interesting. None of these is quite persuasive. What the real cause may be, I cannot decide for myself. But it is into a world of public and scholarly opinion formed by books like *Hitler's Pope* that every new attempt to consider the issue must enter—including this collection of reviews, *The Pius War*. Relatively mild efforts to praise the pope (such as José Sánchez's *Pius XII and the Holocaust* in 2002), like relatively mild efforts to disparage him (such as Martin Rhonheimer's essay in *First Things* in November 2003), are as clueless about the situation in which they appear as the proverbial visitors from Mars. Indeed, there is something willful and maddening in their would-be tone of Olympian detachment. In a world of imbalance, what but pressure on the other side can restore the balance that a true scholar is supposed to love? I am convinced that will we not achieve anything resembling historical accuracy until all the presently existing views are cleared away—and thus, that the job for every honest writer who takes up the topic now is to correct the overblown hatred of Pius XII.

I did not always think so. A minor member of the chattering classes, I entered the Pius War in 2000 with an essay that was far from an exoneration of the pope. Attempting to strike a balance (the *voice* of sweet reason and even-handedness is always easier for a writer to cobble up than the reality), I suggested in an article for *Crisis* magazine that perhaps no one could have been expected to do better than Pius XII, but, even so, what he did was not enough when faced with World War II and the Holocaust.

And there I left it. Although the continued flow of books attacking the pope began to annoy me, they even more began to bore me, and I refused to commission a review of any of them for the *Weekly Standard*, the magazine at which I work. But one day, I bumped into the historian and rabbi David Dalin on the street in Washington, D.C. Over coffee, he mentioned that he had been reading John Cornwell and Susan Zuccotti, and although it wasn't precisely his field—and, anyway, he'd never thought particularly well of Pius XII—still, there was something about these books he didn't trust: some manifest desire to find guilt whether it was due or not, some adventitious and hungry tone that put his teeth on edge.

And at that point, there on M Street, I had an idea. It occurred to me that if a scholarly American reader like David Dalin was feeling this way, then probably others were beginning to as well. A neoconservative and center-right publication, the *Weekly Standard* is widely read by the pundit class in New York and Washington, and so I commissioned David to write an omnibus review of the enormous set of new books on Pius. Magazine editors want, most of all, to get out just enough ahead of opinion that it looks as though they're leading the parade, giving first expression to an idea inchoate but building among readers. More, I imagined the vast majority of neoconservative commentators—together with neoliberal and center-left, for that matter—would nod in agreement when the review appeared.

Events proved me wrong. More prescient than I in understanding where the debate was actually going, David Dalin grew furious the more he read in the popular books. Eventually he turned in an essay that went far beyond any claim I had been willing to make. Published in February 2001, it concluded that Pius XII deserves recognition among Jews as a Righteous Gentile whose church saved hundreds of thousands of lives during the Holocaust.

The reaction, in the arena I had hoped to influence, was brutal, and the *Weekly Standard* found itself leading the parade only in the sense that a man running for his life leads the mob pursuing him. Judith Shulevitz of the *New York Times* responded in the way I had supposed most would, writing a piece for the *Times'* Sunday book section that grumbled a little, but eventually concluded the claims about Pius XII were overwrought and Dalin was basically right: The pope did "more than most to shelter Jews."

But the center-left *New Republic* immediately commissioned Daniel Goldhagen to interrupt the book he was writing on genocides and savage Pius XII instead—which he did in what is said to be the longest essay ever published in the magazine's pages. The neoconservative *Commentary* was so rankled, it did what it would not have done in nearly any other circumstance: publishing a long rebuke of the *Weekly Standard* by a leftist author who had already made many of the same complaints in an article for *Christian Century*. At a Holocaust symposium the next summer, one conservative editor declared he would never read another word David Dalin wrote—because Pius XII was beyond apology. Curiously, this was the same editor who had told me the year before that my own nuanced defense of the pope in *Crisis* seemed exactly the right way to understand the topic. But the momentum of the continuing offensive against Pius was stronger than I had guessed, and in my own journalistic world, David Dalin's essay served mostly to harden opinion toward exactly the opposite of what I had intended.

In a handful of other worlds—particularly conservative Catholic ones—the essay did quite well. But those were the worlds that hardly needed it. For people of that persuasion, the omnipresent assault on Pius XII drives them toward the worst possibilities for their communities: a dread that rampant anti-Catholicism is shortly to unleash itself upon them, a hunger to flee to small fellowships of the saved away from the corruption of the public square, an embracing of a self-image as victims, and a belief that a dark cloud rests over the sum of modern times. "Even a Jewish writer—and a rabbi, too—sees the slander for what it is," they say. And thereby they confirm, for those whom the essay only angered, that David Dalin let himself be used *as a Jew* to advance a sectarian Catholic agenda (mine, presumably, although my friends have had the courtesy not to say that part to my face). And so the whole coil curls up around itself once more, and we get no forwarder.

Perhaps this collection, *The Pius War*, will help. However large it personally looms, the part played by David and myself was small. The attempt to sift through the endless stream of books about Pius XII in recent years was actually carried out by indefatigable reviewers in dozens of magazines and journals, responding to the texts one by one.

So, in addition to essays by David Dalin and myself, this book contains reviews by such scholars as John Jay Hughes and John S. Conway, both students of the Holocaust for many years. The book adds the work of a pair of lawyers who have examined the evidence, Kevin M. Doyle and Ronald Rychlak. It reaches from the German historian Rainer Decker to the American writer Justus George Lawler. The patristics scholar Robert Louis Wilken reads James Carroll's work, and the Thomistic philosopher Russell Hittinger reads David Kertzer's. The widely published author Michael Novak reacts to one particular attack, and William Doino Jr. concludes the book by responding to them all.

Indeed, Doino's annotated bibliography—an eighty-thousand-word walk through the authors who have written on Pius XII and the topics on which they have concentrated—is an extraordinary piece of work. Written especially for *The Pius War*, and strongly aimed toward answering Pius's critics, it will prove a powerful resource for anyone who wants to work in the field.

The only thing that keeps Doino's bibliography from being definitive is the fact that new material seems to arrive every week. The controversy has motivated additional research, and as far as I can tell, all this latest information tells in favor of Pius XII. A recently discovered 1923 letter to the Vatican from Eugenio Pacelli, then nuncio to Germany, for instance, denounces Hitler's *putsch* and warns against his anti-Semitism and anti-Catholicism. A document from April 1933, just months after Hitler obtained power, reveals how Pacelli (then secretary of state) ordered the new German nuncio, Cesare Orsenigo, to protest Nazi anti-Semitism.

Meanwhile, newly examined diplomatic documents show that in 1937 Cardinal Pacelli warned A.W. Klieforth, the American consul to Berlin, that Hitler was "an untrustworthy scoundrel and fundamentally wicked person," to quote Klieforth, who also wrote that Pacelli "did not believe Hitler capable of moderation, and . . . fully supported the German bishops in their anti-Nazi stand." This was matched with the discovery of Pacelli's anti-Nazi report, written the following year for President Roosevelt and filed with Ambassador Joseph Kennedy, which declared that the Church regarded compromise with the Third Reich as "out of the question."

Archives from American espionage agencies have recently confirmed Pius XII's active involvement in plots to overthrow Hitler. A pair of newly found letters, written in 1940 on the letterhead of the Vatican's Secretariat of State, give Pius XII's orders that financial assistance be sent to Campagna for the explicit purpose of assisting interned Jews suffering from Mussolini's racial policies. And the Israeli government has finally released Adolf Eichmann's diaries, portions of which confirm the Vatican's obstruction of the Nazis' roundup of Rome's Jews.

There's more, a regular flow of new material. Intercepts of Nazi communications released from the United States' National Archives include such passages as "Vatican has apparently for a long time been assisting many Jews to escape," in a Nazi dispatch from Rome to Berlin on October 26, 1943, ten days after the Germans' Roman round-up. New oral testimony from such Catholic rescuers as Monsignor John Patrick Carroll-Abbing, Don Aldo Brunacci, Sister Mathilda Spielmann, and Father Giacomo Martegani insists that Pius XII gave them explicit orders and direct assistance to help persecuted Jews in Italy. The posthumous publication this year of Harold Tittmann's memoir, *Inside the Vatican of Pius XII*, is particularly interesting, for in it the American diplomat reveals, for the first time, that Pius XII's wartime conduct drew upon advice from the German resistance.

Out of all this, one might begin to build a new case *for* Pius XII. My own sense is that the anti-Pius books are coming to an end. Even small academic publishers seem to be tiring of the genre, and the market for such books may have at last dried up. Still, I could be wrong. America seems to have an inexhaustible appetite for books about World War II (especially the military aspects) and a nearly equal appetite for books about the Holocaust. Robert Katz's recent *The Battle for Rome: The Germans, the Allies, the Partisans, and the Pope* manages to marry the military strategy and the Holocaust—with a large dose of bitter anti-Catholicism thrown in for good measure, the result of enduring anger about the criminal-libel case he lost in italy over his earlier book blaming Pius for the massacre at the Ardeatine Caves. The success or failure of *The Battle for Rome* will make a useful measure of our current publishing situation.

But, however the market looks, what we really need now is a new biography of Pius XII during those years: a *nonreactive* account of his life and times, a book driven not by the reviewer's instinct to answer charges but the biographer's impulse to tell an accurate story. Before that can be done well, I think, the archives of Pius XII's pontificate will have to be fully catalogued and opened. Documents released here and there are useful, but *useful* is a dangerous word in this context, for the use is always in building an argument: a laying out of evidence to make or rebut a charge, rather than a knowledge of the pope's day-to-day actions. The Vatican has begun to open some archives earlier than scheduled under the various time locks, and it promises to open more.

In the meantime, the reviewers' contributions remain, some of the best of which David Dalin and I have gathered for this volume. But the reviewers' dilemma remains as well: They won the battles, but how are they going to win the war?

Washington, D.C.
February 1, 2004

1

Pius XII and the Jews

David G. Dalin

(an omnibus review from the *Weekly Standard*, February 26, 2001, pp. 31–39)

Even before Pius XII died in 1958, the charge that his papacy had been friendly to the Nazis was circulating in Europe, a piece of standard communist agitprop against the West. It sank for a few years under the flood of tributes, from Jews and gentiles alike, that followed the pope's death, only to bubble up again with the 1963 debut of *The Deputy*, a play by a left-wing German writer (and former member of the Hitler Youth) named Rolf Hochhuth.

The Deputy was fictional and highly polemical, claiming that Pius XII's concern for Vatican finances left him indifferent to the destruction of European Jewry. But Hochhuth's seven-hour play nonetheless received considerable notice, sparking a controversy that lasted through the 1960s. And now, more than thirty years later, that controversy has suddenly broken out again, for reasons not immediately clear.

Indeed, "broken out" doesn't describe the current torrent. In the last eighteen months, nine books that treat Pius XII have appeared: John Cornwell's *Hitler's Pope*, Pierre Blet's *Pius XII and the Second World War*, Garry Wills's *Papal Sin*, Margherita Marchione's *Pope Pius XII*, Ronald J. Rychlak's *Hitler, the War, and the Pope*, Michael Phayer's *The Catholic Church and the Holocaust, 1930–1965*, Susan Zuccotti's *Under His Very Windows*, Ralph McInerny's *The Defamation of Pius XII*, and, most recently, James Carroll's *Constantine's Sword*.

Since four of these—the ones by Blet, Marchione, Rychlak, and McInerny—are defenses of the pope (and two, the books by Wills and Carroll, take up Pius only as part of a broad attack against Catholicism), the picture may look balanced. In fact, to read all nine is to conclude that Pius's defenders have the stronger case—with Rychlak's *Hitler, the War, and the Pope* the best and most careful of the recent works, an elegant tome of serious, critical scholarship.

Still, it is the books vilifying the pope that have received most of the attention, particularly *Hitler's Pope*, a widely reviewed volume marketed with the announcement that Pius XII was "the most dangerous churchman in modern history," without whom "Hitler might never have . . . been able to press forward with the Holocaust." The "silence" of the pope is becoming more and more firmly established as settled opinion in the American media: "Pius XII's elevation of Catholic self-interest over Catholic conscience was the lowest point in modern Catholic history," the *New York Times* remarked, almost in passing, in a review last month of Carroll's *Constantine's Sword*.

Curiously, nearly everyone pressing this line today—from the ex-seminarians John Cornwell and Garry Wills to the ex-priest James Carroll—is a lapsed or angry Catholic. For Jewish leaders of a previous generation, the campaign against Pius XII would have been a source of shock. During and after the war, many well-known Jews—Albert Einstein, Golda Meir, Moshe Sharett, Rabbi Isaac Herzog, and innumerable others—publicly expressed their gratitude to Pius. In his 1967 book *Three Popes and the Jews*, the diplomat Pinchas Lapide (who served as Israeli consul in Milan and interviewed Italian Holocaust survivors) declared the Church under Pius XII "was instrumental in saving at least 700,000, but probably as many as 860,000 Jews from certain death at Nazi hands."

This is not to say that Eugenio Pacelli—the powerful churchman who served as nuncio in Bavaria and Germany from 1917 to 1929, then as Vatican secretary of state from 1930 to 1939, before becoming Pope Pius XII six months before World War II began—was as much a friend to the Jews as John Paul II has been. Nor is it to say that Pius was ultimately successful as a defender of Jews. Despite his desperate efforts to maintain peace, the war came, and, despite his protests against German atrocities, the slaughter of the Holocaust occurred. Even without benefit of hindsight, a careful study reveals that the Catholic Church missed opportunities to influence events, failed to credit fully the Nazis' intentions, and was infected in some of its members with a casual anti-Semitism that would countenance—and, in a few horrifying instances, affirm—the Nazi ideology.

But to make Pius XII a target of our moral outrage against the Nazis, and to count Catholicism among the institutions delegitimized by the horror of the Holocaust, reveals a failure of historical understanding. Almost none of the recent books about Pius XII and the Holocaust is actually about Pius XII and the Holocaust. Their real topic proves to be an intra-Catholic argument about the direction of the Church today, with the Holocaust simply the biggest club available for liberal Catholics to use against traditionalists.

A theological debate about the future of the papacy is obviously something in which non-Catholics should not involve themselves too deeply. But Jews, whatever their feelings about the Catholic Church, have a duty to reject any attempt to usurp the Holocaust and use it for partisan purposes in such a debate—particularly when the attempt disparages the testimony of Holocaust survivors and spreads to inappropriate figures the condemnation that belongs to Hitler and the Nazis.

The technique for recent attacks on Pius XII is simple. It requires only that favorable evidence be read in the worst light and treated to the strictest test, while unfavorable evidence is read in the best light and treated to no test.

So, for instance, when Cornwell sets out in *Hitler's Pope* to prove Pius an anti-Semite (an accusation even the pontiff's bitterest opponents have rarely leveled), he makes much of Pacelli's reference in a 1917 letter to the "Jewish cult"—as though for an Italian Catholic prelate born in 1876 the word "cult" had the same resonances it has in English today, and as though Cornwell himself does not casually refer to the Catholic cult of the Assumption and the cult of the Virgin Mary. (The most immediately helpful part of *Hitler, the War, and the Pope* may be the thirty-page epilogue Rychlak devotes to demolishing this kind of argument in *Hitler's Pope*.)

The same pattern is played out in Susan Zuccotti's *Under His Very Windows*. For example, there exists testimony from a Good Samaritan priest that Bishop Giuseppe Nicolini of Assisi, holding a letter in his hand, declared that the pope had written to request help for Jews during the German roundup of Italian Jews in 1943. But because the priest did not actually read the letter, Zuccotti speculates that the bishop may have been deceiving him—and thus that this testimony should be rejected.

Compare this skeptical approach to evidence with her treatment, for example, of a 1967 interview in which the German diplomat Eitel F. Mollhausen said he had sent information to the Nazis' ambassador to the Vatican, Ernst von Weizsäcker, and "assumed" that Weizsäcker passed it on to Church "officials." Zuccotti takes this as unquestionable proof that the pope had direct foreknowledge of the German roundup. (A fair reading suggests Pius had heard rumors and raised them with the Nazi occupiers. Princess Enza Pignatelli Aragona Cortés reported that when she broke in on the pope with the news of the roundup early on the morning of October 16, 1943, his first words were: "But the Germans had promised not to touch the Jews!")

With this dual standard, recent writers have little trouble arriving at two preordained conclusions. The first is that the Catholic Church must shoulder the blame for the Holocaust: "Pius XII was the most guilty," as Zuccotti puts it. And the second is that Catholicism's guilt is due to aspects of the Church that John Paul II now represents.

Indeed, in the concluding chapter of *Hitler's Pope* and throughout *Papal Sin* and *Constantine's Sword*, the parallel comes clear: John Paul's traditionalism is of a piece with Pius's alleged anti-Semitism; the Vatican's current stand on papal authority is in a direct line with complicity in the Nazis' extermination of the Jews. Faced with such monstrous moral equivalence and misuse of the Holocaust, how can we not object?

It is true that during the controversy over *The Deputy* and again during the Vatican's slow hearing of the case for his canonization (ongoing since 1965), Pius had Jewish detractors. In 1964, for example, Guenter Lewy produced *The Catholic Church and Nazi Germany*, and, in 1966, Saul Friedlander added *Pius XII and the Third Reich*. Both volumes claimed that Pius's anticommunism led him to support Hitler as a bulwark against the Russians.

As accurate information on Soviet atrocities has mounted since 1989, an obsession with Stalinism seems less foolish than it may have in the mid-1960s. But, in fact, the evidence has mounted as well that Pius accurately ranked the threats. In 1942, for example, he told a visitor, "The Communist danger does exist, but at this time the Nazi danger is more serious." He intervened with the American bishops to support lend-lease for the Soviets, and he explicitly refused to bless the Nazi invasion of Russia. (The charge of overheated anticommunism is nonetheless still alive: In *Constantine's Sword*, James Carroll attacks the 1933 concordat Hitler signed for Germany by asking, "Is it conceivable that Pacelli would have negotiated any such agreement with the Bolsheviks in Moscow?"—apparently not realizing that in the mid-1920s, Pacelli tried exactly that.)

In any case, Pius had his Jewish defenders as well. In addition to Lapide's *Three Popes and the Jews*, one might list *A Question of Judgment*, the 1963 pamphlet from the Anti-Defamation League's Joseph Lichten, and the excoriating reviews of Friedlander by Livia Rothkirchen, the historian of Slovakian Jewry at Yad Vashem. Jenö Lévai, the great Hungarian historian, was so angered by accusations of papal silence that he wrote *Hungarian Jewry and the Papacy: Pius XII Did Not Remain Silent* (published in English in 1968), with a powerful introduction by Robert M.W. Kempner, deputy chief U.S. prosecutor at Nuremberg.

In response to the new attacks on Pius, several Jewish scholars have spoken out over the last year. Sir Martin Gilbert told an interviewer that Pius deserves not blame but thanks. Michael Tagliacozzo, the leading authority on Roman Jews during the Holocaust, added, "I have a folder on my table in Israel entitled 'Calumnies Against Pius XII.' . . . Without him, many of our own would not be alive." Richard Breitman (the only historian authorized to study U.S. espionage files from World War II) noted that secret documents prove the extent to which "Hitler distrusted the Holy See because it hid Jews."

Still, Lapide's 1967 book remains the most influential work by a Jew on the topic, and in the thirty-four years since he wrote, much material has become available in the Vatican's archives and elsewhere. New oral-history centers have gathered an impressive body of interviews with Holocaust survivors, military chaplains, and Catholic civilians. Given the recent attacks, the time has come for a new defense of Pius—because, despite allegations to the contrary, the best historical evidence now confirms both that Pius XII was not silent and that almost no one at the time thought him so.

In January 1940, for instance, the pope issued instructions for Vatican Radio to reveal "the dreadful cruelties of uncivilized tyranny" the Nazis were inflicting on Jewish and Catholic Poles. Reporting the broadcast the following week, the *Jewish Advocate* of Boston praised it for what it was: an "outspoken denunciation of German atrocities in Nazi Poland, declaring they affronted the moral conscience of mankind." The *New York Times* editorialized: "Now the Vatican has spoken, with authority that cannot be questioned, and has confirmed the worst intimations of terror which have come out of the Polish darkness." In England, the *Manchester Guardian* hailed Vatican Radio as "tortured Poland's most powerful advocate."

Any fair and thorough reading of the evidence demonstrates that Pius XII was a persistent critic of Nazism. Consider just a few highlights of his opposition before the war:

- Of the forty-four speeches Pacelli gave in Germany as papal nuncio between 1917 and 1929, forty denounced some aspect of the emerging Nazi ideology.
- In March 1935, he wrote an open letter to the bishop of Cologne calling the Nazis "false prophets with the pride of Lucifer."
- That same year, he assailed ideologies "possessed by the superstition of race and blood" to an enormous crowd of pilgrims at Lourdes. At Notre Dame in Paris two years later, he named Germany "that noble and powerful nation whom bad shepherds would lead astray into an ideology of race."
- The Nazis were "diabolical," he told friends privately. Hitler "is completely obsessed," he said to his long-time housekeeper, Sister Pascalina. "All that is not of use to him, he destroys; . . . this man is capable of trampling on corpses." Meeting in 1935 with the heroic anti-Nazi Dietrich von Hildebrand, he declared, "There can be no possible reconciliation" between Christianity and Nazi racism; they are like "fire and water."
- The year after Pacelli became secretary of state in 1930, Vatican Radio was established, essentially under his control. The Vatican newspaper *L'Osservatore Romano* had an uneven record, though it would improve as Pacelli gradually took charge (extensively reporting Kristallnacht in 1938, for example). But the radio station was always good—making such controversial broadcasts as the request that listeners pray for the persecuted Jews in Germany after the 1935 Nuremberg Legislation.
- It was while Pacelli was his predecessor's chief adviser that Pius XI made the famous statement to a group of Belgian pilgrims in 1938 that

"anti-Semitism is inadmissible; spiritually we are all Semites." And it was Pacelli who drafted Pius XI's encyclical *Mit brennender Sorge*, "With Burning Concern," a condemnation of Germany among the harshest ever issued by the Holy See. Indeed, throughout the 1930s, Pacelli was widely lampooned in the Nazi press as Pius XI's "Jew-loving" cardinal because of the more than fifty-five protests he sent the Germans as the Vatican secretary of state.

To these must be added highlights of Pius XII's actions during the war:

- His first encyclical, *Summi Pontificatus*, rushed out in 1939 to beg for peace, was in part a declaration that the proper role of the papacy was to plead to both warring sides rather than to blame one. But it very pointedly quoted St. Paul—"there is neither Gentile nor Jew"—using the word "Jew" specifically in the context of rejecting racial ideology. The *New York Times* greeted the encyclical with a front-page headline on October 28, 1939: "Pope Condemns Dictators, Treaty Violators, Racism." Allied airplanes dropped thousands of copies on Germany in an effort to raise anti-Nazi sentiment.
- In 1939 and 1940, Pius acted as a secret intermediary between the German plotters against Hitler and the British. He would similarly risk warning the Allies about the impending German invasions of Holland, Belgium, and France.
- In March 1940, Pius granted an audience to Joachim von Ribbentrop, the German foreign minister and the only high-ranking Nazi to visit the Vatican. The Germans' understanding of Pius's position, at least, was clear: Ribbentrop chastised the pope for siding with the Allies— whereupon Pius began reading from a long list of German atrocities. "In the burning words he spoke to Herr Ribbentrop," the *New York Times* reported on March 14, Pius "came to the defense of Jews in Germany and Poland."
- When French bishops issued pastoral letters in 1942 attacking deportations, Pius sent his nuncio to protest to the Vichy government against "the inhuman arrests and deportations of Jews from the French-occupied zone to Silesia and parts of Russia." Vatican Radio commented on the bishops' letters six days in a row—at a time when listening to Vatican Radio was a crime in Germany and Poland for which some were put to death. ("Pope Is Said to Plead for Jews Listed for Removal from France," the *New York Times* headline read on August 6, 1942. "Vichy Seizes Jews; Pope Pius Ignored," the *Times* reported three weeks later.) In retaliation, in the fall of 1942, Goebbels's office distributed ten million copies of a pamphlet naming Pius XII as the "pro-Jewish pope" and explicitly citing his interventions in France.

- In the summer of 1944, after the liberation of Rome but before the war's end, Pius told a group of Roman Jews who had come to thank him for his protection: "For centuries, Jews have been unjustly treated and despised. It is time they were treated with justice and humanity, God wills it and the Church wills it. St. Paul tells us that the Jews are our brothers. They should also be welcomed as friends."

As these and hundreds of other examples are disparaged, one by one, in recent books attacking Pius XII, the reader loses sight of the huge bulk of them, their cumulative effect that left no one, the Nazis least of all, in doubt about the pope's position.

A deeper examination reveals the consistent pattern. Writers like Cornwell and Zuccotti see the pope's 1941 Christmas address, for example, as notable primarily for its failure to use the language we would use today. But contemporary observers thought it quite explicit. In its editorial the following day, the *New York Times* declared, "The voice of Pius XII is a lonely voice in the silence and darkness enveloping Europe this Christmas. . . . In calling for a 'real new order' based on 'liberty, justice, and love,' . . . the pope put himself squarely against Hitlerism."

So, too, the pope's Christmas message the following year—in which he expressed his concern "for those hundreds of thousands who, without any fault of their own, sometimes only by reason of their nationality or race, are marked down for death or progressive extinction"—was widely understood to be a public condemnation of the Nazi extermination of the Jews. Indeed, the Germans themselves saw it as such: "His speech is one long attack on everything we stand for. . . . He is clearly speaking on behalf of the Jews. . . . He is virtually accusing the German people of injustice toward the Jews, and makes himself the mouthpiece of the Jewish war criminals," an internal Nazi analysis reads.

This Nazi awareness, moreover, had potentially dire consequences. There were ample precedents for the pope to fear an invasion: Napoleon had besieged the Vatican in 1809, capturing Pius VII at bayonet point; Pius IX fled Rome for his life after the assassination of his chancellor; and Leo XIII was driven into temporary exile in the late nineteenth century.

Still, Pius XII was "ready to let himself be deported to a concentration camp, rather than do anything against his conscience," Mussolini's foreign minister railed. Hitler spoke openly of entering the Vatican to "pack up that whole whoring rabble," and Pius knew of the various Nazi plans to kidnap him. Ernst von Weizsäcker has written that he regularly warned Vatican officials against provoking Berlin. The Nazi ambassador to Italy, Rudolf Rahn, similarly describes one of Hitler's kidnapping plots and the effort by German diplomats to prevent it. General Karl Wolff testified to having received orders from Hitler in 1943 to "occupy as soon as possible the Vatican and Vatican

City, secure the archives and the art treasures, which have a unique value, and transfer the pope, together with the Curia, for their protection, so that they cannot fall into the hands of the Allies and exert a political influence." Early in December 1943, Wolff managed to talk Hitler out of the plan.

In assessing what actions Pius XII might have taken, many (I among them) wish that explicit excommunications had been announced. The Catholic-born Nazis had already incurred automatic excommunication for everything from failure to attend Mass to unconfessed murder to public repudiation of Christianity. And, as his writings and table-talk make clear, Hitler had ceased to consider himself a Catholic—indeed, considered himself an anti-Catholic—long before he came to power. But a papal declaration of excommunication might have done some good.

Then again, it might not. Don Luigi Sturzo, founder of the Christian Democratic movement in wartime Italy, pointed out that the last times "a nominal excommunication was pronounced against a head of state," neither Queen Elizabeth I nor Napoleon had changed policy. And there is reason to believe provocation would, as Margherita Marchione puts it, "have resulted in violent retaliation, the loss of many more Jewish lives, especially those then under the protection of the Church, and an intensification of the persecution of Catholics."

Holocaust survivors such as Marcus Melchior, the chief rabbi of Denmark, argued that "if the pope had spoken out, Hitler would probably have massacred more than six million Jews and perhaps ten times ten million Catholics, if he had the power to do so." Robert M.W. Kempner called upon his experience at the Nuremberg trials to say (in a letter to the editor after *Commentary* published an excerpt from Guenter Lewy in 1964), "Every propaganda move of the Catholic Church against Hitler's Reich would have been not only 'provoking suicide,' . . . but would have hastened the execution of still more Jews and priests."

This is hardly a speculative concern. A Dutch bishops' pastoral letter condemning "the unmerciful and unjust treatment meted out to Jews" was read in Holland's Catholic churches in July 1942. The well-intentioned letter—which declared that it was inspired by Pius XII—backfired. As Pinchas Lapide notes: "The saddest and most thought-provoking conclusion is that whilst the Catholic clergy in Holland protested more loudly, expressly, and frequently against Jewish persecutions than the religious hierarchy of any other Nazi-occupied country, more Jews—some 110,000 or 79 percent of the total—were deported from Holland to death camps."

Bishop Jean Bernard of Luxembourg, an inmate of Dachau from 1941 to 1942, notified the Vatican that "whenever protests were made, treatment of prisoners worsened immediately." Late in 1942, Archbishop Sapieha of Cracow and two other Polish bishops, having experienced the Nazis' savage reprisals, begged Pius not to publish his letters about conditions in Poland. Even Susan Zuccotti admits that in the case of the Roman Jews the pope "might well have been influenced by a concern for Jews in hiding and for their Catholic protectors."

One might ask, of course, what could have been worse than the mass murder of six million Jews? The answer is the slaughter of hundreds of thousands more. And it was toward saving those it could that the Vatican worked. The fate of Italian Jews has become a major topic of Pius's critics, the failure of Catholicism at its home supposedly demonstrating the hypocrisy of any modern papal claim to moral authority. (Notice, for example, Zuccotti's title: *Under His Very Windows.*) But the fact remains that while approximately 80 percent of European Jews perished during World War II, 85 percent of Italian Jews survived.

In the months Rome was under German occupation, Pius XII instructed Italy's clergy to save lives by all means. (A neglected source for Pius's actions during this time is the 1965 memoir *But for the Grace of God*, by Monsignor J. Patrick Carroll-Abbing, who worked under Pius as a rescuer.) Beginning in October 1943, Pius asked churches and convents throughout Italy to shelter Jews. As a result—and despite the fact that Mussolini and the fascists yielded to Hitler's demand for deportations—many Italian Catholics defied the German orders.

In Rome, around 160 convents and monasteries sheltered some 5,000 Jews. Many found refuge at the pope's summer residence at Castel Gandolfo. Sixty Jews lived for nine months at the Gregorian University, and many were sheltered in the cellar of the pontifical biblical institute. Hundreds found sanctuary within the Vatican itself. Following Pius's instructions, individual Italian priests, monks, nuns, cardinals, and bishops were instrumental in preserving thousands of Jewish lives. Cardinal Boetto of Genoa saved at least 800. The bishop of Assisi hid 300 Jews for over two years. The bishop of Campagna and two of his relatives saved 961 more in Fiume.

Cardinal Pietro Palazzini, then assistant vice rector of the Seminario Romano, hid Michael Tagliacozzo and other Italian Jews at the seminary (which was Vatican property) for several months in 1943 and 1944. In 1985, Yad Vashem, Israel's Holocaust Memorial, honored the cardinal as a righteous gentile—and, in accepting the honor, Palazzini stressed that "the merit is entirely Pius XII's, who ordered us to do whatever we could to save the Jews from persecution." Some of the laity helped as well and, in their testimony afterwards, consistently attributed their inspiration to the pope.

Again, the most eloquent testimony is the Nazis' own. Fascist documents published in 1998 (and summarized in Marchione's *Pope Pius XII*) speak of a German plan, dubbed "Rabat-Fohn," to be executed in January 1944. The plan called for the eighth division of the S.S. cavalry, disguised as Italians, to seize St. Peter's and "massacre Pius XII with the entire Vatican"—and specifically names "the papal protest in favor of the Jews" as the cause.

A similar story can be traced across Europe. There is room to argue that more ought to have been attempted by the Catholic Church—for the unanswerable facts remain that Hitler did come to power, World War II did occur, and six million Jews did die. But the place to begin that argument is with the truth that people of the time, Nazis and Jews alike, understood the pope to be the world's most prominent opponent of the Nazi ideology:

- As early as December 1940, in an article in *Time* magazine, Albert Einstein paid tribute to Pius: "Only the Church stood squarely across the path of Hitler's campaign for suppressing the truth. I never had any special interest in the Church before, but now I feel a great affection and admiration because the Church alone has had the courage and persistence to stand for intellectual truth and moral freedom. I am forced thus to confess that what I once despised, I now praise unreservedly."
- In 1943, Chaim Weizmann, who would become Israel's first president, wrote that "the Holy See is lending its powerful help wherever it can, to mitigate the fate of my persecuted co-religionists."
- Moshe Sharett, Israel's second prime minister, met with Pius in the closing days of the war and "told him that my first duty was to thank him, and through him the Catholic Church, on behalf of the Jewish public for all they had done in the various countries to rescue Jews."
- Rabbi Isaac Herzog, chief rabbi of Israel, sent a message in February 1944 declaring, "The people of Israel will never forget what His Holiness and his illustrious delegates, inspired by the eternal principles of religion, which form the very foundation of true civilization, are doing for our unfortunate brothers and sisters in the most tragic hour of our history, which is living proof of Divine Providence in this world."
- In September 1945, Leon Kubowitzky, secretary general of the World Jewish Congress, personally thanked the pope for his interventions, and the World Jewish Congress donated $20,000 to Vatican charities "in recognition of the work of the Holy See in rescuing Jews from fascist and Nazi persecutions."
- In 1955, when Italy celebrated the tenth anniversary of its liberation, the Union of Italian Jewish Communities proclaimed April 17 a "Day of Gratitude" for the pope's wartime assistance.
- On May 26, 1955, the Israeli Philharmonic Orchestra flew to Rome to give in the Vatican a special performance of Beethoven's Seventh Symphony—an expression of the State of Israel's enduring gratitude to the pope for help given the Jewish people during the Holocaust.

This last example is particularly significant. As a matter of state policy, the Israeli Philharmonic has never played the music of Richard Wagner because of his well-known reputation as "Hitler's composer," the cultural patron saint of the Third Reich. During the 1950s especially, the Israeli public, hundreds of thousands of whom were Holocaust survivors, still viewed Wagner as a symbol of the Nazi regime. It is inconceivable that the Israeli government would have paid for the entire orchestra to travel to Rome to pay tribute to "Hitler's pope." On the contrary, the Israeli Philharmonic's unprecedented concert in the Vatican was a unique communal gesture of collective recognition for a great friend of the Jewish people.

Hundreds of other memorials could be cited. In her conclusion to *Under His Very Windows*, Susan Zuccotti dismisses—as wrong-headed, ill-informed, or even devious—the praise Pius XII received from Jewish leaders and scholars, as well as expressions of gratitude from the Jewish chaplains and Holocaust survivors who bore personal witness to the assistance of the pope.

That she does so is disturbing. To deny the legitimacy of their gratitude to Pius XII is tantamount to denying the credibility of their personal testimony and judgment about the Holocaust itself. "More than all others," recalled Elio Toaff, an Italian Jew who lived through the Holocaust and later became chief rabbi of Rome, "we had the opportunity of experiencing the great compassionate goodness and magnanimity of the pope during the unhappy years of the persecution and terror, when it seemed that for us there was no longer an escape."

But Zuccotti is not alone. There is a disturbing element in nearly all the current work on Pius. Except for Rychlak's *Hitler, the War, and the Pope*, none of the recent books—from Cornwell's vicious attack in *Hitler's Pope* to McInerny's uncritical defense in *The Defamation of Pius XII*—is finally about the Holocaust. All are about using the sufferings of Jews fifty years ago to force changes upon the Catholic Church today.

It is the abuse of the Holocaust that must be rejected. A true account of Pius XII would arrive, I believe, at exactly the opposite to Cornwell's conclusion: Pius XII was not Hitler's pope, but the closest Jews had come to having a papal supporter—and at the moment when it mattered most.

Writing in *Yad Vashem Studies* in 1983, John S. Conway—the leading authority on the Vatican's eleven-volume *Acts and Documents of the Holy See During the Second World War*—concluded: "A close study of the many thousands of documents published in these volumes lends little support to the thesis that ecclesiastical self-preservation was the main motive behind the attitudes of the Vatican diplomats. Rather, the picture that emerges is one of a group of intelligent and conscientious men, seeking to pursue the paths of peace and justice, at a time when these ideals were ruthlessly being rendered irrelevant in a world of 'total war.'" These neglected volumes (which the English reader can find summarized in Pierre Blet's *Pius XII and the Second World War*) "will reveal ever more clearly and convincingly"—as John Paul told a group of Jewish leaders in Miami in 1987—"how deeply Pius XII felt the tragedy of the Jewish people, and how hard and effectively he worked to assist them."

The Talmud teaches that "whosoever preserves one life, it is accounted to him by Scripture as if he had preserved a whole world." More than any other twentieth-century leader, Pius fulfilled this Talmudic dictum, when the fate of European Jewry was at stake. No other pope had been so widely praised by Jews—and they were not mistaken. Their gratitude, as well as that of the entire generation of Holocaust survivors, testifies that Pius XII was, genuinely and profoundly, a righteous gentile.

2

Dismantling the Cross

Robert Louis Wilken

(a review of James Carroll's *Constantine's Sword: The Church and the Jews—A History* [Boston: Houghton Mifflin, 2001], from *Commonweal*, January 26, 2001, pp. 22–28; © 2001 Commonweal Foundation, reprinted with permission)

Novelist and National Book Award winner James Carroll claims that *Constantine's Sword* is a work of history, and he even uses the term in his subtitle. But it is evident from the outset and amply displayed in chapter after chapter that the word "history" is a euphemism. This is a book driven by theological animus and padded with irrelevant, distracting material from Carroll's own obsessively chronicled life. Too many pages of the book are self-absorbed meditations on the author's likes (Bob Dylan, John XXIII) and dislikes (Cardinal Francis Spellman and Pius XII), all delivered with pompous solemnity ("I presume to measure the sweep of history against the scope of my own memory.").

The book is filled with information, much of it familiar. Carroll bases his narrative almost wholly on the works of others. If one turns to the notes to check the basis for his comments, the most frequent phrase one finds is "quoted by," whether the passage be from Rosemary Radford Ruether, Salo Baron, Marc Saperstein, Hans Küng, John Cornwell, or others. In a work of such scope it is inevitable that one will have to rely on the scholarship of others, but Carroll displays little understanding of the ambiguities or shortcomings of his sources. *Constantine's Sword* is a six-hundred-page indictment of the Church for its attitudes toward and treatment of the Jews, deploying historical information to support its accusations. It is an effort not to understand but to use history to advance a tendentious agenda.

The central thesis can be stated simply: "Auschwitz is the climax of the story that begins at Golgotha. Just as the climax of *Oedipus Rex* . . . reveals that the hubris that drove the play's action was itself the flaw that shaped the king's character, so we can . . . say that Auschwitz, when seen in the links of causality, reveals that the hatred of Jews has been no incidental anomaly but a central action of Christian history, reaching to the core of Christian character."

Though the author shifts repeatedly from recent events (even Matthew Shepard, the young gay man who was murdered in Wyoming in 1998, appears) and his own experiences to ancient and medieval times, the material in *Constantine's Sword* breaks down into three large historical periods: Christian beginnings and the early Church; the Middle Ages through the Reformation; and the modern age, beginning with the Enlightenment and ending with Pius XII and Edith Stein. At the end Carroll appends a wordy fifty-page proposal for the future entitled "A Call for Vatican III" and an epilogue, "The Faith of a Catholic."

The first section argues that a fatal mistake was made at the very beginning of Christianity. Following the thinking of Ruether, Carroll adopts the view that Christian contempt for the Jews is derived from Christology, in particular the claim that Jesus was the Messiah. Because most Jews did not accept Jesus as Messiah, rejection of the Jews became a defining characteristic of orthodox Christianity. This leads Carroll to conclude that the "death camps are causally linked through two millennia to mistakes made by the first generation of Christians." Hence Christianity is inherently anti-Semitic and the only way forward for the Church is "a revision of what we believe about Jesus." The Church needs to recover the Jesus who lived before Christians imposed an alien creed on his life and teachings, the Jesus who preached a message of love of the God who created not just one group but all human beings.

With this as foundation, Carroll proceeds to Constantine and the Church Fathers. His aim is to show that Christianity's fatal flaw (its belief in the uniqueness of Christ) now takes social and institutional form. But Carroll's evidence is thin and largely rhetorical (especially sermons), not legal or social. Jewish life went on uninterrupted across the Roman Empire, new synagogues were constructed, and Jewish cultural life flourished. In this period Christians were rivals to the Jews, not oppressors. To be sure, the rhetoric of the Church Fathers is sometimes extreme (the synagogue is called "a haunt of infidels," "home of the impious," "under the damnation of God"), and when ancient sermons were read in medieval Europe, they had unforeseen consequences. But there is no basis for seeing in early Christian writings on the Jews a portent of the Inquisition or a premonition of the Final Solution. Christianity and Judaism, it must not be forgotten, had a quarrel over the significance of Jesus of Nazareth and the law. Once Christians embraced Jesus as the Messiah and dispensed with the authority of the law, it was inevitable that Jews, who continued to live by the law, would be the object of criticism. It was the spiritual challenge of a vibrant Judaism that spawned sermons and treatises against the Jews. It is perhaps too much to ask that a writer who consciously overheats his language to arouse the emotions of his readers show some sensitivity to the polemical rhetoric of another age.

Carroll makes the novel, but unhistorical, claim that with the conversion of Constantine, the Cross of Christ replaced the life of Christ in the Christian imagination, and that this set Christians decisively against the Jews. As evidence he notes that the original Nicene Creed (A.D. 325) did not have the words "was crucified" and "died" under Pontius Pilate. What Carroll overlooks is that these phrases occur in almost all early Christian creeds (and in the New Testament), and it is a historical accident that the creed on which Nicaea was based did not include the words "was crucified." Yet Carroll imposes a wholly willful interpretation on the additions made at the Council of Constantinople (A.D. 381). The difference, he writes, "marks a turning point in our inquiry," for now the Son of God came "not to be one of us, not to take on the human condition," but "in order to be crucified." The shift set in motion a dynamic that will "keep Jews at the heart of a quickened, and quickly armed [!], Christian hatred."

But this is pure fantasy, and the reckless use of the term "armed" is an example of Carroll's reliance on innuendo to advance his argument. His treatment of the early Church shows as little understanding of Christian theology as it does of the social setting of early Christian writings against the Jews. The leitmotif of early Christian thought is precisely that the divine Son took on our condition in order that we might share in God's life. In the words of Saint Athanasius: "He became man that we might become divine."

The second part of the book is taken up with an extensive description of Christian mistreatment of Jews in the Middle Ages, beginning with the Crusades, then tracing the rise of tales of blood libel, and ending with the forced conversion of Jews during the Inquisition, their expulsion from Spain in 1492, and the establishment of a Jewish ghetto in Rome. Especially in sermons preached in the later Middle Ages, one can see how old stereotypes of the Jews had deadly consequences. It is a sordid tale and the violence of Christians against Jews in the Middle Ages is a very dark chapter in the Church's history. It can only fill the Christian reader with sorrow and shame and a yearning for repentance.

Carroll does give space to dissenting voices. He notes that Gregory the Great opposed the forced conversion of Jews, that Bernard of Clairvaux spoke out against attacks on the Jews, and that certain bishops valiantly strove to protect the Jews from the passions of the populace. But Carroll seems always to opt for the most malign interpretation and to claim that theological grounds were used to justify whatever Christians did.

What I find most puzzling is Carroll's strained attempt to trace everything back to the Cross. In one of the most astonishing sections of the book he singles out Anselm of Canterbury for particular censure. Anselm, an early scholastic theologian (1033–1109), was the author of a famous book, *Cur Deus Homo* ("Why God Became Man"), in which he argued that Christ's death was a sacrifice offered by God's perfect son to satisfy divine justice. Anselm's preoccupation with Christ's death leads Carroll to the unsupported conclusion that the death of Christ became the central saving event in Christianity, thereby making the situation of the Jews even more precarious. The point of Anselm's book was to demonstrate according to philosophical reason that the Incarnation was necessary (hence "Why did God become man?"), and that the redemption of mankind had to take place as presented in the Gospels. Salvation was possible only through the work of one who was at once true God and true man.

It is apparent in Carroll's discussion of Anselm that there is something much deeper at work here than historical explanation. Any teaching, so the argument goes, that rests on the events in the Gospels, as for example the crucifixion of Christ in Jewish Jerusalem, and claims that in Christ's life, death, and Resurrection God was definitively made known, is incurably anti-Semitic. That is really the message of this book, and in an interlude Carroll illustrates the problem with the words of Jesus in the Gospel of John: "I am the way, and the truth, and the life; no one comes to the Father, but by me."

It is this belief, according to Carroll, that is the source of the Church's anti-Semitism, and also the exclusionary creed adopted at Nicaea (because of its assertion that Christ is God), and the triumphalism of Pope Boniface VIII (and John Paul II). With logic such as this it is pointless to argue over the interpretation of persons or events in the Christian past or present. Christians are guilty for being Christians.

The final section of the book deals with the Enlightenment, the nineteenth-century papacy, especially Pius IX, the Dreyfus case in France, German Catholic intellectuals during the rise of Hitler, the reign of Pius XII and the fate of the Jews during World War II, etc. Carroll tells a familiar and now predictable story (for Pius XII he relies heavily on John Cornwell's discredited *Hitler's Pope*). But some material is less familiar, as for example the discussion of Abbot Ildefons Herwegen of the famous Benedictine monastery of Maria Laach in Germany.

According to Carroll, Herwegen was host to a meeting of Catholic scholars that took place at the monastery in 1933, shortly after the concordat between the Third Reich and the Vatican. Franz von Papen, vice-chancellor of the Reich, was in attendance and the gathering became a celebration of the Reichskonkordat. No doubt many of the Catholics who attended were supporters of the Reich, and some were themselves Nazis. The abbot, according to a speech cited by Carroll, gave his blessing to the "new form of the State." Unfortunately, there was no way to verify this report since Carroll bases his account on an unpublished lecture delivered in Poland three years ago.

But granted that the facts are correct, it is not clear what this incident proves except that during the Third Reich some Catholics (and other Christians) were complicitous with Nazi authorities. That hardly demonstrates that the "arc" of Christian history "curves from Jesus to the Holocaust." Pusillanimity there certainly was and moral myopia and misguided nationalism, but nothing that gives evidence of theological anti-Semitism. Carroll forces everything through a very particular sieve, or to use his image, all actions that relate to the Jews are seen through the single lens of "religious hatred." "The church's failure to denounce publicly or privately early Nazi violence aimed at Jews . . . is rooted in the church's own anti-Semitism." There is no question that Christian teaching helped create an environment in which Nazi ideology could take root. For too many centuries Christians had grown accustomed to depicting the Jews as inferior, as adherents of a decadent religion, as the killers of Christ. In the years leading up to the World War II, resistance of Christian leaders to Nazi ideology was often too little and too late. But Nazism was an anti-Christian ideology, and something more will be required to draw a direct line from the Gospels to the Final Solution.

Which brings me to Carroll's conclusion. He proposes the convening of a Vatican Council III. This council, he says, will be "centrally Catholic," but will also include "Jews and Protestants, people of other faiths and of no faith, clergy and laity and, emphatically, women." One purpose of the council will be for the Church to purge itself of the "anti-Jewish consequences of the New Testament." For the Church that "betrayed Jesus in the first generation has been betraying him ever since." Repentance not only requires transforming the Church into an egalitarian and democratic institution ("conversation is our hope"), it will mean a thorough revision of Christian belief. In particular the Church must dismantle the Cross (and by that Carroll means "removing the horizontal beam"), banishing it as a symbol of Christian faith, and abandon her belief that Christ is the savior of the world.

The question of the Jews is only the first item on the agenda. The council must also address the oppression of women, patriarchal autocracy, dishonesty, clericalism, exclusion of the laity in decision making, denominational narcissism, harmful views on sexuality, and clerical celibacy, all of which, Carroll believes, stem from the Church's theology of the Jewish people.

But clearly this catalog of vices is driven by something more than the Church's relation to the Jews. If Carroll is genuinely interested in the Church and the Jews, he knows that for almost half a century Christian thinkers, Church leaders, and catechists have made extraordinary efforts to come to terms with the "teaching of contempt." Whether one thinks of the decree *Nostra aetate* of Vatican II and other Catholic statements over the last two decades, or the various declarations of the World Council of Churches and Protestant denominations, the depth and seriousness of Christian engagement with Judaism and the Jewish people is unprecedented in Christian history.

In 1986 Pope John Paul II made a historic visit to the Jewish synagogue of Rome where he called the Jews "our dearly beloved brothers," and on a 1980 visit to Germany he said that the covenant with the people of God is "never revoked by God." Last spring the pope led a service of repentance in Rome in which there was a "confession of sins against the people of Israel," and on his journey to Jerusalem last year he made a pilgrimage to the holiest site of the Jews, the Western Wall of the Temple, and deposited this prayer of confession in a crack in the wall.

Of even greater theological significance, *Nostra aetate* cites Saint Paul's words in Romans 11: "If some of the branches were broken off, and you, a wild olive shoot, were grafted in their place to share the richness of the olive tree, do not boast over the branches. If you do boast, remember it is not you that support the root, but the root that supports you." At Vatican II it would have been easy to transpose Paul's present tense "support" into the past tense, "supported." It is thus of great significance that when *Nostra aetate* paraphrases Paul's words it retains the present tense. The Church received the revelation of the Old Testament from the Jewish people, and she "cannot forget that she draws sustenance from the root of that good olive tree onto which have been engrafted the wild olive branches of the Gentiles." One might have expected, two thousand years later, to read, "drew sustenance" from the Jewish people. But what the decree says is, "draws sustenance from the root of that good olive tree." In these few lines the council laid to rest "supersessionism," the theological idea that Christianity has replaced Judaism.

Constantine's Sword is behind the curve of history. Had this book been written fifty years ago it would have been noteworthy. But its message has been heard, digested, and acted upon. And the new openness of the Church to the Jews has led to a dramatic transformation of relations between Jews and Christians. Just this last year a group of Jewish thinkers produced a remarkable document, the first ever by Jews on Christianity and one that would have been inconceivable before the developments within Christian thinking a generation ago.

Entitled "A Jewish Statement on Christians and Christianity," it speaks directly to Carroll's concerns: "Without the long history of Christian anti-Judaism and Christian violence against Jews, Nazi ideology could not have taken hold nor could it have been carried out. Too many Christians participated in, or were sympathetic to, Nazi atrocities against Jews. Other Christians did not protest sufficiently against these atrocities. But Nazism itself was not an inevitable outcome of Christianity. If the Nazi exterminations of the Jews had been fully successful, it would have turned its murderous rage more directly to Christians. We recognize with gratitude those Christians who risked or sacrificed their lives to save Jews during the Nazi regime. With that in mind, we encourage the continuation of recent efforts in Christian theology to repudiate unequivocally contempt of Judaism and the Jewish people.

We applaud those Christians who reject this teaching of contempt, and we do not blame them for the sins committed by their ancestors."

Carroll knows about the Church's response over the last generation to its dealings with the Jews in the past, but deems it insufficient. He will not be satisfied until the "foundational assumptions of Christian faith" are challenged. The "entire structure of the Gospel narrative," he says, "is unworthy of the story it wants to tell." The Church must free itself from any claim that "salvation, redemption, grace, perfection" have come in Christ. Coincidentally I read these words two days after hearing the epistle from the Mass on Christmas Eve: "For the grace of God has appeared for the salvation of all men" (Titus 2:11). For Carroll repentance can only mean renunciation of Christ and of Christian faith, as he puts it, repentance "without Golgotha, redemption, or sacrifice."

At the end of the day, in spite of the enormous effort to lay bare the sins of the Church over two millennia, *Constantine's Sword* is not really a book about Christian theology of the Jews. Its subject is Christian theology *tout court*, and its polemic springs from the currently fashionable "ideology of religious pluralism"—what might be termed horror at strong opinions. Carroll wants a Christianity that celebrates a "Jesus whose saving act is only disclosure of the divine love available to all," and calls for a pluralism of "belief and worship, of religion and no religion, that honors God by defining God as beyond every human effort to express God." What we have then is a rather conventional cultural critique of Christianity. The Jews are the victims par excellence of the excesses of revealed religion. But what Carroll forgets is that the Jews, too, believe in revelation. If Christians, on the basis of the Scriptures and Christian tradition, cannot confess Jesus as Lord, can the Jews, on the basis of the Scriptures and Jewish tradition, claim that they are the elect people of God? In Carroll's brave new world there will be neither Jews nor Christians.

3

A Dangerous Thing to Do

Ronald J. Rychlak

(a review of Susan Zuccotti's *Under His Very Windows: The Vatican and the Holocaust in Italy* [New Haven: Yale University, 2000], from *Journal of Modern Italian Studies* 7 [Summer 2002], pp. 218–240)

In *Under His Very Windows: The Vatican and the Holocaust in Italy*, Susan Zuccotti reports on research that took her into archives that others had not yet mined. What she found—time and time again—was that Catholic clergy and lay persons defied the Nazis and the fascists by providing food, clothing, and shelter to Jews and other refugees. As a result of these efforts, while approximately 80 percent of European Jews perished during World War II, 85 percent of Italian Jews survived Nazi occupation. Despite this evidence, Zuccotti gives little credit to the leader of the Catholic Church, Pope Pius XII. . . .

Zuccotti's arguments against Pius XII can be answered fairly quickly: She simply ignores overwhelming evidence. She clearly misunderstands what rescue work was like under Nazi occupation. Then comes evidence that she has overlooked or improperly discounted, and finally, she fails to understand the way a moral leader inspires people. In sum, she has developed an unrealistic theory and attempted to shoehorn the factual evidence into it. . . .

Zuccotti's argument that Pius XII was not supportive of rescue work is based upon the lack of an existing, written order from the pope. She writes that if there were a papal order to help Jews, it "would almost certainly have been preserved by someone clever enough to understand that it might someday help the pope's reputation." In making this argument, she severely underestimates the danger to life in a Nazi-controlled nation. It was extremely dangerous to keep papers related to anti-Nazi efforts, and few who worked in the underground did. For instance, in the spring of 1940 there was an attempt to oust Hitler by a group of German generals who wanted to surrender to the English. The negotiations took place with the Vatican's mediation and the direct cooperation of Pius XII. He went so far as to inform the Allies about German troop movements. However, there are no documents on this in the Vatican's published collection. The documents were found only in the British archives. Vatican papers were undoubtedly destroyed.

Anyone who cared for the pope would have destroyed written instructions for him. More important, no one at the time thought Pius XII's reputation would need to be protected. As rescuer John Patrick Carroll-Abbing wrote in his 1965 book: "Never, in those tragic days, could I have foreseen, even in my wildest imaginings, that the man who, more than any other, had tried to alleviate human suffering, had spent himself day by day in his unceasing efforts for peace, would—twenty years later—be made the scapegoat for men trying to free themselves from their own responsibilities and from the collective guilt that obviously weights so heavily upon them." Another author wrote: "Any direct personal order would have had to be kept very quiet to protect those who were actually sheltered." This other author is Susan Zuccotti, in her 1987 book, *The Italians and the Holocaust*.

Zuccotti's failure to understand what life was like under Nazi rule is also seen in two of her other arguments. In 1943, the Vatican won assurances that its properties in Rome would be regarded as extraterritorial, not part of German-occupied Italy. Signs were posted on the buildings to warn German soldiers that they should not search them.

Zuccotti complains that the Vatican put protection notices on all of its buildings, instead of just the 160 or so where refugees were hiding. From this she concludes that the Church was protecting its property, not the refugees. She suggests that the warnings should have been put on only those churches, monasteries, and schools that contained Jews or other refugees. That, however, would have been nothing but a clear indication to the Nazis that refugees were hidden therein. Besides, by putting signs on every building, refugees were informed that the buildings were safe, and they could be put into use at a moment's notice. . . .

In a case built not upon evidence, but upon a lack thereof, it is imperative to review all of the evidence that is known and to give it appropriate consideration. Time and again, Zuccotti fails to do this, which results in the complete failure of her thesis.

Between 1967 and 1974, ninety-eight witnesses who knew Pius XII personally gave sworn testimony, under oath, about his life. This evidence, unlike the published documents, focuses directly on Pius XII's personal efforts on behalf of Jews and others. In other words, these transcripts contain exactly the type of evidence that Zuccotti was seeking, but she did not review them for her book.

No less than forty-two witnesses, including five cardinals, spoke directly of Pius XII's concern for and help given to Jewish people. Some witnesses spoke of papal orders to open buildings. Others testified that Pius knew of and approved of the sheltering of Jews in church buildings. The vice-director of the Vatican newspaper testified that Pius personally opened Vatican buildings, and he authorized convents and monasteries to welcome outsiders. The clear message from each and every witness was that Pope Pius XII was honest, holy, and charitable.

It may be understandable that a researcher would not consult the deposition transcripts. They have not been translated or widely published. You cannot, however, legitimately overlook this most relevant testimony and then turn around and build a case based upon an alleged lack of evidence.

In a related manner, Zuccotti leads her readers to believe that none of the rescuers credited Pius for supporting their work. Again, she is mistaken. Pius has a long list of very credible witnesses on this matter, including two popes. In 1955, a delegation from Israel approached Archbishop Montini, the future Pope Paul VI, to determine whether he would accept an award for his work on behalf of Jews during the war. He declined the honor: "All I did was my duty," he said. "And besides I only acted upon orders from the Holy Father. Nobody deserves a medal for that." Angelo Roncalli (the future Pope John XXIII) made a very similar statement when he was offered thanks for his efforts to save Jewish lives in Istanbul: "In all these painful matters I have referred to the Holy See and simply carried out the pope's orders: first and foremost to save human lives."

Cardinal Pietro Palazzini, then assistant vice-rector of the Seminario Romano, hid Italian Jews there in 1943 and 1944. In 1985, Yad Vashem honored the cardinal as a righteous gentile. In accepting the honor, Palazzini stressed that "the merit is entirely Pius XII's, who ordered us to do whatever we could to save the Jews from persecution." Cardinal Paolo Dezza, head of one of the institutions that sheltered Jews, quotes Pius as saying to him: "Avoid helping the military, . . . but as for the others, help them willingly: civilians, persecuted Jews."

Jewish historian Michael Tagliacozzo, head of the Center on Studies on the Shoah and Resistance in Italy, told about how he was rescued from the Nazis and hidden in the pope's building in Vatican City. He also said that Pius himself ordered the opening of convents and that Pius was the only person to intervene when the Nazis rounded up Roman Jews on October 16, 1943. Hungarian rescuer Tibor Baranski, Italian Senator Adriano Ossicini, founder of the Italian "Christian Left," and Sister Maria Corsetti Ferdinanda, all told similar stories. In her book *Yours Is a Precious Witness*, Sister Margherita Marchione writes that in interview after interview she was told that, "at the request of Pope Pius XII, doors of convents and monasteries were opened to save the Jews when the Nazis occupied Italy."

Zuccotti leaves completely unmentioned the anger Pius XII's protests pro-voked in Nazi ranks. Following the pope's 1942 Christmas statement, one Nazi report stated: "Here he is clearly speaking on behalf of the Jews . . . and makes himself the mouthpiece of the Jewish war criminals." Karl Otto Wolff, S.S. chief in Italy toward the end of the war, testified to having received the orders to invade the Vatican from Hitler himself. The German ambassador to Italy and an aide to the German ambassador to the Holy See both confirmed that Hitler had such plans. Fortunately, he was dissuaded from it, but the re-action from Hitler and other Nazi leaders is strong evidence about how they viewed the pope and the Vatican leadership.

Zuccotti's book was published before the recent release of Adolf Eich-mann's memoirs. The memoirs document the reality of the Holocaust and also confirm that Vatican protests played a crucial part in obstructing Nazi in-tentions for Roman Jews following the notorious roundup on October 16, 1943. Eichmann wrote that the Vatican "vigorously protested the arrest of Jews, requesting the interruption of such action."

At Eichmann's trial, by the way, Israeli Attorney General Gideon Hausner, in his opening statement, said "the pope himself intervened personally in support of the Jews of Rome." A Protestant minister, Heinrich Grober, testi-fied that Pius helped him save Jews. Documents introduced in that trial also show Vatican efforts for a halt to the arrests of Roman Jews. In rejecting Eich-mann's appeals, the Israeli Supreme Court noted the pope's protest regard-ing the deportation of Hungarian Jews. Such evidence overwhelms Zuc-cotti's argument regarding an alleged lack of papal involvement.

Zuccotti also completely overlooks Vatican Radio. Father Michel Riquet, a one-time inmate at Dachau and recognized as a rescuer of six Jewish lives, explained: "Pius XII spoke; Pius XII condemned; Pius XII acted . . . through-out those years of horror, when we listened to Radio Vatican and to the pope's messages, we felt in communion with the pope, in helping perse-cuted Jews and in fighting against Nazi violence." . . .

In February 2001, a new book was released in Italy. The title is "The Jews Saved by Pius XII" (*Gli ebrei salvati da Pio XII*), and it is written by Antonio Gaspari, a respected author of a previous book on the subject. Gaspari re-counts several instances of Pius XII intervening in his personal capacity, through the Vatican state secretariat, to save Jews. In one case, 1,000 German Jews wanted to emigrate to Brazil, and the pontiff paid out of his own pocket the $800 each needed for the trip. In 1939, Pius organized special operations inside the Vatican Information Office to help Jews persecuted by Nazism. Re-garding Zuccotti's thesis that Catholic rescue activity took place without papal support, Gaspari expressly says: "This is a thesis that is impossible to defend."

So how is that Zuccotti argues that Pius XII had no role in rescue efforts, when so many witnesses testified that he did? The answer is that—time and time again—she discounts or dismisses the testimony of people who were there.

On page 264, she discusses a bishop who claimed to have been holding a letter from Pius in his hands, but she suggests that the bishop falsified this claim because he "may have considered it useful to make his assistants believe that they were doing the pope's work."

On page 193, Zuccotti suggests that nuns who credited the pope for having ordered their convents opened to Jewish refugees were "eager that Pius XII receive credit for the work of their order."

On page 143, she discusses a letter from A.L. Eastman, of the World Jewish Congress, thanking the pope for helping free imprisoned Jews. Zuccotti however, dismisses this testimony by saying, "Eastman must have known better."

On page 103, she quotes the papal nuncio in Vichy, praising Pius XII for condemning the persecution of Jews and others. Zuccotti accuses him of fabricating the papal responses.

On page 301, she discusses gratitude from Jewish people to the pope following the war. She attributes their attitude to "benevolent ignorance."

On page 302, in an even more disturbing analysis, she suggests that Jewish chaplains simply lied because they were "anxious to protect and preserve the fragile goodwill between Jews and non-Jews that seems to be emerging from the rubble of the war in Italy."

At other points along the way she dismisses letters of thanks from Jewish people because "the Holy See had done nothing more for the Jewish internees than for non-Jews." Favorable accounts of the pope's efforts to help Jews are dismissed as "less than honest." Testimony from the future Pope Paul VI is dismissed because, according to Zuccotti, he "knew perfectly well" that his statement was wrong.

Zuccotti does not show a lack of papal involvement in rescue efforts. All she has shown is that she does not believe the limited amount of evidence that she has reviewed. Her failure to discuss Castel Gandolfo is worth particular note. Castel Gandolfo, the papal summer home, was used to shelter hundreds and perhaps thousands of Jews during the war. . . . A wartime U.S. intelligence document reported that the "bombardment of Castel Gandolfo resulted in the injury of about 1,000 people and the death of about 300 more. The highness of the figures is due to the fact that the area was crammed with refugees." . . . This information—from U.S. archives—shows a great deal of papal involvement in Jewish rescue operations. No one but Pius XII had authority to open these building to outsiders. As at least one witness testified under oath, the orders came from the pope. Again, in a case built not on evidence, but on the alleged lack of it, Zuccotti's failure to address this clear papal intervention is inexcusable.

In some cases, Zuccotti simply misconstrued the evidence. For instance, she gives considerable attention to a Jewish family's request for permission to stay in an Italian convent. She discusses Montini's note of October 1, 1943, about this matter and his efforts, but she says nothing of Pius XII's own involvement, which is confirmed by a notation at the bottom of that note ("Ex. Aud. SS.mi.

1.X.43"). In fact, below this indication that the matter was discussed with the pope is a further notation: "Si veda se possible aiutario," indicating that Pius gave his permission for the convent to admit a male Jew, despite a normal prohibition on men in the convent.

Similarly, Zuccotti tells us that French priest-rescuer Father Marie-Benoît received virtually no support from Rome, but he is on record as saying just the opposite. In 1976, on the centennial of Pius XII's birth, Father Marie-Benoît prepared a statement that spoke in glowing terms of the Holy Father and his undertakings on behalf of Jews. Marie-Benoît noted that Pius listened to his plan to save Jews with great attention and promised to take care of the matter personally.

Among the published documents, Zuccotti encountered evidence that the Vatican provided money to help Marie-Benoît. She says this is difficult to interpret and supposes that the amount must have been "exceedingly sparse." However, Fernande Leboucher, who worked with Father Marie-Benoît as perhaps his closest collaborator, wrote a book about their rescue work. In fact, she called upon him for help in putting the book together. Leboucher estimated that a total of some four million dollars was channeled from the Vatican to Marie-Benoît and his operation. The evidence is certainly not as one-sided as Zuccotti would have us believe.

In arguing that Pius cannot be associated with Catholic rescue efforts because she cannot find existing written documents in the pope's handwriting, Zuccotti is actually advancing an argument that was made by Holocaust denier David Irving. He once offered a reward for anyone who could find a document from Hitler linking him to the extermination of Jews. By the same token, everyone who helped rescue Jews knew that the pope approved of this work. He inspired them. He encouraged them. Zuccotti's theory was bad logic for the Holocaust denier, and it is bad logic for her.

Moreover, Zuccotti applies her demand for written documents quite inconsistently. When evidence of papal support for the Jews is offered, she demands documentation, but when people say bad things about the pope, she is all too eager to accept it. For instance, in her conclusion, Zuccotti repeats an old canard. It is said that the pope was unwilling to speak out against the Nazis because this would create a conflict of conscience for the German soldiers. There is no document to back this up, and no one who has spent any time trying to know Pius XII can believe that this was a primary influence upon him. Zuccotti's only citation for this claim is Guenter Lewy. According to Lewy, a correspondent for the Vatican newspaper in Berlin, Eduardo Senatro, at a public discussion in Berlin in 1964, said that Pius had told him this. The problem is that Senatro was not from the Vatican newspaper, but from an Italian (Fascist) newspaper. He had no particular relationship with the pope. Senatro, who had never made such a claim in his own newspaper, later wrote a letter correcting statements attributed to him at that 1964 occasion.

Similarly, Zuccotti is all too quick to accept Robert Katz's claim that Pius knew of the October 16, 1943, roundup before it took place. As an initial matter, the Pacelli family successfully sued Katz for defamation. He was fined and given a suspended prison sentence. No true scholar can feel good about relying on his work, but even if we take Katz at his word, the story has many holes in it. Katz claimed to have talked to a German diplomat (Eitel Mollhausen) who claimed to have told the German ambassador to the Holy See, Baron Ernst von Weizsäcker, about the roundup in advance. Katz then suggests that Weizsäcker told Vatican officials, and they must have told the pope. There is no writing to prove this. Weizsäcker never mentioned it in his memoirs, and Italian Princess Enza Pignatelli Aragona Cortés, who told the pope about the roundup after it took place, reports that he was shocked. . . .

Zuccotti reveals her bias and refusal to acknowledge beneficial actions for Jews that were taken by the pope or others from the very start of her book. For instance, she notes that many authors who disagree with her have translated the Italian word *stirpe*, which was used in several official Church statements, as meaning "race." On page two of her book, however, Zuccotti explains that *stirpe* does not exactly correlate with the English word *race*, but should be understood as meaning *descent*. Her clear suggestion is that when the pope or various Church officials used the word *stirpe*, they were not saying *race* and therefore were not speaking on behalf of Jewish people. She thus argues that those who have defended the pope were wrong. Pius XI's anti-Nazi encyclical, *Mit brennender Sorge*, used a German word that Zuccotti does translate as meaning race ("Rasse"). This time, however, her analysis is changed. She argues that since the Church did not actually consider Jews as a distinct race but rather as a religion, "it is unlikely that any reference to observant Jews was intended." Regardless of the word used, she finds a basis for her criticism of the pope and the Church. . . .

In August 1944, Pulitzer Prize–winning *New York Times* reporter Anne O'Hare McCormick wrote from liberated Rome that Pius enjoyed an "enhanced" reputation because during the Nazi occupation he had made "hiding someone 'on the run' the thing to do" and had given Jews "first priority." Even Zuccotti agrees that Catholic rescuers "invariably believed that they were acting according to the pope's will." He encouraged, inspired, and authorized them to do what they could to help, but in conformity with the Catholic social doctrine of subsidiarity, details were usually left to be decided at the local level. That is not to say, however, that Pius was uninvolved in rescue efforts.

From the earliest days of the war, the stance of the pope was well known. Despite Zuccotti's claim to the contrary, Pius XII's first encyclical, *Summi Pontificatus*, released just weeks after the outbreak of war, *did* expressly mention Jews. The pope wrote that in the Church there is "neither Gentile nor Jew, circumcision nor uncircumcision. . . . But Christ is all and in all."

This equating of Gentiles and Jews was a clear rejection of Hitler's fundamental ideology, and everyone knew it. "The Encyclical," wrote Heinrich Müller, head of the Gestapo, "is directed exclusively against Germany, both in ideology and in regard to the German-Polish dispute. How dangerous it is for our foreign relations as well as our domestic affairs is beyond discussion." A headline in the London *Daily Telegraph* read: "Pope condemns Nazi theory." French aircraft dropped 88,000 copies of the encyclical over parts of German territory. It even earned a three-column, above-the-fold headline in the *New York Times*: "Pope Condemns Dictators, Treaty Violators, Racism; Urges Restoring of Poland."

At Christmas time 1941, the *New York Times* wrote: "The voice of Pius XII is a lonely voice in the silence and darkness enveloping Europe this Christmas. . . . [T]he pope put himself squarely against Hitlerism." That same paper, one year later wrote: "This Christmas more than ever he is a lonely voice crying out of the silence of a continent."

In August of 1943, *Time* magazine wrote, "It is scarcely deniable that the Church Apostolic, through the encyclicals and other papal pronouncements, has been fighting totalitarianism more knowingly, devoutly, and authoritatively, and for a longer time, than any other organized power." Following the liberation of Rome in October 1944, the *New York Times* wrote: "Under the pope's direction the Holy See did an exemplary job of sheltering and championing the victims of the Nazi-Fascist regime." And contrary to Zuccotti's bald assertion, Pius XII frequently condemned anti-Semitism following the war. Pius continued to condemn racism throughout his life. In 1957, he received a delegation from the American Jewish Committee. The committee's representatives described the pope as a "great friend" in the battle against racism and anti-Semitism in the United States. The pope, in turn, praised the committee's work and issued a strong statement condemning anti-Semitism.

Passionate assertions do not substitute for factual substantiation. At the end of the day, we have Zuccotti on one side arguing that there is no evidence of papal involvement. On the other side we have a mountain of testimony from rescuers, victims, Germans, Jews, priests, nuns, the *New York Times* (and other papers), seven cardinals, and two popes. To ignore the testimony of those who were there is to deny history. With this subject, that is a very dangerous thing to do.

4

A New Syllabus of Errors

Justus George Lawler

(a review of Garry Wills's *Papal Sin* [New York: Doubleday, 2000], from *The Month*, February 2001, pp. 80–83)

Though there has been well over a score of reviews of Garry Wills's *Papal Sin: Structures of Deceit*, the book has been assessed generally along the predictable lines of a given reviewer's perspective on the last two centuries of Catholic history. However, if the larger thesis encapsulated in the title is to be accepted, there must be an appraisal of its historical and factual foundations.

I will concentrate here only on the more significant asseverations, and bypass incidental errors such as the reference to "Pope John Paul VI" or Wills's confusing Mary Tudor with Mary Stuart—perhaps too many Bloody Marys or distraction by an aria from Donizetti's *Maria Stuarda*; similarly with the misreading of the tag for putting a biblical text in a real-life context: here in Wills's version, "Sitz *am* Leben." Nor will I focus on the innumerable reversals of view that have over the years characterized his journalistic forays into the religious arena. . . .

Rather, I am concerned with significant errors that indicate, at the least, that Wills has not done his homework, or at the most, that he is practicing the deceit he so freely denounces in ecclesiastical officials. As to the latter, we read that "in 1937 . . . Pius XI signed the Lateran treaty . . . at a time when Mussolini *wanted church approval for his actions.*" (All italics added.)

But as every Catholic elementary school student used to know, the treaty was actually signed by Cardinal Gasparri in 1929. However, in 1929 Mussolini had had control of the government for only six years, and there was little widespread criticism—"made the trains run on time" was the complacent outsiders' view—and thus no need for "church approval." But by 1937

Mussolini was reviled in most of Western Europe, in Africa, and in North America. His war in Abyssinia had been condemned by the League of Nations; the deposed emperor, Haile Selassie, was a universally pitied but revered figure on the world stage; and Mussolini had forged an alliance with Hitler that among other evils led Italy in that very year to join Germany in the infamous bombing of Guernica. All this suggests 1937 as an opportune time for seeking "church approval." To drive the point—and the chronology—home, Wills adds in a footnote "that Mussolini so wanted church approval in the middle of the 1930s that he moved *almost* to the right of the Pope."

In passing, it should be noted that the year 1937 has now assumed canonical status. Karen Armstrong, credentialised by her publishers as a "former nun," introduces it in a *New York Times* op-ed piece (July 16, 2000) where it is joined to other chronological gaffes to support her position on Jerusalem in peace negotiations. Thus she observes: "The city *only* became central to Judaism after its destruction by Nebuchadnezzar in 586 B.C."—off by "only" four centuries, since virtually all biblical scholars date the Davidic kingdom from c. 1000 B.C. Perhaps we have a new guild of Catholic historical revisionists aborning; if so, its charter members might want to bone up on Richard Hofstadter on "paranoid style" and Harold Bloom on the "school of resentment."

Wills informs his readers that Don Luigi Bosco was the leader of a Catholic party who was "undercut" in *the aftermath* of the allegedly pro-Mussolini Lateran treaty—though de Gasperi (another party leader and later postwar premier), a close friend of the deceit-ridden Pius XI as well as of "Don Luigi," affirmed that even the latter would have approved the treaty. The reference is of course to Don Luigi Sturzo, founder of the *Partito Popolare* who went into exile in 1924, five years *before* the actual signing of the treaty. (Perhaps our mythic Luigi Bosco was exiled to the equally mythic Bocobel of Nabokov's *Pale Fire*.) What is odd here, however, is not so much the presence of more impossible chronology, but the conflation of a nineteenth-century founder of a religious order, Don John Bosco, with the founder of a twentieth-century political party.

I recall citing Sturzo's monumental treatise, *Church and State*, in a 1952 essay on Yves Congar's *Vraie et fausse Réforme*, which bears on the present discussion—though it doesn't get into "papal sins": "Clement XIV is the last of the popes whose acts have been subjected even by Catholic historians to open criticism. It is fortunate that we find this precedent in respect of a recent pope, so that no irreverence can be imputed to anyone using the same historical method toward some of his successors"—but "historical method," not historical retribution. (Ironically the article appeared in the August 15 issue of *Commonweal*—the feast of Mary's Assumption, according to Wills, one of the titular honorifics "heaped on her so that she might preside over papal structures of deceit.")

I do not know if this confusion over Don Luigi betrays some latent stereotype; but such would certainly seem lurking behind the description of Paul VI "with his sad sunken eyes in their smudgy Italian sockets." (One addicted to Willsian journalese might read "smudgy Italian sockets" as indicative of a "dim bulb.") Pope Paul is mise en scène (sin?) here as the pontiff responsible for appointing the commission whose views were ignored in the writing of the encyclical *Humanae Vitae*. But as to whether even these members of the papal commission were guilty of wrongdoing Wills does not waver: "A cultivated submission to the papacy had been, for them, a structure of deceit, keeping them from honesty with themselves, letting them live within a lie." So omnipresent is this structure that even this highly educated body of people is "surprised" at the notion that the Church can and must change. But such a "surprise" is simply unbelievable to anyone living through the period: Scores of articles, innumerable debates, and many books published in the English-speaking world (*Contraception and Holiness*, edited by Archbishop Roberts, for one), all affirmed that on this issue change was a ubiquitous reality.

The fecklessness of employing the reductivism of Wills's title is brought out in his treatment of Pius IX and the "dogmas" proclaimed during his reign. In this account simplistic historical theory goes hand in hand with simplistic practice of the journalist's art. So many curial villains, so many papal sins, so much "toadyism" by so many "lackeys" (Cardinal Newman's terms), so many Vatican conspirators crowd the stage that one loses sight of the actual events in the salvoes of derogatory expletives and epithets that Wills fires. One is reminded of a description by Newman, also one of Wills's "heroes," of a vexatious editor, Richard Simpson (whom Wills confuses with Lord Acton): "He will always be flicking his whip at bishops, cutting them in tender places, throwing stones at Sacred Congregations, and, as he rides along the high road, discharging peashooters at cardinals who happen by bad luck to look out of their window."

Pius IX's first defection was the justly denounced *Syllabus errorum*, a self-contradictory and literally preposterous (pre-Trent and post-Enlightenment) document that condemned virtually every advance of democracy and of human rights. But it is not enough for Wills to describe it; he must weave around it a tissue of tendentious embroidery to support his thesis of papal sin and structures of deceit.

His first fudging is to blur the document's origins in a suggestion of Cardinal Pecci, who is unmentioned because he later becomes the open-minded successor of Pius IX—even as John XXIII succeeded Pius XII. If one is going to prove the ubiquity of "papal sin," one has to be highly selective in one's choice of villains—or willing to portray the innocent as the villain. Papal sin becomes identical with Wills's papal spin. Thus we are to conclude that Pius's propositions had nothing to do with the innominable Pecci but were based on a "list drawn up by an opportunistic ex-liberal,

Phillipe Gerbet, who had scrambled to the right . . . after the condemnation of de Lammenais" (*sic*: twice repeated). But this villainous opportunist, who "was not respected" and had "grandiose" aspirations, was in fact known as a second Fénelon, was highly praised by Sainte-Beuve, and had been the closest collaborator of de Lamennais at La Chesnale—the latter described by E. Hocédez as "the most influential factor in theological renewal in the early nineteenth century."

Pius IX harkened to Gerbet rather than to "mature theologians like Abbot Guéranger and Monsignor Pie"—both of whom may have been mature, but neither of whom could be described as a theologian. Guéranger, who also "scrambled to the right after the condemnation" of de Lamennais, was a collator of obscure liturgical texts to which he added commentaries famously inaccurate. As for Pie, his writings contain little more than (eponymously) unctuous pieties.

Now, with a fanfare from Copland for the common Catholic, come the ultimate exposé of papal sin and its, so to speak, cardinal instance: the decree on infallibility. Again, deceit (accompanied by historical error) abounds. Monsignor Pie, notwithstanding his advocacy of "the Pope-King," is among the "moderates." While Bishop Dupanloup of Orleans, who continues to wear the red hat Wills had conferred on him in *Bare Ruined Choirs*, is leader of the opposition—why Pius IX would have elevated to the cardinalate a bishop who was consistently antagonistic to him goes unexplained. One of the most vocal debaters was, according to Wills, "Cardinal Strossmayer, the Bavarian leader of bishops against infallibility." Unfortunately, Strossmayer was neither a Cardinal nor a Bavarian. He was a Croatian, a recognised leader in the Panslavic movement and intent on bringing about a reunion of Orthodox and Catholics—which, as subsequently with Anglicans and Lutherans, the infallibility decree would render almost impossible. (Witness failed efforts of John Paul II to receive an invitation to Moscow from the Russian Orthodox patriarch.)

After months of debate, Wills correctly informs the reader that "only three negative votes were cast at the last session." (In passing, one notes a nice touch missing. One of the three was a bishop from Arkansas; and so the headlines bannered that Little Rock had opposed Big Rock.) But Wills ceases neither to toil nor to spin as another "papal sin" is ferreted out: "Even if all the bishops who first assembled for the Council had remained for the final vote, they would not have been representative of the entire church, since the pope had named many more bishops from Italy and Spain than from the more distant and less docile lands."

In support of this structural deceit are mustered detailed statistics gleaned from Gertrude Himmelfarb's dissertation on Lord Acton. But overlooked in this assumption of a duplicitous conspiracy to weigh the scales in favour of his loyal countrymen is the fact that Pius IX appointed more non-Italian cardinals than any of his predecessors in modern history. As for the statistical evidence, the distinguished church historian, Rober Aubert, assesses the numerical accounts quite differently: "By dint of their [the Italian delegates] numbers they lent decisive support to the informal compromise faction. This group, conciliatory from the outset, finally succeeded in having a more flexible formula accepted, which occupied a middle ground between the neo-ultramontane and anti-Curial extremists."

Wills continues: "The Council would be broken off when war against Austria made France withdraw its troops, so that an independent Italy's warriors came flooding up to the very gates of the Vatican City." One can overlook the metaphoric mélange of flooding warriors—maybe through the *cloaca maxima* of the Vatican—but one cannot overlook another curious conflation: The Franco-Austrian war of 1859 is identified with the Franco-Prussian war of 1870. This latter "as every schoolboy knows" brought the end of the council and the end of the Papal States. The saw in quotation marks is from Macauley, one of those historians Wills commends for "declaring that history was no longer . . . committed to official versions of the past." It should be added: "and no longer committed to *unofficial* versions either."

But perhaps as with Shakespeare and the Hundred Years War or the War of the Roses, one can get a more vivid sense of the events surrounding the council from the poet Paul Claudel in *Le Père Humilié*, the third play of his *Orestea*. The "Father" of the title is Pius IX, and the central character is a blind young Jewish woman, Pensée, in love with one of the pope's nephews, whom she upbraids for his indifference to a unified Italy: "You're fighting against this people which is struggling to live." The nephew replies: "I can't stand against my Father"; to which she retorts: "Is that futile old man, to whom time and progress mean nothing forever going to put himself between you and life?"

In the aftermath of the council, the opposition bishops who had left the city to avoid "standing against" the Holy Father eventually accepted the decree. Lord Acton's mentor and fellow agitator against infallibility, Dr. Döllinger, was excommunicated along with several thousand "Old Catholics" whom the learned doctor had inspired but, as a matter of conscience, refused to join. Noblesse oblige left Acton untouched, and he later went on to a professorship at Cambridge where he initiated the *Cambridge Modern History*, but never saw its publication, as was equally true of his projected history of liberty, since renowned as "the greatest book never written." Acton's supporter, Gladstone, published an attack on the decree on infallibility to which Newman replied in a subtly argued open letter addressed to the leading Catholic peer, the Duke of Norfolk—thus employing an earl marshal in a rejoinder to a prime minister. It was a whim of the same Duke of Norfolk that later resulted in Newman's elevation to the cardinalate by Leo XIII, as it had earlier been a whim of Newman in his reactionary Anglican

days to oppose Catholic Emancipation, which the then duke of Norfolk supported. In Newman's long history, there is no end of Howards.

Finally, for the record, and to refute the historically warped concept of
fixed structures of deceit, I would note two post–Vatican I transformations.
First, that of Cardinal Manning, the "majority whip" at the council who later
condemned "a Catholic presbyterianism," which reduced the episcopal college to "only the pope's vicariate." And second, as mentioned earlier, that of
Cardinal Pecci, who as Leo XIII made peace—in an understandably mixed
fashion—with the Enlightenment and with post-Revolutionary France, and
who wrote an encyclical on social reform whose very title would have made
Pius IX shudder: "Concerning the New Things." A sense of the shock that
Leo's reign caused is amusingly brought out in André Gide's *Les Caves du
Vatican*, in which a young impersonator, a clerical Felix Krull, cons elderly
ladies into donating cash and jewels to ransom the true pope and drive from
the throne the sham pope, Leo XIII, patently a creature of evil Jesuit plotters—no doubt caught in their own unique structures of deceit.

In the past Catholics were wont to refer to "holy mother the Church"; in
the present they "botanise upon their mother's grave"—a Wordsworthian
mot. But it is more fitting to close with Newman, who is *not* among the reigning pontiff's many candidates for canonisation. When he was "shelved" in
Birmingham he discussed the prospects of a Catholic magazine: "Nothing
would be better than a historical review, but who would bear it: Unless one
doctored all one's facts one would be a bad Catholic." Now it is by doctor-
ing the facts that one proves oneself a "good Catholic." How prophetic; but
even more, how pathetic.

5

Desperately Seeking Culprits

Russell Hittinger

(a review of David I. Kertzer's *The Popes Against the Jews: The Vatican's Role in the Rise of Modern Anti-Semitism* [New York: Knopf, 2001], from the *Journal of the Historical Society*, published by Blackwell Publishing, Spring 2002, pp. 215–227)

Unlike several other highly publicized and mostly accusatory books published on this subject since 1998, David Kertzer's *The Popes Against the Jews: The Vatican's Role in the Rise of Modern Anti-Semitism* does not treat the wartime record of Pope Pius XII. Author of *The Kidnapping of Edgardo Mortara* (1999), the controversial case of a Jewish boy who was baptised by a domestic servant and later adopted by Pius IX, Kertzer specializes in an earlier period of Italian history. . . . As the title indicates, his purpose in this new book is nothing less than an indictment of the modern papacy itself.

The four early chapters (pp. 25–106) on the laws and policies of the Papal States during the nineteenth century are quite useful, and indeed, fascinating. "There is no clearer way to discover the popes' attitudes and policies toward the Jews," Kertzer proposes, "than seeing how the popes dealt with them when they had the power to do what they liked." This is exactly the right kind of question for an historian to ask.

For the most part, Kertzer gives the reader a properly textured account of how Jews were treated in Rome and elsewhere in the papal dominions before 1870, when Rome fell to the House of Savoy. He shows that the Jews were treated with religious and political contempt. In particular, the Roman government played fast and loose with the long-established principle that Jewish children were not to be baptized against the will of their parents. The principle was sidestepped by inducing the head of the household to convert,

47

which then gave ecclesiastical authorities justification for ordering the rest of the family to follow suit. If further evidence be needed, Kertzer shows clearly enough that the popes were not able to create anything resembling a modern regime of civil liberties in their own temporal dominions. . . .

Unfortunately, his overarching thesis requires him to say more. Kertzer is driven to prove that the teachings and policies of modern popes were a bridge to modern anti-Semitism. As he himself admits, the thesis must stand or fall on what happens after the collapse of the Papal States, beginning with the pontificate of Leo XIII (1878). Once he picks up this part of the story (at chapter 6), Kertzer's work ceases to be history in any useful sense of the term. . . .

After four chapters that contain no evidence of papal teaching or approbation of anti-Semitism, Kertzer pauses to give his own criteria for what ought to count as modern anti-Semitism: "But even if we identify modern anti-Semitism with racism, it does not follow that racism is the only significant feature of modern anti-Semitism. In fact, there are other, equally important components of *the ideology that produced* the first modern anti-Semitic political movement in the last two decades of the nineteenth century." Does Kertzer mean to say that in modern times anti-Judaism was partially but still significantly causative of anti-Semitism (already admitted by Cardinal Cassidy)? Does he wish to argue that the Vatican did not provide an accurate understanding of anti-Semitism (an arguable point)? Or does he want to abandon the distinction altogether?

It is entirely unclear. In the chapter entitled "Race" (pp. 205–212) he implies all three. Having subordinated historical research to a quarrel with the Church's 1998 *We Remember* statement about the Holocaust, a pamphlet that was never intended to be a history in the first place, Kertzer loses control over his thesis. The rubrics are expanded and contracted for no other apparent purpose than to insinuate that the popes were proponents or at least servants of modern anti-Semitism. Only those readers willing to assume that Catholicism was from the outset an anti-Semitic ideology waiting for its modern teeth will be able to abide this Procrustean bed.

The second problem is Kertzer's use, but more often his neglect, of sources. At the outset, he promises to "stick as close to the popes as I can get" (p. 19). "If I fail to bring their worldview to life," he says, "I will have failed to fully accomplish my task" (p. 12). Beginning at chapter 6, the popes only make cameo appearances in the story. We should not be surprised, for Kertzer declined to read their public documents. If he had consulted the eight-volume *Enchiridion delle Encicliche,* he would have discovered that between 1775 and 1939 there were ten popes who issued some 277 encyclicals and other teaching documents. By my count, at least 158 of these documents deal with issues of political and social order: religious liberty, Catholic schools, civil and ecclesiastical courts, rights of parents, Freemasons, social-contract theories, labor unions, the respective virtues and vices of monarchical and republican forms of government, and morality of dueling, to mention only a few. These teaching documents are an irreplaceable source of information about what Rome had to say about the evolution of modern states and societies in the most important century of their development.

Remarkably, there is no indication that Kertzer has laid eyes on any of these documents. Four encyclicals are mentioned (not always by name) without citation of the original source. On three occasions, Kertzer alludes to the *Syllabus errorum*, which Pius IX appended to the encyclical *Quanta cura* (1864). It is indeed a rich source for understanding Rome's view of political modernity in the wake of the revolutions of 1848. None of the propositions concerning the states' suppression of civil and natural rights is quoted or even mentioned. This is not to say that Kertzer deliberately left out evidence; the note indicates that he fished the information out of an encyclopedia, which is to say that he did not read the document.

What is worse, Kertzer neglects serious treatment of the one encyclical that bears directly on his project, *Mit brennender Sorge* (1937). Kertzer acknowledges that in *Mit brennender* Pius XI criticized the Nazi regime, but insists that the pope made "no direct attack on anti-Semitism" (p. 277). My copy of the encyclical contains a discussion of why the Scriptures and the Incarnation itself forbid any racial derogation of the "chosen people." Perhaps Pius XI should have said more, but Kertzer could hardly have known what he said at all—for in the notes we see that the six words he quotes from the encyclical are lifted out of John Cornwell's *Hitler's Pope*.

What can explain Kertzer's failure to read the public documents of the modern popes? Perhaps someone told him that he would find nothing favoring his thesis. Indeed, putting scriptural quotations aside, Jews are mentioned no more than a half-dozen times before 1937. Between 1775 and 1937, this is the only sentence in more than two hundred teaching documents that casts the Jews in an unfavorable light: "But it knew well that none of the metropolitans or the senior bishops would agree to ordain new bishops who were elected in the municipal districts by laity, heretics, unbelievers, and Jews as the published decrees commanded." Here, we have quoted Pius VI's *Charitas* (1791). In the second year of the French Revolution, the pope was complaining that the regime's *Civil Constitution of the Clergy* made clergy subject to election by taxpayers, regardless of their religion or complete lack of religion. Unless one supposes that Jews are entitled to elect Catholic clergy, the passage hardly demeans either the natural or civil rights of Jews. In fact, the public documents show clearly that Jews hardly registered on the papal radar screen during the time in which the older polities became states as we now know them. Were the popes preoccupied with Jacobins, Liberals, Masons, Socialists, and Laicists? Yes, of course. But not Jews.

Rather than reading the public documents, which cut against his thesis at every point, Kertzer decides to characterize Leo XIII as a public-relations artist rather than a teacher (pp. 166–168). It is well known, of course, that the modern political and social doctrine of the Church begins with Leo. Since Kertzer's thesis is that the Church and the papacy began their slide into modern anti-Semitism at this very time, we should think that the historian would immediately repair to the 110 Leonine encyclicals, if for no other reason than curiosity. Instead, Kertzer argues that Leo kept a public distance from anti-Semitic movements while secretly giving them room to develop. In other words, there is no point bothering with the pope's public teachings.

Without reference to any source, primary or secondary, he contends that Leo XIII "believed that the Jews' divinely ordained place was in the ghetto" (p. 222). Regarding an interview that Leo gave to a French journalist, Kertzer writes: "In warning of a new plague that was affecting modern society, which he termed 'the kingdom of money,' and insisting on the need to defend against it, the pope—without naming the Jews—tapped in to one of the main themes of the Catholic anti-Semitic campaign of the time" (p. 316). Again, Kertzer's characterization of the interview is not drawn from an original source. The hapless innuendo that Leo was agitating anti-Semitism evinces not the slightest awareness of Leo's great encyclicals against the laissez-faire policies of European governments. A few months earlier, he had issued *Rerum novarum*, on the plight of the workers. Kertzer manages to make even the most liberal moments of the modern papal mind mere subterfuge for anti-Semitism; papal teachings against greed and exploitation of workers are weirdly interpreted as a kind of *sub silentio* targeting of the Jews.

As for the infamous Dreyfus affair at the turn of the century, Kertzer fails to quote or cite a single sentence from Leo's letters to the French Church and people: *Au Milieu des Sollicitudes* (1892), *Notre consolation* (1892), *Depuis le jour* (1899). While he mentions in passing that Leo had a "growing concern" about the French right wing, and specifically about the anti-Semitic screed being published by the Assumptionist Fathers' journal *La Croix*, Kertzer can only conclude that this was a matter of politics and public opinion—spin control, rather than a principled position on Leo's part. But Kertzer has no familiarity with the Leonine documents that set forth the principles. He lacks the knowledge necessary for making such a judgment. Since his judgments are scurrilous, one must wonder whether his publisher looked at the notes carefully enough to detect that Kertzer relies on second- and third-hand material.

Kertzer also completely overlooks what is surely the most important and interesting right-wing movement in the Catholic world at that time, Charles Maurras's Action française. Founded in 1899 during the Dreyfus affair, Action française represents better than any other movement the passage of the monarchical party to the ideology of extreme nationalism. Maurras distinguished between the legal nation (*pays légal*) and the authentic nation (*pays réel*). For Maurras, the authentic nation must be recovered from the Protestants, revolutionaries, Freemasons, and Jews who control the legal nation.

Pius X accused the movement of "hatred." In 1914 seven of Maurras's publications were put on the index. His supporters were excommunicated by Pius XI in 1927, and the Jesuit Cardinal Billot was forced to resign because of his support for the movement.

The history of Action française can help us understand just how the older Christian nativism had become colored by secularism and nationalism. Some of the most important Catholic thinkers of the twentieth century—Charles Péguy and Jacques Maritain, to name but two—were formed in the crucible of this dispute. Indeed, its effect can be detected in many of Pius XI's encyclicals. What is certain, however, is that there can be no credible history of papal ideas about the political right wing without careful study of this movement and Rome's thirty-year effort to stifle it. It is certainly necessary for someone like Kertzer, who is in search of incriminating ideas, and who asserts, without evidence or citation, that for the Vatican fascist regimes were "embraced as a God-given bulwark against the great socialist evil" (p. 15).

Instead of the public documents and history, Kertzer purports to give a "secret" history consisting of diplomatic cables, private audiences with popes, and form letters from papal secretaries conveying papal benedictions to priests and laymen who had an anti-Semitic agenda. From these, Kertzer does not merely charge that the popes were not doing enough to resist and correct anti-Semitism in countries like France and Austria (not to mention the anti-Semitism expressed in ecclesiastical newspapers sponsored by the Vatican); he also implies that popes supported or found nothing untoward in these developments. Throughout the book, the popes are depicted as omniscient and omnipotent figures, capable of putting Austria and France, the Roman Curia, bishops, monsignors, and journalists into line by the snap of a papal finger; their silence about a particular renegade priest or political movement is interpreted as another instance of papal causality in world affairs. But, again, for Kertzer, the one thing the pope is not is a teacher. . . .

The Popes Against the Jews pursues an important subject—in recent literature, one that has been obscured by artless polemic. Whatever might be the author's sincerity (there can be no doubt about his moral passion), this work does not rise to the level of history. He has no control over the metahistorical criteria to which the data are supposed to conform. His research into the material data is slipshod, his inferences are rarely sound, and often drawn irresponsibly. The book does not throw light on a history already too obscured by legend and witch hunt.

6

The Land of What If

Kevin M. Doyle

(a review of Georges Passelecq and Bernard Suchecky's *The Hidden Encyclical* [New York: Harcourt Brace, 1997], from the *New Oxford Review*, July–August 1998, pp. 20–24)

The land of *what if* is a poignant place from which to contemplate the Shoah. To ask what if the Allies had bombed the railways, or what if all immigration quotas had been suspended, is to enter a world in which six million of God's chosen people have *not* been slaughtered. The view from *what if* can help us see afresh the full horror of what did happen. Danger, though, lies in the move from *what if* to *if only*. From there, we may facilely assume an ethical authority and second-guess moral actors in a world half a century away, a world too often rendered in the starkest monochrome.

The Hidden Encyclical, a new translation of a 1995 French book, hails from this land of *what if*. It merits discussion because it so well illustrates how contemporary study of the Holocaust can both unfairly vilify the Church and, perhaps more destructively, instill a false sense of our moral superiority today. The authors of *The Hidden Encyclical* are two Belgians, ecumenist George Passelecq and historian Bernard Suchecky. They tell the story of Pius XI's commissioning an antiracism encyclical in June 1938, three and one-half years before Hitler's persecution of the Jews escalated into industrialized murder.

In 1938 the American Jesuit John LaFarge was visiting Rome on assignment for *America* magazine. LaFarge's pioneering book *Interracial Justice* had greatly impressed Pius, who summoned LaFarge for a private audience. Binding the priest to secrecy, the pope outlined his vision of the encyclical, but told LaFarge to say "what you would say if you yourself were pope."

LaFarge set to work in Paris, collaborating with two other Jesuits. The resulting text was entitled *Humani Generis Unitas*, and it devoted about one-quarter of its text explicitly to race, racism, and anti-Semitism—the latter of which it managed to both denounce and perpetrate. For *Humani Generis Unitas* at once championed Jews' "human rights" and cast Jews as accursed and hostile. The Jewish community was a source of "spiritual contagion," a people whose presence gave rise to "problems" to be solved, albeit justly, by civil powers. Such was the flawed document LaFarge brought back to Rome and submitted to Jesuit Superior General Ledochowski in September 1938.

Pius XI died in February 1939, before, however, having a chance to publish, adapt, reject, or perhaps even read *Humani Generis Unitas*. Cardinal Secretary of State Pacelli became Pius XII. *Humani Generis Unitas*, thought last to be on Pius XI's desk, receded into nonhistory, coming to public light only in 1972 and 1973 when the *National Catholic Reporter* ran a series on portions of it. (*The Hidden Encyclical* reprints *Humani Generis Unitas* fully for the first time in English.)

Why was *Humani Generis Unitas* not published before Pius XI died? (Did Ledochowski intentionally stall delivery of the draft to the ailing Pius XI?) Why didn't Pius XII publish *Humani Generis Unitas*? What if it had been published?

Exploring these and other questions, the authors of *The Hidden Encyclical* display a daunting lack of rigor and fairness precisely where analytical depth and historical context are needed. So, for example, the authors perpetuate the all-too-common impression that Church fear of communism owed merely to some worry that conquering Reds might seize the scapulars and melt down the monstrances. In fact, by 1938, Joseph Stalin's body count exceeded ten million. The authors also fault *Mit Brennender Sorge*, Pius XI's 1937 encyclical, both for its focus on the persecution of German Catholicism and for its not denouncing National Socialism as irreformable. Such judgment reeks of hindsight and loses force under close historical scrutiny.

Because Jews, even before the genocide, were Hitler's most oppressed victims, one can easily overlook the terror visited on others. Before *Mit Brennender Sorge*, though, even a writer in the *Nation* would report that "the [Nazi] persecution of the Catholics is less open than that of the Jews, but it is almost as virulent." Such virulence had meant not only show trials of the clergy and ravaged Catholic institutions; it had meant countless beatings and even brazen murders of Catholic leaders. Brutalized for speaking up even for herself, whom could the Church have served by overtly broadening its battlefront?

Additionally, *Mit Brennender Sorge* did condemn whoever "exalts race," and insisted on "recognition of natural rights," because "God's sun shines on every human face." By stating these principles, Pius XI placed the Church in direct opposition to the fundamental errors Nazism rode into infamy.

This likely contributed to the Nazis' deeming *Mit Brennender Sorge* subversive, defamatory, illegal under the Vatican-German Concordat, and subject to suppression. It certainly accounted for the American Jewish Committee's *Contemporary Jewish Record* citing "the Papal Encyclical against Racialism" as contributing to greater defense of the Jews in the American Catholic press by the spring of 1939.

Speculating on why *Humani Generis Unitas* was not published, *The Hidden Encyclical* pays scant attention to a small intervening event: the Second World War, a conflict costing upwards to fifty or sixty million lives (and in which Passelecq served with the Belgian Resistance). Lacking in retrospective imagination, *The Hidden Encyclical* fails to consider how, for the Vatican in the middle quarters of 1939, the imminent catastrophe of such global conflict might have eclipsed the crime of racial persecution.

Even Guenter Lewy, on whose *The Catholic Church and Nazi Germany* the authors very regrettably rely, acknowledged Pius XII's peace-brokering initiatives. Forcing a full-blown rhetorical showdown with the fanatical Hitler over anti-Semitism was not likely to enhance these efforts. Given the Nazis' genius for retaliation, such a confrontation was far more likely to mean greater torment for Jews whose emigration the Vatican was making possible (mostly converts in this prewar period).

Most fundamentally perhaps, *The Hidden Encyclical* bungles the crucial variable in its *what if* formula: the degree of anti-Semitism among the laity with whom any encyclical would have achieved its greatest impact. The authors assume that prewar rank-and-file Catholics typically viewed their Jewish contemporaries through a poisonous scrim of deicidal hate theology.

This assumption is common. It grounds the notion that catechetical conditioning drove Catholics who joined in, or acceded to, the Final Solution. Relatedly, it anchors the argument that a sufficiently strident pontifical protest might have brought the murder to a halt. This assumption, of course, does not help explain how Hitler systematically murdered five million non-Jews—Gypsies, Russian POWs, Polish Catholic intellectuals, handicapped, and mentally ill citizens.

More important, the assumption of a near-universal Catholic anti-Semitism tramples much historical fact. It comports with neither German Catholic voting patterns nor the record of Germany's Catholic Center Party, which is remembered for its tragic decision to allow Chancellor Hitler extraordinary powers after the burning of the Reichstag but forgotten for its earlier and subsequent protest against Nazi treatment of Jews. It clashes with internal Nazi reports of both Catholic citizens' "greatest indignation" over government Jew-baiting and Catholic breach of the boycott against Jewish merchants. It conflicts even with the overwhelming disapproval by American Catholics polled on Germany's mistreatment of Jews in 1938, a time when Charles Coughlin still fouled the airwaves. *The Hidden Encyclical* declines to wrestle with any of this troublesome evidence.

Imagining *what if* is hard, complicated work. Try this one out: What if Pius XII had published an encyclical within sixty days of the Second World War's outbreak? Suppose this encyclical's opening entrusted to the Lord's protection those united to the Church "in belief in God," even if not "in love for the person of Christ." What if the encyclical dwelled at length on the "Equality of the Races," while railing against a "corrupting paganism" and "Deification of the State"? Imagine the encyclical took care to preserve the pose of Vatican neutrality—thus later allowing the Holy See, inter alia, to aid until at least 1943 those Germans trying to overthrow Hitler, tip Britain off to Germany's imminent invasion of the Low Countries, and intervene diplomatically on behalf of Jews throughout Europe. But imagine also that the encyclical openly commiserated with newly invaded Poland, that it was so pro-Ally in substance that France leafleted German troops with it.

Finally, at the risk of seeming too fantastic, what if John LaFarge himself, *Humani Generis Unitas*'s drafter, wrote glowingly about this other encyclical in *America?* Fancy that LaFarge took as granted that this "dangerous" encyclical addressed racism in Europe and left for speculation merely its respective application to particular regimes. Fancy that LaFarge worried only that Americans would conveniently overlook that "German Racism as applied to the Jew is but a match for American Racism as applied to the Negro."

Does all this *what if* amount to an *if only?* Given this scenario, could Hitler have possibly perpetrated his singularly evil slaughter of Europe's Jewish community? Answer: Sadly, yes. Be sure of it. Pius XII issued *Summi Pontificatus* on October 20, 1939. You have now read an accurate recounting of it.

You will not find such a recounting in *The Hidden Encyclical.* The authors' omission is not startling, given what has gone before. From the early 1960s, when *The Deputy*, an antihistorical German play attacking Pius XII, debuted to mixed reviews, it has been open season on the wartime Church. To be sure, the Church's record was uneven, containing moments of inspiring heroism and sinful failure. Still, criticism has too often been one-sided and factually selective.

More, criticism, not only of the Church but also of the Allies and Jewish leaders, has too often ignored the moral complexities faced by people of good will who lived and struggled in Hitler's shadow. The Nazi juggernaut displayed a diabolical genius for retaliation, recrimination, and retribution. While devoid of conscience, it discerned ethical pressure points cleverly enough to ensnare potential resisters in unconscionable dilemmas. To ignore this not only subverts truth but keeps us from today learning from the Holocaust.

For only two questions can lead to our growth as moral persons as we meditate on the Holocaust: "What would *I* have done? What should *I* have done?" These questions must be asked honestly and humbly.

A study of the Holocaust's profound evil must itself be profound. If not, we risk the Holocaust's serving as a flattering diversion that falsely reassures us that we could not partake in, or succumb to, any comparable evil today.

Yet genocide persists; witness Cambodia, Rwanda, and Bosnia. And, beyond all reckoning, scandalous economic inequality takes a lethal toll, despite technological advances unimaginable a century ago. How easily, then, the Holocaust becomes a refuge rather than a challenge. At a Holocaust museum, rather than ask "What *am* I doing?" we can train our moral gaze on the past. A no-cost pity for victims long dead can combine with our self-congratulatory disgust toward perpetrators and bystanders, toward what *they* did and did not do.

We stand at the display case, shaking our heads and clucking our tongues. For a moment, we are exalted on the cheap—as we defile the memory of the slaughtered and ignore the needs of the living.

7

Something Deeply Shameful

John Jay Hughes

(a review of Michael Phayer's *The Catholic Church and the Holocaust, 1930–1965* [Bloomington: Indiana University, 2000], from *Inside the Vatican*, December 2000, pp. 48–52)

Of the making of books attacking Pope Pius XII for alleged complicity in the death of six million Jews there appears to be no end. Hard on the heels of British journalist John Cornwell's *Hitler's Pope*, a riveting tissue of half-truths, gross misinterpretations, and outright falsehoods brilliantly crafted to produce a *frisson* of horror and indignation in even the most jaded reader, comes this volume by a professor of history at Marquette University in Milwaukee.

Michael Phayer portrays the wartime pontiff as part Hamlet, his resolution sicklied o'er with the pale cast of thought; part cautious functionary whose "greatest failure lay in his attempt to use a diplomatic remedy for a moral outrage"; and occasional rescuer when circumstances allowed him to act without danger to himself or his entourage. Determining the pope's occasional action, in Phayer's view, and his too-frequent inaction, was the pontiff's obsessive fear of communism, which he sought to combat by preserving a strong Germany, the country he learned to love as nuncio, first in Munich then in Berlin from 1917 to 1929, but which under its Nazi rulers he greatly feared; and his desire to protect the city of Rome, Vatican City, and his own person.

Phayer repudiates Rolf Hochhuth's portrayal of a pope with "aristocratic coldness" and an "icy glint" in his eyes; and Cornwell's charge that Pius XII was "the perfect pope for Hitler because the pontiff's anti-Semitism allowed the dictator to carry out genocide while he kept silent." "Jews and Gentiles alike who had audiences with the pope recalled his warm personality, and documents record a number of occasions when the pope wept openly," he writes. "If Pius was tainted with anti-Semitism, it did not keep him from aiding Jews during and after the Holocaust. . . . To hold that the pope always acted negatively toward Jews is to close one's eyes to the historical record."

The burden of Phayer's complaint is not that pope did nothing, but that what he did fell far short of what was possible and, for a pope, required. Moreover, in contrast to Cornwell, who used no German sources at all (save those available in English translation), Phayer conducted much of his research in Germany and frequently cites German works. His interpretation of these sources is, however, another matter.

Phayer spreads his net far beyond Rome, examining the record in Germany, France, and the Balkans. He highlights the work of individual rescuers, especially women (about whom he has written two previous books). Here too, however, Phayer charges that far more could have been done if Pius XII had informed potential rescuers about Nazi atrocities and encouraged protests and resistance. Extending his study to the postwar years, Phayer repeats long-familiar and oft-refuted charges that "the Vatican" actively assisted Nazi criminals to escape justice.

Dealing adequately with such a wide-ranging indictment would require an entire book. The most that a reviewer can do is examine, first Phayer's methodology, and then some of his principal charges. On the first page of his book Phayer acknowledges help from other scholars, who "generously provided me with many corrections and alternative points of view." Failure to consider other points of view is a major weakness in the book. Here are three examples, although many others could be cited:

- When the Nazis, in the fall of 1941, ordered all Jews to wear the star of David, Cardinal Bertram of Breslau told his clergy that if Nazis openly protested the presence in church of (baptized) Jews, the latter were to be told to attend an early Mass not frequented by Nazis. Phayer's comment: "Nazis would be accommodated at the expense of Catholics of Jewish descent." He fails to consider a more plausible interpretation: the desire to spare such Jews public humiliation.
- Phayer writes that the Austrian Bishop Hudal, a well-known Nazi sympathizer and as such an embarrassment to the Vatican, "won an appointment as rector of the Collegia del Anima in Rome." In reality the appointment was intended to isolate Hudal by confining him to a post of little significance or influence—a practice that a historian as widely read as Phayer should know is common in all large organizations, the Vatican included.
- Phayer's most serious failure to consider alternative points of view is his treatment of Ernst von Weizsäcker, Hitler's wartime ambassador to the Holy See. Like many anti-Nazi Germans who held government posts in Hitler's Germany, Weizsäcker used his position to sabotage Nazi policy

when he could. Many of these heroic covert resisters paid with their lives. Weizsäcker survived the war, only to be sentenced to imprisonment by the Nuremberg War Crimes Tribunal. A number of historians consider Weizsäcker's treatment a miscarriage of justice. Deeply convinced (as he wrote to his mother) that "Hitler's persecution of the Jews [was] a violation of all the rules and laws of Christianity," Weizsäcker did everything in his power to save Jews. This forced him to play a double game: on the one hand assuring Berlin that the pope remained well disposed toward Germany and was not much concerned with the Jews; while at the same time urging Pius XII to work quietly behind the scenes, avoiding any public protest that, Weizsäcker knew, would only enrage Hitler and thus hasten the Jews' destruction. Phayer shows some awareness of this double game, referring at one point to "the cagey Weizsäcker." By failing to take sufficient account of Weizsäcker's delicate position, however, Phayer undermines his argument at a crucial point.

Because a review cannot analyze more than a fraction of Phayer's charges, we must now examine what he himself calls "for many the litmus test of the pope's response to genocide during the war." During the night of October 15–16, 1943, the S.S. rounded up 1,259 Roman Jews. Early in the morning of October 16 the Italian Princess Enza Pignatelli Aragona Cortés went to the pope to seek help. She reported later that he was both shocked and furious. As she left, Pius was already on the telephone ordering his secretary of state to make an immediate protest to Ambassador Weizsäcker, demanding that the arrests be stopped. Weizsäcker responded that if the pope wished to save any Jews he must avoid a public protest. That would send Hitler into a frenzy and doom even more Jews. The British minister to the Holy See, Osborne, confirmed the unpublicized papal protest in a message to his superiors in London, telling them that as a result of the pope's action "large numbers" of Jews were released.

Ignoring this clear record of vigorous papal action, Phayer writes: "Nothing came of anything the Holy See said about the fateful days beginning on October 16, 1943. Having known in advance what would befall the Roman Jews, the pope said nothing to forestall it. Afterward he said nothing to condemn it."

There is no hard evidence that the pope knew in advance about the Nazi action against the Roman Jews. The claim that he did (which Phayer repeats from previous authors) goes back to Robert Katz, author of two books defaming Pius XII. After the pope's death his niece sued Katz for libeling her uncle. The Italian court found Katz guilty and imposed a large fine and a suspended prison sentence. Further evidence that the pope had no advance knowledge of the October 16 raid is the statement of Princess Enza Pignatelli Aragona Cortés that Pius XII was in a state of shock when she told him what the Nazis had done.

Ten days after the October 16 roundup, *Osservatore Romano* published a statement in the then-customary rotund Vatican-speak: "With the augmentation of so much evil, the universal and paternal charity of the Supreme Pontiff has become, it might be said, ever more active; it knows neither boundaries nor nationality, neither religion nor race."

Fearful that even this convoluted statement might enrage Hitler, Weizsäcker sent a telegram to Berlin on October 28 saying that the pope, despite pleas from various quarters, "has not allowed himself to be carried away [into] making any demonstrative statements against the deportation of the Jews." The telegram also mentioned the *Osservatore Romano* statement just quoted, saying that "hardly anyone will understand the text as referring specifically to the Jewish question."

This telegram was seized upon long ago by authors eager to condemn Pius XII. Repeated from author to author, it is now widely considered to be the smoking gun that definitively convicts the pope of silence and inactivity in the face of the Holocaust. In reality the telegram was one of what Weizsäcker's deputy, Albrecht von Kessel, called his chief's "tactical lies," designed to protect both the pope and the Jews by persuading the authorities in Berlin that the pontiff was well disposed toward Germany and would do nothing to injure its cause. Weizsäcker knew of Nazi plans to kidnap the pope. He also knew that at the very moment he sent this telegram thousands of Jews were hiding in Roman monasteries and convents. Phayer himself estimates their number between 4,000 and 5,000. He adds at once, however, that there is no evidence that Pius XII ever ordered their rescue: "Written instructions to this effect have never surfaced."

Seldom can a serious historian have written a sentence so breathtaking in its naiveté. Is Phayer not aware that one of the principal arguments of today's Holocaust deniers is that no written instructions from Hitler ordering the mass slaughter of Jews have ever surfaced? The British writer David Irving recently lost a costly suit for libel against the American historian Deborah Lipstadt, who had criticized Irving for using this very argument. There is abundant testimony from Pius XII's subordinates that they had clear directions from the pope to do everything possible for the Jews. Angelo Roncalli, then apostolic delegate in Turkey and Pius's successor as John XXIII, responded to praise for his work in saving Jews: "In all these painful matters I have referred to the Holy See and simply carried out the pope's orders: first and foremost to save human lives." (Phayer knows better: "It is difficult to take this in a literal sense.") There are some things one does not put in writing—in Rome as well as in Berlin.

Finally, the charge that no one in Rome knew of the pope's protest against the roundup of Roman Jews, or understood the *Osservatore Romano* statement ten days later to refer to the pope's intervention, is directly refuted by the diary of an American nun, then resident in Rome. Published in 1945 under the pseudonym "Jane Scrivener," it contains an entry on October 19, just three days after the roundup, that verifies the old adage that in the Eternal City everything is a mystery and nothing a secret: "It is understood that the pope has asked the German Ambassador to make an effort to help the Jews. It is difficult for von Weizsäcker, of course, as the S.S. are independent of him. However, he did have some measure of success, for we hear that the women and children will be released."

Like all Pius XII's critics, Phayer argues that when the pope did speak about Nazi persecution of the Jews he did so in such vague terms that few people understood. Typical is Phayer's comment about the pope's statement, in his 1942 Christmas address, about "the hundreds of thousands who, through no fault of their own, and solely because of their nation and race, have been condemned to death or progressive extinction." Phayer's comment is "Pope Pius's radio talk contained twenty-seven words about the Holocaust out of twenty-six pages of text. The part about the Holocaust, buried in a sea of verbosity, did not mention Jews. A few months later, Pius wrote to Bishop von Preysing in Berlin [the most anti-Nazi of the German bishops] saying that his address was well understood. In reality, no one, certainly not the Germans, took it as a protest against their slaughter of the Jews."

Phayer's grasp of reality, never strong, completely deserts him at this point. Mussolini's foreign minister and son-in-law, Count Ciano, wrote in his diary that the duce was furious at the pope's speech. The then German ambassador to the Holy See, Diego von Bergen, protested, and no one from his embassy attended the pope's Christmas midnight Mass. In Berlin an official report called the pope's speech "one long attack on everything we stand for. Here he is clearly speaking on behalf of the Jews . . . and makes himself the mouthpiece of the Jewish war criminals."

Finally, the *New York Times* commented on the speech: "This Christmas more than ever [Pope Pius XII] is a lonely voice crying out of the silence of a continent. . . . No one would expect the pope to speak as a political leader, or a war leader, or in any other role than that of a preacher ordained to stand above the battle, tied impartially, as he says, to all people and willing to collaborate in any new order which will bring a just peace. . . . Pope Pius expresses as passionately as any leader on our side the war aims of the struggle for freedom when he says that those who aim at building a new world must fight for free choice of government and religious order. They must refuse that the state should make of individuals a herd of whom the state disposes as if they were a lifeless thing."

A historian who claims, in the face of all this evidence, that the pope was not understood has forfeited all claim to credibility.

Pius XII's major public statements were infrequent. His own radio station and newspaper, however, regularly informed the world about Nazi atrocities.

The English Catholic Robert Speaight, in a monograph about the wartime broadcasts of Vatican Radio, spoke of "the satisfaction of a Catholic in a Protestant country in being able to affirm, at least in the battle against Nazism, that the Vatican was on the side of the Allies." The French Jesuit Michel Riquet, who personally saved six Jews before his imprisonment in Dachau, testified in 1964 about the invigorating effect on the pope's words and actions on resisters and rescuers: "Pius XII spoke; Pius XII condemned; Pius XII acted. . . . Throughout those years of horror, when we listened to Radio Vatican and to the pope's messages, we felt in communion with the pope, in helping persecuted Jews and in fighting against Nazi violence."

There are many situations in which it is not necessary to speak explicitly in order to be understood. During the July 2000 Republican political convention, and the campaign that followed, President Clinton's name was scarcely mentioned. Instead we heard about "restoring dignity and integrity to the office of the president." No one was in any doubt what those statements referred to.

Moreover, conditions in a tyrannical totalitarian regime, especially in wartime, sharpen people's ears to a degree hardly conceivable to those who live in open societies like our own. There was a striking example during the short-lived Czech overthrow of Communist rule in 1968. Television showed the new prime minister addressing parliament. His opening word brought prolonged, tumultuous applause. The announcer explained, for the benefit of viewers unable to understand Czech, that the prime minister had addressed his audience not as "comrades" but as "fellow citizens." A single word constituted a declaration of protest and independence immediately intelligible to all.

In excoriating German bishops and their flocks for not doing enough, Phayer takes little account of the pressures under which they lived. A never-delivered letter to an English friend, written by the martyred German Protestant resistance hero Count Helmut von Moltke in March 1943, vividly describes the difficulties of any resistance in wartime Germany: inability to communicate by telephone, post, or messenger; the danger of speaking openly even to trusted friends (who might be arrested and tortured); the exhaustion of people whose energies were fully occupied with the ordinary tasks of day-to-day survival. Most telling is von Moltke's account of the terror visited by Hitler on his own people: nineteen guillotines executing an estimated fifty people daily, the relatives cowed into silence for fear of suffering the same fate. . . .

Running like a scarlet thread through Phayer's book is the pope's obsessive fear of communism. . . . Like many academics today, Phayer regards anticommunism as a taint. Is he unaware of *The Black Book of Communism*, published in France in 1997 and now available in English translation, which estimates communism's victims worldwide at one hundred million? This figure, which dwarfs the number of Hitler's victims, suggests that the pope's concern may have had more justification than Phayer is willing to allow. That the pope ever considered supporting Nazi Germany against the Soviet Union is, however, sheer fantasy.

Despite strong pressure to do so, not once did Pius XII call Hitler's war against the Soviets a crusade. Following Germany's attack on Russia in June 1941 the Vatican polemic against communism virtually disappeared. The contrast with the pastoral letters of German bishops during the same period is striking. Moreover, the pope informed his bishops in the United States that the church's continuing opposition to communism should be no barrier to Catholic support for President Roosevelt's Lend-Lease program in aid of the western Allies. . . .

In his chapter "Answering for the Holocaust," Phayer criticizes the German bishops for rejecting the notion of collective guilt after the war, and Pius XII for supporting them. It seems to have escaped him that rejection of collective guilt was the basis for the statement of Vatican II (which Phayer toward the end of his book warmly applauds) that "neither all Jews indiscriminately at [Jesus' death], nor Jews today, can be charged with the crimes committed during his passion. . . . The Church deplores all hatreds, persecutions, displays of anti-Semitism leveled at any time or from any source against the Jews." The rejection of collective guilt was correct, theologically and philosophically. Guilt is always personal, even when the number of those guilty is large.

Phayer also criticizes Pius XII for asking mercy for war criminals condemned to death. Though Phayer does not mention it, the pope also asked the Polish government to suspend its death sentence against Arthur Geiser, responsible for the deaths of numerous priests. The present pope regularly asks mercy for criminals sentenced to death for crimes of unspeakable bestiality and cruelty. Does Phayer disapprove of these pleas as well? Pius XII also supported efforts to bring war criminals to justice. Through the American Jesuit, Edmund A. Walsh, the pope submitted to the War Crimes Tribunal at Nuremberg a dossier, authenticated by the papal secretary of state, documenting Nazi crimes against the Catholic Church.

Phayer repeats the charges of other authors, long known and oft refuted, that the Vatican helped Nazi war criminals escape justice after the war. In his reading of the record, "the Vatican" includes anything and anyone Catholic, from the Trapp Family Singers and the Vienna Boys' Choir to the notorious loose cannon, Austrian Bishop Hudal. A game played by such rules is hard to lose. While Hudal may have aided a few war criminals, neither he nor anyone else Phayer mentions in this connection acted with Vatican approval. Phayer's principal source is a 1992 book, *The Unholy Trinity* by John Loftus and Mark Aarons. They cite material from the U.S. National Archives. This gives their charges an aura of authenticity—until one learns that they are citing a collection of unproved reports collected by James J. Angleton, postwar OSS bureau chief in Rome and passed on to his superiors in Washington. Much of this material was forged by one

Virgilio Scattolini, author of an Italian book called *The Secret Diplomacy of the Vatican*, for which Scattolini received a prison sentence.

Enough already! Were all the judgments and decisions of Pope Pius XII wise and prudent? Who would venture an affirmative answer? Did he make mistakes? Undoubtedly. Papal infallibility, as not even all Catholics know, does not extend to policies or the prudential judgments of a pope. . . .

The worst aspect of Phayer's book remains unmentioned: the dust jacket. Drawn by a Holocaust survivor, it portrays a uniformed Nazi guard holding a whip and next to him a faceless Catholic prelate, both standing on the corpse of an emaciated victim wearing the Jewish Star of David. To the left of the figures is an inscription, in epitaph style: "A.D. 1933–1945 The Concordat."

Phayer says in his acknowledgments that he chose the drawing himself. Clearly designed to enrage and inflame, it is the visible portrayal of a historical falsehood. The Concordat was never an alliance with Hitler. On the contrary, it was a treaty guaranteeing church freedom and rights. Without it neither the Holy See nor the German bishops would have had any legal basis for the countless protests against Nazi policies that so enraged Hitler that he promised, in his Table Talk, to scrap the treaty at the war's conclusion.

By choosing this mendacious drawing to introduce his book, Phayer has placed his work on the level of the viciously anti-Semitic nineteenth-century forgery, *Protocols of the Elders of Zion*. Is it not clear that something deeply shameful is going on?

8

How Not to Deal with History

John S. Conway

(an editorial on the Vatican's Pius XII Commission, from the *American Jewish Congress Monthly*, November–December 2001, pp. 9–13)

The suspending of the deliberations of the Joint Catholic-Jewish Commission was a setback for the desirable goal of improved relations between Catholics and Jews through collaborative investigations of contentious historical issues. It is to be hoped that the flurry of recriminations and unwarranted accusations that were voiced subsequently will soon be forgotten and the whole incident regarded as no more than a regrettable stumble. But because there are significant issues involved for all historians, this commentary may be of some help to those who have not been able to pay close attention to this controversy.

As is well known, debate has recently been stirred up again over the policies of the Vatican during the Second World War, and more specifically, over the alleged failure of Pope Pius XII to adopt an attitude of protest against the Nazi persecution of the Jews, culminating in the Holocaust. In the past few months, no fewer than ten books on this topic have been published, and more are now in the works. It is interesting to note that the most vigorous attacks have come from such authors as John Cornwell, Michael Phayer, and James Carroll, who belong to what may be called the "liberal" wing of the Catholic Church, and who take a highly critical view of the pope, Eugenio Pacelli, personally, or stress the deficiencies of the Vatican structures. At the same time, among the defenders of the wartime policies of Pius XII are several Jewish scholars, such as Pinchas Lapide, William Rubinstein, or, more recently, Rabbi David Dalin. Thus, among both Jewish and Catholic experts, there are considerable differences of view, with the result that, so far, no historical consensus has been achieved. Not surprisingly these unresolved arguments have proved disappointing to those Catholic loyalists who believe the pope's attitudes to be beyond reproach or, alternately, to some Jewish commentators who seek vindication of their own critical appraisal.

This controversy arose at the time when the present leaders of the Catholic Church, led by Pope John Paul II himself, are engaged in striking measures to improve relations with the Jewish people. In the eyes of one Jewish scholar, these efforts constitute "the most remarkable progress in Catholic-Jewish relations that seasoned observers can ever remember, . . . and are a genuine and sincere effort of the leadership of the Church to promote awareness of the Holocaust among Catholics and a climate of healing between the two communities."

It was in part a result of this new approach that in 1998 Cardinal Cassidy, then president of the Pontifical Commission on Religious Relations with the Jews, proposed that a team of Catholic and Jewish historians should together review what was already published on the sensitive issue of the Vatican's wartime activities, and if so desired, "pose questions about unresolved matters." This unprecedented team of six scholars, three Catholic and three Jewish, began its work in October 1999. Five men and one woman were selected by their respective agencies: on the one side by Cardinal Cassidy's Pontifical Commission, and on the other by the International Jewish Committee for Interreligious Consultation. The Catholic members were all American citizens, and apparently were asked to serve because of a known sympathy for the aims of Catholic-Jewish reconciliation. So far so good.

But the terms of their mandate were less satisfactory. They were invited to look first and foremost at the eleven volumes of documents from the Vatican archives dealing with this subject that were published between 1965 and 1981. These large collections of documents, entitled *Actes et Documents du Saint Siège relatifs a la seconde guerre mondiale,* had been compiled and edited by an international team of four Jesuits, Fathers Blet, Graham, Schneider, and Martini, acting on the explicit instructions of Pope Paul VI. The purpose of this publication was clearly to provide the documentation to refute the criticisms and attacks launched in the early 1960s against Pope Pius XII's wartime policies, beginning with Rolf Hochhuth's sensational drama *The Deputy.*

In order to undertake this task, the Jesuit editors were given unique and unprecedented access to the otherwise closed Vatican archives. According to Father Graham, they were able to see all the documents they wanted and were not subject to any censorship or pressure to produce results favorable to the Vatican authorities. But the very fact that these editors were all Jesuits and that no one else was allowed to see the documents in question raised objections from outsiders. Despite assurances to the contrary, suspicions remained that the whole venture had been a well-organized effort at damage control.

The documents themselves are drawn from the files of the Vatican's Secretariat of State and consist mainly of the telegrams and memoranda exchanged between the Holy See and its representatives, principally the nuncios or apostolic delegates accredited to the various governments around the world. These exchanges are almost all in Italian, though documents in English, German, French, and even Latin also appear. The editorial introduction to each volume is, however, in French. Acting on a traditional principle, the editors included only those documents that originated in one of their own diplomatic service's offices, or related ecclesiastical structures, and hence did not print, but only referred in a footnote to other documents, however significant, supplied by outsiders, such as, for example, statements presented to the Vatican's representatives by Jewish contacts. Had these been included, it is possible that much criticism of these Vatican volumes might have been averted, even though in fact these valuable documents have usually appeared in print elsewhere.

The scope of these eleven volumes is twofold. The editors sought to present the documentary evidence on two main subjects: first, the efforts made by the Vatican, from the beginning of Pope Pius XII's reign in March 1939, to preserve peace, or, after the outbreak of war in September 1939, to prevent the spread of hostilities. These efforts included the hope that the Vatican could play an effective part in any mediated peace settlement—as it had sought to do in the First World War. Also included were the various endeavors to mitigate the effects of the war, such as the extensive efforts designed to secure agreement to making Rome an open city and hence spared from bombing attacks. The second theme was to record the Vatican's endeavors to assist the victims of the war. Almost daily exchanges on this subject occurred throughout the Vatican's network of diplomatic contacts.

It is in this latter context that the Vatican's actions on behalf of the stricken Jewish communities are to be found. Although, at first, the prime concern was to seek to provide relief supplies and assistance to the Catholic victims of Nazi aggression in Poland, very soon the horizons widened. Catholics of Jewish origin soon came to the Vatican's notice, through appeals to find them some refugee haven in a Catholic country overseas.

But from 1941 onwards, it is clear that the Vatican's leaders were aware of the scale of persecution inflicted on all the Jews, and were prepared to instruct their officials to offer help, including protests against these atrocities to those governments where such papal pressure might be effective. The documents relating to Slovakia, Roumania, Hungary, and France are a clear indication that these interventions went beyond a defense merely of Catholic interests or persons. These interventions were all the more notable since the Vatican officials were well aware that the Catholic leaders in these countries were unsympathetic to the plight of the Jews. In Slovakia, for instance, the situation was made more difficult by the fact that the president of Slovakia was Monsignor Josef Tiso, a well-known anti-Semite. Energetic representations were made by the papal apostolic delegate in Bratislava, Monsignor Burzio, in 1942 and 1943. But the results were disappointingly negative. Indeed, in July 1942, Monsignor Tardini, one of the Vatican's senior staff members, bitterly commented: "It is a great misfortune that the president of Slovakia is a priest. Everyone knows that the Holy See cannot bring Hitler to heel. But who will understand that we can't even control a priest?"

From 1942 onwards, the pope's prudent and fearful stance brought him to the conclusion that a more outspoken policy of protest would lead to increased repercussions or vengeance from the Nazis and hence inflict still more suffering on the victims. The overall picture to be drawn from these volumes is therefore of the significant reduction of papal influence during these years of war and terror. The evidence makes clear that, despite the pope's sincere efforts to mitigate the effects of the war and to bring relief to its victims, his initiatives were spurned and his advice ignored as the forces of violence and destruction escalated.

Particularly in the later volumes, and especially for the period of nine months when the German army occupied Rome, the sense of foreboding and frustration is very evident. The pope and his officials were imprisoned within the Vatican's boundaries, surrounded by German troops. Their offices were infiltrated with Nazi spies and their communications censored. At any moment, they feared, the pope might be carried off into captivity and exile. This claustrophobic nightmare was only in part moderated after Rome was liberated by Allied troops in June 1944 and its precious architectural heritage preserved from any further bombing raids. But the premonition of apocalyptic doom that the end of the war might bring, through the use of new and even more terrible weapons of destruction, was still present. The powerlessness of the papacy to prevent any such final catastrophe was an unwelcome but undeniable reality.

The critics of Pius XII and his wartime policies, beginning with Hochhuth in the 1960s and repeated by the more recent authors, have ignored these considerations. Instead they claim that a more vigorous and prophetic stance of protest against the Nazi atrocities would not only have been effective but would have resulted in the saving of many more lives, particularly Jewish lives. Several of the recent books contain numerous passages advancing such hypotheses as: "If only the pope had protested at this juncture . . . " or "The papacy should have taken steps . . . "

Historical evidence to back up such claims is however lacking, and certainly is not to be drawn from the *Actes et Documents*. Rather such notions are the product of wishful thinking. In effect these claims vastly exaggerate the moral and political power of the papacy and fail to recognize its greatly diminished influence during the Second World War. And while no one can say what might have happened if the Vatican and its local representatives had adopted other policies, it is necessary to recognize that such optimistic speculations have been put forward mainly for nonhistorical reasons.

It would seem that many of the Vatican's critics, whether Jewish or Catholic, are unfamiliar with the already published documentary sources. This is hardly surprising since these volumes appeared at irregular intervals over a fifteen-year period, and the language barrier, particularly for English-speaking commentators, is clearly evident. This was also the case for some of the members of the Joint Commission who apparently found themselves "linguistically challenged."

But, more seriously, this series of documents, and the historical value of the contents, has suffered the same fate as befell other significant collections of documents relating to the policies and actions of various governments in both the First and Second World Wars. Starting in 1919, all the major European states authorized the publication of extensive documentary series, designed to provide the evidence of their nation's purity of motives and tactics in the crisis of 1914 that led to the outbreak of war. The self-justifying and apologetic purpose was obvious. And even though these collections were edited by distinguished historians, they inevitably came to be regarded as self-serving and biased presentations. Their appearance did not in fact prevent or deflect criticism, and the charges continued to be made that such editions, prepared by "in-house" professionals, were carefully screened to suppress publication of any embarrassing material that would damage their nation's reputation, if necessary by the removal of incriminating documents altogether. Officially sponsored document collections of this kind were suspect.

It was exactly this consideration that led the Joint Commission to refrain deliberately from inviting any member of the Vatican's staff from joining their team, including the sole survivor of the four Jesuits, Father Pierre Blet, or the current "expert" in the Vatican, Father Peter Gumpel, S.J., the officially appointed relator in charge of evaluating the cause for the beatification of Pope Pius XII, who for several years has been assembling documents for this purpose. It would seem that the presupposition was made that an independent panel of experts would be able to reach an accurate version of events that would carry greater credibility, especially in hostile circles.

The issue of credibility has been a sensitive and indeed vital issue throughout the history of this controversy over the past forty years. But it has to be placed in a wider context than merely the question of the authenticity of the Jesuits' selection of documents. We have to recognize—and indeed to sympathize with—the continuing and sincerely motivated search, particularly by survivors of the Holocaust, but also by the Jewish community at large, and a growing number of Christians, for some overall explanation for the unprecedented persecution and destruction of so many million Jews at the hands of the Nazis and their accomplices. There is a widely shared view that the horrors of the Holocaust may be made more tolerable if the failures of other governments and agencies to halt the Nazi atrocities can be pinpointed and brought to light. What might appear to be a search for scapegoats should, in reality, be appreciated as a kind of therapeutic necessity to bring relief for the unmitigated suffering involved—regardless of the historical facts of the case.

It is in this context that the view has grown up that, if only Pope Pius and his officials had been more energetic in protesting the Nazi crimes, or in mobilizing Catholics to take inhibitory action, the Holocaust might never have happened, or at least that its devastating effects would have been modified or lessened. The concomitant expectation is that evidence to support such a hypothesis exists in the Vatican's files. If the previous publication did not lead to this conclusion, it was because of the officially sponsored nature of the project, or because the editors were determined not to reveal "the smoking gun," which advocates of this theory believe still exists hidden in the Vatican vaults. Hence the demand put forward that the Vatican should give access to its unpublished files and open its archives for this period to all comers, so that, once and for all, the issue can be resolved.

The view that an independent, but part-time, group such as the Joint Commission could reach a more conclusive verdict than the editorial team that labored for so long in the 1960s and 1970s is, by any objective standard, a questionable one. But it had its own political dynamic. Necessarily the Joint Commission felt impelled to adapt a critical stance toward their predecessors' labors. But in the end, their preliminary report on the *Actes et documents,* which was presented to the Vatican in October 2000, sought clarification of forty-seven specific issues that they felt had not been adequately answered in the printed collection.

Even while expressing appreciation for the work of the four Jesuit editors, the Joint Commission members adopted the professionally understandable point of view that another look based on wider access was desirable. And this in turn led on to their explicit request, echoing demands frequently made by the Vatican's critics, that full disclosure and unfettered research should be made possible through the release of all relevant documentation, and that the Vatican archives for the period should be opened up, thereby allowing the truth to emerge. Any continued refusal to accede to this request would seemingly confirm the impression that there are still secrets or scandals that the Vatican wants to conceal.

This suggestion, or request, however, also rests on the questionable assumption that such a wider enquiry would in fact discover materials substantially different from those already published. If such a freer enquiry found only that the earlier editors had been correct in their selection, then the Vatican's original case would be vindicated, and any new investigation would be superfluous. On the other hand, as one of the Joint Commission members noted: "Every documentary collection is based on a selection of material; inevitably, scholars want to make their own selection, and decide for themselves what is relevant. Further, historians also need to know what material was not in the published volumes—again highlighting the need to see the unpublished material. And finally, the original selection was made by scholars of another era—in some instances working more than thirty years ago. Once again, an argument for access."

This is the counsel of perfection. No historian is happy about archival closures. All would like to see free and open access on an unlimited scale. But the reality is otherwise. All governments and agencies have rules about the extent to which their records are open to public scrutiny. In many democratic countries, such as the United States, Canada, or Britain, their government collections are not made available for research purposes until thirty years after their inception. But even here there are exceptions when materials are withheld and no reasons are provided. The situation in countries such as Russia is even more erratic.

In the case of the Vatican, the world's oldest diplomatic entity made up its own rules. Until the end of the nineteenth century, the Vatican guarded its archives with total secrecy. Only during the reign of Pope Leo XIII (1878–1903) was it recognized that the mission of the Church could be enhanced by opening up the rich treasures of the past, even if this involved revelations about past scandals, such as the Galileo affair. As a result, the Vatican authorities came to the decision that public access could be granted, as a privilege, not a right, after a suitable interval had elapsed. Because the Vatican's history is usually divided into the periods of the reigns of successive popes, it was decided that the records of each reign would be collected and then made available en bloc to interested scholars.

But no automatic date of transfer was set by edict. Rather, when this transfer is to take place is left up to the current holder of the pontificate. So far, in the twentieth century, the records are now released for the reigns of Leo XIII (1878–1903), Pius X (1903–1914), and Benedict XV (1914–1922). Rumor has it that the papers of Pius XI are now being worked on, which would bring the story up to 1939. But no one has ventured to suggest a time frame when the records of Pius XII (1939–1958) will become available.

The Vatican archives are hence open only up to 1922 [*editors' note: more have been opened since this article was written*]. The records of the more than seventy-five subsequent years remain closed "for technical reasons." It would seem clear that the Vatican has too few archivists and that the resources devoted to this project are inadequate. Doubtless, for such lengthy reigns as those of both Pius XI and Pius XII, the work of preparing the papers for transfer a public reading room is a massive task. But seventy-five years seems excessive.

One further factor has to be noted: The Vatican archives fall under the supervision of the secretary of state, Cardinal Sodano, who is the most senior official of the curia under the pope. He thus outranks the newly appointed Cardinal Walter Kasper, the current president of the Pontifical Commission for Religious Relations with the Jews. There could therefore be no question that the latter could do no more than pass on to the former the request made by the Joint Commission for the opening up of the archives for the period of the Second World War. Nine months after the submission of the Preliminary Report, Cardinal Kasper wrote to the Joint Commission to say that the archives would remain closed. A month later, the five remaining members of the Joint Commission decided to suspend their work—at least for the present period.

When the Joint Commission was established two years ago, the then-president of the Pontifical Commission, Cardinal Cassidy, expressed the hope that Jewish and Catholic historians meeting together could move the controversy away from inaccuracy and media sensationalism. The Vatican's understanding was that each scholar would read the eleven published volumes and add their authority to the findings of the earlier editors.

Cardinal Cassidy and his staff were therefore disappointed when the Joint Commission failed to do what it was charged to do, either because of other commitments or because its members did not know Italian. But the cardinal would have to be exceedingly naive if he did not realize that the Joint Commission would inevitably take up the long-standing and deeply felt view voiced among the Jewish community that only the release of the relevant documents and unfettered access to these materials would suffice. The Vatican authorities could surely have foreseen (or even shared) the view that coming to terms with such a traumatic past requires special steps to secure full disclosure of the sources. The refusal of the Joint Commission's very polite request was bound to have repercussions. The justification given—that the archivists are not yet ready to deal with the documents of that period—must appear specious and self-serving. The subsequent outburst of Father Peter Gumpel, accusing the Joint Commission members of "irresponsible behaviour," of misrepresentation of the Vatican's intentions, or of being engaged in a "campaign with a clear propagandistic goal to damage the Holy See," is surely egregious.

On the other side, it remains to be clarified as to when the Commission members were made aware that the records of the reign of Pius XII could not and would not be opened within a matter of months. It is inconceivable, in fact, that they were not fully aware of this situation during their deliberations. Their expectation that the Vatican authorities would yield to this form of pressure from an outside group was surely unrealistic, and could even be considered provocative.

And it is far from clear that they had thought through the consequences for the appropriate officials, from the secretary of state, Cardinal Sodano, or the librarian and archivist, Cardinal Jorge Mejia. Acceptance of this recommendation would not only have meant the abandonment of the Vatican's established procedures, but probably would have led to other demands for a similar favorable treatment by the advocates of other causes. In any case, giving priority to this one issue, for what is clearly a political not a historical reason, might set an unwelcome precedent. It would also involve a massive reallocation of personnel and resources. In view of these considerations, it was surely impolitic for one of the Joint Commission members to accuse the Vatican of "sending a message that would confirm many people's worst suspicion that there is something to hide." Similarly it was unfortunate that a commentator from the World Jewish Congress should make reference to a "cover up" or label the Vatican's stance as "a profound moral failure." Such mutual accusations of bad faith or recriminations about lost opportunities to open up the Vatican archives cannot help to advance the cause of improved mutual understanding.

Where do we go from here? The lesson surely to be learned from this unfortunate tale is that this is not the way to deal with history. The pursuit of historical accuracy should not be merged with other agendas drawn from political or theological considerations. Nobody doubts that investigations into the Holocaust, and the role of the Catholic Church in it, should continue. In due course, the Vatican archives for the period will be opened. The issue is not whether, but only when. In the meanwhile, like historians of other epochs, scholars should make more use of the abundant evidence already available, which, as noted above, has been underused since the *Actes et Documents* first appeared. It can only be hoped that the example of scholarly cooperation set by the Joint Commission members will be infectious enough to encourage the continuing study of this significant if painful subject, *sine ira et studio*. As the American Cardinal of Baltimore, William Keeler, commented: "Joint efforts by Catholic and Jewish scholars working together can bear fruit in the long run, provided the dialogue is conducted in the spirit of mutual respect and trust."

9

To Avoid Worse Evils

Rainer Decker

(a review, translated from the German by John Jay Hughes, of John Cornwell's *Hitler's Pope* [New York: Viking, 1999], from *H-Soz-u-Kult* on the online *H-Net Reviews*, February 2000)

In the past year two British writers have captured public attention in Germany. The first is the Oxford professor, Niall Ferguson. His book, *The Pity of War: Explaining World War I*, criticizes England's intervention in the First World War. By posing the contrary-to-fact question, "What would have happened if Germany had won the war?" Ferguson opened new perspectives—for some readers provocative, for others irrelevant.

His older colleague at Cambridge, John Cornwell, travels a well-worn path, indicated by the subtitle of the German edition: *The Pope Who Remained Silent,* which recalls Rolf Hochhuth's play, *The Deputy.* The title of the English original is sharper still: *Hitler's Pope: The Secret History of Pius XII.* Cornwell goes beyond Hochhuth's polemic, mounting a massive attack on Pius XII's conduct that culminates in a systematic indictment of papal centralism, all the way from the First Vatican Council to Pope John Paul II. "It has been the urgent thesis of this book," Cornwell writes, "that when the papacy waxes strong at the expense of the people of God, the Catholic Church declines in moral and spiritual influence to the detriment of us all."

In order to enforce its claim to supremacy over local churches, Cornwell argues, the Vatican entered into negotiations with national states that produced the concordats with Fascist Italy (in 1929) and with Nazi Germany (in 1933). The price for these agreements was recognition of these regimes and silence regarding their murderous policies, especially the Holocaust.

Cornwell argues his case biographically. His sources include two collections of largely unpublished material. The first is testimony collected by the Vatican in connection with the process of beatification for Pius XII. This gives personal and family information about Pacelli, but offers no substantially new insights. The second is the archives of the Vatican Secretariat of State, which are now accessible for the pontificate of Pope Benedict XV, who died in 1922. This material has already been studied, and in part published, by the Italian historian Emma Fattorini in her 1992 book (which Cornwell fails to mention) about Pacelli's work as nuncio in Munich from 1917 to 1923.

After sketching Pacelli's upbringing in Rome by traditionally Catholic parents loyal to the papacy, Cornwell emphasizes the formative influence on the young priest of the conservative papacy of Pius X (1903–1914), whom Pacelli would later canonize. Working in the secretariat of state, Pacelli played a major role, Cornwell contends, in negotiating a concordat with Serbia shortly before the outbreak of World War I. The treaty enabled the curia to circumvent older Austrian laws for the protection of Catholics in the Balkans, thus giving fresh impetus to Serbian nationalism and adding to the incendiary material that exploded in August 1914—a remarkable contribution to the controversy over the blame for the outbreak of war.

Describing Archbishop Pacelli's role as nuncio in Munich (from 1917) and later in Berlin (until 1929), Cornwell describes Pacelli's efforts to negotiate concordats with the German states and the Reich, and emphasizes his experiences with the Munich "Conciliar Republic" in early 1919—which, Cornwell contends, caused the nuncio to link his anticommunism with anti-Semitism. A key document for Cornwell is a letter Pacelli sent to Cardinal Secretary of State Gasparri on April 18, 1919, in which the nuncio passes on and affirms the report of his representative, Monsignor Schioppa, about the "totally chaotic" situation he encountered in a personal meeting with the head of the Communist government, Max Levien.

Cornwell's translation diverges at several points from the original Italian text published by Emma Fattorini—thereby giving the reader "an impression of stereotypical anti-Semitic contempt." For instance, where Fattorini's original text speaks of a "gruppo femminile," a "group of women" or a "female group," Cornwell translates this as "female rabble." His German translator heightens this even farther: "rabble" becomes "scum," so that the passage reads: "The boss of this female scum was Levien's mistress."

Cornwell contends that Pacelli was prejudiced not only against Jews but also against blacks, citing his concern about sexual attacks on civilians by black French or American troops in the Rhineland in 1920 and in Italy in 1944. He never mentions that in October 1939 Pius ordained the first black African bishops of modern times or that from 1950 onward he appointed further native African bishops almost every year.

Cornwell's use of important scholarly material is highly selective. With few exceptions he uses German sources and studies only when they have been translated into English. In the German translation the publishers conceal this defect by citing German works. The account of the Reich Concordat of 1933, for instance, is based almost exclusively on that of Klaus Scholder, which has been translated into English. Cornwell accepts uncritically Scholder's contention that there was a direct connection between the Catholic Center Party's assent to the Enabling Act in March 1933, alleged Roman desires, and the conclusion of the concordat.

Scholder's critic, Konrad Repgen, whose refutation of Scholder is available only in German, is for all practical purposes ignored. At one point Cornwell does consider a contrary position: in footnote 24 to chapter 7. This mentions—only to dismiss at once, as "niggling and not entirely accurate"—Rudolf Morsey's criticism of a passage in the memoirs of the Catholic former Reich Chancellor Heinrich Brüning, in which the latter severely criticizes Pacelli's concordat policy. Significantly, this footnote has been dropped in the German translation—which has given rise to considerable speculation.

Cornwell's charge, that the curia's concordat policy in various countries was intended to support papal centralism, is arguable but one-sided. The policy also had a defensive aspect: defending the church against state control and interference, as seen in the Kulturkampf, still fresh in the curial memory. The Reich Concordat exemplified this defensive aspect, providing a legal basis for challenges to Nazi persecution of the Church. The enhancement of Hitler's prestige that the concordat brought him was fleeting and should not be overemphasized. The Church struggle that started a year or two later left no doubt about Nazism's true ideology. When Cornwell criticizes the passivity of the Vatican (apart from a few expressions of sympathy for the Jews by the aging Pius XI), of the German bishops, and of German Catholics generally in the face of increasing discrimination of the Jews, he is indulging in hindsight. At the time no one foresaw the events of 1941 to 1945. Nonetheless the encyclical *Mit brennender Sorge,* coauthored by Pacelli (secretary of state since 1930), sharply condemned Nazi racial ideology.

Cornwell's description of the wartime policy of the new pope, elected in March 1939, in particular of his alleged "silence," is the weakest part of the book. At least he reports Pius XII's role, long known to historians but not to the public at large, in mediating in the winter of 1939–1940 between military opponents of Hitler in Germany and the British government, in the hope of obtaining favorable peace terms following Hitler's overthrow. (This from *Hitler's Pope!*) This was fraught with extreme danger had the plot become known—not only for the pope personally but for the Catholic Church in both Germany and Italy. Cornwell is thus correct when he says that the pontiff's actions during World War II were not dictated by cowardice. Must we therefore accept the further charge that anti-Bolshevism and latent anti-Semitism were the leading motives for the pope's "silence"?

Two statements by Pius XII in May 1940, not mentioned by Cornwell, are relevant here. The first is a memorandum he wrote on May 11, the day after the telegrams of sympathy he sent to the monarchs of the Benelux countries following the German attack of their lands. Written for the benefit of his immediate collaborators, it described a conversation he had with the Italian consul in Warsaw, who had just returned to Italy. "He [the consul] confirmed, as did his wife, that one could not imagine the cruelty and sadism of the Germans, or more accurately of the Gestapo—led by a genuine criminal, Himmler, and composed of the most repulsive personalities—who were tormenting the Polish people and trying to destroy them." Two days later, in a conversation with the Italian Ambassador Alfieri, the pope defended his telegrams and then addressed the situation in Poland. "They [the Italians] have full and exact knowledge of what is gong on in Poland. We ought to utter fiery protests against this, and the only thing that prevents our doing so is the knowledge that anything we said would worsen the victims' fate."

The pope's words are a clear statement of the reason he refrained from denouncing the Nazi regime. This motive runs like a golden thread through all the Vatican documents and is most clearly expressed in the Pope's 1943 letter to Bishop Preysing of Berlin: "*ad maiora mala vitanda*—to avoid worse evils." Cornwell completely ignores all of these statements. About the pope's veiled reference to the murder of the Jews and the oppression of the Poles in his 1942 Christmas address, Cornwell writes: "Hitler himself could not have wished for a more convoluted and innocuous reaction from the Vicar of Christ to the greatest crime in human history." If that were true, we would have no explanation for the biting analysis of this speech by "Hitler's Pope" in a memorandum prepared by the Reich Security Office for Ribbentrop's Foreign Ministry. This culminated in the sentence: "[The Pope] is virtually accusing the German people of injustice against the Poles and Jews and makes himself the mouthpiece and advocate of these genuine war criminals." This too Cornwell totally ignores.

Also one-sided, indeed in essential points false, is Cornwell's account of the Vatican's action in connection with the arrest and deportation of more than one thousand Jews in mid-October 1943. "To his everlasting shame," Cornwell writes, "and to the shame of the Catholic Church, Pacelli disdained to recognize the Jews of Rome as members of his Roman flock." Quite apart from the question of whether such a value judgment belongs in a book claiming to be a work of scholarship, the sources show that Cornwell's statement of the facts, as well as his evaluation of them, is false. One example: His charge that the pope "was prepared to countenance the deaths of a thousand Roman Jews to prevent the consequences of a Communist takeover in Rome."

Cornwell claims that the German ambassador to the Holy See, Ernst von Weizsäcker, and his trusted first secretary, Albrecht von Kessel, "urged Pacelli that day [October 16] to make 'an official protest.'" In support of this claim Cornwell cites a telegram sent by Mollhausen, consul at the German embassy, to the foreign office in Berlin.

Cornwell's own footnote shows, however, that this telegram had been sent on October 7, and thus said nothing about any plan urged on the Vatican by German diplomats. In the conversation that Weizsäcker had with the secretary of state, Cardinal Maglione, on October 16, the ambassador did *not* urge the pope to act energetically, as Cornwell claims. His citation of Maglione's record of this meeting, and his interpretation of it, is distorted. In reality, at this meeting Weizsäcker explicitly urged the pope *not* to protest, since—in the ambassador's opinion—this could not cancel the arrests and indeed would make the situation worse: The Nazi persecutors, appealing to Hitler's "supreme authority," would intensify the persecution, and the pope himself would be in danger. Instead Weizsäcker hoped, by working behind the scenes and by sending Berlin reports about bad publicity and Vatican displeasure, to get the order for the Jews' deportation changed into forced labor (in which he failed) and to prevent future arrests (in which he had partial success). In the months following, the Nazis respected international law guaranteeing the neutrality of Vatican City, making it possible to offer refuge both in the Vatican and in many religious houses in Rome to hundreds of anti-fascists and Jews, and thus saving lives.

The view of Weizsäcker and Kessel, that protests would do no good and would actually make matters worse, was consistent from the start of the war. Cornwell's German translator seems to have been aware that the author falsified the strategy of the two diplomats, for on p. 365 of the German translation there is a phrase, lacking in the English original, that says that the pope refrained from protesting the roundup of Roman Jews "on the explicit advice of Weizsäcker." The German translation is more historically accurate at this point. But the translator has overlooked Cornwell's claim on previous pages that Weizsäcker demanded papal protests.

Among the sources that support the account just given of the role played by the German diplomats at the Vatican is the impressive statement of Kessel during the controversy over Hochhuth's play in 1963—and never mentioned by Cornwell: "Von Weizsäcker had to fight on two fronts. He had to advise the Holy See, i.e. the Pope, not to undertake any ill-considered actions—anything, that is, which had not been thought through to its ultimate, possible deadly consequences. And at the same time Weizsäcker had to convince the Nazis, i.e. Hitler, by carefully framed reports that the Vatican was well disposed, in Hitler's eyes weak. His reports to Berlin represented the Vatican's countless actions on behalf of the Jews as so insignificant that they need not be taken seriously."

This means that all of Weizsäcker's reports about the Vatican's political attitude must be read with a sharply critical eye. Kessel's statement continues: "Finally all of us at the German Embassy to the Vatican, despite our different judgments of the situation, were united in the conviction that a flaming protest by Pius XII against the persecution of the Jews would in all probability have brought him and the curia into acute danger. And at that late date, in the autumn of 1943, such a protest could not possibly have saved a single Jewish life. Hitler, like an encircled predatory animal, would have increased his cruelty in the measure in which he encountered resistance."

In hindsight one can ask whether this view of the matter was not too pessimistic. But that does not diminish the integrity of those who held this view. Cornwell is not interested in subtleties or ambiguities. He gives readers no opportunity to judge for themselves, to doubt, or to presume. Everything is black and white. He wishes to contribute to intra-Catholic dialogue with the goal of "genuine collegiality and pluralism" in the Catholic Church. That is a legitimate aspiration. Does this book contribute to this end, however? Is it conceivable that a more collegial and pluralistic Catholic Church would have opposed Nazism more vigorously that a Rome-centered church? The example of the German Protestant Church does not support such a supposition. It points in exactly the opposite direction.

10

Bigotry's New Low

Michael Novak

(a column on Daniel Goldhagen's essay "What Would Jesus Have Done?" in the *New Republic*, January 21, 2002, pp. 21–45, subsequently expanded into Goldhagen's book, *A Moral Reckoning: The Role of the Catholic Church in the Holocaust and Its Unfulfilled Duty of Repair* [New York: Knopf, 2002], from *National Review Online*, January 28, 2002)

The government of the United States, George Washington wrote to the Hebrew Congregation of Newport in 1790, "gives to bigotry no sanction." But now the *New Republic* does. "Anti-Catholicism," Peter Vierek once shrewdly remarked, "is the anti-Semitism of the intellectuals." In its January 21 issue, the *New Republic* has sunk into the swamp of bigotry as low as it could go. it gave twenty-five pages to Daniel Jonah Goldhagen so that he could offer Catholics a theological interpretation of what their faith entails and hint broadly that the Church deserves destruction as an ally of the anti-Christ and enemy of humankind.

In Goldhagen's fevered view, the startling uniqueness of Adolf Hitler's totalitarian racial hatred, a uniqueness that preoccupied a generation of philosophers of history, has been diminished until Hitler for him is only a later "chapter" in the long history of Catholic perfidy and nefariousness toward the Jews. So Judeo-centered is Goldhagen's theology, moreover, that in his view Catholic faith is reduced to its doctrines about the Jews, as these are imagined in his own passionate mind.

It's true that Goldhagen has reasons for internal agony and unquenchable anger. Relatives were brutally exterminated by the Nazis simply for being Jews. The scope and the execution of the Shoah are vile beyond description, worthy of all our anger, inexhaustibly so, and his, too. It's also true that many evils, sufferings, and humiliations were inflicted upon Jews by Catholics down the centuries, for which tears, repentances, and askings of pardon are in order; for which no amount of tears, repentances, and askings of pardon could suffice in justice. Mercy must be pleaded for.

The calm and objective assessment of wrong—with due regard for every circumstance—was not, however, Goldhagen's aim, neither as moral judge nor as historian. His tirade is theological in form, making an argument about the theological nature of Catholicism, its doctrines, its criteria for martyrdom and for sainthood, its proper relation to Judaism, its conception of what its mission as Church is (its ecclesiology), its relation to truth, and its ideal relation to other religions.

In its title (chosen perhaps by his editors, but well justified by his closing questions), Goldhagen opens with a theological taunt: "What would Jesus do?" There is no evidence in Goldhagen's work, nor in the recent history of the *New Republic*, that such a question is one he or the magazine takes seriously. Nor is there any sign that he or the magazine has examined the life, work, and words of Jesus to see just what Jesus in fact did in the circumstances of his day closest to those of today. In other words, not a serious question but a taunt.

Regarding Roman imperialism, the subjection of the Jews, the Roman practices of slavery and torture (such as Jesus was made to suffer himself), according to the New Testament, Jesus was, well, silent. "My kingdom is not of this world. If it were of this world, do you doubt that my Father would send legions of angels to my aid?" His silence infuriated his accusers.

Unlike Jesus, Pius XII was not silent regarding the Jews. As secretary of state to Pius XI, he had a determining hand in the letter condemning Hitler, "With Burning Concern" (*Mit Brennender Sorge*). Through the broadcasts of Vatican Radio, regularly amplified for the English-speaking world through the *Tablet* of London and the British intelligence and broadcasting services, Pius XII was the first to tell the world about the sufferings of Jews (by name) and other minorities, including during the war years more millions of Catholics than Jews. Much that the *New York Times* and the London *Times* published about the plight of Jews, Poles, and other civilians during the early war years came from the Vatican, through its radio broadcasts, papal statements, and the pope's newspaper (totally dependent on Mussolini for newsprint and less free than Vatican Radio), *Osservatore Romano.*

Even those scholars who minimize what the pope did have had to admit that his personal efforts saved thousands of Jews (in Hungary, Goldhagen admits)—too little, too late, they say. Was not what Schindler and Raul Wallenberg did also too little, too late, and yet altogether noble?

Why didn't Pope Pius XII just warn all Europeans that mass extermination was happening, Goldhagen asks, so that they might hear the warning and get away while they could? It is touching, the power that Goldhagen attributes to the pope. Nearly all the popes of the twentieth century had had the experience of giving warnings about the impending madness of war and the barbarity it would lead to. The popes did not gain the impression that people were listening to them with bated breath. They were totally ignored.

During the preceding 150 years, beginning when Napoleon dragged Pius VI as a prisoner to Paris and kept him in solitary confinement, pope after pope was threatened with violence and humiliation by secular rulers. Memories of the thorough destruction of the Church in France after the Revolution of 1789—monks and nuns driven from their religious houses, seminaries turned into barracks, churches used as stables, libraries and colleges confiscated, and scores of thousands of the devout slaughtered—were still fresh. As late as 1890, young nuns in France taking their vows did not have their hair cut off in the traditional ceremony, in the expectation that they might be driven from the convent at any time and would need to have their hair at normal length.

Pius XII quite bravely had resisted advice to take refuge in America for the duration, living within daily danger of imprisonment by Mussolini and Hitler. He formulated a clear policy and stuck to it faithfully throughout the war. Some Poles, especially, were outraged that all through 1939 and 1940, the pope never spoke out forcefully in their explicit defense, even though hundreds of thousands of them were already being herded into concentration camps, work trains bound for Germany, prisons, or simply slaughtered in villages, especially priests, nuns, and intellectuals of any sort. Nor did the pope single out the fate of the Gypsies, or the handicapped, or any single group. Knowing Hitler well from firsthand experience in Germany, he knew what statements would only make Hitler redouble his depredations.

One may argue with Pius XII's principles, but one cannot argue that they marked out the course from which he did not waver: (1) neutrality as between the belligerent powers, in the case that papal mediation might one day be sought; (2) timely and clear enunciation of relevant moral principles (platitudes, as Goldhagen calls them, meaning the timeless moral law); and (3) the denunciation of egregious abuses of moral principles, such as mass murders, the imprisonment of civilians solely for racial or religious or ethnic reasons, and mass bombings from airplanes of civilian populations in cities. Many people at the time—the British ambassador who was living inside the Vatican, for instance—told the pope to his face that his words were not concrete and vivid enough and that he should say more. Judging by how clearly the Nazis and the Allies interpreted what he had already said, the pope argued that his words were getting through loud and clear, and that the course he had chosen was the course most likely to do the most good.

The pope did not lack courage, and he did not lack clarity of mind. Mistaken he may have been. Open to criticism like any other mortal, he certainly was. He prayed much and suffered much internally under the pressure. But he did not waver. After the war, he received immense plaudits from the citizens of Italy, including the Jewish community of Rome, the nation of Israel, the Israeli Philharmonic that traveled to the Vatican in 1955 to give a concert in gratitude, and Jewish and other groups throughout the world. The rabbi of Rome became a Catholic, in large measure through being stirred by the assistance given Jews by the pope and friendships formed in the process.

Though I am not a professional historian, I have read enough on Pius XII—and have a sizable personal library on the period—that I see the transparent tendentiousness of nearly every historical point that Goldhagen raises. In every case, he selects accounts or facts that set the pope in the light he wishes to put popes into, and ignores facts, testimonies, and accounts that sharply contradict his version of events.

Yet let us suppose for a moment that every accusation Goldhagen makes against Pius XII is true. So then we had, as the *New Republic*'s publisher Martin Peretz has it, a "wicked man" as pope. Well, it wouldn't have been the first one. Indeed, Goldhagen says there is a danger in concentrating on Pius XII, because his personal behavior isn't the issue. What is wrong with Christianity runs through all the popes. It infects the core of Christian theology itself. It corrupts the very essence of the Church. What Goldhagen calls for is nothing less than the extermination of the Church as it now is and has been since the beginning. *Ecrasez l'infame.*

The great sin of which Goldhagen accuses the Church is its "supersessionist creed," namely, its clear teaching that the New Covenant supersedes the Old Covenant. Even to speak of "New" and "Old," Goldhagen quotes a soulmate, "is inherently supersessionist."

As John Paul II has made clear, however, the Jewish Testament remains valid; God can no more become unfaithful to His covenant with the Jews than He can to His covenant with Christians. The relation between Jews and Christians, therefore, is asymmetrical. Christians must understand and accept Jewish faith, in order to accept Christian faith. Their God is also the God of Abraham, Isaac, and Jacob. Apart from the background, principles, and prophecies of the Jewish Testament, the Christian Testament does not make sense. Christians, in order to be Christians, must be Jews in belief (though not in circumcision and ritual), in a way that, in order to be Jews, Jews need not be Christians. That is the asymmetry.

To put this another way, in order to go deeper into their own faith as Christians, it is both common and altogether necessary for Christians to go deeper into the Jewish Testament and plumb all they can of Judaism, the Judaism of serious reflection today, as well as of yesteryear. For this reason, Christians today need a vital, believing Jewish community that will lead them into the depths of Jewish faith. The reverse can scarcely be said of Jews, many of whom feel no need whatever, in order to be Jews, to study Christian doctrine or history.

Goldhagen puzzles over what the Church can mean when it says, "Church," in a way that is separate from the individual "sons and daughters of the Church," who include popes and bishops and priests, as well as laity. What is left over, beyond the sociological individuals who make up the Church? Well, once upon a time, Saul of Tarsus was holding the coats of Jewish youths who were stoning to death a young Christian, Stephen. A bit later, when Saul was riding on his horse toward Damascus, a bright light overcame him and, fallen from his horse, he recognized the voice of Jesus, who asked him, "Saul, Saul, why persecutest thou me?" Saul had not been persecuting Jesus, but only Stephen. It burst upon him that Jesus was saying that what was done to any Christian was done to Him, Jesus, the Son of God. An invisible vitality links all Christians as one in Christ.

Christians believe that Jesus is God, the Second Person of the Holy Trinity, the One indivisible God. They believe that God lives in every baptized Christian (and many other persons of good will, who love God with all their hearts and minds and souls). When they say "Church," they mean primarily this presence of God. They do not attribute sin to God, only to those who are false to what is in them. Thus, only secondarily do they mean, in the ordinary sociological sense, all those sinners who make up the actual lists of parishes, dioceses, and worldwide tribunals. It would be otiose to expect non-Catholics to use this language, or even to find it believable (or intelligible). But since Goldhagen asked, it seemed a duty to mention it.

Goldhagen might recall that something similar was once said of Israel, the unblemished Beloved of Yahweh, even when individual Israelites turned to worship idols, and rejected Moses and the Law. Even then God faithfully loved Israel.

Goldhagen's center of gravity is the Jewish Covenant. It is obviously not easy for him to see the world from a different center of gravity. It is quite wrong of him to try to force Christians into his frame of reference. After the trial, suffering, death, and resurrection of Jesus Christ, which confirmed his three years of teaching, it would not be reasonable to ask Christians to renounce the centrality to their faith of the Second Covenant.

Had Goldhagen been content as a historian merely to assess both the pluses and the minuses of the moral life of Pius XII, and even if given his own preoccupations he had come down hard on Pius XII, he would not be liable to the charge of bigotry. Indeed, he himself tries to defend himself against this charge, as if in foreknowledge that he may deserve it, by reporting the apology for sins of anti-Semitism voiced by the bishops of France in 1997—an apology that many of us accept as our own and that John Paul II has renewed in many words and deeds.

The reason Goldhagen is quite guilty of the charge of anti-Catholicism lies in the breadth and passion of the smears he spreads across a broad history, the distortion and hysteria of his tone, the extremity of his rage, and the lack of proportion in his judgments—dwarfing Hitler and making Pius XII a giant of evil, and then diminishing Pius XII so as to indict the whole of Christian theology down the ages. It is disingenuous of him to stop at Christ, the good and gentle Christ of his parody, and at the edges of the Christian Testament, which is our main source for knowledge about the character and teachings of Christ.

Goldhagen went over the top in disqualifying Catholics from any moral standing, so long as they hold to Catholic faith as it is. He wants a new type of Catholicism to supersede the old. In this, he reminds me not a little of Voltaire and other haters of the Church. The Enlightenment, too, was supersessionist in its self-conception, its light triumphing over the darkness of Rome—and not just of Rome, but of Jerusalem as well.

We have all had to learn that we must accept one another's reality as we are, without trying to make others over into our own image of what they ought to be. We can appeal to one another in argument and in debate, in mutual searching, and even in mutual fraternal correction of one another's oversights and errors. But mutual honor and respect are the first preconditions of dialogue. It is sad that the *New Republic* went over to the side of a bigotry that makes dialogue impossible. After many centuries of woe, we need every moment of dialogue that we can get.

11

Pius XII and the Nazis

Joseph Bottum

(an omnibus review from *Crisis*, November 2000, pp. 13–17)

He was a cosseted Renaissance prince, and he looked like an El Greco painting, as whip-thin and dangerous as a pistol, as ascetic as a razor.

He was a Victorian Italian, born in 1876, and entirely a product of his place and time. But he was also "a big man," in the sense in which a 1920s American industrialist might have used the phrase—one of those people, instantly recognizable to another, who understands exactly how people and organizations work: a getter of things done.

He was hard and competent, perhaps the most sheerly competent man ever to hold his position, though he also showed a sentimental streak from time to time, and he trained himself to a habitual charity by force of will. He was more long-sighted than most such quick and decisive men, but short-sighted sometimes as well, as they all eventually prove. He lived in a castle and flew in an airplane. He spent three hours a day in prayer. He could never learn to ride a horse. Six months before Hitler's total war of modern tanks and dive-bombers smashed its way across Europe, he assumed control of a vast medieval institution whose international operations were best suited to solve the question of what to do about Charlemagne.

Most of all, he was an insider. Inside the Church, inside the diplomatic corps, inside politics, inside the world. He knew how a president's office operates and what a banker does, how a scholar functions and what an army colonel thinks. He came from a powerful and important family, who groomed him for great things from the beginning. At every point, his teachers and elders recognized his discretion, his self-possession, his superiority, and his strength. And they always responded by taking him further, and further, and further in.

Early in his career, he was the highest example of a type you sometimes spot at an embassy party or a state reception. The kind of young politician you can almost sense—like an ultraviolet color just beyond seeing, a batsqueak just beyond hearing—is destined for power. The kind of young diplomat who has quickly become the ambassador's right-hand man and is standing near the entrance talking quietly with the other ambassadors' right-hand men. The kind of young priest who will run his eye over you as you walk in, weigh you to the last scruple, file you away for future use in the endless careful cabinets of his mind, and pray for your soul that night on his knees. He had something finer, harder, sharper than vanity: a will that had come out on the far side of personal ambition and turned into institutional ambition, an ambition for God.

Later in life, he wore round, silver-framed glasses that made his eyes seem never to blink. He had the kind of physical courage that allowed him to stare down an armed assassin and the kind of mental courage that allowed him to keep the secret of the generals' plot against Hitler from even his own closest advisors. He had an enormous right to expect loyalty and personal freedom, and for six years he was trapped inside a hundred acres in the middle of Rome, walking every day the same path through his garden—spied upon by half a dozen major intelligence services, his mail opened, his employees bribed, his telephone lines tapped, his papers copied, his radio signals jammed. He hated extemporaneous speaking. He kept his own counsel.

He was a saint and a failure, a success and a sinner, a man designed by nature to be the finest wielder of the delicate tools of civilized diplomacy the Vatican had ever known—and confronted during his papacy with only blind, monstrous barbarity, like a fencing master forced to duel a panzer tank. He was the most important man in the world and utterly beside the point. From the time he became pope in 1939 until his death in 1958, every thread of world history passed through his hands. But for the most part those threads proved steel cables, and he could never make them bend.

His name was Eugenio Pacelli—reigning as Pope Pius XII—and he was either one of the greatest disasters to sit on the throne of St. Peter or one of the greatest men to live in the twentieth century.

Perhaps the most curious thing about the man, however, is exactly this division, for there seems no third option, no middle ground for us to choose. Whenever the topic of his pontificate is raised, Pius XII is either unreservedly lauded as the only significant resister of Hitler to survive on the European continent, or unrelentingly denounced as a cowardly failure who passively or even actively participated in the Nazis' destruction of six million Jews.

So, in the mid-1960s, Broadway gave us Rolf Hochhuth's widely discussed play *The Deputy*, which presented the guilty silence of the Catholic Church during the war as an obvious matter of history, and Hollywood gave us *The Sound of Music*, which presented the Catholic Church as the sole source of shelter for refugees from the Nazis. For the recent British writer John Cornwell, Pius XII is "the most dangerous churchman in modern history," without whom "Hitler might never have come to power or been able to press forward with the Holocaust." But for the Israeli diplomat Pinchas Lapide in his 1967 volume *Three Popes and the Jews*, the pontificate of Pius XII "was instrumental in saving at least 700,000, but probably as many as 860,000 Jews from certain death at Nazi hands."

These absolute extremes are why Pius XII's papacy is a topic we seem to have forced upon us over and over. The spring of 2000 alone saw the appearance of four books on the question: Cornwell's extremely bitter *Hitler's Pope*, Pierre Blet's careful *Pius XII and the Second World War*, Garry Wills's unhesitating *Papal Sin*, and Margherita Marchione's hagiographical *Pope Pius XII: Architect for Peace*.

And with the fall of 2000, another set of books on the subject arrived, like the annual falling of leaves: Ronald J. Rychlak's systematic response to Pius's critics in *Hitler, the War, and the Pope*, Susan Zuccotti's somewhat belated attempt to join the recent bandwagon of papal detractors with *Under His Very Windows*, Michael Phayer's curious effort to extend the attack to include everything Catholic before the reforms of the Second Vatican Council in *The Catholic Church and the Holocaust, 1930-1965*, and Ralph McInerny's splenetic defense in *The Defamation of Pius XII*.

On the whole, the defenders of Pius seem to have the stronger case. Indeed, the best of these books is Rychlak's *Hitler, the War, and the Pope*, and in his epilogue Rychlak provides a devastating, point-by-point refutation of Cornwell's *Hitler's Pope*.

But "on the whole" is not an option in the argument over Pius. And—to get down to the nub of the matter—"on the whole" *shouldn't* be an option. The phrase implies a moderated view of the role played by the Church during World War II. And where is there room for moderation?

On the one hand, if from concern for Vatican finances (as Hochhuth claims), lust for power (as Cornwell has it), or hatred of the Communists and latent anti-Semitism (as Zuccotti argues), Pius XII significantly failed to do what could have been done to prevent the war or to save Europe's Jews from the Nazis, then he is guilty and dishonorable, a scandal to believers and a stumbling block to nonbelievers. Indeed, he is in this case more blameworthy than anyone except the Nazis themselves, for it was his task— as it was not, in a certain way, the British prime minister's or the American president's—to present a model of moral response.

On the other hand, if Pius XII was a holy and able religious leader who succeeded in saving lives and did the best that could be done when, armed with nothing but a traditional moral authority, he was faced with a set of monsters dedicated to the destruction of traditional morality, then attacks from the likes of Hochhuth and Cornwell are obscene, the twisted slanders of a saint.

Between the camps holding these divergent views, the facts are hotly disputed—but the number of facts actually in dispute proves, upon examination, to be surprisingly small. Ordained a priest at twenty-two in 1899, Eugenio Pacelli was one of those talented men that hierarchies exist to find, train, and promote. Pius X made him a monsignor in 1904, Benedict XV consecrated him a bishop in 1917, and Pius XI raised him to cardinal in 1929.

Ever since 1848, the Catholic Church had found itself faced across Europe with a swirl of communists, socialists, Catholic center parties, and traditional Protestant animus. And the Vatican's solution—even as the Papal States ceased to exist as an independent nation—was to sidestep domestic politics and negotiate as a foreign power with each European state. It was, in its way, a brilliant idea for preventing the seizures of schools and monasteries the Church had suffered in France—and for winning, at a single stroke, protections that would have required years to obtain politically as domestic legislation. But the governments after World War I were not the kind that had existed before. And instead of changing its technique, the Vatican after 1917 *accelerated* its negotiation of concordats with any government that made the least claim to legitimacy—as though dictators, fascists, communists, military cabals, and impossibly fragile coalitions could be bound with international law.

Pacelli's relations with Germany began in 1917 when Benedict XV sent him as nuncio to Bavaria. In 1920, he was named apostolic nuncio for all Germany, and he signed concordats with Bavaria in 1924 and Prussia in 1929. That was the same year the Lateran Accords were completed with Italy, recognizing the Vatican as a sovereign state. In 1930, Pacelli returned to Rome to become Pius XI's secretary of state, where he concluded the general concordat with Germany—led now by Hitler—in 1933.

For all that, Pacelli seems to have understood that the new governments were not entirely compatible with Christianity. Before Hitler's accession, Pacelli gave forty-four major addresses in Germany, forty of which condemned some aspect of Nazism. He was deeply involved in the drafting of *Mit brennender Sorge (With Burning Anxiety)*, Pius XI's 1937 encyclical condemning German racialism and nationalism. In 1935, at Lourdes, Pacelli denounced ideologies "possessed by the superstition of race and blood." At Notre Dame in Paris in 1937, he called Germany "that noble and powerful nation whom bad shepherds would lead astray into an ideology of race."

In March 1939, Pacelli was elected pope, and six months later the war he dreaded began with the invasion of Poland. For the next six years, he would speak constantly of peace, always peace, anything but war—denouncing, for instance, the Allies' demand for total surrender. He was, at root, a diplomat and believed that clever negotiations, subtle pressures, and behind-the-scenes manipulations could ameliorate almost any horror in a time of peace. Many of his best gifts were useless during war.

On March 3, 1940, for example, Pius celebrated his first papal anniversary by attending a patriotic Polish concert of Chopin pieces and was overheard to say, "Poor Poland is being crucified between two thieves." This was a week before Ribbentrop's official visit to the Vatican, during which Pius read out a list of Germany's racial crimes and concordat violations in Poland. It was all very strong and powerful—for a world before the Nazis, for a world at peace. A month later, the blitzkrieg swept across France. Italy joined the war.

The Vatican's radio and newspaper, the *Osservatore Romano*, poured out denunciations of atrocities, and Pius's Christmas message of 1941 deplored "the dishonor to human dignity, liberty, and life." By 1942, the Nazis' systematic plans for the Jews were clear. When the prime minister of Slovakia complained, "I don't understand why you want to stop me from ridding Slovakia of . . . this pack of criminals and gangsters," the nuncio replied, "Your Excellency is no doubt aware of the atrocious fate awaiting these deported Jews. . . . All the world knows of it." In Holland, in July 1942, the Catholic bishops issued an official protest against deportations—and the Germans retaliated by seizing and deporting the Jewish converts who had previously been exempt (among them, Edith Stein). The pope's 1942 Christmas message pleaded for "the hundreds of thousands who, through no fault of their own, only because of their nationality or descent, are condemned to death."

The Nazis, at least, seemed to understand what Pius meant. His 1943 theological encyclical *Mystici Corporis* was banned in Belgium for containing such lines as "we must recognize as Brothers in Christ . . . those not yet one with us in the Body of Christ." In an April 30 letter, Pius wrote, "We give to the pastors who are working on the local level the duty of determining if and to what degree the danger of reprisals . . . seem to advise caution." The prudential decision may have been mistaken, but it was a strongly indicated one, and it matched his personal style. "I have repeatedly considered excommunicating Nazism," he told an Italian military chaplain, "in order to castigate before the civilized world the bestiality of Judaeocide. But after many tears and prayers, I have concluded that a protest would not only fail to help the persecuted, it might well worsen the lot of the Jews." His personal bravery was never in question. In September 1943, the Germans seized Rome and assigned an officer to "advise" the pope—whose sole response was, "Tell your chiefs that the pope is not afraid of concentration camps." "Papal caution and circumspection," Pinchas Lapide later wrote, "saved close to 90 percent of Roman Jewry; would papal clamor have saved more—or, conversely, would it have endangered those Jews then in precarious hiding?"

It is not so much these facts that are in dispute between the two camps of Pius interpreters. It is rather mostly "a question of judgment," as the Jewish scholar (and Polish refugee from the Nazis) Joseph Lichten entitled his 1963 essay defending Pius XII. How are we to take statements made on Vatican Radio and in the *Osservatore Romano?* To whom are we to ascribe the ultimate credit for the good done by some nuncios and bishops in Greece and France? To whom are we to ascribe the ultimate blame for the evil done by some clergy in Slovakia and Croatia? The argument about the Church during World War II turns primarily on what facts are to be taken as central and what facts are to be set aside as incidental.

So, for instance, in a private conversation on July 14, 1933, Hitler boasted that the German concordat Pacelli signed on behalf of the Vatican "will be especially significant in the urgent struggle against international Jewry." But then, recorded in the "table talks," we find Hitler's tirade on July 4, 1942: "Once the war is over we will put a swift end to the Concordat. . . . Not only the history of the past, but also present times afford numberless examples of the very hard-boiled diplomats to be found in the service of the Catholic Church, and of how extremely cautious one must be in dealing with him." And which of these are we to take as Hitler's actual view?

In 1939, in the formal letter announcing his election as pope, Pius wrote to Hitler: "At the outset of Our pontificate, we wish to assure you that We have an intimate affection for the German people consigned to your care. . . . [A]s papal nuncio, We labored to organize the relations between the Church and the State in a reciprocal agreement and effective collaboration, . . . a goal at which We aim particularly now with all the ardent desire that the responsibility of Our office charges Us." But Sister Pascalina Lehnert, his longtime secretary, recalls: "On one occasion I asked the Nuncio if he did not think that [Hitler] could . . . perhaps help the German people. The Nuncio shook his head and said: 'I would be very, very much mistaken in thinking that all this could end well. This man is completely obsessed: all that is not of use to him, he destroys; all that he says and writes carries the mark of his egocentricity; this man is capable of trampling on corpses and eliminating all that obstructs him.'" And which of these are we to take as Pacelli's actual view?

The problem for writers in one of the Pius XII camps is always to explain why the writers in the other Pius XII camp cannot see what seems so apparent from the chosen facts. At times, the explanations are almost comic. In a relentless section of *The Defamation of Pius XII*, Ralph McInerny dismisses—as the psychodrama of lapsed Catholic faith—the papal attacks by the likes of the ex-seminarians Garry Wills and John Cornwell, and the ex-priest James Carroll (whose 1997 article in the *New Yorker* began the latest round of attacks on the memory of Pius). Susan Zuccotti devotes her conclusion in *Under His Very Windows* to disparage—as mistaken or even sly—the praise Pius received from such Jews as Pinchas Lapide, Golda Meir, and Albert Einstein.

But if there is a solution to the puzzle of Pius XII, it must lie most of all in the rejection of anachronism. We make a historian's mistake when we insist that the everyday people and busy leaders of some past time should have seen things as sharply as scholars who have devoted their lives to studying the period later can. We stumble when we apply the same moral condemnations to those who instigated the atrocities of World War II and those who did not foresee or prevent them. Judgment is the historians' task, but we err most of all when we substitute not only our judgment but our reactions for that of the observers of the time—when we say, for instance, that because a document is not phrased in a way to evoke a strong reaction from us, the people who reacted strongly to it then must be mistaken.

For someone like John Cornwell, anachronism is almost the only available tool for his anti-Catholic project. In *Hitler's Pope*, he denounced Pius XII for his failure to speak as forcefully about the Jews as John Paul II has done. But that same spring in which *Hitler's Pope* appeared, he wrote an article in the *Times* of London mocking the "sclerotic pontificate" of John Paul II. For Cornwell, it amounts to a double bind in which the Church is dismissed as corrupt because prior popes were not like John Paul II, and John Paul II is dismissed because he leads a Church thereby found corrupt.

But even Ralph McInerny seems not to escape the trap entirely. In *The Defamation of Pius XII*, he devotes four sections to Zionism and the confusing, contradictory statements of Jewish leaders: "If I knew that it would be possible to save all the children in Germany by bringing them over to England, and only half of them by transporting them to [a new Jewish state in Palestine]," the Zionist David Ben Gurion once declared, "then I would opt for the second alternative." McInerny's purpose seems to be a kind of *reductio*: If you want to play the anachronistic game of interpreting statements from the 1930s and 1940s by the standards of today, then there are plenty beside Pius XII open to ridicule and blame.

This is, however, a dangerous strategy. And it is, in any case, an unnecessary one. If we dismiss the errors of anachronism and consider how Pius XII's pontificate was perceived at the time, the defense of the Catholic Church's behavior before and during World War II comes clear. That behavior was not perfect, by any means. It was not always wise even by the standards of the moment, and it seems more often unwise in retrospect. But it was clear and coherent, and *everyone* knew it—the Nazis knew the Church opposed them, the Nazi sympathizers within the Church knew they had lost the fight to influence the papacy, the Allies knew the Vatican was not under Axis control, and the observers of the time knew Pius XII alone stood against the tide.

So, for example, we must take seriously such things as the October 28, 1939, story in the *New York Times*, which observed, "a powerful attack on totalitarianism . . . was made by Pope Pius XII in his first encyclical. . . . It is Germany that stands condemned above any country or movement in this encyclical—the Germany of Hitler and National Socialism." The March 14, 1940 issue reported Ribbentrop's visit to the Vatican with the subhead "Jews Rights Defended." "Vichy Seizes Jews; Pope Pius Ignored," ran the *Times* headline on August 27, 1942. "Pope Said to Help in Ransoming Jews," added the headline of October 17, 1943.

What would make all this clear is a kind of writing about history that we haven't quite had yet (although Rychlak's *Hitler, the War, and the Pope* comes close and is, for now, the magisterial volume on the subject). We need a history that selects not only the actions undertaken during Pius XII's pontificate, but the recorded reaction to them—that refuses to decide how things ought to have been perceived, but limits itself to reporting how they were perceived.

What we will arrive at from such a systematic history is, I believe, an ability to recognize both the sanctity of Pius XII and the failure of all he longed for. An ability to recognize that he did more than anyone else to prevent war, and nonetheless war came. An ability to recognize that the Catholic Church saved more than 700,000 Jews from the Nazis, but nonetheless six million others died. An ability to recognize that no one could have done better than this good, brilliant, powerful man, and nonetheless it was not enough.

An Annotated Bibliography
of Works on Pius XII, the Second
World War, and the Holocaust

William Doino Jr.

INTRODUCTION

This annotated bibliography covers the papacy during the Second World War and the Holocaust. It concentrates on the reign of Pius XII (1939–1958), although, as the topic dictates, it ranges both before and after his pontificate. No bibliography on such an immense subject can be exhaustive, particularly since important new articles and books on the Vatican, fascism, Nazism, and the Holocaust are published almost every month. But I have tried to provide a representative selection of scholarly and popular articles, books, and monographs, arranging them according to particular themes.

Since this bibliography will be read primarily in the United States, English-language translations have been preferred to foreign-language originals (where the translations exist), and American editions have been preferred to British editions. Nevertheless, because so much important documentation and literature exists only outside English, I have included key untranslated sources where I could find them. Full publication data is typically given only the first time a work is mentioned.

I have listed a few authoritative archival sources of particular importance. But for the most part, instead of filling these already overlong pages with lists of the actual archives of particular countries and institutions, or such standard series of documents as the many volumes resulting from the Nuremberg war crimes trials, I have merely named the authors who have best used these sources and who themselves provide excellent listings of these primary sources.

This bibliography devotes considerable attention to Jewish issues. But because the focus is on the papacy, I have not attempted to list the vast literature on other questions of anti-Semitism and the Holocaust. Good places to start, for those interested in pursuing the subject, are the *Encyclopaedia Judaica* (New York: Macmillan, 1992) and *Encyclopedia of the Holocaust* (New York: Macmillan, 1990), together with the depositories of Holocaust documents at Yad Vashem in Jerusalem, the Wiener Library in London, the Centre de Documentation Juive Contemporaine in Paris, and the YIVO Institute for Jewish Research in New York.

Make no mistake: This bibliography offers a positive view of Pius XII and the papacy, a view I believe is supported by the enormous weight of evidence. I have had the good fortune to consult and befriend many distinguished scholars and writers, all of whom have contributed to this bibliography. Three in particular must be mentioned: the late John J. Mulloy, the late Erik von Kuehnelt-Leddihn, and Robert L. Mauro. Without them, this bibliography would not have been possible, and to them, I dedicate this work.

PART 1: PRIMARY SOURCES

1. *Acta Apostolicae Sedis* [Acts of the Apostolic See]. Vatican City: Libreria Editrice Vaticana, 1908–present.

Acta Apostolicae Sedis is the official publication of the Holy See. Canon Law names it authoritative, and it contains all the official texts (in Latin, as well as other languages) of Church documents and papal pronouncements. Volumes 31 to 37 cover the war years, 1939 to 1945.

It is remarkable how little known is the *Acta* among those who comment on the Vatican and the Holocaust. As Cardinal Henri de Lubac notes, "With respect to Pius XII, many writers and journalists . . . seem completely ignorant of the important scholarly publication of the *Acta Apostolicae Sedis*" (*Christian Resistance to Anti-Semitism: Memories from 1940–1944* [San Francisco: Ignatius, 1990], p. 130). Similarly, Jane Scrivener (the pen name of Mother Mary St. Luke, an American nun who lived in Rome during the German occupation) notes in her wartime diaries that if commentators were "to study . . . the monthly *Acta Apostolicae Sedis* . . . they would reach a higher level of objective understanding" (*Inside Rome with the Germans* [New York: Macmillan, 1945], p. 102).

Two summaries of Pius XII's wartime statements that draw heavily on the *Acta* are Zygmunt Jakubowski's *Pope Pius and Poland* (New York: America, 1942), which documents Pius XII's actions on behalf of Poland, and Felicity O'Brien's "The Mind of Pope Pius XII" (*Inside the Vatican*, March–April 2001, pp. 54–59).

2. *Actes et Documents du Saint Siège relatifs à la Seconde Guerre Mondiale* [Records and Documents of the Holy See Relating to the Second World War], edited by four Jesuit scholars: Pierre Blet of France, Robert A. Graham of the United States, Angelo Martini of Italy, and Burkhart Schneider of Germany. 11 volumes. Vatican City: Libreria Editrice Vaticana, 1965–1981.

Initiated under Paul VI and completed under John Paul II, *Actes et Documents* present the Holy See's official activities during the Second World War. (Volume 3 is printed in two parts; thus some authors refer to twelve volumes instead of eleven.) The decision of Paul VI to waive the traditional seventy-five-year time restraint governing the Vatican's secretariat of state archives was unprecedented (it was not done for records from World War I), and the Jesuit editors had uninhibited access. Contained in this collection are Pius XII's wartime addresses and statements; letters, written instructions, and exhortations he sent to his bishops, nuncios, and religious; and exchanges between the Holy See and wartime governments. (Four of the eleven volumes deal with the Vatican's humanitarian assistance.) The texts of *Actes et Documents* are in their original languages (chiefly Italian, French, and German). All together, the volumes contain over 5,000 primary documents and run over 8,000 pages.

The first volume of *Actes et Documents* has been translated into English as *Records and Documents of the Holy See Relating to the Second World War*, edited by Gerard Noel (Washington: Corpus, 1968). No further translations have yet appeared. Pierre Blet, one of the four editors of *Actes et Documents*, has written a summary of the volumes, *Pius XII and the Second World War According to the Archives of the Vatican* (Mahwah: Paulist, 1999), permitting English readers some access.

For background on the Holy See's archival procedures, see *Vatican Archives: An Inventory and Guide to Historical Documents of the Holy See* by Francis X. Blouin Jr. (New York: Oxford University, 1998). In 2003 the Vatican began releasing archives from the pontificate of Pius XI (1922–1939), to be followed by those of Pius XII (1939–1958). Peter Godman's *Hitler and the Vatican: Inside the Secret Archives that Reveal the New Story of the Nazis and the Church* (New York: Free Press, 2004), is an effort to assess these new documents. Though hampered by some faulty assumptions and erroneous interpretations (see "Why *Hitler and the Vatican* Fails as History," Zenit News Agency, March 3, 2004), Godman's book does establish that both Pius XI and Cardinal Pacelli were personally anti-Nazi, concerned about the persecution of Jews and how best to resist the Third Reich.

Better yet is the work of Matteo Luigi Napolitano, one of Italy's leading diplomatic historians, who has written on the newly released archives and devoted a website to their interpretation, www.vaticanfiles.net, which contains many important articles and links. A steady flow of recent articles by Father Giovanni Sale, S.J., for *La Civiltà Cattolica* also draws on the newly released archives. In "La Santa Sede e la legislazione antisemita nella Germania nazista," *Civiltà Cattolica* 2004, volume 1, pp. 116–129, for example, Sale examines Vatican and German Catholic reaction to Hitler's 1933 laws barring Jews from civil service and severely limiting their enrollment in schools and universities, concluding, "It is not true, as some scholars have claimed, that the Holy See did nothing for the Jews." Sale has collected these articles in *Hitler, la Santa Sede e gli ebrei* (Milan: Jaka, 2004).

3. *L'Osservatore Romano* [The Roman Observer]

Known as "the Vatican newspaper," *L'Osservatore Romano* began daily publication in 1861. Throughout its history, *L'Osservatore* has engaged in countless controversies, some political, most religious. After he became Vatican secretary of state in 1930, the future Pius XII, Cardinal Eugenio Pacelli, working closely with Pius XI, took control of the paper.

L'Osservatore Romano's importance in the struggle against fascism and Nazism cannot be denied. As Joseph Dineen, one of Pacelli's earliest biographers, observes: "*Osservatore Romano* had been forthright and downright in its denunciation of Hitler for his excesses against the Jews, his sterilization law, his restrictions upon freedom of speech and assembly and freedom of religious worship. This little newspaper, published within the Vatican State, was one of the few remaining in Europe that dared to criticize Hitler or Mussolini" (*Pius XII: Pope of Peace* [New York: Robert M. McBride, 1939], pp. 201–202). French historian Henri Daniel-Rops writes that after Hitler obtained power, "Hardly a day passed without the *Osservatore Romano* and the Vatican Radio denouncing the doctrines of Nazism and its violence" (*A Fight for God, 1870–1939* [New York: E.P. Dutton, 1965], p. 321).

Similarly, A.C. Jemolo, a noted enemy of Italian Fascism, wrote: "It may be recognized without qualification that there was no heretical principle, no proposition against dogma, against orthodox history or against morals which was even tentatively advanced by fascist men or journals of any authority, which was not immediately refuted by pontifical acts, by very authoritative ecclesiastical reviews or by the *Osservatore Romano*" (*Chiesa e stato in Italia negli ultimi cento anni* [Turin: Einaudi, 1948], pp. 680–681). And Piero Calamandrei, a left-wing political activist who was no friend of the Church, made a remarkable speech in March 1949 to the Italian Constituent Assembly in which he acknowledged: "At a certain moment, during the years of greatest oppression, we were aware that the sole newspaper in which it was still possible to find some accent of liberty, of our own liberty and of the common liberty of all free men, was the *Osservatore Romano*" (ibid., p. 703).

The daily Italian editions are available on microfilm and CD-ROM, and in them, one can find such articles as the October 11, 1930, editorial that declares, "The Party of Hitler Stands Condemned by the Ecclesiastical Authorities. . . .

Belonging to the National Socialist Party of Hitler is irreconcilable with the Catholic conscience"; the series of articles, beginning in 1933, chronicling the Nazi campaign against Jews and other "enemies," culminating in the establishment of a concentration camp at Dachau (described in the March 22, 1933, edition); the front-page article on "The Renewal of Anti-Semitism in Germany," dated July 17, 1935 (preceding the Nuremberg Laws by almost two months); the report of March 23, 1937, on how parish priests throughout Germany read the encyclical *Mit brennender Sorge* from their pulpits on Palm Sunday; the front-page article of July 30, 1938, carrying Pius XI's antiracist speech of July 28, 1938, which condemned Mussolini's "Aryan Manifesto"; the issues of late 1938 (particularly November 11–19), which exposed the racism and anti-Semitism of Kristallnacht; the statements of American and British leaders denouncing German anti-Semitism in no uncertain terms (see in particular the issue of December 30, 1938, containing extracts from a speech of President Roosevelt's secretary of the interior, Harold Ickes, defending the "thousands of unhappy Jews robbed and tortured by a brutal dictatorship"); the editorials and articles on behalf of Poland (particularly October 15, 1940) after the Nazis' invasion; and the issues of December 6, 1940, and February 27, 1941, which document Pius XII's condemnation of euthanasia and the Vatican's rejection of German literature promoting euthanasia.

L'Osservatore was among the first publications to report on the Nazi plans for European Jewry. On November 13, 1938, shortly after Kristallnacht, the paper quoted a chilling, although unofficial, statement from the Nazi gauleiter in Bavaria, that the German struggle against Jews would continue "until their extermination." A year later, as John Morley observes, "The Vatican newspaper . . . carried various articles in late 1939 and early 1940 announcing and describing the German plans for 'The Jewish Reservation of Lublin.' . . . The very first of these articles related that the Jews from the Reich, Austria, Bohemia, Moravia, Slovakia, and Poland would be moved to the Lublin area. A later article indicated that the process brought sorrow and tragedy to the Jews involved" (*Vatican Diplomacy and the Jews During the Holocaust 1939–1943* [New York: KTAV, 1980], p. 109). See *L'Osservatore Romano* of November 29, 1939, p. 1; December 23, 1939, p. 6; January 7, 1940, p. 4; February 5–6, 1940, p. 6; and February 17, 1940, p. 4, which announced the deportation of 900 Jews from Stettin to Lublin, commenting: "It is believed that similar measures will be extended to other German cities in order to completely eliminate the Jewish element from the Reich."

On May 12, 1940, the front page of *L'Osservatore Romano* published Pius XII's open telegrams to the leaders of Holland, Belgium, and Luxembourg, supporting them after the Nazis invaded their countries. This was accompanied by a scathing editorial that read: "Rumors about new dangers threatening neutral countries found unexpected confirmation this morning. The frontiers of Holland, Belgium, and Luxembourg have been crossed by German troops. . . . The

German move has . . . not a semblance of justification. . . . States are occupied against their will and turned into bloody battlefields; peace, prosperity, and lives are thrown to the winds. War bursts the dams and submerges countries with floods of fire and blood. It is dreadful! The deepest feelings of humanity, Christian charity, Christian brotherhood of nations are stung and protest in pain" (as translated by the *Tablet* of London, May 25, 1940, p. 530). See also José Sánchez's *Pius XII and the Holocaust: Understanding the Controversy* (Washington: Catholic University, 2002), p. 52, which points out that the telegrams denounced the Nazi invasion as "against right" and "against all justice" and that *L'Osservatore* further declared "the total war launched by Germany has clearly revealed itself as a pitiless war of extermination conducted in defiance of the laws of war" (*Osservatore Romano*, May 12, 1940, pp. 1, 13–14).

As the Nazi persecution of the Jews developed into the Final Solution, Pius XII spoke out against it in his 1942 Christmas address and June 2, 1943, allocution to the College of Cardinals, both published in full in *L'Osservatore* (issues of December 25, 1942, pp. 1–3 and June 3, 1943, p. 1). Guido Gonella, Italy's leading antifascist writer (who was jailed by Mussolini) was hired by *L'Osservatore* to write interpretive articles on the pope's major addresses. The best of these articles were later collected in Gonella's book, *The Papacy and World Peace: A Study of the Christmas Messages of Pope Pius XII* (London: Hollis and Carter, 1945).

During the German occupation of Rome, *L'Osservatore* declared: "the pope has in vain endeavored, as is well known, to avert the outbreak of war, . . . he has used all possible means at his disposal in order to alleviate the sufferings which in any manner resulted from the heinous world conflagration. With the aggravation of so much misery, the activities of universal and paternal succor by the pope have multiplied; they know no limitations, neither of nationality, nor religion, nor race. This manifold and ceaseless activity of the pope has, of late, grown still further in depth, due to the increased suffering of so many unfortunate people" (October 25–26, 1943, p. 1; see also the accompanying editorial, "La strage degli innocenti").

Pinchas Lapide comments: "These words, in 1943, had only one clear meaning to tens of thousands of Romans—many of whom sheltered Jews in their homes—who avidly read Italy's only non-fascist newspaper, both on, but even more between, the lines: The Pope wants all Catholics to do all they possibly can to hide and save Jews from the clutches of the Germans" (*Three Popes and the Jews* [New York: Hawthorn, 1967], p. 261).

On December 3 and 4, 1943, *L'Osservatore* also published front-page condemnations of Italy's anti-Semitic decrees, and subsequent articles outlined how Pius XII had coordinated efforts with the Italian bishops to condemn Nazi-fascist atrocities: "Following the pope's appeals, the Italian episcopate has frequently and sharply protested against these atrocities, and condemned them" (*Tablet*, October 28, 1944, p. 212; see also January 15, 1944, p. 30, as well as June 24, 1944, p. 306). Pius XII also had antiracist pastoral statements of Catholic bishops published in *L'Osservatore*. See the issues of April 11, 1943, p. 2; June 6, 1943, p. 2; February 25, 1944, p. 2; and April 14, 1944, p. 1.

Throughout the war, both the Nazis and fascists waged a campaign against *L'Osservatore*. After the Germans invaded the Lowlands, "the *Osservatore Romano* protested openly, sales were suppressed outside Vatican City, copies of the paper burned, readers of it thrown into the Trevi Fountain. After Italy entered the war, fascists were forbidden to read it; Professor Gonella, its pro-Ally news columnist, mysteriously disappeared for two days; its editor went about with two bodyguards" (*Current Biography* [New York: H.W. Wilson, 1941], pp. 673–674). On January 26, 1943, the German diplomat Diego von Bergen sent a telegram to German Foreign Minister Joachim von Ribbentrop that denounced "the *Osservatore Romano*, which day in and day out pours out its poison against Germany" (cited by Anthony Rhodes, *The Vatican in the Age of the Dictators* [New York: Holt, Rinehart and Winston, 1973], p. 273). These facts need to be clearly emphasized because a number of authors have tried to diminish the wartime record of *L'Osservatore* (see, for example, Susan Zuccotti's "*L'Osservatore Romano* and the Holocaust, 1939–1945," *Holocaust and Genocide Studies*, Fall 2003, pp. 249–277).

General studies of the newspaper include Francesco Leoni's *L'Osservatore Romano: Origini ed evoluzione* (Guida: Napoli, 1970) and Fritz Sandmann's *L'Osservatore Romano e il Nazionalsocialismo 1929–1939* (Rome: Cinque Lune, 1976). The wartime editor of *L'Osservatore*, Giuseppe Dalla Torre, provides a firsthand account of these years in his *Memorie* (Milan: Mondadori, 1965). His struggles against totalitarianism, backed by Pius XII, were widely recognized at his death (see, for example, "Count Giuseppe Dalla Torre, Editor, Dies at 82; Directed *L'Osservatore Romano* in Vatican City for 41 Years; Ran Anti-Fascist Editorials during Mussolini Regime," *New York Times*, October 19, 1967, p. 42).

4. Vatican Radio

Inaugurated by Pius XI on February 12, 1931, Vatican Radio was designed to bring papal teachings and sociopolitical analysis to a worldwide audience. In his monograph *Voice of the Vatican* (London: Sword of the Spirit, 1942), Robert Speaight expressed British appreciation for the "persistence with which it continued to tell the truth" about the Nazi regime, noting how it "withstood every pressure brought against it by the Italian fascists and their German masters" (p. 3).

Marilyn J. Matelski adds, "Some of the most courageous broadcasts aired by Radio Vaticana at this time were those that unveiled the horrors of the Nazi Holocaust. On January 20, 1940, an American Jesuit became the first announcer in world radio to report the imprisonment of Jewish and Polish prisoners in 'sealed ghettos.' From that point on, Vatican Radio continued to feature stories on concentration camps and other Nazi torture chambers. From 1940 to 1946, Vatican Radio also ran an Information Office, transmitting almost 1.25 million shortwave messages to locate prisoners of war and other missing persons. Later the radio station combined its information services with the International Refugee Organization, forming a team Tracing Service to reunite war-torn families and friends" (*Messages from the Underground* [Westport: Praeger, 1997], p. 6). See also Matelski's *Vatican Radio: Propagation by the Airwaves* (Westport: Praeger, 1995).

Since its inception, Vatican Radio has been run by the Society of Jesus. But although the Jesuits were "in principle responsible for the content of their broadcasts, those broadcasts clearly committed the authority of Rome as well" (Jean Lacouture, *The Jesuits: A Multibiography* [Washington: Counterpoint, 1995], p. 387). Moreover, Pius XII himself authored some of the station's wartime broadcasts and explicitly ordered the January 1940 reports on Nazi atrocities in Poland. See Robert Graham's "La Radio Vaticana tra Londra e Berlino: Un dossier della guerra delle onde: 1940–1941," *Civiltà Cattolica* 1976, volume 1, pp. 132–150; also *Actes et Documents* 3, part 1, p. 204, containing the notes on Pius XII's directives for Vatican Radio, recorded by his assistant Giovanni Montini (the future Paul VI).

Certain polemicists have claimed (1) that the Vatican never explicitly condemned Hitler and the Final Solution and refused to use the word "Jew," and (2) Pius XII ended the station's anti-Nazi broadcasts in 1941 because he believed them to be too harsh. See, for example, Carlo Falconi's *The Silence of Pius XII* (1965; English translation, Boston: Little Brown, 1970), pp. 31–45, and Saul Friedlander's *Pius XII and the Third Reich: A Documentation* (New York: Knopf, 1966), pp. 77–78.

Both claims are false. On September 28, less than one month after the Nazi invasion of Poland, the exiled Polish bishop, Cardinal Hlond, was given free use of Vatican Radio. "To allow him to say what he said from a neutral station was almost an act of war by a neutral state," Owen Chadwick comments in *Britain and the Vatican During the Second World War* (Cambridge: Cambridge University, 1986) pp. 80–81. Hlond spoke such lines as: "Martyred Poland, you have fallen to violence while you fought for the sacred cause of freedom. . . . Your tragedy rouses the conscience of the world. . . . On these radio waves, which run across the world, carrying truth from the hill of the Vatican, I cry to you. Poland, you are not beaten! By the will of God you will rise with glory my beloved, my martyred Poland!" (quoted by French ambassador to the Vatican, François Charles-Roux, in *Huit Ans au Vatican 1932–1940* [Paris: Flammarion, 1947], pp. 344–345).

In October 1939, "the Jesuit-operated Vatican Radio started to broadcast first-hand accounts of atrocities perpetrated by the Nazis in Poland as reported to the Holy See by its own informants in that country," Harold H. Tittmann Jr.

noted in his *Inside the Vatican: The Memoir of an American Diplomat During World War II* (New York: Doubleday, 2004), pp. 111–112. In January 1940, Vatican Radio explicitly declared: "Jews and Poles are being herded into separate 'ghettos,' hermetically sealed and pitifully inadequate for the economic subsistence of the millions destined to live there. . . . It adds up to a fearful total and a tremendous responsibility: one more grievous affront to the moral conscience of mankind; one more contemptuous insult to the law of nations; one more open thrust at the heart of the Father of the Christian family [Pope Pius XII], who grieves with his dear Poland, and begs for peace with decency and justice from the throne of grace" (text in *The Persecution of the Catholic Church in German-Occupied Poland* [London: Burns and Oates, 1941], p. 115–117).

On January 24, the *Manchester Guardian* reported, "Tormented Poland has found a most powerful advocate. The Vatican broadcast, which has been issued in four languages, must make a deep impression on the consciences of the Christian world." The broadcast was "a warning to all who value our civilization that Europe is in deadly danger." On the same day, the *New York Times* informed its readers: "Vatican City radio station made two broadcasts today, adding many details to the atrocities that supposedly are being committed in German-occupied Poland. It is now clear that the papacy is throwing the whole weight of its publicizing facilities into an exposé of conditions which, yesterday's broadcast said, 'profoundly pained' the pope." The Germans, on the other hand, delivered a strong protest to the Holy See and threatened that there would be strong reprisals in Germany. See *The Papacy in the Modern World* by J. Derek Holmes (New York: Crossroad, 1981), pp. 128–129.

In September of 1940, Vatican Radio attacked "All Who Pledge a 'New Order'" (*New York Times*, September 17, 1940, p. 5). On October 6, 1940, while Germany was celebrating the first anniversary of its invasion of Poland, Vatican Radio declared that "Hitler's war unfortunately is not a just war, and therefore God's blessing cannot be upon it" ("Hier spricht Deutschland," October 6, 1940, "Vatikan-Funkspiegel" no. 00396, P.A. Bonn. Pol. Verschluss, 23; cited by Guenter Lewy, *The Catholic Church and Nazi Germany* [1964; reprinted New York: Da Capo, 2000], pp. 247 and 390 n. 112).

On October 15, 1940, Vatican Radio denounced "the immoral principles of Nazism" (Pierre Blet, *Pius XII and the Second World War*, p. 99). On March 30, 1941, it explicitly condemned "the wickedness of Hitler" (*Tablet*, April 5, 1941, p. 264). On August 1, 1941, the radio station condemned "this scandal . . . the treatment of the Jews" (quoted in Jean Lacouture, *Jesuits: A Multibiography*, p. 387), and in the summer of 1942, after France's bishops publicly condemned the Nazi persecution and deportation of the Jews, Pius XII personally ordered that these declarations be read over Vatican Radio (Henri de Lubac, *Christian Resistance to Anti-Semitism*, p. 162).

On February 20, 1943, Vatican Radio condemned Nazi actions in Vichy France as "barbarous" and declared that "the Catholic Church will 'never recognize a regime based on forced labor,' which uproots populations and disperses families" (*New York Times*, February 21, 1943, p. 19). On March 2, 1943, Vatican Radio broadcast to Germany a program entitled "The Watcher in the Night of the Age," which emphasized Pius XII's opposition to the war and his support for its multitude of victims—and asked Catholics everywhere to emulate him (*Catholic Mind*, June 1943, pp. 19–21). On June 21, 1943, Vatican Radio broadcast into Germany a lengthy text "defining the rights of the Jews under the Natural Law" (*Tablet*, July 3, 1943, p. 8). That same month it added: "He who makes a distinction between Jews and other men is unfaithful to God and is in conflict with God's commands" (*New York Times*, June 27, 1943, p. 16; see also *American Jewish Yearbook, 1943–1944* [Philadelphia: Jewish Publication Society, 1944], p. 292). And a few days later, on July 6, 1943, Vatican Radio condemned the "heresy of racism" (*Catholic Mind*, August 1943, pp. 120–121).

On January 29, 1944, Vatican Radio broadcast a long and detailed condemnation of new anti-Semitic legislation (see *Is the Catholic Church Anti-Social? A Debate Between G.G. Coulton and Arnold Lunn* [London: Catholic Book Club, 1947], p. 193). And on February 8, 1944, "Vatican Radio, commenting on the fascist raid on St. Paul's Basilica last Thursday in which sixty-four Italian officers and Jews who had received sanctuary there were arrested, said tonight that the Church would not yield in offering charity to everyone. The radio referred to the 'hospitality granted to the arrested persons,' and said: 'It is not a paradox, nor is it absurd that the Church is for everybody and for nobody. Charity is above human constitutions. On this point, the priest can never yield. It is the demarcation line between good and evil. Men of honest views will permit us to continue with it'" (*New York Times*, February 9, 1944, p. 7).

The impact of these and similar condemnations is described at length by the French scholars François and Renée Bédarida in "La Voix du Vatican, 1940–1942, Batailles des ondes et Résistance Spirituelle" in the *Revue d'Histoire de l'Eglise de France*, July–December 1978, pp. 215–243. Jesuit Father Michel Riquet, one of the noblest rescuers himself, declared: "Throughout those years of horror, when we listened to Radio Vatican and to the pope's messages, we felt in communion with the pope, in helping persecuted Jews and in fighting against Nazi violence" (*Figaro*, January 4, 1964; see also Riquet's *Le Chrétien face aux ruines* [Paris: Spes, 1946]).

When the British government asked the Vatican on June 10, 1941, if it was true that Vatican Radio's wartime reporting had ceased because of German protests, "Pius XII replied that there was no agreement between the Holy See and the Axis powers and that it had not been stated that no one could speak, day after day, about what was happening in Germany. The pope further replied that he was not unaware that some broadcasts were exposing German Catholics and religious to harsh reprisals" (Blet, *Pius XII and the Second*

World War, p. 103). Indeed, as Pinchas Lapide reports, "Radio Vatican went right on saying such home truths as: 'The Church does not accept regimes based on forced labor, on the uprooting of populations, on individual or collective deportations' (February 26, 1943)" (*Three Popes and the Jews*, p. 246).

5. Papal Encyclicals, Addresses, and Decrees

During the reign of communism, fascism, and Nazism, the Holy See issued major statements, particularly in the form of encyclical letters, against these ideologies, contrasting them to the Christian concept of social justice. An English-language collection is *Principles for Peace: Selections from Papal Documents from Leo XIII to Pius XII*, edited by Harry C. Koenig (Washington: National Catholic Welfare Conference, 1943). In Koenig's collection are found Leo XIII's encyclical *Rerum Novarum* (1891) on the condition of the working classes, Pius X's address decrying the outbreak of World War I, and Pope Benedict XV's rarely cited 1916 condemnation of anti-Semitism. Pius XI's antifascist encyclical *Non abbiamo bisogno* (1931), and his famous 1937 encyclicals, *Mit brennender Sorge*, against Nazism, and *Divini Redemptoris*, against communism, are also included—as are excerpts from Pius XII's series of addresses on behalf of peace and against the Nazi invasion of Poland, together with long passages from his first encyclical, *Summi Pontificatus* (October 1939), which condemned racism and totalitarianism.

An excellent collection of Pius XII's teachings, published during the war, is *Pius XII on World Problems* by James W. Naughton, S.J. (New York: America, 1943). A postwar collection is *The Mind of Pius XII*, edited by Robert C. Pollock (New York: Crown, 1955). In addition to their place in the *Acta Apostolicae Sedis*, Pius XII's major addresses can be found in his *Discorsi e Radiomessaggi di Sua Santità Pio XII, 1939–1958* (Vatican City: Tipografia Poliglotta Vaticana, 1940–1958, 20 volumes; particularly helpful is the index to the collection).

Many of the pontiff's speeches also appeared in *L'Osservatore Romano* and were broadcast over Vatican Radio. For English-language versions of papal encyclicals, see *The Papal Encyclicals 1740 to 1981*, a five-volume set edited by Sister M. Claudia Carlen (Wilmington: McGrath, 1981). A companion work is *Papal Pronouncements, A Guide: 1740–1978*, two volumes also edited by Carlen (Ann Arbor: Pieran, 1990).

For Pius XII's early years, nothing surpasses Sister Carlen's *Guide to the Documents of Pius XII* (Westminster: Newman, 1951), which lists nearly all the official statements, allocutions, and informal addresses during the first ten years of Pius XII's pontificate—along with the exact references to the official and semi-official Vatican publications in which they appeared. See also *The Major Addresses of Pope Pius XII*, two volumes, edited by Vincent A. Yzermans (St. Paul: North Central, 1961); *The Pope Speaks: The Teachings of Pius XII*, edited by Michael Chinigo (New York: Pantheon, 1957); and *Pius XII: Selected Encyclicals and Addresses* (1949; reprinted Harrison: Roman Catholic Books, n.d.). *The Papal Encyclicals in Their Historical Context*, edited by Anne Fremantle (New York: Putnam's Sons, 1956), is a solid interpretive work, particularly good at explaining the encyclical letters of the wartime popes.

6. Contemporary Newspapers and Journals

Contemporary wartime newspapers, documentary news services, and journals are among the most valuable sources of information on the Vatican's actions during the war and how they were perceived. The most accurate English-language source of Vatican news at the time was the *Tablet* (the foremost Catholic weekly in Great Britain). During Hitler's reign from 1933 to 1945, the *Tablet* published many statements by Pius XI and Pius XII, as well as by the nuncios, bishops, and religious who acted in coordination with them. (A valuable service the paper provided was to translate articles from the non-English anti-Nazi Catholic press.) For a brief history of the *Tablet*, upon its 150th anniversary, see *The Tablet: A Commemorative History* by Michael Walsh (London: Tablet, 1990).

The Nazis persecuted those caught reading the *Tablet*. The case of the Austrian priest Jacob Gapp (recently beatified by John Paul II) is particularly tragic. Arrested in 1943 by the Nazis for distributing copies of the *Tablet*, Gapp was brutally interrogated for two days, during which he stoutly defended the *Tablet*: "It is a good Catholic journal." Enraged by his remarks, the Nazis decapitated Gapp in Berlin at the Ploetzensee Prison on August 13, 1943. See "Modern Martyr Championed Catholic Press" by John M. Samaha, S.M., in *Lay Witness*, June 2000, pp. 38–39.

Of the secular English-language newspapers, the *Times* of London and the *New York Times* are the most important. Both hailed Pius XII's leadership during the war and regarded him as a champion of civilized values and outspoken opponent of totalitarianism. On October 1, 1942, the *Times* editorialized: "A study of the words which Pope Pius XII has addressed since his accession in encyclicals and allocutions to the Catholics of various nations leaves no room for doubt. He condemns the worship of force and its concrete manifestation in the suppression of national liberties and in the persecution of the Jewish race" (p. 5). For an analysis of coverage during the war, see *"N.Y. Times* Articles Refute *Hitler's Pope*" by Robert L. Mauro in the *Wanderer*, October 7, 1999, p. 8, and the comprehensive monograph "Pius XII and the Jews: The War Years, as Reported by the *New York Times*" by Stephen M. DiGiovanni in the *Catholic Social Science Review* 6 (2000), pp. 341–376.

For the Jewish press's attitude toward Pius XII, see Dimitri Cavalli's "The Good Samaritan: Jewish Praise for Pope Pius XII," *Inside the Vatican*, October 2000, pp. 72–77. Cavalli spent many hours paging through wartime Jewish publications at the New York Public Library and discovered the highly favorable attention the pope received before, during, and after World War II. Among the examples: "Vatican Radio Denounces Nazi Acts in Poland" (*Jewish Advocate* of Boston, January 26, 1940); "Laval Spurns Pope: 25,000 Jews in France Arrested for Deportation" (*Canadian Jewish Chronicle*, September 4, 1942); "Vatican Gives Assurance for Aid to Jews" (*California Jewish Voice*, February 12, 1943); "Jewish Hostages in Rome: Vatican Protests" (*Jewish Chronicle* of London, October 29, 1943—a headline of particular significance, as it reported on the pope's support of persecuted Jews during the German occupation of Rome); "Hungary Gets Pope's Appeal" (*Jewish Advocate*, July 20, 1944), etc.

The Catholic Periodical and Literature Index is a valuable guide; important articles from such publications as *America*, *Commonweal*, and the *Catholic Mind* are all extensively referenced. Leading Catholic periodicals from abroad such as *Etudes* (France), *Stimmen der Zeit* (Germany), and the Italian Jesuit journal *La Civiltà Cattolica* have also been indexed. For an excellent history of the latter journal, which has been the source of much discussion, see *La Civiltà Cattolica: 150 anni al servizio della Chiesa 1850–1999* by Giuseppe De Rosa (Rome: Civiltà Cattolica, 1999). The French news service *Documentation Catholique* was in the forefront in publicizing the Vatican's condemnations of anti-Semitism and totalitarianism during the 1930s and 1940s, as was the English-language service *Facts on File*. Available from Great Britain for over 150 years, *Keesing's Contemporary Archives* is also a valuable resource.

PART 2: THE PAPACY BEFORE PIUS XII

A good overall history is *The Popes: A Concise Biographical History*, edited by Eric John (1964; updated Harrison: Roman Catholic Books, 1994). Three other respectable, although occasionally uneven, histories are: *The Oxford Dictionary of Popes*, edited by J.N.D. Kelly (Oxford: Oxford University, 1986); *Saints and Sinners: A History of the Popes* by Eamon Duffy (New Haven: Yale University, 1997; updated 2002), and the *Encyclopedia of the Vatican and Papacy*, edited by Frank J. Coppa (Westport: Greenwood, 1999). Coppa's *The Modern Papacy Since 1789* (London: Longman, 1998) is an interesting, if debatable, work. More sympathetic to the papacy are *Vicars of Christ* by Charles Coulombe (New York: Citadel, 2003) and two works by J. Derek Holmes: *The Triumph of the Holy See: A Short History of the Papacy in the Nineteenth Century* (London: Burns and Oates, 1978) and *The Papacy in the Modern World: 1914–1978* (New York: Crossroad, 1981).

Francis Sugrue's knowledgeable *Popes in the Modern World* (New York: Thomas Y. Crowell, 1961) covers the pontificates of Pius IX through John XXIII. W.A. Purdy's *The Church on the Move* (London: Hollis and Carter, 1966) is a sensitive and penetrating look at the character and policies of Pius

XII and John XXIII, far superior to Carlo Falconi's popular (but secular-minded) *The Popes in the Twentieth Century: From Pius X to John XXIII* (London: Weidenfeld and Nicolson, 1967).

Igino Cardinale's *The Holy See and the International Order* (Gerrards Cross: Smythe, 1976) is an important diplomatic study. A collection of serious essays, with an introduction by Robert A. Graham, S.J., can be found in *Papal Diplomacy in the Modern Age*, edited by J.F. Pollard and Peter C. Kent (Westport: Praeger, 1994). A comparable earlier collection, outstanding in many regards, is *The Catholic Church in World Affairs*, edited by Waldemar Gurian and M.A. Fitzsimons (South Bend: University of Notre Dame, 1954). For events that set the stage for Church-State relations in the twentieth century, see Owen Chadwick's *A History of the Popes, 1830–1914* (Oxford: Clarendon, 1998). For texts of the earlier popes' encyclicals, see the volumes of the *Enchiridion delle encicliche* (Bologna: EDB, 1994–1998), edited by Erminio Lora and Rita Simionati.

1. Benedict XV

The most informed biographies of the three wartime-era pontiffs—Benedict XV, Pius XI and Pius XII—are those written by contemporaries. For Benedict XV, who reigned during the First World War, the best are *Benedict XV: The Pope of Peace* by Henry E.G. Rope (London: Catholic Book Club, 1940) and the heavily documented *Life of Benedict XV* by Walter H. Peters (Milwaukee: Bruce, 1959).

A sympathetic modern account is J.F. Pollard's *The Unknown Pope: Benedict XV (1914–1922) and the Pursuit of Peace* (London: Geoffrey Chapman, 1999). Annie Lacroix-Riz's outrageous *Le Vatican, l'Europe et le Reich de la Première Guerre mondiale à la guerre froide* (Paris: Armand Colin, 1996) speculates that the Vatican and Germany worked together from the end of the First World War for a German domination of Europe. No one who has seriously studied the life of Benedict XV, who established the modern papacy's universal peace efforts, has ever believed her curious conclusion. In *The Kaiser's Memoirs* (New York: Harper and Brothers, 1922), Wilhelm II praises Benedict's nuncio, Pacelli, but claims for himself the peace initiative during World War I that the Vatican proposed through Pacelli. Pacelli corrected the record in a signed note in *L'Osservatore Romano*, October 19, 1922. For an analysis of Vatican diplomacy during the First World War, see Charles J. Herber's commentary in the *Catholic Historical Review*, January 1979, pp. 20–48.

2. Pius XI

For Pius XI, two early works are *The Life of Pius XI* by Angelo Novelli (Yonkers: Mt. Carmel, 1925), and Dennis Gwynn's *Pius XI* (London: Holmes,

1932). *His Holiness, Pope Pius XI* by René Fontenelle (London: Methuen, 1938) is a shortened English version of Fontenelle's much longer *Pie XI* (Paris: Spes, 1939), the standard life. William Teeling's *Pope Pius XI and World Affairs* (New York: Frederick A. Stokes, 1937) is a neglected study that offers valuable insights. Philip Hughes's *Pope Pius the Eleventh* (New York: Sheed and Ward, 1937) is an excellent biography by a first-rate historian. Lord Clonmore's *Pope Pius XI and World Peace* (New York: E.P. Dutton, 1938) is also outstanding, particularly on Pius XI's opposition to anti-Semitism and totalitarian ideologies. An interesting firsthand portrait is found in *A Reporter at the Papal Court: A Narrative of the Reign of Pope Pius XI* by Thomas Morgan (New York: Longmans, Green, 1937).

Also containing information not available elsewhere are Lilian Browne-Olf's *Pius XI: Apostle of Peace* (New York: Macmillan, 1938) and M. Vincenti's *Pio XI* (Rome: Alba, 1941). Rarely cited but interesting is Zsolt Aradi's *Pius XI: The Pope and the Man* (New York: Hanover, 1958). In 1969, the thirtieth anniversary of Pius XI's death, a collection of articles was published in Italy as *Pio XI nel trentesimo della morte (1939–1969)* (Milan: Opera diocesano per la preservazione e diffusione della fede, 1969). More recent collections include *Il Pontificato di Pio XI a cinquant'anni di distanza*, edited by G. Bianchi (Milan: Vita e pensiero, 1991) and *Achille Ratti, Pape Pie XI* (Rome: Ecole française de Rome, 1996), organized by the French School in Rome. A reliable modern biography is Robin Anderson's *Between Two Wars: The Story of Pope Pius XI* (Chicago: Franciscan Herald, 1977).

Important books dealing with particular aspects of Pius XI's pontificate include Daniel A. Binchy's masterful *Church and State in Fascist Italy* (Oxford: Oxford University, 1941; reprinted with a new introduction in 1970), written by a highly ·informed contemporary observer; *Church and State* by Luigi Sturzo (London: Centenary, 1939), a classic work on the subject; *Pio XI e Mussolini* by Giulio de' Rossi dell'Arno (Rome: Corso, 1954); *Church and State in Italy, 1850–1950* by A.C. Jemolo (Oxford: Blackwell, 1960); *The Rome-Berlin Axis: A Study of the Relations between Hitler and Mussolini* by Elizabeth Wiskemann (London: Collins, 1966); *La Chiesa e il Fascismo. Documenti e interpretazioni* by Pietro Scoppola (Bari: Laterza, 1971); *The Papacy and Totalitarianism Between the Two World Wars*, edited by Charles F. Delzell (New York: John Wiley and Sons, 1974); Peter C. Kent's *The Pope and the Duce* (New York: St. Martin's, 1981); J.F. Pollard's *The Vatican and Italian Fascism 1929–1932: A Study in Conflict* (Cambridge: Cambridge University, 1985); *Between Pope and Duce: Catholic Students in Fascist Italy* by Richard J. Wolff (New York: Peter Lang, 1990); and F.W. Deakin's *The Brutal Friendship: Mussolini, Hitler and the Fall of Italian Fascism* (London: Phoenix, 2000). Note also Meir Michaelis's *Mussolini and the Jews: German-Italian Relations and the Jewish Question in Italy, 1922–1945* (Oxford: Clarendon, 1978), which is sensitive and informed on the papacy's role during the period.

a. The Concordat with Germany

In later sections of this bibliography, Pius XII's connection with the German concordat will be discussed. But for the relation of his predecessor, Pius XI, to the 1933 concordat, the best source is Stewart A. Stehlin's *Weimar and the Vatican, 1919–1933: German-Vatican Relations in the Interwar Years* (Princeton: Princeton University, 1983). Less reliable is *Controversial Concordats: The Vatican's Relations with Napoleon, Mussolini and Hitler*, edited by Frank J. Coppa (Washington: Catholic University, 1999). This book, however, does have an outstanding bibliography, including references to important literature largely unknown in the English-speaking world. For the general history of the Church's concordats, see the definitive *Enchiridion dei Concordati: Due secoli di Storia dei rapporti Chiese-Stato* (Bologna: EDB, 2003), edited by Ermino Lora.

b. Mit brennender Sorge

A defining moment in Pius XI's pontificate was the publication of the encyclical *Mit brennender Sorge* (1937). For a complete English translation, see *The Persecution of the Catholic Church in the Third Reich* (1940; reprinted Fort Collins: Roger A. McCaffrey, 2002), pp. 523–537, and many other sources. The literature surrounding this famous anti-Nazi encyclical—in which Eugenio Pacelli (the future Pius XII) was heavily involved—is immense. For an introduction, see *"Mit brennender Sorge*: März 1937–März 1962" by Robert Leiber (Pacelli's confidential aide) in *Stimmen der Zeit*, March 1962, pp. 417–426, and Angelo Martini's "Il cardinale Faulhaber e l'enciclica di Pio XI contra il nazismo" in *La Civiltà Cattolica* 1964, volume 4, pp. 421–432. For textual analysis and interpretation of the evolution of the encyclical, see *Pius XI und der Nationalsozialismus. Die Enzyklika 'Mit brennender Sorge' vom 14 März 1937* by Heinz-Albert Raem (Paderborn: Ferdinand Schöningh, 1979).

Unlike other encyclicals, which are typically in Latin, *Mit brennender Sorge* was written and published in German. Dated and signed by Pius XI on Passion Sunday, March 14, 1937, it was smuggled into Germany and read from every Catholic pulpit on Palm Sunday, March 21, 1937. The Nazis reacted furiously, condemning the encyclical as "a call to do battle against the Reich government" (*Documents on German Foreign Policy 1918–1945*, Series D [1937–1945], 1:633). "That Hitler clearly realized its import," writes Pinchas Lapide, "was obvious from the next day's *Völkischer Beobachter*, which carried a vitriolic counterattack on the 'Jew-God and His deputy in Rome'" (*Three Popes and the Jews*, p. 110).

Other contemporary reactions confirm its impact. *Mit brennender Sorge* was written, said Nathaniel Micklem, "in no uncertain tone" (*National Socialism*

and the Roman Catholic Church [Oxford: Oxford University, 1939], p. 170).
The Anglican dean of Chichester, A.S. Duncan-Jones, described it as of "shattering force" (*The Struggle for Religious Freedom in Germany* [London: Gollancz, 1938], p. 225). It is "impossible, in a few words to do justice to that encyclical," commented Michael Power. "In one tremendous flash of light it illuminated, as no other account will ever be able to do, the whole nature and extent of the attack upon the Church, the width and depth of the gulf that separates National Socialism from the Christianity of Christ" (*Religion in the Reich* [London: Longmans, Green, 1939], p. 82).

Robert d'Harcourt, who was present in a German church when the encyclical was read out, described its effect in *The German Catholics* (London: Burns, Oates and Washbourne, 1939). In his diaries, German Jewish survivor Victor Klemperer recorded that although the encyclical was banned by the Nazis, it was circulated underground and that "everyone has already read it" (entry for May 22, 1937, in *I Will Bear Witness: A Diary of the Nazi Years: 1933–1941* [New York: Random House, 1988], p. 221).

Peter Hoffman believes it had a formidable impact upon Claus von Stauffenberg (who tried to overthrow Hitler): He "knew the encyclical, had thought about it, and identified with it" (*Stauffenberg: A Family History, 1905–1944* [Cambridge: Cambridge University, 1995], p. 317 n. 37). The teachings of *Mit brennender Sorge* also had an impact on Catholic academics. See, in particular, Andrew J. Krzesinski's *National Cultures, Nazism and the Church* (Boston: Bruce Humphries, 1944). For more on the encyclical, see John S. Conway's *The Nazi Persecution of the Churches 1933–1945* (1968; reprinted Vancouver: Regent College, 1997), pp. 165–167.

c. *"Spiritually we are all Semites"*

Pius XI taught against anti-Semitism both before and after *Mit brennender Sorge*. On March 25, 1928, a decree from the Holy Office declared: "Moved by the spirit of charity, the Apostolic See has protected the people [of Israel] against unjust persecutions, and since it condemns all jealousy and strife among peoples, it accordingly condemns with all its might the hatred directed against a people which was chosen by God; that particular hatred, in fact, which today commonly goes by the name of anti-Semitism" (*Acta Apostolicae Sedis* 20, pp. 103–104).

On September 6, 1938, during a speech to a group of Belgian pilgrims, Pius XI, reflecting on the words of the Mass dealing with the sacrifice of Abraham, exclaimed: "Note that Abraham is called our patriarch, our ancestor. Anti-Semitism is not compatible with the thought and the sublime realization expressed in this text. It is a deplorable movement, a movement which we, as Christians, must have no part in. . . . By Christ and in Christ, we are the spiritual offspring of Abraham. No, it is not possible for Christians to take part in anti-Semitism. . . . Anti-Semitism is inadmissible. Spiritually, we are all Semites" (*La Libre Belgique*, September 14, 1938; reproduced in *Documentation Catholique*, December 5, 1938, pp. 1459–1461). Commenting on this statement, Jacques Maritain wrote: "Spiritually we are Semites—no stronger word has been uttered by a Christian against anti-Semitism, and this Christian was the successor to the Apostle Peter" (*Virginia Quarterly Review*, Spring 1939, p. 167).

Because this text did not immediately appear in the Italian Catholic press, some authors have speculated that some of Pius XI's subordinates—perhaps even his cardinal secretary of state, Eugenio Pacelli—tried to suppress it. See, for instance, Susan Zuccotti's *Under His Very Windows* (New Haven: Yale University, 2000), p. 45. But the reason that Pius XI's statement did not appear in the Catholic press was that it was a spontaneous comment and not an official part of his prepared text. Because certain of Benedict XV's spontaneous comments had been quoted out of context during World War I, the Catholic press established a strict policy—requested by the Holy See—of not immediately publishing any *unofficial* statements by the pope, however significant. But news of the pope's heartfelt plea nevertheless spread rapidly, and the phrase, "spiritually we are all Semites" soon became well known.

Moreover, Pius XI's declaration was given publicity in countries outside Italy, with papal approval. See, for example, the report in the *Tablet*, "The Holy Father on the Jews," September 24, 1938, pp. 397–398. In his introduction to Pius XI's statement for *La Libre Belgique*, the Belgian paper that first published it, Monsignor Picard stated the "text we are offering has no official character. . . . We would not have made it public had not the Holy Father asked us to do so." The roles of Cardinal Pacelli and Pius XI in authorizing the publication of papal texts in the Catholic press is described by Lilian Browne-Olf in *Pius XI: Apostle of Peace*, pp. 197–198.

d. The Hidden Encyclical

One reason there is so much confusion about Pius XI's pontificate is because of a book, *The Hidden Encyclical of Pius XI* by Georges Passelecq and Bernard Suchecky (New York: Harcourt, Brace, 1997; a translation of the 1995 French original). This work purports to explain how Pius XI, toward the end of his pontificate, planned to publish an encyclical condemning anti-Semitism, but the project was scuttled at Pius XI's death by Pius XII.

It is true that Pius XI had discussed a possible encyclical with an American Jesuit, Father John Lafarge, and that Lafarge later brought in several other colleagues to work on a possible text. But there never was a completed text approved by Pius XI—he was too ill at the time to finalize anything—and the project never advanced beyond several drafts, which contradicted each other in numerous parts. There is no hard evidence that Pius XI or Pius XII ever saw these drafts, and Lafarge's autobiography never speaks of a completed text of a new encyclical, much less that it was "hidden." See *The Manner is Ordinary* by John Lafarge (New York: Harcourt, Brace, 1954), pp. 272–274.

For more details, at times speculative, see the *National Catholic Reporter*, December 15 and 22, 1972, and January 19, 1973, as well as the Vatican's response in Burkhart Schneider's "Un 'encyclica mancata,'" *Osservatore Romano*, April 5, 1973. For two modern, though flawed, commentaries, see "The Lost Encyclical" by Roland Hill, *Tablet*, August 11, 1997, and "The Hidden Encyclical of Pius XI against Racism and Anti-Semitism Uncovered—Once Again!" by Frank Coppa, *Catholic Historical Review*, January 1998, pp. 63–72.

After Pius XI died on February 10, 1939, a papal transition took place; world events were quickly changing, and Pius XII addressed these concerns in his first encyclical, *Summi Pontificatus*, which Father Lafarge himself hailed as the papal statement most needed to fight ethnic and racial bigotry ("Mankind is Called to Unity in Christ," *America*, November 11, 1939, pp. 120–121).

On the mythology surrounding the so-called "hidden encyclical"—as well as the failure of scholars to acknowledge *Summi Pontificatus* as being as good as anything Pius XI had planned—see "The Encyclical That Never Was," *Catholic World Report*, November 1995, pp. 8–9; Kevin Doyle's review of the Suchecky-Passeleq book in the *New Oxford Review*, July–August 1998, pp. 20–24; Ronald Rychlak's comments in *First Things*, June–July 2001, p. 39–40; and especially a book answering Suchecky and Passeleq, *Wider den Rassismus*, edited by Anton Rauscher (Paderborn: Ferdinand Schöningh, 2001). See the related "An Encyclical on Racism That Almost Was: Interview with Anton Rauscher," Zenit News Agency, April 6, 2001, and John Jay Hughes's review of Rauscher in the *Catholic Historical Review*, October 2001, pp. 710–712.

e. *Pius XI and the Jewish Community*

The writer David Kertzer has recently attempted to portray Pius XI (Achille Ratti) as an anti-Semite in *The Popes Against the Jews: The Vatican's Role in the Rise of Modern Anti-Semitism* (New York: Knopf, 2001). The charge is unsustainable.

After Ratti became Pius XI, he issued two forceful and explicit condemnations of anti-Semitism (in 1928 and 1938). In the spring of 1933, the year Hitler took power, Pius XI met with Rabbi Allesandro da Fano of Milan to express his solidarity with the Jewish community. The *Jewish Chronicle* reported: "The pope received in audience a delegation from the Agudath Israel, consisting of Consul General Guggenheim of Basle and Rabbi Allesandro da Fano of Milan, the President of the Board of Rabbis in Italy, and had a long private talk with them about the situation of the Jews in Germany. It is understood that the pope was extremely concerned about the sufferings imposed on the Jews and expressed his sympathy with them and his desire to help. Rabbi da Fano, who is eighty-six years of age, is a personal friend of the pope, and was his teacher of Hebrew when the pope was Director of the Catholic Ambrosian Library in Milan" ("The Pope's Desire to Help," *Jewish Chronicle*, May 12, 1933, p. 28).

Later that year, the *Jewish Chronicle* further reported: "The pope, having received reports of the persistence of anti-Semitic persecution in Germany, has publicly expressed his disapproval of the movement. He stated that these persecutions are a poor testimony to the civilization of a great people. He recalled the fact that Jesus Christ, the Madonna, the apostles and the prophets and many saints were all of the Hebrew race, and that the Bible is a Hebrew creation. The Aryan races, he declared, had no claim to superiority over the Semites" ("The Pope Denounces Anti-Semitism," *Jewish Chronicle*, September 1, 1933, p. 28).

On April 13, 1938, the pope had the Sacred Congregation for Seminaries and Universities address a letter to all rectors of Catholic universities and faculties to refute the pseudoscience with which Nazism justified its racist ideologies (text in *The Canon Law Digest, 1933–1942* [Milwaukee: Bruce, 1943], volume 2, pp. 395–396; see also *La Croix*, May 11, 1938; *Documentation Catholique*, May 20, 1938, pp. 579–580; *Civiltà Cattolica* 1938, volume 1, pp. 83–84; and *Nouvelle Revue Théologique* 66 [1939], pp. 235–236).

On July 14, 1938, Mussolini's regime issued its infamous Manifesto of the Racial Scientists, which marked Italian Fascism's embrace of Nazi-style racism and explicitly denied that Jews were members of the human race. The next day, Pius XI branded the manifesto "a true form of apostasy. It is no longer merely one or another erroneous idea; it is the entire spirit of the doctrine that is contrary to the Faith of Christ" (*Osservatore Romano*, July 17, 1938, p. 1; also *New York Times*, July 17, 1938, p. 1).

In a speech on July 21, 1938, Pius XI stated, "Catholic means universal, not racist, nationalistic, separatist. . . . The spirit of Faith must fight against the spirit of separatism and exaggerated nationalism, which are detestable, and which, just because they are not Christian, end up by not even being human" (*Osservatore Romano*, July 23, 1938, p. 1; *New York Times*, July 22, 1938). See also Camille Cianfarra's book, *The Vatican and the War* (New York: E.P. Dutton, 1944), which comments: "As the enslaved Italian press obeyed fascist party instructions to vilify the Jews, Pius XI fought with truly amazing vigor. . . . The papal appeal contained in the July 21 speech was a signal for a campaign throughout Italy against the racial laws" (pp. 133–134).

In a discourse to the members of the Collegio de Propaganda Fide on July 28, 1938, Pius XI again stated: "Catholic means universal, not racist, not nationalistic in the separatist meaning of these two tributes. . . . We do not wish to separate anything in the human family. . . . The 'humankind' reveals precisely what the human race is. It must be stated that people are first and foremost all one great and single species, one great and single family of living beings. . . . There is only one human, universal 'catholic' race . . . and with it and in it, different variations. . . . This is the Church's response" (*Osservatore Romano*, July 30, 1938, p. 1). And on August 21, Pius XI urged missionaries to "guard against 'exaggerated nationalism' as against a real curse" (*Osservatore Romano*, August 22–23, 1938, p. 1). For Pius XI's other major speeches, see *Discorsi di Pio XI*, 3 volumes, edited by Domenico Bertetto (Turin: Società Editrice Internazionale, 1959–1960).

Pius XI condemned the essence of Mussolini's anti-Semitic decrees, and he did so well before they were actually codified into law. Moreover, the pontiff's words were not only meant for baptized Jews but *all* Jews, regardless of their standing with the Church. If the Vatican's official documents to Mussolini's government often address Jewish converts, that is because the Vatican had legal standing to do so, under the Lateran Accords of 1929—not because Vatican diplomats were indifferent to the needs of unconverted Jews. Moreover, precisely because they understood the means by which the Church could protect them under the terms of the Lateran Accords, a flood of Jews entered the Church after the anti-Semitic laws in Italy were implemented. (See *Church and State in Fascist Italy* by Daniel Binchy, pp. 626–627.)

Two diplomats who had extensive personal contacts with Pius XI during this time—Zsolt Aradi (of the Hungarian Legation) and Ivone Kirkpatrick (of the British Foreign Office)—both confirm the pontiff's personal revulsion against anti-Semitism. See Aradi's *Pius XI*, pp. 221–222, and Kirkpatrick's *The Inner Circle* (London: Macmillan, 1959), pp. 47–48.

Certainly, Pius XI's enemies, who listened intently to all his speeches, knew who were being defended. After the pope made one of his many appeals, Nazi propagandist Julius Streicher railed, "The Jews have now found protection in the Catholic Church, which is trying to convince non-Jewish humanity that distinct races do not exist. . . . The pope has made the false conception his own—that of racial equality—and the Jews, with the help of Marxists and Freemasons, are doing their best to boost it. But the pope's attitude will surprise no one who is familiar with the shrewd schemes of Vatican politics" (translated from the Nazi journal *Der Stürmer*, and published in the *Tablet*, September 3, 1938, p. 301).

Similarly, in a speech to a huge crowd in Trieste on September 18, 1938, Mussolini defended Italy's new anti-Semitic policy and warned its opponents: "In the end the world perhaps will be more astounded by our generosity than by our rigor, at least (here his voice became ominous) unless Semites beyond the frontier and in our country, and, above all, their unexpected friends who defend them from too many chairs of learning, compel us to change our course radically" (*New York Times*, September 19, 1938). The *Times* added: "Mussolini . . . evidently was still smarting under the taunt flung at him by the pope, who charged that fascism was supinely following Germany in racial questions, for he reserved his strongest and most heated words for those who hold or who spread such a belief. 'Those who try to make it believed,' he stormed, 'that we have obeyed or initiated—or worse, have been influenced—are poor halfwits to whom we accord our contempt and our pity.' This invective was perhaps not intended for Pope Pius XI alone but certainly included him because the pope in a speech on July 28 expressed his surprise that Italy thought it necessary to ape Germany." (For additional commentary, see "In Defense of Pius XI" by Richard Escobales, *Catholic International*, August 2003, pp. 92–96.)

Denis Mack Smith, Mussolini's noted biographer, adds: "Every [Fascist] newspaper was obliged to carry articles justifying persecution and forbidden to print the protest which arrived from the pope. . . . When the Vatican remonstrated strongly, Mussolini warned that racialism was by now a fascist dogma that left no room for compromise. To spite the pope—whose death, he said, he was hoping for soon—he tried to persuade himself that religion, and indeed any belief in God, was on the decline: if Italians still went to Church, 'that was merely because they knew that the Duce wanted them to,' they were anticlerical at heart, and if he gave the word, were ready to get rid of the pope for good. . . . Sometimes he now acknowledged that he was an outright disbeliever, and once told a startled cabinet that Islam was perhaps a more effective religion than Christianity. The papacy was a malignant tumor in the body of Italy and must 'be rooted out once and for all,' because there was no room for both the pope and himself" (*Mussolini: A Biography* [New York: Knopf, 1982], pp. 222–223).

See also Jasper Riddley's *Mussolini* (New York: St. Martins, 1997), pp. 290 and 302; Charles F. Delzell's *Mussolini's Enemies: The Italian Anti-Fascist Resistance* (1961; reprinted New York: Howard Fertig: 1974); *Mussolini: A Study in Power* by Ivone Kirkpatrick (New York: Hawthorn, 1964); and Patrick J. Gallo's *Enemies: Mussolini and the Antifascists* (New York: Xlibris, 2002).

Pius XI was not intimidated and continued to lash out at "stupid racialism" and "barbarian Hitlerism" (*Tablet*, February 18, 1939, p. 205; see also Eamon Duffy's *Saints and Sinners*, p. 261). For Pius XI's last dramatic speeches against fascism and Nazism, see his addresses of September 18, 1938 (against the totalitarian state), September 29, 1938 (offering his life for the peace of the world), October 1, 1938 (again pleading for peace), October 20, 1938 (comparing Hitler to Julian the Apostate), and especially his Christmas address of December 24, 1938 (denouncing the Fascist government's crimes once again, alluding to Hitler's visit to Rome [in May 1938], and condemning the swastika as "a cross which is the enemy of the Cross of Christ"). Excerpts of these speeches are published in *Principles for Peace*, pp. 546–551. For more on Pius XI's opposition to Hitler's visit to Rome, see Giovanni Sale's "La mancata visita di Hitler in Vaticano," *Civiltà Cattolica* 2003, volume 4, pp. 10–23, and "Pius XI Snubbed Hitler's Bid for Papal Audience," Zenit News Agency, July 23, 2001.

When Mussolini's anti-Semitic decrees began depriving Jews of employ-ment in Italy, Pius XI, on his own initiative, admitted Professor Vito Volterra, a famous Italian Jewish mathematician, into the Pontifical Acad-emy of Science and proposed that Dr. Tullio-Levi-Civita, Italy's greatest physicist, also be taken in (see "Scholars at the Vatican," *Commonweal*, De-cember 4, 1942, pp. 187–188). When Lord Rothschild, a prominent British Jewish leader, organized a protest meeting in London against Kristallnacht (November 9–10, 1938), Eugenio Pacelli, Vatican secretary of state, acting on behalf of Pius XI, who was then ill, sent a statement of solidarity with persecuted Jews; the statement was read publicly at the meeting. See *Actes et Documents* 6, pp. 12–13, and 539, and Peter Gumpel's comments in "Historian's Accusations Against Wartime Holy See Are Refuted," Zenit News Agency, November 21, 2002.

Also of note is Pius XI's support for British efforts to help Jewish and other refugees (see "Pope Backs Britons on Aid to Refugees—Message Approving Baldwin Fund is Read at Meeting of All Parties and Faiths—Immediate Need is Cited," *New York Times*, December 10, 1938, p. 6). Rarely mentioned by the Vatican's detractors is that the Holy See sent out requests to its represen-tatives throughout the world to assist those fleeing oppression and racial per-secution; see Cardinal Pacelli's circular telegrams of November 30, 1938, and January 10, 1939, in *Actes et Documents* 6, pp. 48–50, and Pius XI's letter to the cardinal archbishops of Boston, Philadelphia, Chicago, Quebec, and Buenos Aires, pp. 50ff.

On January 13, 1939, Pius XI met with a British delegation including Prime Minister Chamberlain and Viscount Halifax. The *New York Times* editorial-ized that the meeting "was intended as recognition of a moral alignment which unites those who strive to buttress the established moral order against a new worship of force, race or state" (January 16, 1939, p. 14).

On February 11, 1939, the day after Pius XI died, the *New York Times* re-ported: "He [Pius XI] told them [the British delegation] exactly what he thought of reactionary regimes and of the resistance that the democracies must make to dangerous forces in the world. He talked of racial persecu-tion and the pressing need of helping refugees. He turned to bless his vis-itors. Almost all of them dropped to their knees, although they had previ-ously agreed only to bow. . . . They walked through the long halls, none of them speaking—Chamberlain, the Unitarian; Halifax, the Anglo-Catholic, and others who never dreamed that they could be so deeply moved—and two of the delegation were in tears as they emerged into the sunshine of Rome." Up until the day he died, Pius XI was preparing further attacks against Nazism and the totalitarian creed, as John XXIII revealed years later (see "Warning on Nazis by Pius XI Bared: Pope John Reveals Deathbed Notes Likening Hitler's Methods to Nero's," *New York Times*, February 10, 1959, p. 11).

The assessment of Pius XI's pontificate at the time was quite high. As Daniel Binchy comments: "The papacy . . . increased its prestige among non-Catholics, by its brave challenge to totalitarianism during the last years of Pius XI's reign. . . . Even the [Anglican] Bishop of Durham, whom we have already met as a severe critic of the Italian Church, publicly rejoiced that the brave words of Pastor Niemöller and Cardinal Faulhaber against the racialist myth should have been 'lately endorsed with unique authority and impressiveness by the Sovereign Pontiff himself' [letter to the *Times* of London, August 12, 1938]; while the *Church Times*, in whose eyes Pius XI was rarely fortunate enough to find favor, described his speeches against anti-Semitism as 'of great historical and moral importance' [August 5, 1938]. In other countries, notably France and the United States, praise was still more abundantly bestowed, and it is no exaggeration to say that at the death of Pius XI the Church he ruled stood higher in the world's esteem than at any time since the Reformation" (*Church and State in Fascist Italy*, pp. 702–703). For similar American tributes, see *Pope Pius XI and American Public Opinion*, edited by Robert J. Cuddihy and George N. Shuster (New York: Funk and Wagnalls, 1939).

In January 1939, the *National Jewish Monthly* reported that "the only bright spot in Italy has been the Vatican, where fine humanitarian statements by the pope have been issuing regularly" (pp. 157 and 183). The February 1939 issue of B'nai B'rith's *National Monthly* placed Pius XI on its cover under the title, "Pope Pius XI Attacks Fascism." At the time of Pius XI's death (February 10, 1939), Bernard Joseph, on behalf of the Executive of the Jewish Agency (the future government of Israel), wrote to the Latin patriarch in Jerusalem on February 12, 1939: "In common with the whole of civilized humanity, the Jewish people mourns the loss of one of the greatest exponents of the cause of international peace and good will. . . . More than once did we have occasion to be deeply grateful for the attitude which he took up against the persecution of racial minorities and, in particular, for the deep concern which he expressed for the fate of the persecuted Jews of Central Europe. His noble efforts on their behalf will ensure for him for all time a warm place in the memories of the Jewish people wherever they live" (Pinchas Lapide, *Three Popes and the Jews*, p. 116).

See also the obituary, "Pope Pius and the Jews: A Champion of Toleration," published in the *Jewish Chronicle* of London, February 17, 1939, p. 16, including a separate tribute by Cecil Roth, eminent Jewish historian, who wrote movingly of his private audience with the aged pontiff, during which Pius XI assured Roth of the papacy's opposition to anti-Semitism. Roth hailed Pius XI as that "courageous voice raised unfalteringly and unwearyingly . . . protesting against oppression, condemning racial madness, and reminding the world of the ultimate spiritual values above States and statecraft. . . . This was an aspect which he appreciated to the full, and earned his memory an undying claim to the gratitude of the Jewish people."

f. The Contrast between Pius XI and Pius XII

Those unsympathetic to Pius XII sometimes compare him unfavorably to Pius XI. The leading proponents of this view are Peter C. Kent and Frank Coppa; see Kent's "A Tale of Two Popes: Pope Pius XI, Pius XII and the Rome-Berlin Axis," *Journal of Contemporary History* 23 (1988), pp. 589–608, and Coppa's "Pope Pius XI's 'Encyclical' *Humani Generis Unitas* Against Racism and Anti-Semitism and the 'Silence' of Pope Pius XII," *Journal of Church and State*, Autumn 1998, pp. 775ff. For earlier versions of the contrast, see William Harrigan's two essays, "Nazi Germany and the Holy See, 1933–1936," *Catholic Historical Review* 47 (1961), pp. 164–198, and "Pius XII's Efforts to Effect a Détente in German-Vatican Relations, 1939–1940," *Catholic Historical Review* 49 (1963), pp. 173–191; and George O. Kent's "Pope Pius XII and Germany: Some Aspects of German-Vatican Relations," *American Historical Review*, October 1964, pp. 59–78.

While all popes differ, Pius XI worked intimately and consistently with his secretary of state, Eugenio Pacelli, on all of his major statements, including those against Nazism and anti-Semitism. A case in point: When Theodore Innitzer, the archbishop of Vienna, made statements interpreted as sympathizing with Hitler's Germany, Pius XI and Cardinal Pacelli immediately forced him to retract. *L'Osservatore Romano* on April 1, 1938, declared that the remarks by the Austrian prelate were wholly unwarranted and made without the approval of the Holy See. The same day, "the Holy See broadcast a blistering attack on the Austrian episcopate for violating its teaching role. Immediately thereafter, Pius XI summoned Innitzer to Rome where he and Pacelli chastised the primate for his poor judgment and wishful thinking" (Evan Burr Bukey in *Hitler's Austria: Popular Sentiment in the Nazi Era, 1938–1945* [Chapel Hill: University of North Carolina, 2000], p. 98). In the words of the British minister to the Holy See, Innitzer "was severely hauled over the coals by the Vatican" and "told to go back and eat his words" (Confidential Letter to Oliver Harvey from D'Arcy Osborne, British Public Record Office, FO 371/67917 60675). Innitzer signed a public retraction. The *Encyclopaedia Britannica* notes: "After a rebuke from Pius XI, Innitzer ceased to approve Nazism. His home subsequently became a refuge for Jews, while he strove to alleviate public distress and to restore the Austrian church' (*Micropaedia*, volume 5, p. 321). See also the *Tablet*, October 22, 1938, p. 522, reporting on the Nazi mob attack on Innitzer's residence in Vienna; also the issue of January 19, 1946, p. 31, for Innitzer's work on behalf of Austrian Jews.

Pius XI and Pacelli also intervened forcefully to repress anti-Semitism in Poland (see "Pope's Action in Warsaw: Check to Spread of Racialism," *Jewish*

Chronicle, August 5, 1938, pp. 23–24). Pius XI specifically groomed Pacelli to become his successor: "On a number of occasions, Pius XI indicated that Cardinal Pacelli would make an ideal pope, going so far as to say that if he were sure the conclave would elect Pacelli as his successor, he would retire" (*Hitler, the War, and the Pope* by Ronald Rychlak [Columbus: Genesis, 2000], p. 106; see also Robin Anderson's *Between Two Wars: The Story of Pope Pius XI*, pp. xiii, xxviii, 67, 84–85, 135, 140, and 142).

Another author affirms: "The relationship between Pope Pius XI and his Secretary of State was especially close toward the end of the former's reign. Pius XI made no secret of his admiration for his highly intellectual subordinate and repeatedly made clear that he had no doubt as to who should be his own successor: 'Our Secretary of State works a great deal, he works well, he works quickly. . . . He will make a fine Pope!'" (quoted by John Dombrowski in *Faith and Reason*, Winter 1988, p. 358, citing "Pius XII," *Osservatore Romano*, March 18, 1976, p. 8, and *Actes et Documents* 1, p. 5).

The strongest evidence of Pius XI's support for Pacelli comes from Monsignor Domenico Tardini, then secretary of the Congregation for Extraordinary Ecclesiastical Affairs, who wrote on February 22, 1939—soon after Pius XI's death (February 10), but before the election of his successor: "Many times His Holiness Pius XI spoke to me about his successor. For him, there was no doubt. His secretary of state had to become the next pope. The Holy Father told me that it was to prepare him for the tiara that he often sent him abroad, and even to the two Americas. One day, in October–November 1936, when his Eminence [Cardinal Pacelli] was in the United States, Pius XI highly praised his secretary of state and, looking me straight in the eye with his penetrating eyes, concluded by saying: "He will be a magnificent pope' (*Sarà un bel papa*). He did not say: 'He would be' or 'He could be' but 'he will be' without admitting any doubt. He said this on 12 November" (cited in Pierre Blet's *Pius XII and the Second World War*, p. 7).

Cardinal Eugenio Pacelli was elected pope on March 2, 1939. The next day, the Berlin *Morgenpost* reported: "The election of Cardinal Pacelli is not accepted with favor in Germany because he was always opposed to Nazism and practically determined the policies of the Vatican under his predecessor." For a highly favorable American assessment, see "New Pope, a Roman Aristocrat, Known for Humility and Sagacity," *New York Times*, March 3, 1939, p. 4. Two years later, the editor of *Current Biography* confirmed this view: "The election of Cardinal Eugenio Pacelli on March 2, 1939, meant continuance of his predecessor's policy, which, as papal secretary of state, he had helped to effect: a policy of opposition to race prejudice, religious persecution, wars of aggression. Cannons roared, the bells of Rome rang out, congratulations poured in. But there was small rejoicing in Germany, for the Reich had made it clear that of all candidates the 'pro-Ally' Pacelli would be least acceptable" (*Current Biography 1941*, edited by Maxine Block [New York: H.W. Wilson, 1941]).

Soon after Pacelli assumed the papal throne, the Vatican made clear it would continue Pius XI's policies. "At the beginning of World War II, Pius XII arranged a meeting at the Quirinal Palace with the King of Italy, and specifically excluded Mussolini from the session. . . . The pope's words: 'I don't want anyone present at the meeting who signed the racial laws'" (firsthand testimony of Adriano Ossicini, antifascist leader who was arrested by Mussolini, as recounted in *L'Avvenire*, June 27, 1996; English language summary in "More Echoes on Pope Pius XII, Nazi Holocaust," Zenit News Agency, June 27, 1996).

On the consistency of Pius XI and Pius XII's policies, the *New York Times* correspondent Camille Cianfarra spoke of "being an eyewitness to the struggle that both Pius XI and Pius XII waged against Nazism and fascism. . . . I heard those two pontiffs condemn time and again the totalitarian system of government and witnessed the birth and rapid growth of very close cooperation between the Vatican and Washington to prevent the war, and, later, to minimize it" (*The Vatican and the War*, p. 8). Similarly, Archbishop Philip M. Hannan, a seminarian at the North American College in Rome from 1936 to 1940, remembers the election of Pius XII: "There was great need to continue the opposition of the Church to all the dictatorships, and Cardinal Pacelli was completely linked with the policy of Pius XI" (*Rome: Living Under the Axis* [McKees Rocks: St. Andrews, 2003], p. 285).

PART 3: THE PAPACY OF PIUS XII

1. Biographies of Pius XII

While the definitive biography of Pius XII has yet to be written, many books can be recommended in varying degrees. Joseph Dineen's *Pius XII* (New York: R.M. McBride, 1939) is the best early biography (see, in particular, the excellent chapter on relations with America); Kees van Hoek's *Pius XII: Priest and Statesman* (London: Burns, Oates and Washbourne, 1940) is a good short life.

At the end of the Second World War, a spate of biographies appeared, of which the best are *The Life of Pope Pius XII* by Charles Hugo Doyle (New York: Didier, 1945) and Jan Olav Smit's *Angelic Shepherd: The Life of Pope Pius XII* (New York: Dodd and Mead, 1950). Wilhelm Sandfuchs's *Papst Pius XII* (Karlsruhe: Badenia, 1949) is a neglected work by an important German scholar.

In *Keeper of the Keys: Life of Pope Pius XII* (Milwaukee: Bruce, 1946), Thomas McDermott comments: "It has been said, in ignorance or malice, that the Holy See, terrified by the Nazi victories, favored the Axis during the early years of the war. Voluminous evidence to the contrary might be introduced, and the accusers still not be convinced, for prejudice like death is not open to argument. These sentences, however, broadcast by the Vatican Radio *in the fall of 1940, when Hitler and Mussolini were at the zenith of their power and conquest*, should be of some weight. 'Those who allege that they will be able to create a new order [then the Nazi boast] in the world are prefacing the destruction of the people whom they allegedly wish to make happy. It is a world order as dry as the desert and it is being achieved by the exploitation of human life. What these false benefactors call life is death.' It should also be pointed out that the Holy See through *L'Osservatore Romano* bluntly denied every claim of the Axis radio and press that the Pope favored its designs and principles. The Holy Father, through his bountiful charity to the oppressed and the enslaved, clearly demonstrated that his sympathies were not with the victors but their victims" (p. 194).

In 1951, the distinguished historian Oscar Halecki wrote what is still the best available biography in English: *Eugenio Pacelli: Pope of Peace* (New York: Creative Age, 1951; revised edition 1954). The Italian scholar Igino Giordani subsequently wrote another major biography *Pio XII: un grande papa* (Turin: Società Editrice Internazionale, 1961). Ernesto Buon-aiuti's earlier work, *Pio XII* (Rome: Universale di Roma, 1946) is also important. Toward the end of Pius XII's life, Katherine Burton published a popular biography, *Witness of the Light: The Life of Pope Pius XII* (New York: Longmans, Green, 1958), as did Louis de Wohl after the pontiff's death, *Pope Pius XII: The World's Shepherd* (New York: Farrar, Straus and Cudahy, 1961).

Retrospectives of Pius XII's pontificate include Nazareno Padellaro's *Portrait of Pius XII* (London: Catholic Book Club, 1956), which is excellent on Pius XII's personal strength and political courage, although it occasionally mistranslates Italian quotations. Alden Hatch and Seamus Walshe's *Crown of Glory: The Life of Pope Pius XII* (New York: Hawthorn, 1957) is good on the war years and also contains a remarkable epilogue by Hatch entitled "A Protestant Looks at the Pope," which predicts Pius XII will ultimately be judged a great pope. Cardinal Richard Cushing, a close friend of Pius XII, published a salute in *Pope Pius XII* (Boston: St. Paul, 1959).

In 1968, the German Jesuit Burkhart Schneider, one of the four editors of the Holy See's wartime *Actes et Documents*, wrote his own study, which has since been updated, with an afterward by David Dalin: *Pio XII: Con un contributo del rabbino David Dalin in difesa del pontefice* (Rome: San Paolo, 2002). The Austrian scholar Herbert Schambeck has edited an outstanding collection of essays, *Pius XII* (Berlin: Duncker und Humblot, 1977). The Italian Andrea Riccardi has edited a similar collection, *Pio XII* (Rome: Paoline, 1984), as has the French scholar Jean Chelini, *Pie XII et la Cité* (Aix-Marseille: Presses universitaires, 1988).

2. Firsthand Accounts

Essential to understanding the character and policies of Pius XII are the sworn depositions and other documents relating to Pius XII's possible beatification and canonization, now residing in Rome under the supervision of the Vatican's Congregation for the Causes of Saints. Ronald Rychlak comments: "The original transcripts take up just over 1,700 pages which are spread over seven volumes. . . . The clear message from each and every witness is that Eugenio Pacelli—Pius XII—was an honest, holy, and charitable man—even saintly" (*Hitler, the War, and the Pope*, pp. 286–287). For more on the cause of Pope Pius XII, see *Making Saints: How the Catholic Church Determines Who Becomes a Saint, Who Doesn't and Why* by Kenneth L. Woodward (New York: Simon and Schuster, 1990), pp. 280–308; see also "German Jesuit Nears End of Campaign for Beatifying Pope Pius XII," Associated Press, May 14, 2003.

a. Accounts of Vatican Staff

1. Robert Leiber

Father Robert Leiber, S.J., Pius XII's personal assistant and confidant from the pontiff's earlier days as nuncio to Germany, spoke with Pius XII two or three times a day and is one of the most important witnesses on his behalf. When Pius XII died in 1958, Leiber published what remains the finest obituary of the pope, "Pius XII," *Stimmen der Zeit*, November 1958, pp. 81–100, later translated in *The Storm Over the Deputy: Essays and Articles About Hochhuth's Explosive Drama*, edited by Eric Bentley (New York: Grove, 1964), pp. 173–194.

Leiber also documented his knowledge of Pius XII's support for persecuted Jews in "Pio XII e gli ebrei di Roma, 1943–1944," *Civiltà Cattolica* 1961, volume 1, pp. 449–458. See as well Leiber's "Der Papst und die Verfolgung der Juden" in *Summa iniuria oder durfte der Papst schweigen? Hochhuths 'Stellvertreter' in der öffentlichen Kritik*, edited by Fritz J. Raddatz (Hamburg: Rowohlt, 1963), pp. 101–107. Also worth noting are Leiber's comments in "Pius XII and the Third Reich," *Look*, May 17, 1966, pp. 36–50: "The pope sided very unequivocally with the Jews at the time. He spent his entire private fortune on their behalf. . . . Pius spent what he inherited himself, as a Pacelli, from his family."

In an earlier article, Leiber noted that in 1933, the year Hitler came to power, Eugenio Pacelli was secretary of state, and the first initiative of the Holy See toward the government in Berlin was made on behalf of Jews, and against anti-Semitism (*Stimmen der Zeit*, March 1962, p. 420). After Pacelli became pope, Leiber worked closely with Pius XII, and the anti-Nazi German resistance, on plots to overthrow Hitler. See *The Conspiracy Against*

Hitler in the Twilight War by Harold C. Deutsch (Minneapolis: University of Minnesota, 1968), especially chapter 4, and *Spies in the Vatican: Espionage and Intrigue from Napoleon to the Holocaust* by David Alvarez (Lawrence: University Press of Kansas, 2002).

Because Leiber is such an important supporter of Pius XII, a number of papal detractors have questioned his testimony; still others have suggested he was critical of Pius. In fact, all of Leiber's documented writings and statements attest to his belief that Pius XII was a great and courageous pontiff (see the remarks of Peter Gumpel, official relator for the cause of Pius XII, in the article by the Austrian news agency Kathpress, "Heiliger Stuhl öffnet Deutschland," October 30, 2002). In early 2003, a document emerged from the newly released archives of the pontificate of Pius XI revealing that, just as Father Leiber had maintained, Cardinal Pacelli sent explicit instructions to the papal nuncio in Germany, on April 4, 1933, to oppose Nazi anti-Semitism (see "New Proofs of Pius XII's Efforts to Assist Jews: 1933 Letter Targets 'Anti-Semitic Excesses' in Germany," Zenit News Agency, February 17, 2003).

2. Pascalina Lehnert

The warm recollections of Pius XII by his housekeeper, Sister Pascalina Lehnert, were published as *Ich durfte Ihm dienen: Erinnerungen an Papst Pius XII* (Würzburg: n.p., 1982) and translated into Italian as *Pio XII, il privilegio di servirlo* (Milan: Rusconi, 1984). Particularly revealing is her description of Pacelli's opposition to all forms of political tyranny and his prophetic insight into Nazism. See, especially, pp. 42–43, for Pacelli's explicit warnings against Hitler in 1929—four years before he came to power.

Sister Pascalina's authentic memoirs are not to be confused with a concoction appearing under the title *La Popessa* (New York: Warner, 1983) by R. René Arlington and Paul I. Murphy. As one critic noted, *La Popessa* "is a world apart from the genuine memoirs of the nun; it is a world of arbitrary invention, carried at times to the wildest extremes" (Michael O'Carroll, *Pius XII: Greatness Dishonored* [Dublin: Laetare, 1980], p. 244). Among other lurid fantasies, the book claims that before becoming pope, Eugenio Pacelli gave money to a young Adolf Hitler; in fact, the two never met.

3. Luigi Maglione

Cardinal Luigi Maglione, Pius XII's secretary of state during the war, never wrote his memoirs because of his untimely death in 1944, but his interaction with Pius XII, and humanitarian interventions, are extensively documented in *Actes et Documents*, especially volumes 6, 8, 9, and 10. For more on Maglione, see the obituary in *L'Osservatore Romano*, August 23, 1944, p. 1; also Bruno Wuestenberg's "Luigi Kardinal Maglione, Staatssekretär Pius' XII.

1939–1944" in *Die Aussenminister der Päpste*, edited by Wilhelm Sandfuchs (Munich: G. Olzog, 1962), pp. 124–130. Maglione's assistant, Domenico Tardini, left behind a powerful tribute in *Memories of Pius XII* (Westminster: Newman, 1961). On Tardini himself, see Carlo Felice Casula's biography *Domenico Tardini, 1888–1961* (Rome: Studium, 1988).

4. Giovanni Battista Montini

Another of Maglione's assistants was Giovanni Battista Montini, who later became Pope Paul VI. On Montini, Peter Hebblethwaite's massive biography, *Paul VI: The First Modern Pope* (Mahwah: Paulist, 1993), documents his wartime experiences and high regard for Pius XII, as testified to by Montini's letter to the *Tablet* (June 29, 1963, p. 714), which vigorously defended Pius XII against Hochhuth's play *The Deputy*.

During Paul VI's visit to Israel in 1964, he declared: "Everybody knows what Pius XII did for the defense of all those who were caught in [World War II's] tribulations, without distinction. And yet you know suspicions and even accusations have been leveled against this great Pontiff. We are happy to have the opportunity to state on this day and in this place that there is nothing more unjust than this slight against such a venerated memory. Those who intimately knew this admirable man know how far could go his sensibility, his compassion for human suffering, his courage, his delicacy of heart. Those who after the war came with tears in their eyes to thank him for saving their lives also knew it" (*Insegnamenti di Paolo VI* [Vatican City: Libreria Editrice Vaticana, 1976], volume 2, pp. 53–54; for an English-language summary, see the January 6, 1964, *New York Times*, p. 1, which commented: "The pope's defense of Pope Pius XII's efforts to save Jews during World War II were widely and favorably commented on both privately and publicly [throughout Israel]"). For more on Paul VI's trip to Israel, see *Paul VI—Rom und Jerusalem. Konzil, Pilgerfahrt, Dialog der Religionen* (Trier: Paulinus, 2001) by Thomas Brechenmacher and Hardy Ostry, especially pp. 73–74.

Paul VI also praised Pius XII's wartime rescue efforts in an allocution on January 10, 1975, in which he said: "There are also many who can testify what the Catholic Church did, at Rome itself, under the forceful leadership of Pope Pius XII—we witnessed this ourselves—and what numerous bishops, priests and faithful of the different countries of Europe did, often at the risk of their lives, to snatch innocent Jews from persecution" (*Acta Apostolicae Sedis* 67, p. 95).

Twenty years before, in 1955, when a delegation from Israel approached Montini to ask whether he would accept an award for his own work on behalf of Jews during the war, he declined the offer, explaining: "All I did was my duty. And besides I only acted upon orders from the Holy Father. Nobody deserves a medal for that" (quoted in Lapide's *Three Popes and the*

Jews, p. 137; see also Alexander Ramati's comments in *The Assisi Underground: The Priests Who Rescued Jews* [New York: Stein and Day, 1978], pp. 178–179).

For a further tribute by Paul VI to Pius XII's wartime conduct, see the allocution of March 12, 1964 (reprinted in *Heights of Heroism in the Life of Pope Pius XII* by the Daughters of St. Paul [Boston: St. Paul, 1964]). For more on Paul VI and his wartime rescue efforts, see *Apostle for Our Time* by John G. Clancy (New York: Kennedy, 1963) and *Pope Paul VI* by Alden Hatch (New York: Random House, 1966), especially pp. 65–82.

Also important is the statement by Pasquale Macchi, the private secretary of Pope Paul VI, testifying to both Pius XII's and Paul VI's support for persecuted Jews: "Paolo VI non andò sul Monte Herzl ma onorò le Vittime della Shoah," *Corriere della Sera*, June 6, 2000. See also "Paul VI and His Legacy: Interview with Papal Biographer Andrea Tornielli," Zenit News Agency, September 17, 2003. Tornielli is the author of *Paolo VI: Il Timoniere del Concilio* (Casale Monferrato: Piemme, 2003).

5. Quirino Paganuzzi

Monsignor Paganuzzi, a chaplain of the Supreme Military Order of Malta, testified that he was asked by the Vatican to deliver a package of anti-Nazi papal declarations that Pius XII wanted publicized in Poland. When Paganuzzi finally delivered Pius XII's message, however, Archbishop Sapieha of Cracow suppressed it.

Paganuzzi first revealed the incident for an Italian periodical in the spring of 1964, commenting: "As always, Msgr. Sapieha's welcome was most affectionate. . . . However, he didn't waste much time in conventionalities. He opened the packets [from Pius XII, with statements condemning Nazi Germany], read them, and commented on them in his pleasant voice. Then he opened the door of the large stove against the wall, started a fire, and threw the papers on to it. All the rest of the material shared the same fate. On seeing my astonished face, he said in explanation: 'I'm most grateful to the Holy Father, . . . no one is more grateful than we Poles for the pope's interest in us, . . . but we have no need of any outward show of the pope's loving concern for our misfortunes, when it only serves to augment them. . . . But he doesn't know that if I give publicity to these things, and if they are found in my house, the head of every Pole wouldn't be enough for the reprisals Gauleiter Frank will order'" (*Vita*, April 15, 1964, as translated by Carlo Falconi in *The Silence of Pius XII*, p. 149).

For further documentation on Paganuzzi's meeting with Sapieha—which was also witnessed and confirmed by a German military chaplain named Father Joseph Kaul—see Paganuzzi's diaries, which originally appeared in book form in 1970 under the title *Pro Papa Pio* (reprinted Rome: Nuovo

Omicrom, 1998). See also *Processo al Vicario* (Turin: Sale, 1965) by Rosario F. Esposito, and the extensive account provided by Margherita Marchione in *Consensus and Controversy: Defending Pope Pius XII* (Mahwah: Paulist, 2002), pp. 24–28.

Actes et Documents confirms Paganuzzi's contacts with the Polish hierarchy and their results. In a letter to Pius XII dated October 28, 1942, Archbishop Sapieha expressed his warm gratitude and understanding of what the Holy Father had done and was doing in Poland, but explained the reason for the Polish hierarchy's reserve: "We very much regret that we cannot publicly communicate to our faithful your Holiness' letters, as this would only afford an opportunity for fresh persecutions; and the fact that we have been suspected of being in secret communication with the Holy See has already led to victimization" (*Actes et Documents* 3, part 2, pp. 669–670).

6. Pirro Scavizzi

The testimony of Don Pirro Scavizzi, an Italian field chaplain, offers further evidence that the pope was extremely concerned about the ongoing reprisals the Nazis were inflicting as the result of the Vatican's public statements.

Scavizzi wrote: "When I volunteered as a chaplain at the age of nearly sixty. . . . I was enabled to see at close quarters the appalling cruelties of the Hitlerite organizations, especially of the SS, and so to inform the Holy Father. I was able to deliver important papal documents in Austria, Germany, Poland and the Ukraine, as well as secret and practical arrangements to defend and help the persecuted, and especially the Jews; for the work of exterminating them was taking its tragic course. My hospital train came to Rome twice to 'unload the hopelessly wounded' and I went to see Pius XII secretly to tell him everything without any preliminary formalities. Before my eyes he wept like a child and prayed like a saint. . . . The pope, standing beside me, listened with deep emotion; then raised his hands and said: 'Tell everyone, everyone you can, that the pope is in anguish for them and with them! . . . Serious threats of reprisal have come to our ears, not against our person, but against our unhappy sons who are now under Nazi domination'" (*La Parrocchia*, May 1964, as translated by Carlo Falconi, *The Silence of Pius XII*, pp. 150–151 and 238. See also "Nazi Reprisal Against Jews Held Fear of Pope Pius XII," *Religious News Service*, May 20, 1964, which, referring to the same article by Scavizzi, quotes Pius XII's concern that a rash action by him could "arouse the most ferocious rage against the Jews and multiply acts of cruelty"). For more on Scavizzi's heroic life, as well as his gratitude and support of Pius XII, see Michele Manzo's biography, *Don Pirro Scavizzi: Prete Romano, 1884–1964* (Casale Monferrato: Piemme, 1997).

As a result of such warnings, Pius XII weighed everything he said in the interests of those vulnerable to Nazi retaliation. As he told the College of

Cardinals in 1943: "Every single word in our statements addressed to the competent authorities, and every one of our public utterances, has had to be weighed and pondered by us with deep gravity, in the very interest of those who are suffering, so as not to render their position even more difficult and unbearable than before, be it unwittingly and unintentionally" (from a June 2, 1943, allocution, as translated in the *Tablet*, June 12, 1943, p. 282; the full text of the speech is in the *Acta Apostolicae Sedis* 35, pp. 165–171).

Almost identical concerns were voiced by Pius XII in two letters to German prelates: his letter of April 30, 1943, to Bishop von Preysing of Berlin (published in *Actes et Documents* 2, pp. 318–327), and in his letter of March 3, 1944, to Archbishop Joseph Frings (*Actes et Documents* 2, pp. 363–367). Indeed, as early as the spring of 1940, Pius XII had already expressed his concern to Italian ambassador Dino Alfieri that the Nazis were easily provoked to savage reprisals (against Christians as well as Jews) as a result of statements emanating from the Holy See. (See the Holy See's notes from the May 13, 1940, discussion in *Actes et Documents* 1, pp. 453–455.)

On point here is the testimony of Monsignor Jean Bernard, the bishop of Luxembourg, who spent two years in a concentration camp at Dachau: "The detained priests trembled every time news reached us of some protest by a religious authority, but particularly by the Vatican. We all had the impression that our warders made us atone heavily for the fury these protests evoked . . . whenever the way we were treated was suddenly brutalized, the Protestant pastors among the prisoners used to vent their indignation at the Catholic priests: 'Again your big naive pope and those simpletons, your bishops, are shooting off their mouths . . . why don't they get the idea, once and for all, and shut up. They play the heroes, but we have to pay the bill'" (from Bernard's prison memoirs, *Pfarrerblock* [Munich: Pustet, 1962], as cited by Pinchas Lapide in *Three Popes and the Jews*, p. 247).

Lapide himself stated that "he had heard a German general on trial [for war crimes] admit that reprisals for public protests were official policy" (cited by Michael O'Carroll in *Pius XII: Greatness Dishonored*, p. 151 n. 9). See also "When Protest Can Only Harm" by Emilia Paola Pacelli, *Osservatore Romano*, November 15, 2000, p. 10 (English edition) and "Pius XII and the Holocaust: Fear of Reprisals and Generic Diplomacy" by Killian McDonnell, *Gregorianum* 83 (2002), pp. 313–334, an interesting if flawed article on Pius XII's use of language.

7. Eugene Tisserant

The French Cardinal Eugene Tisserant is often quoted against Pius XII for the private letter he wrote in May 1940 to Cardinal Suhard, saying, among other things: "I fear that history will reproach the Holy See for having practiced a policy of selfish convenience and little else." But Tisserant himself later emphatically stated that he was not criticizing Pius XII but those who refused to follow the pope's lead: "The pope's attitude was beyond discussion. My remarks did not involve his person, but certain members of the Curia. In the dramatic period of the war, and what a period that was, Pius XII was able to guide the Church with invincible strength" (Tisserant interview, *Informations Catholiques Internationales*, April 15, 1964; also see O'Carroll's *Pius XII: Greatness Dishonored*, pp. 14 and 69).

Tisserant declared that Pius XII had done exactly what his critics had asked for: "It seems evident to me that principles, reaffirmed by Pope Pacelli in his first encyclical [*Summi Pontificatus*] and repeated forcefully in every circumstance, above all in the Christmas messages of the war years, constitute the most concrete condemnation of the Hitlerian type of absolutism" (*New York Times*, February 26, 1964, p. 41). See also "1944 Talk on Racial Stand by Pius XII is Published," *New York Times*, April 4, 1964, p. 7, containing excerpts from a wartime address by Tisserant, showing that he praised Pius XII for having "underlined the doctrine that 'men have the same rights, whatever their origin might be' and that 'many times he helped those who were being persecuted because of their birth.'"

8. Other Staff

For testimony from one of Pius XII's personal doctors, who confirms the pope's concern for persecuted Jews, see Aga Hruska's *Der Tragische Karneval* (Vienna: Ibera, 1998), pp. 320–323.

The most famous Italian refuge used during the war was Castel Gandolfo, the papal summer palace. "This summer home of the Holy Father was soon completely filled, as he had given orders that no one was to be refused," wrote Monsignor Carroll-Abbing (*A Chance to Live: The Story of the Lost Children of the War* [London: Longmans, Green, 1952], p. 82), who ministered there. In her diary, dated February 3, 1944, Jane Scrivener, an American nun working in Rome with the Vatican at the time, records: "The Pontifical Villa at Castel Gandolfo has been bombed. . . . The news was telegraphed in to the Vatican, and the pope gave orders to the staff at the Villa to give all possible help to the refugees" (*Inside Rome with the Germans*, p. 103).

The wartime director of Castel Gandolfo was Emilio Bonomelli, whose book, *I papi in campagna* (Rome: Gherardo Casini, 1953), expressly notes that persecuted Jews were among those under his care (p. 439). Ronald Rychlak comments: "Castel Gandolfo, the papal summer home, was used to shelter hundreds, perhaps thousands, of Jews during the war. . . . A wartime U.S. intelligence document reported that the 'bombardment of Castel Gandolfo resulted in the injury of about 1,000 people and the death of about 300 more. The highness of the figures is due to the fact that the area is crammed with refugees.' The intelligence reports also indicate that Pius himself protested the bombing. This information—from U.S. archives—shows a great deal of papal involvement in Jewish rescue operations. No one but Pope Pius XII had the authority to open these buildings to outsiders" (*Journal of Modern Italian Studies*, Summer 2002, p. 224).

That persecuted Jews were among the estimated 12,000 refugees who stayed at Castel Gandolfo during the war is clearly documented in the Vatican's wartime archives (*Actes et Documents* 10, p. 129); moreover the Jesuit Father Stein, director of Castel Gandolfo's observatory during the war, was an emissary for some of the Vatican's humanitarian actions (*Actes et Documents* 8, p. 228 n. 1, and 9, p. 47 n. 6). At Castel Gandolfo there stands "an enormous wooded cross, beautifully decorated. This Christian symbol of suffering love was given to Pius XII at the end of the war by the Jews who lived there during those terrifying days. It was their way of expressing their deep gratitude and veneration for this pope who had heroically defied the Gestapo and had saved their lives" (November 30, 1988, statement of Timothy O'Donnell, president of Christendom College, cited in *The Pope and the Holocaust* [Alexandria: Family Apostolate, 1997] by John S. Rader and Kateryna Fedoryka, p. 122). For additional details, see also "Castel Gandolfo Celebrates 400 Years of Papal Residence," *Catholic World News*, December 31, 1996; *Hitler, the War, and the Pope* by Ronald Rychlak, p. 202; and *The Incredible Mission of Father Benoît* by Fernande Leboucher (London: William Kimber, 1969), p. 137.

b. Accounts of Catholic Rescuers

1. Tibor Baranski

Baranski, executive secretary of the Jewish Protection Movement of the Holy See in Hungary during World War II, has been honored by Yad Vashem as a "Righteous Gentile" and is one of the most powerful witnesses on behalf of Pius XII. In interviews, articles, and a forthcoming book, Baranski makes clear that everything he did for persecuted Jews was done on the explicit instructions of Pius XII. "Charges that Pius was not involved are 'simple lies; nothing else,' and claims that Pius should have done more for Jews are, according to Baranski, 'slanderous.' Baranski personally saw at least two letters from Pius XII instructing [Angelo] Rotta [papal nuncio to Hungary] to do his very best to protect Jews. . . . He adds: 'These two letters were not written by the authorities at the Vatican, but they were handwritten ones by Pope Pius himself.' He goes on to note that 'all other nuncios of the Nazi-occupied countries received similar letters.' . . . Baranski, who says that he was 'fantastically near' to Wallenberg, reports that if Wallenberg were alive today, he would defend Pope Pius XII" ("A Righteous Gentile Defends Pius XII," Zenit News Agency, October 5, 2002). See also Harvey Rosenfeld's biography,

Raul Wallenberg: Angel of Rescue (Buffalo: Prometheus, 1982), pp. 72–81, which recounts Baranski's testimony in detail, and the profile, "Hungarian Catholic Given Highest Honors in Israel" by Kay Lyons, *Western New York Catholic Visitor*, March 4, 1979, pp. 6A–7A, which reaffirms Baranski's testimony ("I was really acting in accordance with the orders of Pope Pius XII").

2. Don Aldo Brunacci

Brunacci, a priest-rescuer of Jews from Assisi, has testified that Pius XII wrote a letter to his bishop explicitly instructing the clergy to rescue and protect persecuted Jews. Because those caught by the Nazis carrying incriminating documents were severely punished, these papal orders had to be carried out with the greatest discretion. Brunacci writes: "One Thursday in September, 1943, after the usual monthly clergy meeting in the seminary, the bishop [Giuseppe Nicolini of Assisi] called me aside in the alcove next to the chapter room and, showing me a letter of the Secretariat of State of His Holiness, said to me: We must organize to give aid to the persecuted and particularly to the Jews. This is the will of the Holy Father Pius XII. It has to be with the maximum of secrecy and prudence. No one even among the priests should know about it [the papal letter]" (from Brunacci's lecture, "Giornata degli ebrei d'Italia: Ricordi di un protagonista," given in Assisi on March 15, 1982, printed in *Ebrei in Assisi durante la guerra. Ricordi di un protagonista* [Assisi: n.p., 1985], pp. 7–15). Also see Brunacci's similar testimony in "Rescue Italian Style" by Mae Briskin in *Jewish Monthly*, May 1986, pp. 20–25, and "Assisi 2002: An Encounter with History" by Gerald Schwartz, *Canadian Jewish News*, September 5, 2002, pp. B60–B61.

The *L'Osservatore Romano* published a profile—"Un colloquio ad Assisi con don Aldo Brunacci" by Mario Spinelli, February 8, 2003, p. 11—of Brunacci, who, as a living witness, recounted his rescue activities, revealing new details about the support he and his bishop received from Pius XII. Note, finally, Brunacci's powerful interview, "The Secret Letter," *Inside the Vatican*, January 2004, pp. 74–76, in which he reaffirms Pius XII's direct support for his bishop and rescuers like himself, concluding, "The work of Pope Pius XII was a majestic work, a work of deeds, not of words."

3. J. Patrick Carroll-Abbing

Monsignor Carroll-Abbing, of the Boys Town of Italy, was stationed in Rome during the German occupation (September 1943 to June 1944) and had direct and frequent access to Pius XII. In his memoirs, *But for the Grace of God* (New York: Delacorte, 1965), Carroll-Abbing describes the pope's protests against the Nazi seizure of Jews and his extensive relief efforts, and also documents Pius XII's orders to his subordinates: "Almost immediately word came from the Vatican that, because of the emergency, nuns would be allowed to give hospitality in their convents to Jewish men as well as their families. . . . With each day that passed, Monsignor Vitucci and I found ourselves becoming increasingly involved in the problems of the hideaways. The word had passed from one good sister to another, from one convent to another. Soon we were in touch with many of the more than a hundred and fifty religious institutions that were sheltering the Jews" (pp. 55–56).

In an interview given shortly before his death, Carroll-Abbing, in a direct rebuttal to those who claim those acts were done spontaneously and without the explicit instructions of the pope, declared: "I spoke to Pope Pius XII many times during the war, in person, face-to-face, and he told me not once but many, many times to assist the Jews." And again he stressed: "I can personally testify to you that the pope gave me direct face-to-face verbal orders to rescue Jews." Carroll-Abbing insisted that the pope ordered him to help all Jews, not just baptized converts to the Church: "Most of the Jews under my care were unbaptized committed Jews and the pope knew that because I told him that they wanted to continue to practice their faith while in hiding, and the pope explicitly told me, 'Father, do what is necessary to allow them to practice their faith, according to their sacred Jewish rites'" (*Inside the Vatican*, August–September 2001, pp. 10–11).

In an earlier book, *A Chance to Live*, Carroll-Abbing had already recorded his own assistance to victims of the war, documented Pius XII's order that "no one was to be refused" shelter, gave many examples of the pope's direct assistance to relief workers, and spoke of "the luminous and sublime example of the Holy Father" who "gave supreme comfort to these elect souls, to these apostles of charity. . . . He spurred them to ever greater achievements" (pp. 77–87). During the war, Carroll-Abbing organized an extensive rescue network for refugees, Jewish victims of persecution, and escaped Allied prisoners of war. For these efforts, on the Day of Liberation, Italy bestowed on Monsignor Carroll-Abbing the Silver Medal for Military Valor "on the field of battle" (see the official website of Boys Town of Italy: www.boystown.it).

4. Paolo Dezza

In a published tribute to Pius XII, Cardinal Dezza stated that he had received direct orders from the pontiff to rescue Jews: "I recall that when in 1943 came the German domination of Rome—I was rector of the Pontifical Gregorian University, and it was I who accepted the refugees—Pius XII said to me: 'Father, avoid receiving soldiers, since, as the Gregorian is a pontifical university and linked to the Holy See, we for our part must keep ourselves out of this side. But for the others, most willingly: civilians, persecuted Jews.' In fact many were received" (*Osservatore della Domenica*, June 28, 1964, pp. 68–69). In the same article, Dezza—who had been appointed to his post by the pope in 1941—also declared Pius XII told him that he considered Nazism an even greater threat than communism, and also revealed how he explicitly defended the persecuted in his confrontational meeting with German Foreign Minister Ribbentrop in March 1940.

Dezza thus confirms the *New York Times* story of March 14, 1940—headlined, "Pope is Emphatic about Just Peace: Jews Rights Defended"—which reads: "Twice in two days Pope Pius has gone out of his way to speak of the necessity for justice as well as peace, and Vatican circles take this as an emphasis of his stern demand to Joachim von Ribbentrop, German Foreign Minister, that Germany right the injustice she has done before there can be peace. . . . It was also learned today for the first time that the pontiff, in the burning words he spoke to Herr von Ribbentrop about religious persecution, also came to the defense of the Jews in Germany and Poland" (p. 8).

Shortly before he died, Dezza spoke of how deeply Pius XII concerned himself with the fate of the Jews and how conscientious he was in deciding how best to assist them. The danger of reprisals was ever present in the pope's mind, according to Dezza: "He showed me letters he received from German Cardinals and priests that warned him that the Third Reich would meet his protests with harsh reprisals against Catholics as well as Jews" ("Pope Pius XII Knew of Nazi Atrocities, Confessor Says," Zenit News Agency, April 7, 1998). Even so, said Dezza, the pope continued to defend Jews publicly and privately, in ways he thought best protected them.

5. Pierre-Marie Benoît

Among the most celebrated of Catholic rescuers, Father Pierre-Marie Benoît (also known by his Italian name, Padre Benedetto) was a Capuchin priest who spent the war years in France and Italy, dedicating himself to Jewish rescue and assistance. When Rome was liberated in June 1944, the Jewish community held an official synagogue ceremony in honor of Benoît, and Yad Vashem recognized him a righteous gentile in 1966. For testimony about Benoît's high regard for Pius XII and the support the Vatican gave him, see James Rorty's "Father Benoît: Ambassador of the Jews," *Commentary*, December 1946, pp. 507–513, and Fernande Leboucher's 1969 *The Incredible Mission of Father Benoît*.

Leboucher—who was Benoît's most effective collaborator and who wrote her book in cooperation with Benoît—documents how the priest-rescuer received the full support of Pius XII. "The Vatican offered to supply whatever funds would be needed for Fr. Benoît's work. It is estimated that a total of some four million dollars was thus channeled from the Vatican to DELASEM [the Italian Jewish refugee organization, taken over by Benoît], much of which came from the American Catholic Refugees Committee, an official Catholic collection and distribution agency whose funds were at the disposal of Pope Pius XII" (pp. 167–168).

On July 16, 1943, Benoît met with Pius XII and, according to Benoît's own testimony, received the pope's support. See "Resumé de Mon Activité en faveur des Juifs Persecutés, 1940–1944" by Father Marie-Benoît, "Yad Vashem Martyrs and Heroes Remembrance Authority" at Yad Vashem Archives, Testimony of Father Marie Benoît, B/19-4. See also Benoît's testimony given in *Livre d'Or des Congrégations francaises: 1939–1945* (Paris: DRAC, 1948), as well as Benoît's statements to interviewer Nicola Caracciolo about the meeting: "I spoke of the French police, who were acting pretty much against the Jews and working with the Germans. . . . The Italian police were protecting them instead. The pope made this observation: 'No one would have believed that in France there would have been such an attitude.' In addition, he told me, 'I will study this and have it studied, your requests'—and that sort of thing" (*Uncertain Refuge: Italy and the Jews During the Holocaust* by Nicola Caracciolo, translated from the 1986 original by Florette Rechnitz Koffler and Richard Koffler [Urbana: University of Illinois, 1995], p. 39).

Benoît had requested the pope to assist in a rescue effort to transfer tens of thousands of endangered Jews to safe territory. Because of military actions outside the Vatican's control, the operation became impossible, but the pope's attitude of support is significant (on this issue, see Justus George Lawler's remarks in *Popes and Politics: Reform, Resentment, and the Holocaust* [New York: Continuum, 2002], pp. 47–49).

Commenting on this testimony, John Morley, generally a detractor of the Vatican's wartime diplomacy, comments: "Pius XII appeared well-disposed to all of the priest's requests. This benevolent attitude toward the Jews of France was very reassuring to Jewish leaders" (*Vatican Diplomacy and the Jews During the Holocaust 1939–1945*, pp. 64–65). Ralph Stewart adds: "Some people have tried to make the claim that Father Marie-Benoît was critical of Pius XII during the war. Not only do his various writings deny that allegation but also an AFP report which came out of the Vatican as recently as March of 1976 indicates that Father Marie-Benoît spoke in glowing terms of the Holy Father. In fact on the occasion of the centenary of Eugenio Pacelli's birth, he sent a report which praised the various undertakings of the pope on behalf of the Jews during the war" (*Pope Pius XII and the Jews* [New Hope: St. Joseph Canonical Foundation, 1990], p. 74).

For the text of Benoît's July 15, 1943, letter to Pius XII (the day before his meeting with the pope), see *Actes et Documents* 9, pp. 393–397. The letter, describing Benoît's rescue activities, says in part: "When the Jews learned that I would be coming back to Rome, they formulated a plan which chose me to act as their intermediary to express to the Holy Father their profound gratitude for the charity and devotion which had been shown them." For further details on Benoît, see "Where Justice is Due: Italian Repugnance to Racist Doctrine" by Richard Arvay, *Commonweal*, June 8, 1945, pp. 182–186.

Both Sam Waagenaar's *The Pope's Jews* (La Salle: Open Court, 1974), pp. 418–419, and Susan Zuccotti's *Under His Very Windows*, pp. 184 and 371 n. 30, cite a letter ("Alcune precisazioni di Padre Benedetto," *Israel*, July 6, 1961, p. 5) that suggests Benoît received no real assistance from the Vatican. And both Waagenaar and Zuccotti claim Benoît wrote the letter because he was upset about postwar claims made by Father Robert Leiber (in an article for *La Civiltà Cattolica* 1961, volume 1, pp. 449–458) concerning Vatican support for DELASEM.

The provenance and editing of the letter are unknown. It has Benoît acknowledging that he has not read the Leiber article in *La Civiltà Cattolica*, for instance, and it refers to Monsignor Antonio Riberi as the apostolic nuncio to Italy (the wartime nuncio was Franceso Borgongini-Duca—a fact that all rescuers in Italy, and certainly Father Benoît, would have known). Most important, the letter's claim denying Vatican funding is (1) flatly contradicted by the testimony of Benoît's chief collaborator, Fernande Leboucher; and (2) disproved by the Vatican's own archives: An official at the Vatican secretariat of state confirmed on January 9, 1944, that the Holy See had been supplying Father Benoît money and foodstuffs for Jewish refugees during the German occupation. See the note of the secretariat of state, January 9, 1944, attached to document 412 in *Actes et Documents* 9, pp. 544–545: "Since the arrival of this group of Jews in Rome, the Holy See has occupied itself about them by furnishing money and foodstuffs to Fr. Benoît. . . . His Excellency Monsignor Riberi [a Vatican official] follows this matter."

Acknowledging this evidence, Zuccotti speculates "any Vatican contributions must be regarded as exceedingly sparse" (*Under His Very Windows*, p. 184). But Fernande Leboucher estimates the assistance totalled four million dollars. (For more on Leboucher, see "Grateful Jews Help Care for a Holocaust 'Guardian Angel,'" *New York Times*, September 9, 2001, p. 8–14, and the obituary, *New York Times*, September 4, 2002, p. 8-B.)

Raffaele Cantoni's tribute to Pius XII, "Ha fatto tutto il possibile per salvare gli uomini," *Osservatore della Domenica*, June 28, 1964, pp. 67–68, is also telling. Cantoni, who worked with Benoît, was one of DELASEM's most courageous wartime Jewish leaders—he was arrested and barely survived imprisonment—and his testimony on behalf of Pius's efforts is an eloquent answer to those who have tried to diminish the pontiff's support for persecuted Italian Jews.

It is also significant that Father Pancrazio Pfeiffer, Pius XII's confidante and assistant, "was in touch with the Capuchin Padre Benedetto [a.k.a. Benoît]" (*Rome '44: The Battle for the Eternal City* by Raleigh Trevelyan [New York: Viking, 1981], p. 118). See also Trevelyan's "The Ordeal of Italian Jewry," *New York Times* book review, April 12, 1987, p. 22, a sharp review of Susan Zuccotti's *The Italians and the Holocaust: Persecution, Rescue and Survival* (1987; reprinted Lincoln: Bison, 1996). As James Rorty put it in *Commentary*,

December 1946, p. 513, "The Nazis were never sure how much support Benoît was getting, or would get, from the Vatican. The record shows that he got a good deal."

6. Pietro Palazzini

Cardinal Palazzini, a wartime assistant to the rector of the Seminario Romano, received the Medal of the Righteous Among the Nations from Yad Vashem in Israel for his rescue efforts on behalf of persecuted Jews. At the time he accepted the honor in 1985, he told members of the Sacred Congregation for the Causes of Saints: "The merit is entirely Pius XII's, who ordered us to do whatever we could to save the Jews from persecution" (cited by Father Peter Gumpel, a collaborator of Palazzini's, in *Inside the Vatican*, June 1997, p. 25). In his memoirs, published in Italian in 1995, Palazzini declared that his rescue efforts, as well as those of others in Rome, were directly inspired by the pope: "The guidelines provided by Pope Pius XII were to save human lives, on whatever side they may be." He concluded, "Thus, in the last analysis it was Pius XII himself who allowed this great work of charity," adding, "The refuge offered to so many people would not have been possible without his moral support, which was much more than tacit consent" (*Il Clero e l'occupazione tedesca di Roma* [Rome: Apes, 1995], pp. 35, 29, and 17).

7. Pancrazio Pfeiffer

According to Carroll-Abbing, one of the men used by Pius XII to protest the Nazi roundup of Rome's Jews and intervene for persecuted victims was Father Pancrazio Pfeiffer, superior general of the Salvatorian Fathers, who also served as Pius XII's personal liaison to the German military command in Rome. Because Pfeiffer died tragically in an automobile accident toward the end of the war and thus never took part in the postwar analysis of Pius XII's conduct, many historians have overlooked him. But those who knew him or have researched his life have chronicled his collaborative efforts with Pius XII to rescue Jews and others during the war. See the article "Pfeiffer's List" by Robert Graham, *30 Days*, June 1994, pp. 42–46. Prince Constantine of Bavaria's book on Pius XII, *The Pope* (London: Allan Wingate, 1954) contains an excellent section on Pfeiffer, whom he describes as an "agent for the pope on behalf of the victims of persecution and the fugitives in hiding" (p. 213).

At Pfeiffer's death in May 1945, Vatican Radio paid tribute: "He came into contact with the Commander of the German occupying forces [in Rome in 1943–1944]. From that day onwards, he placed his religious and spiritual qualities at the service of many who had been arrested or already condemned to death. He helped countless people in this way, and saved their lives, among them many Jews and other Italian personages. He championed the cause of all the victims, irrespective of their standing" (*Tablet*, May 26, 1945, p. 247). An article on Father Pfeiffer for a special edition of the *Osservatore della Domenica* on June 28, 1964, concluded: "Pius XII gave carte blanche to Father Pancrazio. . . . He had free access to German headquarters as well as to the person of the pope. . . . Nobody will ever know how many Jews he managed to save, hide or shelter, at papal behest, thanks to the authority he carried" (p. 61).

8. Angelo Roncalli

Archbishop Angelo Roncalli, who would later become Pope John XXIII, helped rescue Jews while serving as an apostolic delegate in Turkey and Greece. In 1957, he told Israeli consul Pinchas Lapide: "In all these painful matters I have referred to the Holy See and simply carried out the pope's orders: first and foremost to save human lives" (*Three Popes and the Jews*, p. 181).

In a signed statement of May 18, 2002, addressed to the reiator for the cause of Pius XII, Archbishop Loris Capovilla, who was the private secretary of Pope John XXIII, wrote: "With regard to the actions in favor of the Jews, affected particularly in Istanbul in the years 1935–1944, which was recognized and praised by Hebrew communities in Jerusalem, Istanbul, and the United States, it is obligatory to recognize that Roncalli was and declared himself the executor of the thought and the directives of Pius XII. He [Roncalli] repeated, in fact: 'The papal representative is the eye, the ear, the mouth, the heart and the effective hand of the pope.'" Capovilla continued that Roncalli's rescue efforts on behalf of Jews make sense "only if they are referred above everything else to Pius XII, of whom Roncalli was the careful and most faithful interpreter. Any strictly personal action, even though it be heroic, of Roncalli himself, would otherwise be inconceivable."

Thus, the claim, for instance, of the historian Stanford Shaw that Roncalli undertook these actions "without any encouragement from the Vatican" (*Turkey and the Holocaust* [New York: New York University, 1993], p. 278) is erroneous. Michael Bar-Zohar's *Beyond Hitler's Grasp: The Heroic Rescue of Bulgaria's Jews* (Holbrook: Adams, 1998) credits Roncalli with rescuing Jews in Bulgaria in coordination with King Boris. See also the excellent article by Peter Hoffmann, "Roncalli in the Second World War: Peace Initiatives, the Greek Famine and the Persecution of the Jews," *Journal of Ecclesiastical History*, January 1989, pp. 74–99, which attributes Roncalli's initiatives to the Vatican.

John XXIII—whose traditionalism can be seen in his *Journal of a Soul* (New York: McGraw-Hill, 1965)—has not been well-served by his biographers. Thomas Cahill, for instance, romanticizes John as a revolutionary in *Pope John XXIII* (New York: Penguin, 2002); worse yet, he glowingly contrasts John against the supposedly backward Pius XII, whom Cahill offensively brands "a moral pygmy." This was not the opinion of John XXIII himself: "To Pius XII," he declared, "and to the mystery of grace which he served during a great pontificate of almost twenty years, belongs the merit of having lavished on the flock of Christ luminous treasures of heavenly wisdom and of the most intense zeal. . . . [T]he threefold title, 'excellent doctor, lover of the divine law, light of the holy Church' is most fitting to the pontiff of our eventful age" (statement of December 24, 1958, cited in O'Carroll's *Pius XII: Greatness Dishonored*, foreword; see *Discorsi, messaggi, colloqui del Santo Padre Giovanni XXIII* [Vatican City: Tipografia Poliglotta Vaticana, 1961–1967], volume 1, p. 101).

See also "Pope Pays Tribute to Pius XII," *New York Times*, October 10, 1961, p. 40. John P. Donnelly adds: "Pope John's program and its concern for the modern world naturally enough found much of its inspiration in Pope John's predecessor under whom he served for 19 years, and from whom came much of the intellectual foundation on which the Council is built. No one was more generous in acknowledging this debt than Pope John himself" (*Days of Devotion: Daily Meditations From the Good Shepherd Pope John XXIII* [New York: Viking, 1996], p. 12).

Despite this clear testimony, a number of authors have imagined that John XXIII disliked Pius XII and regretted his wartime actions; Hannah Arendt, for example, writes: "There is finally the report that in the months preceding his death he was given Hochhuth's play *The Deputy* to read and then was asked what one could do against it. Whereupon he allegedly replied: 'Do against it? What can you do against the truth?'" (*Men in Dark Times* [New York: Harcourt, Brace, 1968], p. 63).

The story is an invention. Loris Francesco Capovilla, Pope John's private secretary, who was at his bedside till the end, denounced it as "a lie." (See Ronald Rychlak's review of James Carroll's *Constantine's Sword* in the *Washington Post*, February 12, 2001, p. C3.) The historian Felicity O'Brien adds: "The postulator of John XXIII's cause for canonization, Fr. Luca De Rosa, OFM, states that the story is 'absolutely untrue.' He adds that Pope John was, in fact, 'full of admiration and devotion' for Pius XII. Archbishop Loris Capovilla, formerly private secretary to Pope John, also categorically denies that Pope John ever said any such thing. Pope John had repeatedly said that everything he himself did for the Jews during the war had been on the orders of Pius XII" (Letter to the Editor, *Catholic Times* [Manchester, England], July 20, 1997). For further information on John XXIII's close relationship with Pius XII see "John XXIII: Pope of World Peace" by Sister Margherita Marchione, *Columbia*, January 2003, pp. 19–21. Also of note: "A Great Defender of the Poor, 'Good Pope John' was More Conservative Than Most Realize" by Antonio Gaspari, *Inside the Vatican*, August–September 2000, p. 70.

For a sampling of John XXIII's own writings which touch upon his wartime experiences, see *Pope John XXIII: Letters to His Family*; translated from the Italian by Dorothy White (London: Geoffrey Chapman, 1970); *La predicazione a Istanbul: omelie, discorsi e note pastorali, 1935–1944* by

Angelo G. Roncalli, edited by Alberto Melloni (Florence: Leo S. Olschki, 1993); and *Mission to France: 1944–1953* by Angelo G. Roncalli, translated by Dorothy White (London: Geoffrey Chapman, 1966).

Since Alden Hatch published the well-received *A Man Named John: The Life of Pope John XXIII* (New York: Hawthorn, 1963), two major biographies on Roncalli have appeared: *Pope John XXIII: Shepherd of the Modern World* by Peter Hebblethwaite (New York: Doubleday, 1985; revised edition published in 1994) and *John XXIII: The Official Biography* by Mario Benigni and Goffredo Zanchi (Boston: Pauline, 2001). While both of these are valuable, the best studies of John XXIII remain in the writings of Archbishop Capovilla, especially his *The Heart and Mind of John XXIII* (New York: Hawthorn, 1964) and *John XXIII: Witness to the Tenderness of God* (Montreal: Mediaspaul, 2001).

c. Accounts of the Persecuted

Among the most important witnesses who suffered under fascist and Nazi brutality is Dr. Guido Mendes, a lifelong Jewish friend of Eugenio Pacelli. Both Mendes and Pacelli studied at the Liceo Visconti [the former Collegio Romano Gymnasium] in Rome during the 1890s. "Their paths separated after their school years—Pacelli going into the Church and Mendes to medical school. They next met in the First World War whilst he was an officer in the Medical Corps and the pope already a monsignor. In 1938, with the beginning of the persecution of the Italian Jews, Pacelli's aide [Giovanni Battista Montini, the future Pope Paul VI] called him from the Vatican to ask the Mendes family if they needed help. The Mendes later escaped to Switzerland, and the Vatican secured them certificates to Palestine in 1939" (*Jerusalem Post*, October 10, 1958). In 1963, after Rolf Hochhuth's play *The Deputy* appeared, Dr. Mendes, then eighty-seven, utterly repudiated it and again praised his late friend in public (*Jewish Chronicle* of London, October 11, 1963).

Also interesting are the memoirs of the musician Bruno Walter, *Theme and Variations: An Autobiography* (New York: Knopf, 1966), which recount a little-known episode involving the future Pius XII—when the then-papal nuncio to Germany rescued a wrongly imprisoned Jewish musician during World War I (p. 221).

A picture of Pacelli after he became secretary of state in 1930 is provided by Dietrich von Hildebrand, the anti-Nazi Catholic philosopher whom Hitler tried to assassinate. In her biography *The Soul of a Lion: Dietrich von Hildebrand* (San Francisco: Ignatius, 2000), his wife Alice von Hildebrand records the 1935 conversation in which Pacelli told her husband "that there could be no possible reconciliation between Christianity and racism; they were like 'fire and water'" (p. 286). "One of the great privileges in my life was the close contact with the Nuncio in Germany," von Hildebrand wrote of his earlier acquaintance with Pacelli, "I had the opportunity of discussing several questions with him, either in his palace or taking walks with him. He also came to our home once. His personality emanated an intense spiritual life, which impressed everyone who came into contact with him. He was one of those personalities who in their sublime spirituality seem to be free from the weight of matter. On the other hand, he had a keen interest in the most varied problems, approaching every question in an unconventional way, which was extremely inspiring. I still remember with joy our discussion when I was preparing my first lecture on marriage" (*The Book of Catholic Authors: Informal Self-Portraits of Famous Catholic Writers*, edited by Walter Romig [Grosse Point: Romig, 1962], p. 212).

During his 1936 visit to America, Cardinal Pacelli met with two officials of the American Jewish Committee, Lewis Strauss and Joseph Proskauer, and reaffirmed Pope Benedict's 1916 condemnation of anti-Semitism, promising to make its teachings better known. See the archives of the American Jewish Committee as described in Naomi Cohen's official history, *Not Free to Desist: A History of the American Jewish Committee, 1906–1966* (Philadelphia: Jewish Publication Society, 1972), pp. 180, 214–215, and 578. For an analysis of Pacelli's involvement in the Vatican's 1916 condemnation of anti-Semitism, as well as the text of the statement, see Rychlak's *Hitler, the War, and the Pope*, pp. 299–300 and 439, footnotes 141–142, and *Principles for Peace*, pp. 198–199.

Indispensable are the memoirs of Eugenio Zolli, the former chief rabbi of Rome, published as *Before the Dawn* (New York: Sheed and Ward, 1954). See also "1954 Autobiography of Rabbi who Converted is [Re] Published," Zenit News Agency, February 16, 2004. Zolli's book provides dramatic firsthand evidence that Pius XII offered Vatican gold if it was necessary to ransom Jews threatened by the Nazis. Zolli also documents Pius XII's orders to his subordinates: "The Holy Father sent by hand a letter to the bishops instructing them to lift the enclosure from convents and monasteries, so they could become refuges for the Jews" (pp. 140–141). These memoirs conclude by affirming: "There is no place of sorrow where the spirit of love of Pius XII has not been reached. Volumes could be written on the multiform works of succor of Pius XII" (p. 186).

Because Zolli and his wife were baptized and received into the Catholic Church on February 17, 1945, his high-profile conversion has generated controversy, as can be seen in *The Chief Rabbi, the Pope, and the Holocaust: An Era in Vatican-Jewish Relations* by Robert G. Weisbord and Wallace P. Sillanpoa (New Brunswick: Transaction, 1991). Much of the controversy was anticipated by Father Arthur Klyber in his article "A Chief Rabbi's Conversion" in the August 1945 issue of *Liguorian*, which was condensed to form the introduction to *Before the Dawn*.

Inside the Vatican, February 1999, pp. 78–83, contains a rare interview with the rabbi's daughter, Miriam, which corrects a number of uninformed views about her father and reiterates his admiration for Pius XII. The story of Zolli's conversion is told in Paolo Dezza's moving article, "Eugenio Zolli: Da gran rabbino a testimone di Cristo (1881–1956)," *Civiltà Cattolica* 1981, volume 2, pp. 340–349. See also the recent biography of Zolli, *Il rabbino che si arresse a Christo. La storia di Eugenio Zolli, rabbino capo a Roma durante la seconda guerra mondiale* (Milan: San Paolo, 2002) and the interview with its author, Judith Cabaud, in "The Christian Rabbi," *Inside the Vatican*, June–July 2002, pp. 44–46.

For an outstanding article on Zolli that appeared in the German press, see "Der Oberrabiner, der sich taufen liess" in the *Deutsche Tagespost*, November 28, 2002. See also Alberto Latorre's "Eugenio Zolli: apostata o profeta?" *Studia Patavina*, September–December 2002, pp. 579–614. Not to be forgotten is Zolli's own book, *Antisemitismo* (Rome: A.V.E., 1946), with its section on Pius XII's protection of Italian Jews (pp. 244–247), which begins: "World Jewry owes a great debt of gratitude to Pius XII for his repeated and pressing appeals for justice on behalf of the Jews, and, when these did not prevail, for his strong protests against evil laws and procedures."

The foremost authority on the Nazi roundup of Rome's Jews—and a survivor of the raid himself—is Michael Tagliacozzo, author of "La Comunità di Roma sotto l'incubo della svastica: La grande razzia del 16 ottobre 1943," in *Gli ebrei in Italia durante il fascismo: Quaderni del Centro di Documentazione Ebraica Contemporanea*, November 1963, pp. 8–37; see also his "La persecuzione degli ebrei a Roma" in *L'occupazione tedesca e gli ebrei di Roma: Documenti e fatti*, edited by Liliana Picciotto Fargion (Rome: Carucci, 1979), pp. 149–171.

Tagliacozzo also wrote a monograph (prepared for fellow historian Meir Michaelis and dated June 16, 1975) entitled, "Ebrei refugiati nelle zone exterratoriali del Vaticano," which documents the life-saving efforts of the Vatican. (The Tagliacozzo archives in Israel have preserved a wealth of such documentation.) As Michaelis wrote, drawing on Tagliacozzo's scholarship, "The open-door policy of the Holy See saved the lives of nearly 5,000 Jewish Romans. According to Michael Tagliacozzo, the foremost authority on the subject, 477 were sheltered in the Vatican and its enclaves, while another 4,238 found refuge in the numerous monasteries and convents in Rome" (*Mussolini and the Jews: German-Italian Relations and the Jewish Question in Italy, 1922–1945* [Oxford: Clarendon, 1978], p. 365).

Both having lived through the Roman terror and studied the primary documents relating to it, Tagliacozzo has had nothing but praise for Pius XII. "I know that many criticize Pope Pacelli," he said in a recent interview. "I have a folder on my table in Israel entitled 'Calumnies Against Pius XII,' but my judgment cannot but be positive. Pope Pacelli was the only one who intervened to impede the deportation of Jews on October 16, 1943, and he did very much to hide and save thousands of us."

After explaining how the relevant "documents clearly prove" that Pius XII's protests were decisive in rescuing 80 percent of Roman Jewry, Tagliacozzo dismissed the notion that the pope was not behind the rescue effort: "There was much confusion in those days, but all knew that the pope and the Church would have helped us. After the Nazis' action, the pontiff, who had already ordered the opening of convents, schools and churches to rescue the persecuted, opened cloistered convents to allow the persecuted to hide. Monsignor Giovanni Buttinelli, of the parish of the Transfiguration, told me that the pontiff had recommended that parish priests be told to shelter Jews. I personally knew a Jewish family that, after the Nazis' request for 50 kilos of gold, decided to hide the women and children in a cloistered convent on Via Garibaldi. The nuns said they were happy to take the mother and girl but they could not care for a little boy. However, under the pope's order, which dispensed the convent from cloister, they also hid the boy." Tagliacozzo, it should be noted, was rescued from starvation and death by Pius XII's assistants, led by Cardinal Palazzini. "I remember they treated me wonderfully," recalls Tagliacozzo. "After not having eaten for two days, Father Palazzini gave me a meal with all God's goods: a bowl of vegetable soup, bread, cheese, fruit. I had never eaten so well" ("Jewish Historian Praises Pius XII's Wartime Conduct," Zenit News Agency, October 26, 2000).

Also valuable is *Rumor and Reflection* (New York: Simon and Schuster, 1952), the wartime diaries of Bernard Berenson, the celebrated Jewish humanist and art historian who lived in Italy during the years 1941 to 1944. His book is a wonderful example of how a civilized mind can maintain its humanity even in the face of fascist and Nazi brutality. Berenson's diary records the interventions of the pope on behalf of the Jews: "The pope summoned Weizsäcker, the German Ambassador, and told him that if his government insisted on applying here in Italy all the Nuremberg laws against Jews he at Christmastime would radiophone a discourse that they would not like" (entry for December 20, 1943). "Both the pope and the cardinal of Florence have spoken courageously and clearly, . . . the rump of Nazi fascism [has] suddenly become aware that its days are numbered, . . . how lawless, brutal, even bestial it has been, including foul torture of its victims, has been clearly referred to in the allocution of the Florentine Cardinal" (entry for December 26, 1943).

One of the brightest chapters in Jewish-Catholic relations is the intense cooperation between the two to rescue the persecuted as the Holocaust unfolded. Many Catholic periodicals opened up their pages to Jewish leaders, who revealed the ongoing horrors of Nazi anti-Semitism (see, for example, Maurice Edelman's "Persecution Stalks the Jews Across the Face of Europe," *America*, September 19, 1942, pp. 654–655). "In World War II," writes Robert Graham, "the Jewish community, both national and international, was in close, continuous, and fruitful contact with the Vatican and the Catholic population as never before in history. Repeatedly, the world Jewish organizations dedicated to rescue work received a sympathetic hearing and substantial help from Pius XII" ("Relations of Pius XII and the Catholic Community with Jewish Organizations" in *The Italian Refuge: Rescue of Jews During the Holocaust*, edited by Ivo Herzer [Washington: Catholic University, 1989], pp. 231–253; Graham provides many examples of such cooperation).

Documentation of Jewish testimonials on behalf of Pius and his diplomats exist in abundance. In the *New Oxford Review*, July–August 2002, pp. 33–39, Dimitri Cavalli writes: "Many examples from *Actes et Documents* and other sources can be cited. On April 14, 1942, the leaders of the Jewish inmates at the Ferramonti concentration camp in southern Italy wrote to the Vatican, thanking the pope who sent an 'abundant supply of clothing and linen' to the children of a camp (volume 8, pp. 505–507). On February 23, 1943, Monsignor Joseph Marcone, the Vatican's 'apostolic visitor' in Croatia, reported that Chief Rabbi Freiberger expressed his gratitude to the Vatican for helping a group of Croatian Jewish children, including Freiberger's son, find refuge in Turkey (volume 9, p. 139). In his February 14, 1944, letter to Cassulo, Chief Rabbi Alexander Safran of Bucharest, Romania acknowledged the concern of the 'Supreme Pontiff, who offered a large sum to the sufferings of Romanian Jews' (volume 10, pp. 291–292). On July 21, 1944, several weeks after the liberation of Rome, the National Jewish Welfare Board cabled the Vatican, lauding Pius XII for saving most of Rome's Jews (volume 10, pp. 358–359)." See also Cavalli's "The Good Samaritan: Jewish Praise for Pope Pius XII," *Inside the Vatican*, October 2000, pp. 72–77. For similar documentation, see Felicity O'Brien's "Justice for Pius XII," *Tablet*, May 4, 1996, p. 578.

Confronted with such evidence, detractors of Pius XII have sought to diminish and even discredit Jewish praise for Pius in a number of ways. Some claim that privately Jews were far more reserved about Pius than their public comments would suggest; others, that Jews were unaware of Pius XII's real record and naively credited him with charitable acts; some go so far as to accuse these Jews of deliberately lying in order to foster Vatican support for Israel or reduce anti-Semitism.

Responding, Rabbi David Dalin has stated: "To deny the legitimacy of their gratitude to Pius XII is tantamount to denying the credibility of their personal testimony and judgment about the Holocaust itself" ("Pius XII and the Jews," *Weekly Standard*, February 26, 2001, p. 39). Primary Holocaust archives confirm Dalin's position that Jewish support for Pius XII was sincere, objective, and justified. A report, dated November 16, 1943, of the Information Section of the Jewish Agency, Jerusalem, on Jewish refugees in liberated southern Italy, relates the following eyewitness report from a Jewish survivor: "Source, a student, who escaped after the German occupation of Yugoslavia in 1941 from Zagreb to Italy, was interned from February 1943 until his departure on the 10th October, 1943, in the civil internment camp Ferramonti di Tarsia, in the province of Cosenza. He states, . . . 'The internees were effectively protected by the Vatican against German interference. In May 1943, the Nuntius Granduca Borgongini [sic; referring to Monsignor Francesco Borgongini Duca, the apostolic nuncio in Italy] visited the camp and conveyed to the refugees the pope's assurance of protection. . . . After the announcement of the Italian capitulation the refugees made off for hiding places in the neighboring hills, leaving behind in the camp only old people, in order to escape probable German brutalities. When German troops attempted to enter the camp, they were opposed by Italian clergymen who explained to the Germans that the internees had been placed under the protection of the Vatican'" (Central Zionist Archives, Jerusalem, 1939–1945, printed in *Archives of the Holocaust: An International Collection of Selected Documents*, volume 4, edited by Francis R. Nicosia [New York: Garland, 1990], pp. 185–186).

On February 18, 1944, Maurice L. Perlzweig of the World Jewish Congress wrote the apostolic delegate in Washington: "It is scarcely necessary for me to assure your Excellency that the repeated interventions of the Holy Father on behalf of the Jewish communities in Europe has evoked the profoundest sentiments of appreciation and gratitude from Jews throughout the world. These acts of courage and consecrated statesmanship on the part of His Holiness will always remain a precious memory in the life of the Jewish people" (*Actes et Documents* 10, p. 140).

Similarly, in a statement to German scholar Edgar Alexander, the author of *Hitler and the Pope: Pius XII and the Jews* (New York: Thomas Nelson and Sons, 1964), the World Jewish Congress said: "Throughout the World War II years, and particularly in the period 1943–1945, interventions were frequently made with Pope Pius XII by the World Jewish Congress in an effort to save, shelter and succor Jews hounded by the Nazis. In all instances the appeals were graciously and sympathetically received. The responses to these pleas and the subsequent information channeled to the WJC by the pope's envoys in the USA, Britain and elsewhere, indicates that the action was taken and the machinery of the Vatican put into operation on behalf of Jews. Constant contact with the Vatican was, for instance, maintained from early 1944 on the question first of Hungarian asylum to Jewish refugees from Poland and Slovakia and, later, on the desperate issue of preventing the mass deportations of Jews from Hungary. As the result of one intervention by Dr. Goldmann early in 1944, the Holy See notified its Nuncios in Budapest and Bratislava to watch the situation and interest themselves, as far as they could in the welfare of Jewish refugees. About that time, an interoffice memo written by one of the WJC officers closely involved in these matters said: 'The Catholic Church in Europe has been extraordinarily helpful to us in a multitude of ways. From Hinsley in London to Pacelli [Pope Pius XII] in Rome, to say nothing of the anonymous priests in Holland, France and elsewhere, they had done very notable things for us'" (letter from Monty Jacobs of the World Jewish Congress to Dr. Alexander, dated March 24, 1959).

Pius XII reciprocated by greeting and addressing the Jewish community numerous times after the war. See Pius XII's allocution to a group of Jewish refugees on the brotherhood of man, November 29, 1945 (*Acta Apostolicae Sedis* 37, pp. 317–318; *Osservatore Romano*, November 30, 1945, p. 1; for English extracts, see *Tablet*, December 8, 1945, p. 277, and *Catholic World*, January 1946, pp. 370–371). See also Pius XII's address to representatives of the United Jewish Appeal on relief work in Europe and Palestine, February 9, 1948 (*Osservatore Romano*, February 9–10, 1948, and in summary in English, *Tablet*, February 14, 1948, p. 105, and *New York Times*, February 10, 1948, p. 13).

Also significant in this regard is Pius XII's speech of August 3, 1946, to the members of the Supreme Arab Committee on Palestine, in which the pope explicitly condemned anti-Semitism: "There can be no doubt that peace can only come about in truth and justice. This presupposes respect for the rights of others and for certain vested positions and traditions, especially in the religious sphere, as well as the scrupulous fulfillment of the duties and obligations to which all inhabitants are subject. That is why, having received again during these last days numerous appeals and claims, from various parts of the world and from various motives, it is unnecessary to tell you that we condemn all recourse to force and to violence, from wherever it may come, as also we have condemned on several occasions in the past the persecutions which a fanatical anti-Semitism unleashed against the Jewish people" (*Tablet*, August 24, 1946, p. 97; the full text appears in the *Acta Apostolicae Sedis* 38 [September 14, 1946], pp. 322–323, and *L'Osservatore Romano*, August 15, 1946, p. 1; for English extracts, see the *New York Times*, August 15, 1946, p. C3).

On May 26, 1955, the Israeli Philharmonic Orchestra was received by Pope Pius XII in the Vatican's Consistory Hall and performed the second movement of Beethoven's Seventh Symphony. "Conductor Paul Klecki had requested that the Orchestra on its first visit to Italy play for the pope as a gesture of gratitude for the help his Church had given to all those persecuted by Nazi fascism" ("Pope Delighted by IPO Playing," *Jerusalem Post*, May 29, 1955, p. 1). See also *Osservatore Romano*, May 27, 1955, p. 1, and the subsequent commentary in the *Tablet*, June 11, 1955, p. 582, and July 30, 1955, p. 116, and the obituary of Klecki (also spelled Kletzki) in the *New York Times*, March 7, 1973, p. 46. *L'Osservatore* subsequently carried an article ("Riconoscimenti o polemica?" July 17, 1955, pp. 1–2) recounting this and many other gestures of Jewish gratitude to Pius XII. A rarely seen photograph of Pius XII and the Israeli Philharmonic Orchestra appears in *Shepherd of Souls: A Pictorial Life of Pope Pius XII* by Margherita Marchione (Mahwah: Paulist, 2002), p. 140.

d. Accounts of Foreign Diplomats

A revealing insight into the character of Eugenio Pacelli shortly before he became pope can be found in *The Inner Circle* (London: Macmillan, 1959), the memoirs of Ivone Kirkpatrick, who served as British chargé d'affaires to the Vatican from 1930 to 1933. Writing of his private conversations with Pius XI, Kirkpatrick comments on how the pope "told me in pungent terms what he thought of Hitler's persecution of the Jews" (p. 47). Kirkpatrick continues: "Similarly I saw his successor, who was then Cardinal Secretary of State, far more often than business justified. He received the diplomatists accredited to the Holy See every Thursday, and I usually called upon him once a fortnight for a general conversation. He was particularly interested and well informed about Germany, where he had been Nuncio for many years. When Hitler became Chancellor I asked him whether responsibility would cause him [Hitler] to put a little water into his wine. 'I'm afraid not,' he replied, 'we shall see that with every year power will make him more extreme and difficult to deal with'" (p. 48).

Robert Murphy, an American diplomat stationed in Munich during the 1920s, also recalled: "The titular head of the Munich consular corps was the Papal Nuncio, Monsignor Eugenio Pacelli, who later became Pope Pius XII. . . . Monsignor Pacelli, through his intimate knowledge of international politics, was one of the first to recognize that the future of Europe depended largely upon what happened in Germany. I had many enlightening conversations with him in Munich, and two decades later I was to renew my association with him after he became pope, when I entered Rome with American troops in 1944 as President Roosevelt's personal representative" (*Diplomat Among Warriors* [New York: Doubleday, 1964] p. 19).

In April 1938, Cardinal Pacelli met with Joseph P. Kennedy (United States ambassador to Britain from 1938 to 1940) and handed him a report, intended for President Roosevelt. In this document, Pacelli made clear that Nazism represented a grave danger to the civilized world, denounced "the new pagans arising amongst the young Arian [*sic*] generations," warned that the Nazi program struck at the "fundamental principle of the freedom of the practice of religion," and declared that any compromise with the Nazis was "out of the question." (The report, accompanied by Kennedy's cover letter dated April 19, 1938, was duly delivered to the president.)

On March 3, 1939, the day after Pacelli became pope, A.W. Klieforth, the American consul to Berlin, filed a report with the United States State Department, describing a three-hour meeting in 1937 with the future pope. Pacelli, wrote Klieforth, "regarded Hitler not only as an untrustworthy scoundrel but as a fundamentally wicked person." Klieforth further noted that Pacelli "did not believe Hitler capable of moderation, in spite of appearances, and he fully supported the German bishops in their anti-Nazi stand." For details on both documents, see "Personal, Private Views" by Charles Gallagher, *America*, September 1, 2003, pp. 8–10; and "Wartime Pope's anti-Nazi stand was strong in 'private contacts'" by Frances D'Emilio, Associated Press, August 21, 2003. Klieforth's son, also a diplomat, has confirmed the meeting, adding new details: "What was divulged was critical, sensitive information because among other things, it proved that the pope-to-be was anti-Nazi and hated Hitler. . . . Cardinal Pacelli thought the whole Nazi ideology an abomination because it persecuted the Jews and it persecuted the Church" ("San Diego Diplomat Defends Pope Pius XII," *The Southern Cross*, January 15, 2004, pp. 2, 21).

In 1954, Kazimierz Papée, Poland's wartime ambassador to the Holy See, published *Pius XII a Polska* (Rome: Studium, 1954), a documentary chronicle that corrects numerous distortions about Pius XII's attitude toward Poland. The reflections of François Charles-Roux, the opinionated French ambassador to the Vatican during the 1930s, are found in his memoir, *Huit Ans au Vatican, 1932–1940*. Significant is Charles-Roux's extraordinary praise for Pius XII's first encyclical, *Summi Pontificatus*, which Charles-Roux hailed for taking a position "against exacerbated nationalism, the idolatry of the state, totalitarianism, racism, the cult of brutal force, contempt of international agreements, against all the characteristics of Hitler's political system; he laid the responsibility for the scourge of the war on these aberrations" (pp. 351–352). Also notable is the testimony of the ambassador's son: "Rev. Fr. Jean Charles-Roux, now a Rosminian priest living in London and whose father was French ambassador to the Holy See in the 30s, lived with his family in Rome during the fateful prewar period. He recalls that the Pope [then Cardinal Pacelli] told his father as early as 1935 that the new regime in Germany was 'diabolical'" ("The Real Story of Pius XII and the Jews" by James Bogle, *Salisbury Review*, Spring 1996, reprinted in *Catalyst*, volume 23, number 10).

Charles-Roux's successor as French ambassador, Wladimir D'Ormesson, wrote a stirring defense of Pius XII: "Pie XII tel que je l'ai connu" in *Revue d'Histoire Diplomatique* 82 (1968), pp. 5–34; see also D'Ormesson's *De Saint-Pétersbourg à Rome* (Paris: Plon, 1969), which praises Pius XII's kindness, simplicity, spiritual grandeur, and concern "for all of Europe and for the future of Western civilization" (p. 196).

One of the finest memoirs to come out of World War II is Dino Alfieri's *Dictators Face to Face* (New York: Elek, 1954). Alfieri was Mussolini's ambassador to the Vatican and, later, to Hitler—and was also part of the rebel group opposed to both dictators, for which he almost lost his life. His book contains a vivid description of an interview in which Hitler railed against Pius XII's anti-Nazi initiatives, and declared: "Ours are two different worlds. The pope goes his way, I go mine" (p. 60). Alfieri also provides detailed information on the meetings Pius XII and his secretary of state, Cardinal Maglione, had with German Foreign Minister Joachim von Ribbentrop in March of 1940. Both the pope and Maglione demanded an end to Nazi atrocities in Germany and Poland, and at times the exchange became "heated and polemical" (p. 12). In May of the same year, Alfieri himself had a private audience with Pius XII at which the pope "did not hide his grave anxiety about the policy of the National-Socialist Government" (p. 16).

Also important are the writings of Germany's ambassador to the Vatican, Ernst von Weizsäcker's *Memoirs*, translated by John Andrews (Chicago: Henry Regnery, 1951), especially p. 270 and pp. 281–293; also the references to Pius XII in *Die Weizsäcker-Papiere 1933–1950* (Frankfurt: Ullstein, 1974), edited by Leonidas E. Hill III. Hill's "The Vatican Embassy of Ernst von Weizsäcker, 1943–1945," *Journal of Modern History* 39 (1967), pp. 138–159, is now somewhat superseded, but still important for understanding Weizsäcker's character and relationship with the Holy See. See also the article on Weizsäcker in the *L'Osservatore Romano*, May 16–17, 1949, replying to disinformation about Weizsäcker and the Vatican from the Communist press.

Arrested by the Allied authorities as a war criminal in 1947, Weizsäcker was put on trial at Nuremberg. He had a conflicted character. Having served as a German diplomat under Hitler, Weizsäcker was clearly implicated, yet there was also evidence of his resistance. Knowing of his opposition to Nazi ideology, many people testified to his good character, including priest-rescuer Father Marie Benoît and even some Jewish survivors. Nevertheless, Weizsäcker was found guilty of collaboration and sentenced to seven years' imprisonment. Some later scholars believe this to be a miscarriage of justice. The fact that the sentence was soon reduced (Weizsäcker was released from prison in 1950) indicates that some at the time thought so as well.

But of interest here is that during the trial both Weizsäcker and his chief assistant, Albrecht von Kessel, strongly defended Pius XII, particularly the pope's record regarding Jews. Commenting on the International Red Cross and the Vatican, Weizsäcker testified: "It is a matter of course, and everybody knows it, that these two agencies of world significance and reputation and worldwide influence would have undertaken any possible step that they considered feasible and useful to save the Jews." In his own statement, von Kessel affirmed: "I am convinced . . . that his Holiness the Pope did, day and night, think of a manner in which he could help the unfortunate Jews in Rome." (For an analysis of Weizsäcker's and von Kessel's testimony, with these quotations and all the relevant documentation, see Michael O'Carroll's *Pius XII: Greatness Dishonored*, pp. 80–81 and 94–97.)

Also revealing are the diaries of Count Galeazzo Ciano, Mussolini's foreign minister, who noted during the war that the pope "is even ready to be deported to a concentration camp but will do nothing against his own conscience" (*Diario 1937–1943*, edited by R. De Felice [Milan: Rizzoli, 1980], p. 430).

After the war, the Catholic philosopher Jacques Maritain, who briefly served as France's ambassador to the Vatican—and who is often wrongly represented as a critic of Pius XII's wartime policy—wrote a remarkable letter to the papal assistant Giovanni Battista Montini (later Paul VI) on the need for the Church to address the issue of postwar anti-Semitism. In a key part of the letter, dealing with the war years, Maritain went out of his way to praise "the tireless charity with which the Holy Father has tried with all his might to save and protect the persecuted," and he praised Pius's "condemnations against racism that have won for him the gratitude of Jews and all those who care for the human race."

Significantly, Maritain hailed Pius XII's wartime diplomacy on behalf of persecuted Jews, realizing it was "for very good reasons, and in the interests of a higher good, and in order not to make persecution even worse, and not to create insurmountable obstacles in the way of the rescue that he [Pius XII] was pursuing" (letter of July 12, 1946, to Montini, quoted in *Ecumenist*, Spring 2002, pp. 1–3). Maritain went on to request a new papal statement against anti-Semitism, and within weeks Pius XII issued his August 3, 1946, condemnation. For more on Maritain's opposition to anti-Semitism, see his articles, "On Anti-Semitism," *Commonweal*, September 25, 1942, pp. 534–537, and "A Letter on Anti-Semitism," *Commonweal*, February 27, 1948, pp. 489–492. For Maritain's influence on Catholic-Jewish relations, see *Jacques Maritain and the Jews*, edited by Robert Royal (South Bend: University of Notre Dame, 1993).

Two diplomats attached to the Holy See during the war were Sir Francis D'Arcy Osborne, the British minister to the Vatican, and Myron C. Taylor, the personal representative of President Roosevelt. Osborne's private papers and official diplomatic telegrams are summarized by Owen Chadwick in his *Britain and the Vatican During the Second World War.* Chadwick documents both the disagreements between Osborne and the Holy See about specific tactics and their mutual desire to see an end to Nazism. One of the most significant documents to emerge from the British archives is Osborne's telegram of September 11, 1942 (shortly after the Nazis began deporting Jews from France) in which he tells his government: "The pope today confirmed for me that the nuncio at Vichy [Valerio Valeri] had protested against persecution of Jews in France" (British Foreign Office, document 371-32680).

This establishes three things that Pius XII's detractors have denied: (1) that the pope was aware and concerned about the persecuted Jews; (2) that the pope was in direct contact with his nuncio in France, who was carrying out Pius XII's will in protesting the anti-Jewish measures; and (3) that the pope wanted to make crystal clear to Allied diplomats that he sided unequivocally with the Jews. (Evidence exists that the pope expressed the same views to Myron Taylor; see "Pope has Long Talk with Taylor: Move to Aid Jews in France Seen," *New York Times*, September 20, 1942, p. 1.)

On a personal level, there was also mutual esteem between the British diplomat and Pius XII. Osborne told T.J. Kiernan, Irish minister to the Vatican, that he would have liked to be a Catholic for one reason: "So that I might receive Holy Communion from Pius XII" (*Pope Pius XII* by T.J. Kiernan [Dublin: Clonmore and Reynolds, 1958], p. 46). After Rolf Hochhuth's play *The Deputy* appeared, Osborne wrote a letter to the *Times* (May 20, 1963) providing his final evaluation of Pius: "So far from being a cool (which, I suppose, implies cold-blooded and inhumane) diplomatist, Pius XII was the most warmly humane, kind, generous, sympathetic (and incidentally saintly) character that it has been my privilege to meet in the course of a long life. I knew that his sensitive nature was acutely and incessantly alive to the tragic volume of human suffering caused by the war and, without the slightest doubt, he would have been ready and glad to give his life to redeem humanity from its consequences. And this quite irrespective of nationality or faith. . . . I feel assured that Pope Pius XII has been grossly misjudged in Herr Hochhuth's drama." Also notable is *Vatican Assignment* by Alec Randall (London: Heinemann, 1956), another British envoy with warm recollections of Pius XII.

The voluminous papers of Myron C. Taylor are preserved in eight containers at the Library of Congress in Washington, D.C., and also at the Franklin D. Roosevelt Library at Hyde Park, New York. The latter's Vatican files consist of wartime reports, memoranda, and correspondence with Roosevelt, Pius XII, and others, and are a rich source of information.

A selection can be found in the *Wartime Correspondence Between President Roosevelt and Pope Pius XII*, with an introduction and explanatory notes by Myron C. Taylor (New York: Macmillan, 1947). In his long and thoughtful introduction, Taylor wrote: "President Roosevelt and Pope Pius XII carried on their parallel endeavors for more than five years, which all but covered the entire span of the most deadly attack on the foundations of Christian civilization and the most exhausting strife in mankind's annals. . . . The world was fortunate indeed to have had in its darkest hour the vitality of leadership of which the parallel endeavors were a part—a leadership which placed these vital activities upon so high a moral, spiritual, and humanitarian plane" (pp. 8–9). See also *Vaticano e Stati Uniti, 1939–1952: dalle carte di Myron C. Taylor*, edited by Ennio Di Nolfo (Milan: Franco Angeli, 1978); revised and updated (with an attached CD-ROM of documents) as *Dear Pope* (Rome: Inedita, 2003).

The posthumous memoirs of Taylor's assistant, Harold Tittmann Jr., also reveal the high esteem the two had for Pius XII, as well as his wartime record, correcting numerous claims found in the anti-Pius literature. See *Inside the Vatican of Pius XII: The Memoir of an American Diplomat During World War II*, edited by his son, Harold Tittmann III, in 2004. Rebutting the numerous attacks which have been made against the wartime pontiff, Tittmann affirms that Pius XII "detested the Nazi ideology and everything it stood for," and praises his diplomacy: "The Holy Father chose the better path . . . and thereby saved many lives" (pp. 123–124).

e. Accounts of Foreign Statesmen

Both as secretary of state and pope, Eugenio Pacelli left a lasting impression on the leaders of nations. In his book, *Austrian Requiem* (London: Gollancz, 1947), Kurt Schuschnigg—the chancellor of Austria who strongly opposed Hitler's takeover of his country and spent the war years in a concentration camp—comments: "With Cardinal Pacelli . . . I discussed the relations of state and Church and found great understanding for the particular difficulties of Austria—more understanding than I found with the sometimes stormy but mostly overcautious and timorous hierarchy and clergy at home. . . . Cardinal Pacelli belongs among the most impressive personalities that I have ever met in my life: as a man, as intellect, as priest, in short as the prototype of a timeless but at the same time very modern prince of the Church" (p. 107).

The Hungarian Prime Minister Nicholas de Kallay recorded the concerns of Pius XII expressed at a meeting on April 3, 1943: "His Holiness brought up the matter of conditions in Germany. He depicted the conditions prevailing in Germany, which fill him with great sadness, in dramatic words. He finds incomprehensible all that which Germany does with regard to the Church, the Jews, and the people in the occupied territories, first of all the Poles. These measures not only are interference in the affairs of the Church but also are in opposition to the principles of a Christian world order based on the word of God. [Pius XII] is filled with sadness . . . so long as Germany and the German occupation authorities disregard the most elementary principles of human and moral laws. . . . He is quite aware of the terrible dangers of Bolshevism, but he feels that, in spite of the Soviet regime, the soul of the large masses of the Russian people has remained more Christian than the soul of the German people" (from the archives of the Hungarian Foreign Ministry, as cited by Robert A. Graham in *The Vatican and Communism During World War II: What Really Happened?* [San Francisco: Ignatius, 1996], pp. 156–157). See also Kallay's memoirs, *Hungarian Premier: A Personal Account of the Second World War* (Oxford: Oxford University, 1954), p. 169. For an analysis of the Pius XII-Kallay meeting, see Angelo Martini's "Un giudizio sconosciuto di Pio XII sul Nazismo" in *La Civiltà Cattolica* 1977, volume 2, pp. 324–338.

Anyone wishing to learn the effectiveness of Pius XII's opposition to the Nazi regime need only study the writings of leading Nazis. "From the beginning Hitler and his closest followers were motivated by a pathological hatred of the Catholic Church, which they appraised correctly as the most dangerous opponent to what they hoped to do in Germany," states Church historian Peter Gumpel. "Proof of this, among other things, are Hitler's (already published) discussions with those closest to him (known as "Tischgespräche" [or "Table Talk"]), Joseph Goebbel's diary, Martin Bormann's decrees, Alfred Rosenberg's delirious diatribes, and Heinrich Himmler's orders to the SS and Gestapo" (Zenit News Agency, May 2, 2000).

Perhaps the most important work in this genre is the diary of Adolf Eichmann, the notorious SS lieutenant colonel executed in 1962 in Israel for crimes against the Jewish people and humanity. Eichmann wrote his memoirs in an Israeli prison, during and after his trial in 1961. The Israeli government finally released them in 2000. The diaries record not only the stark, horrifying reality of the Holocaust but also establish, unintentionally, the courage of those who fought it. Commenting on events in Rome during the German occupation, Eichmann writes: "The Church was vigorously protesting the arrest of Jews of Italian citizenship, requesting that such actions be interrupted immediately throughout Rome and its surroundings. To the contrary, the pope would denounce it publicly. . . . The objections given and the excessive delay in the steps necessary to complete the implementation of the operation, resulted in a great part of Italian Jews being able to hide and escape capture" ("Eichmann's Diary Reveals Church's Assistance to Jews," Zenit News Agency, March 1, 2000).

At Eichmann's trial in 1961, Israeli Attorney General Gideon Hausner declared it already established that "the pope himself interceded for the Jews of Rome" (*The Trial of Adolf Eichmann, Record of the Proceedings in the District Court of Jerusalem* [Jerusalem: Israeli Ministry of Justice, 1992], volume 1, p. 83). See also *6,000,000 Accusers; Israel's Case Against Eichmann. The Opening Speech and Legal Argument of Mr. Gideon Hausner, Attorney-General*, edited by Shabtai Rosenne (Jerusalem: Jerusalem Post, 1961), and Hausner's memoirs, *Justice in Jerusalem* (New York: Schocken, 1968).

For more on the Axis view of Pius XII, see Albrecht von Kessel's *Verborgene Saat: Aufzeichnungen aus dem Widerstand 1933 bis 1945* (Berlin: Peter Steinbach, Ullstein, 1992); German consul Eitel Möllhausen's *La Carta perdente* (Rome: Sestante, 1948); the *Memoirs* of diplomat Franz von Papen (New York: E.P. Dutton, 1953); German Field Marshal Albert Kesselring's *A Soldier's Record* (New York: William Morrow, 1954); *The Interpreter: Memoirs of Doktor Eugen Dollmann* (London: Hutchinson, 1967); and Silvio Bertoldi's *I tedeschi in Italia* (1964; updated and reprinted Milan: Rizzoli, 1994). All of this literature should be read with some skepticism, as many of the principals had a personal interest in disassociating themselves from the crimes of Hitler.

On the Allied side, the well-known memoirs and biographies of Churchill and De Gaulle speak highly of Pius, and many of the generals who prosecuted the war shared that assessment. See in particular the memoirs of American General Mark S. Clark, American commander of the Fifth Army, *Calculated Risk* (New York: Harper, 1950): "I saw the Pope on many occasions thereafter during my stay in Italy and developed a great admiration for his statesmanship, his wisdom, and his infinite humaneness" (pp. 373–374). In *The Alexander Memoirs: 1940–1945* (New York: McGraw-Hill, 1962), Field Marshal Earl Alexander of Tunis not only praises the pope but makes revealing comments about Pius XII's understanding of what the Allies had to do to win the war. Commenting on the destruction of one of Rome's oldest Catholic monasteries, Alexander wrote: "The bombs of the Allied air forces had left nothing of the building standing except part of one of the outer walls—all else was a heap of rubble. Yet amidst this appalling destruction St.

Benedict's tomb, in the centre of the monastery, went utterly unscathed. After the capture and liberation of Rome I was able to tell the late Pope [Pius XII] of its survival. He was deeply moved. He assured me, moreover, that he well understood the military necessity for the bombing and the inevitable destruction of the monastery. I well remember that, when the Allies were in occupation of Rome, crowds of our soldiers went to the Vatican to see the pope, who daily gave them his blessing. Thinking that it might be too great a strain on him I said one day: 'I hope that all these Allied soldiers are not too great a burden for your Holiness,' and added, 'although of course, so many of them are Catholics,' He replied: 'No! No! Let them all come to me—I love them all'" (p. 122). Shortly after Pius XII's death, Field Marshal Montgomery, who had befriended Pius, wrote in the October 12 issue of London's *Sunday Times*: "He was a great and good man, and I loved him."

f. Accounts of Other Observers

On November 7, 2000, the German Catholic news agency KNA released a remarkable interview with Nikolaus Kunkel, a German officer stationed in Rome during the Nazi round-up of the city's Jews (October 16, 1943). Kunkel, a lieutenant on the staff of General Rainer Stahel, the German army commander of Rome, revealed: (1) the Nazis were seriously considering occupying the Vatican and arresting Pius XII during their nine-month occupation of Rome; (2) in spite of this threat, the pope forcefully intervened behind the scenes (through Father Pancrazio Pfeiffer, superior general of the Salvatorians, and Bishop Hudal, rector of the Santa Maria dell'Anima) to rescue Rome's Jews; (3) as a result of the pope's actions, General Stahel persuaded the Nazi authorities to stop the anti-Jewish raids at once, with the result that the vast majority of Rome's Jews survived; and (4) had Pius XII publicized these efforts, that strategy certainly, according to Kunkel, would have backfired and caused immense harm, thus preventing the papal rescue effort.

This testimony, from an eyewitness involved in the operation, directly contradicts claims that a more "public" action by the pope after the anti-Jewish roundup would have somehow proved beneficial. For details, see "Most of Rome's Jews Were Saved from Hitler's Final Solution" (a translation of Kunkel's interview) in *L'Osservatore Romano* weekly edition in English, January 24, 2001, p. 11. For analysis of the details and timeline of these events, see Ronald Rychlak in the *Journal of Modern Italian Studies*, Summer 2002, pp. 232–233 n. 43.

The posthumous memoirs of the Austrian Bishop Alois Hudal, *Römische Tagebücher: Lebensbeichte eines alten Bischofs* (Stuttgart: Leopold Stocker, 1976) are not well known but essential to understanding the man. Hudal was a very conflicted figure who was, on the one hand, notoriously sympathetic to the Germans, yet was also known to have assisted Jews during the German occupation. In fact, when the Germans began rounding up Rome's Jews in October of 1943, Pius XII immediately had his nephew Carlo Pacelli induce Hudal to write a letter of protest to the German authorities, demonstrating the Vatican's strong opposition. The pope, who had always kept Hudal at a distance because of his political views, in this case ingeniously exploited Hudal's sympathies, knowing that the Germans would listen. (For the effectiveness of Hudal's letter in blocking further roundups of Rome's Jews, see Michael O'Carroll's *Pius XII: Greatness Dishonored*, pp. 96–97.)

For many years scholars wondered whether Hudal had really written the letter himself. Hudal's memoirs settle the matter by affirming that he wrote the letter, at the behest of the pope's messenger, Carlo Pacelli (see Hudal *Römische Tagebücher*, pp. 114–115, and *Actes et Documents* 9, p. 510 n. 4). After the war, Hudal was accused of assisting fleeing Germans suspected of war crimes. For more on Hudal's connections, see "Bischof Hudal und SS-Führer Meyer. Ein kirchenpolitischer Friedensversuch 1942/43" by Hanjakob Stehle in *Vierteljahreshefte für Zeitgeschichte* 35 (1987), pp. 299–322. Peter Godman's *Hitler and the Vatican* reveals the many contradictory views of Hudal.

Simon Wiesenthal, the highly respected authority on Nazi war criminals, has written, "There is no evidence that Pope Pius XII ordered or knew about" Hudal's assistance to such German criminals after the war (*New York Times*, March 13, 1984, p. A26), and Matteo Sanfilippo of the University of Viterbo has prepared an authoritative report demonstrating the Vatican strongly opposed Hudal's efforts to assist such criminals. See his "Los papeles de Hudal como fuente para la historia de la migración de alemanes y nazis después de la Segunda Guerra Mundial," published by the investigative Argentine body, CEANA (www.ceana.org.ar). Far from sympathizing with suspected Nazi war criminals after the war, Pius XII in fact authorized the American Jesuit Edmund Walsh to help prosecute them at Nuremberg; see chapter 11 of Louis Gallagher's biography, *Edmund A. Walsh, S.J.* (New York: Benziger, 1962). Indeed, in his memoirs Hudal criticizes the Vatican for refusing to support his attempt to bring about a rapprochement between the Church and the Nazis (see pp. 13–20, 107–151, 191–262).

On October 18, 1943, just two days after the Nazi roundup of Rome's Jews, an observer, M. de Wyss, wrote in her diary that "the Jews have implored help from the pope and that Pius XII has asked the German Ambassador Weizsäcker to stop this ill treatment and violence." De Wyss emphasizes that the one institution which stood firm was the Church: "The population is half crazy: young men and their families look desperately for hiding places, get them, then look for better ones. Everybody is in a cold sweat, in haste and in despair. Terror-struck, homeless men (hardly one between the ages of eighteen and fifty lives in his own house) ask everyone possible for help. The Germans seem to have given new assurances to the Vatican: large placards on doors of convents and churches, strictly prohibit entry to German officers and men. Papal territories and properties have to be left alone. Up to now this has been observed, and consequently convents and seminaries have become the most 'sought after' hide-outs." And on October 24: "Jews are still persecuted, though less . . . because, it is said, the pope interceded in their behalf" (*Rome Under the Terror* [London: Robert Hale, 1945], pp. 144–145 and 150).

Journalists who covered Pius XII during the war have also left behind testimony. In *The Vatican and its Role in World Affairs* (New York: E.P. Dutton, 1950), Charles Pichon, France's leading wartime correspondent, documents the pontiff's fierce opposition to Nazism and fascism, his repeated interventions for the war's victims, and above all his outspoken condemnations of totalitarianism. "The pontifical texts condemned most strongly the anti-Semitic persecutions, the oppression of invaded lands, the inhuman conduct of the war, and also the deification of earthly things which were made into idols: the Land and the Race, the State and the Class" (p. 167).

Anne O'Hare McCormick was for over three decades a writer for the *New York Times* in Rome. Her *Vatican Journal 1921–1954* (New York: Farrar, Straus and Cudahy, 1957) collects her columns, which display an extraordinary insight and sympathy into the policies of the wartime pontiffs, particularly Pius XII. In a dispatch entitled "Position of Pope in Italy Has Been Enhanced by War" dated August 21, 1944, after the liberation of Rome, McCormick commented: "The Romans give credit to the pontiff for the sparing of the city. . . . But this is not the only cause for the popularity of Pius XII. During the nine months between the armistice and the entry into Rome, the Vatican was a refuge for thousands of fugitives from the Nazi-fascist reign of terror. Jews received first priority—Italian Jews and Jews who escaped here from Germany and other occupied countries—but all the hunted found sanctuary in the Vatican and its hundreds of convents and monasteries in the Rome region. What the pope did was to create an attitude in favor of the persecuted and hunted that the city was quick to adopt, so that hiding someone 'on the run' became the thing to do. This secret sharing of danger cleared away fascism more effectively than an official purge. The Vatican is still sheltering refugees. Almost 100,000 homeless persons from the war zone and devastated areas are fed there every day" (pp. 119–120).

The writings of American correspondent William Shirer—especially his *Berlin Diary* (New York: Knopf, 1941) and his bestselling *The Rise and Fall of the Third Reich* (New York: Simon and Schuster, 1960)—portray the Church of Pius XII as clearly anti-Nazi, as does Howard K. Smith's *Last Train to Berlin* (New York: Knopf, 1942). Lowell Thomas's documentary chronicle of his radio broadcasts, *History as You Heard It* (Garden City: Doubleday, 1957) contains many favorable references to the Church's struggle against Hitler. Barrett McGurn's *A Reporter Looks at the Vatican* (New York: Coward-McCann, 1962) is a unique and highly valuable work by a journalist who knew and covered Pope Pius XII firsthand. McGurn analyzes the early postwar criticisms of the pope and concludes that Pius XII was very probably a saint.

The recent memoirs of Gerhart Riegner, *Ne jamais désespérer: soixante années au service du peuple juif et des droits de l'homme* (Paris: Cerf, 1998), the World Jewish Congress leader who first revealed news of the Holocaust to the world, have drawn considerable attention. The controversy centers around Riegner's claim that the Jesuit editors of the Vatican's *Actes et Documents* may have omitted important documentary evidence surrounding the pope's knowledge of the Holocaust. (See, for instance, "Jewish Memoir Says Vatican Holocaust Files Incomplete," *Catholic World News*, October 9, 1998.)

In *Hitler's Pope: The Secret History of Pius XII* (New York: Viking, 1999), John Cornwell seized upon this claim. Against this, however, Ronald Rychlak argues that documentary evidence not only exonerates Pius XII and the editors of *Actes et Documents*, but demonstrates how conscientious they were. Rychlak comments: "On pages 259, 281, and 376–77 [of *Hitler's Pope*], Cornwell refers to a memorandum of Gerhart Riegner for transmission to the Holy See, dated March 18, 1942. It described Nazi persecution of Jewish people, and Cornwell points out that this memorandum was not published by the Vatican in its collection of wartime documents (*Actes et Documents*). By the same token, the letter of thanks [following Vatican intervention for Jews] that Riegner sent to Nuncio M. Filippo Bernadini on April 8, 1942, was also not published" (*Hitler, the War, and the Pope*, p. 426).

In fact, well before the Jesuits had collected and published the Vatican documents for the year 1942, Riegner's memorandum had already been translated and published in full in Saul Friedlander's *Pius XII and the Third Reich*, pp. 104–110. Riegner's memo, moreover, is noted and referred to in the *Actes et Documents* 8, p. 466.

PART 4: MAJOR ATTACKERS

Many commentators suggest that the attack on Pius XII began with Rolf Hochhuth's 1963 play *Der Stellvertreter*, which depicted Pius XII as "silent" and indifferent toward the Nazi extermination of Jews. (The play is known in the English-speaking world as *The Deputy* or *The Representative*.)

But in fact, the attack began much earlier, from communist propagandists at the end of the Second World War, and it has recently reemerged through a group of contemporary polemicists. Thus, the attack against Pope Pius XII has taken place in three waves:

1. Communist Origins

Throughout—and especially toward the end of—World War II, the communists conducted a concerted effort to depict Pius XII as pro-Nazi and thus shatter his reputation. This antipapal campaign was amply documented at the time. Stephen DiGiovanni notes that on February 2, 1944, the *New York*

Times reported that the previous day's issue of *Izvestia* (the Soviet communist paper) claimed that the Vatican had consistently supported fascism and charged that Pius XII "had supported the Nazi Regime and had worked for the destruction of other states. . . . [The] *Times* reported the *Izvestia* charges, gave them no credence, and, in later pieces, expressed consternation that anyone could believe the charges as anything other than Communist propaganda" (*Catholic Social Science Review* 6 [2000], p. 366).

Indeed, on February 4, 1944, the *Times* editorialized that the United States and Great Britain "have no doubt where the real sympathy of the Vatican lies in this struggle. They recognize the inescapable neutrality of the pope's position; but they have had no difficulty in finding in his eloquent declarations clear evidence of his detestation for those who have violated the rights of the little nations who have committed bestial acts from one end of Europe to the other and who have attempted to elevate the dogma of Totalitarianism to the dignity of a new religion. *Izvestia*'s attack is damaging to the unity on which victory depends."

Anti-Catholic agitators produced a whole body of antipapal literature at the time, now largely forgotten but important from an historical standpoint. Examples include Joseph McCabe's *The Pope Helps Hitler to World-Power: How the Cross Courted the Swastika for Eight Years* (Girard: Haldemon-Julius, 1941); the novelist H.G. Wells's *Crux Ansata: An Indictment of the Roman Catholic Church* (New York: Agora, 1944); Avro Manhattan's massive *The Catholic Church Against the Twentieth Century* (London: Watts, 1947), and Edmond Paris's *Le Vatican Contre L'Europe* (Paris: Fischbacher, 1959). The anti-Catholic and communist canards about papal conduct during World War II were amply reported in the Catholic press. See the *Tablet*, January 6, 1945, p. 8; May 5, 1945, p. 212; May 12, 1945, p. 225; June 16, 1945, p. 284; July 21, 1945, p. 32; August 11, 1945, p. 68.

After the war, the Soviets hired an agent, Mikhail Markovich Sheinmann, a specialist in antireligious propaganda, to produce a series of tracts—translated into numerous languages—to blacken the reputation of the Holy See. Sheinman's works, particularly *Der Vatikan im Zweiten Weltkrieg* (Berlin: Dietz, 1954; first published in Russian in 1948), contained lurid details about a (nonexistent) "Secret Pact" the Vatican had signed with Hitler. How the communists and their allies grievously corrupted the historical record is explained by Robert Graham in *The Vatican and Communism During World War II*. Graham's 1996 book is a potent antidote to Hansjakob Stehle's *Eastern Politics of the Vatican, 1917–1979* (Athens: Ohio State University, 1981), which swallows many communist-inspired legends.

2. The Deputy

Rolf Hochhuth's play *Der Stellvertreter* premiered in Berlin on February 20, 1963. It depicted an icy and avaricious pontiff maintaining an inexcusable silence during the Holocaust and refusing to make any efforts on behalf of the Jews of Rome. Soon translated into other languages, it had its American premiere in New York on February 26, 1964, under the title *The Deputy*. Intended to ignite intellectual fireworks, it only partially succeeded, for, as critic Frank Rich noted, "The only bomb was on stage, but the publicity turned the show, now forgotten, into a quasi-hit and earned its producer a Tony for his courage" (*New York Times*, October 17, 1998, p. A-15).

Paulist father and ecumenical leader Thomas Stransky recalled: "Reactions did not strictly follow religious lines" (preface to Pierre Blet's *Pius XII and the Second World War*, p. xiii). Indeed, many Jews rejected Hochhuth's thesis of a silent and indifferent pope. Cardinal Montini of Milan, Pius XII's assistant during the war and soon to become Pope Paul VI, wrote a letter to the *Tablet* (June 29, 1963) that accused Hochhuth of "an inadequate grasp of the psychological, political realities" in "those appalling conditions of war and Nazi oppression." Among others who repudiated *The Deputy* were Wladimir d'Ormesson, Sir Francis d'Arcy Osborne (whose March 20, 1963, letter to the London *Times* was printed, on official orders, in the program for the West End performance of Hochhuth's play), Albrecht von Kessel, attached to the wartime German embassy, Ambassador Grippenberg of Finland, Gunnar Haggelof of Sweden, and Mr. Kanayama, minister for Japan (see Michael O'Carroll's *Pius XII: Greatness Dishonored*, p. 21).

In the same year that *The Deputy* appeared, a collection of (uneven) German responses appeared: *Summa iniuria oder durfte der Papst schweigen?: Hochhuth's 'Stellvertreter' in der öffentlichen Kritik* (Hamburg: Rowohlt, 1963). A similar work published in America, *The Storm Over the Deputy: Essays and Articles About Hochhuth's Explosive Drama* (New York: Grove, 1964), edited by Eric Bentley, has everyone from Alfred Kazin and Lionel Abel to Karl Jaspers and Golo Mann weigh in on the play (in almost unanimous approval of Hochhuth's thesis). But the book does include a few exceptional pieces (by the editors of *America* magazine and Father Robert Leiber, Pius XII's personal aide) and also contains an impressive bibliography on the immediate reaction to the play. For a later collection, see *The Deputy Reader: Studies in Moral Responsibility* by Earl Robert Schmidt (Chicago: Scott, Foresman, 1965).

Because so much documentary evidence was not then available, some of Pius XII's early defenders conceded far too much to Hochhuth. See, for example, *Commonweal*, February 28, 1964, pp. 647–662, and also the commentaries on the play in *Continuum*, Summer 1963, and in *Blackfriars*, October 1963. But much of the discussion at the time was just plain bad. One of the worst examples is "The Vicar: A Controversy and a Lesson," an embarrassingly sanctimonious endorsement of the play by the Catholic pacifist Gordon Zahn in the *Critic*, October–November 1963, pp. 42–46 (note the cogent and eloquent refutation of Zahn by Warren Reich, also in the *Critic*, December 1963, p. 4).

Among the better critiques at the time were "As We Await *The Deputy*," *America*, November 9, 1963, pp. 570–582, by Monsignor John M. Oesterreicher, founder of the Institute of Judeo-Christian Studies at Seton Hall University, and "Rolf Hochhuth: Equivocal 'Deputy,' a Study of the Anti-Semitic and Anti-Catholic Mental Baggage of a Playwright" by Edgar Alexander (an anti-Nazi German refugee), also in *America*, October 12, 1963, pp. 416–423. (On the uproar Alexander created, see *America*, June 27, 1964.)

"The Roots of the Dilemma" by John Lukacs (*Continuum*, Summer 1964) is a profound analysis by a great historian. Leonidas E. Hill's "History and Rolf Hochhuth's *The Deputy*" in *From an Ancient to a Modern Theatre*, edited by R.G. Collins (Winnipeg: University of Manitoba, 1972), pp. 145–157, is limited but does have some important insights. Erik von Kuehnelt-Leddihn's sizzling critique of the play was published in the appendix to his book, *The Timeless Christian* (Chicago: Franciscan Herald, 1969), pp. 184–194. See also Desmond Fisher's rebuttal in *Pope Pius XII and the Jews* (Glen Rock: Paulist, 1963).

The *Tablet* also published a solid refutation, "History on the Stage," March 16, 1963, noting that Monsignor Erich Klausener, then editor of the Berlin weekly *Petrusblatt*, whose father had been murdered by Hitler, and Father Robert Leiber, Pius XII's personal assistant, both categorically repudiated Hochhuth's accusations. Monsignor Walter Adolph, an assistant to the anti-Nazi German bishop Konrad von Preysing, became the leading German critic of *The Deputy*, and wrote *Verfälschte Geschichte: Antwort an Rolf Hochhuth, mit Dokumenten und authentischen Berichten* (Berlin: Morus, 1963).

A particularly eloquent critique of *The Deputy* appeared in *Catholic Mind*, June 1964, pp. 26–31, which pointed out: "The play makes a great issue of the pope's 'silence' concerning Hitler's unspeakable crimes against the Jews. . . . Out of curiosity then, we consulted the issues of the *Catholic Review* which were published in late 1943. In the issue of November 5, there appears a story entitled 'Holy See Eager to Rescue Hebrews,' and tells of the arrest of Roman Jews, the concern of the Vatican, and the pope's offer of gold to ransom Jewish hostages. The same issue contains a reprint of an appeal for prayers on behalf of the pope, made by Rabbi Lazaron of the Baltimore Hebrew Congregation. Speaking of Pius XII as a prisoner in the Vatican, the rabbi affirmed, 'The pope has condemned anti-Semitism and all its works. Bishops of the Church have appeared in the streets of Antwerp, Brussels, The Hague and Paris with the shield of David on their arms. Humble priests . . . have joined with Protestant ministers in protecting Jews . . . at the risk of their own lives. Indeed, many priests and ministers have been jailed and not a few killed in their effort to protect the Jews'" (pp. 26–27).

Jesuit historian Angelo Martini also wrote a fine critique of Hochhuth's play, "La vera storia e 'Il Vicario' di Rolf Hochhuth," *Civiltà Cattolica* 1964, volume 2, pp. 437–454. But the best response to Hochhuth allegations remains the

June 28, 1964, issue of *Osservatore della Domenica*, which devoted a special section to Pius XII's wartime record, discrediting the playwright's accusations with precise evidence and facts, including firsthand testimony from those who worked with Pius XII to rescue Jews and others. (See also the earlier response, "Vatican Answers Criticism of Pius," *New York Times*, March 1, 1964, p. 13.)

Rarely mentioned in the criticism surrounding Hochhuth's play is that a year after it premiered, another play, *The Comforter*, was performed at Blackfriars Theatre in New York (see "Blackfriars to Stage 'Deputy' Rebuttal," *New York Times*, August 24, 1964, p. 22; the play was performed on October 13, 1964). Written by Redemptorist priest Edward A. Molloy, it presented Pius XII as a humane man, reenacting how much he did in defense of the Jews during the Holocaust. (See "Priest Who Wrote Play as Reply to 'The Deputy' Calls for Truth," *New York Times*, October 17, 1964, p. 19. The play can be found in the archives of Providence College in Rhode Island. See also Fr. Molloy's obituary in the *Boston Globe*, March 7, 1986.)

Historian Eamon Duffy has written that modern scholarship has "decisively established the falsehood of Hochhuth's specific allegations" (*Saints and Sinners*, p. 264). The Vatican did protest the deportation of Rome's Jews ("in the name of humanity, in Christian charity," to quote Cardinal Maglione's plea to the German ambassador, *Actes et Documents* 9, pp. 505–506)—as newly released documents confirm again: "Vatican has apparently for a long time been assisting many Jews to escape," reads a Nazi dispatch, intercepted by the Allies, from Rome to Berlin, on October 26, 1943 (National Archives and Records Administration, College Park, Maryland, CIA Selected Documents, 1941–1947, Box 4).

But the myths continue. In early 2002, the leftist Greek filmmaker Constantin Costa-Gravas released his film *Amen* (also called *Eyewitness*), based on Hochhuth's play. The film, despite an aggressive public-relations campaign, was an international flop. See the devastating criticism in the French *Histoire du Christianisme*, March 2002, pp. 4–26; "Critiquing a Film that Faults Pius XII on the Holocaust: Interview with French Historian Jean-Yves Riou," Zenit News Agency, February 18, 2002; Peter Gumpel's remarks in "Thumbs Down on the New Film about Pius XII" (Zenit News Agency, February 18, 2002); "Pius XII Film False and Damaging to Church," the *Universe*, March 10, 2002; Ronald Rychlak's excellent rebuttal, "The Church and the Holocaust" in the European edition of the *Wall Street Journal*, March 28, 2002; and Gerri Pare's intelligent critique for the *Catholic News Service*, "Amen," January 22, 2003.

When discussing Hochhuth and *The Deputy*, it is worth mentioning that four years after it appeared, Hochhuth published another play, *Die Soldaten* ("The Soldiers," 1967), which tried to indict Winston Churchill. (See "Hochhuth Plays Slurs Churchill, So London Theater Can't Use it," *New York Times*, April 25, 1967, p. 39). The reaction was swift and severe: "Hochhuth was publicly disgraced in Britain and elsewhere when, with exactly the same anti-historical methods which he used against Pius XII, . . . he accused Winston Churchill of having ordered the murder of the Polish General [Wladyslaw] Sikorski and then that of the pilot, whose plane crashed close to Gibraltar, causing the death of the general. But the pilot in fact survived and brought charges against Hochhuth. After serious examination of the case, Hochhuth was discredited" ("Pius XII as He Really Was," Peter Gumpel, *Tablet,* February 13, 1999).

Another source adds, "Hochhuth's . . . accusation resulted in a libel action brought by the surviving pilot of the crashed aircraft which involved the author [Hochhuth] and the producers of the play in London in a costly financial settlement" ("Rolf Hochhuth" by Martin Esslin in *Makers of Modern Culture* [New York: Facts on File, 1981], p. 233). For details of the verdict against Hochhuth, see "Pilot of General Sikorski's Aircraft Claims Libel Damages from German Playwright," *Times,* May 3, 1972, p. 3; "£50,000 Award to General Sikorski's Pilot," *Times,* May 4, 1972, p. 1; and "$130,000 Awarded to Pilot for Libel in Hochhuth Play," *New York Times,* May 4, 1972, p. 48. Michael O'Carroll adds: "David Frost, the well-known television interviewer, has stated that possibly his best performance ever was the night he fairly thoroughly dismantled Hochhuth before the cameras, above all for waiting until Churchill's death to make such a foul slander; he also waited until Pius XII was dead" (*Pius XII: Greatness Dishonored,* p. 151). For background on the whole affair, see Carlos Thompson's *The Assassination of Winston Churchill* (Gerrards Cross: Smythe, 1969) and "Book About Churchill Calls Hochhuth Charge a Fantasy," *New York Times,* May 6, 1969, p. 6.

3.After *The Deputy*

Hochhuth's play precipitated the publication of a number of books that attempted to support his thesis in a more scholarly way, particularly Guenter Lewy's 1964 *The Catholic Church and Nazi Germany,* Carlo Falconi's *The Silence of Pius XII* (translated in 1970 from the 1965 Italian original), and Saul Friedlander's 1966 *Pius XII and the Third Reich.*

None of these volumes makes significant use of the *Actes et Documents* (which were also precipitated by Hochhuth's play). The most extensive rebuttal to Guenter Lewy's book appeared in the German Jesuit periodical *Stimmen der Zeit,* 176 (1965), pp. 29–41, written by Ludwig Volk, Germany's greatest postwar Church historian. Both Pierre Blet and Robert Graham— two of the four Jesuit editors of *Actes et Documents*—wrote sharp critiques of Friedlander's book, and even the restrained John S. Conway said of Friedlander that his "arbitrariness in selection [of documents] is matched by a bias in interpretation which extends even to the translations in the various editions of his book" (*The Nazi Persecution of the Churches,* p. 450).

Also from this era are Robert Katz's two books: *Death in Rome* (New York: Macmillan, 1967) and *Black Sabbath: A Journey Through a Crime Against Humanity* (New York: Macmillan, 1969). *Black Sabbath* is Katz's analysis of the Nazi roundup of Rome's Jewish community on the morning of October 16, 1943, which resulted in the deportation and death of over a thousand Jews. The book made many claims, particularly that the Jewish community itself was largely responsible for its own fate, due to naiveté and stupidity, and that the Vatican was alerted to the roundup well before it occurred but refused to take any action to prevent it.

Both claims have been discredited. See *Dante Almansi: President of the Union of Italian Jewish Communities, November 13, 1939, to October 1, 1944: note prepared by his son Renato J. Almansi: A Refutation of Black Sabbath by Robert Katz* (New York: n.p., 1971; a manuscript by the son of one of the Italian Jewish leaders disparaged in Katz's book), as well as Renato J. Almansi's "Mio padre, Dante Almansi," *La Rassegna Mensile di Israel*, May–June 1976, pp. 251–252. For the Vatican's record during the roundup, see Giovanni Sale's "Roma 1943: occupazione nazista e deportazione degli ebrei romani," *Civiltà Cattolica* 2003, volume 4, pp. 417–429, and David Dalin's "A Friend of the Jews" (*First Things*, August/September 2002, pp. 66–71). Also see the scathing criticism *Black Sabbath* received from M.M. Bernet in a *New York Times* book review (August 31, 1969, p. 6), which denounced the book as "hostile," "uninformed," and "downright offensive;" see also the follow-up letter supporting this criticism of *Black Sabbath* by Renato J. Almansi, *New York Times* book review section, September 28, 1969, p. 50.

Katz's *Death in Rome* concerned Pius XII's alleged failure to prevent the massacre of 335 Italians in the Ardeatine Caves in March 1944. (See "Book Accusing Pius Decried by Vatican," *New York Times*, January 25, 1967, p. 7.) When a movie based on the book, called *Massacre in Rome*, appeared in 1973, Countess Elena Pacelli Rossignani, the niece of Pius XII, instituted a calumny suit. Robert Graham, who testified at the trial, commented: "After 10 years the highest court closed the matter by confirming the original sentence—at least for Katz: 13 months in jail (suspended), a 400,000 Lire fine, and court costs" ("A Valiant Lady's Struggle on a Matter of Honor," *Columbia*, December 1983, p. 6). See also Graham's refutation of Katz's allegations, "La rappresaglia nazista alle Fosse Ardeatine: P. Pfeiffer, messaggero della carità di Pio XII" (*Civiltà Cattolica* 1973, volume 4, pp. 467–474).

More recently, Katz has published *The Battle for Rome: The Germans, the Allies, the Partisans, and the Pope—September 1943–June 1944* (New York: Simon and Schuster, 2003), which repackages the outdated charges of his two previous books. (See Ronald Rychlak's "New Anti-Pius XII Book by an Old Critic," *Catalyst*, May 2004, and José Sánchez's "Occupied in Terror," *America*, January 5–12, 2004, pp. 15–16). Only toward the end (pp. 353–354) does Katz summarize the court case against him—and does so in a very partial manner, claiming that his participation in a general amnesty in Italy meant that the verdict against him had been "annulled." In fact, his guilt remained the conclusion of the Italian courts, as proved by the continued assessment against him of court costs (not covered under the amnesty).

A few reviews endorsed *The Battle for Rome* (particularly Richard Cohen's egregious "A Pope of Many Silences," *Commonweal*, November 21, 2003, pp. 22–24), while others accepted uncritically Katz's peculiar account of his earlier defamation trial (particularly Carlo D'Este's review in the *New York Times*, January 11, 2004, p. A12). But the substance of Katz's charges was answered by the simultaneous publication of Patrick Gallo's *For Love and Country: The Italian Resistance* (Lanham: University Press of America, 2003), a well-documented study decisively refuting Katz's interpretation of the pope's conduct during the German occupation of Rome, establishing Pius XII's prominent role in the anti-Nazi resistance.

By the late 1960s, the attack on Pius XII seemed to have been turned back with the discrediting of *The Deputy*. One of the few books to appear in the next generation of scholarship was John F. Morley's *Vatican Diplomacy and the Jews During the Holocaust, 1939–1943* (New York: KTAV, 1980), which concluded that the Vatican "failed the Jews during the Holocaust by not doing all that it was possible for it to do on their behalf" (p. 209). Morley was among the first to draw attention to the Vatican's *Actes et Documents*, though his narrative ends in 1943 and was completed before the last two volumes of *Actes et Documents* were published.

Because Morley is a Catholic priest, and because he used primary documents, many regarded his book to be the authoritative voice of Catholic scholarship on the issue. But the same year Morley published his work, the Irish scholar Father Michael O'Carroll published *Pius XII: Greatness Dishonored*, which used many of the same documents but came to a far more positive evaluation. Moreover, Father Robert Graham, one of the editors of *Actes et Documents*, wrote two highly critical reviews of Morley's book, "Father Morley's Book is Strange and Unfair" in the *Long Island Catholic*, August 14, 1980, and another in *America*, August 9, 1980.

Critics suggest that three main flaws injure Morley's work. First, an inconsistent and tendentious interpretation of events: Morley, for example, repeatedly upbraids the Vatican for not confronting the Nazis on the persecution of Jews, but then, acknowledging evidence that the German Nuncio Orsenigo did precisely that in a face-to-face meeting with Hitler, comments on its counterproductivity. (On this protest, see Orsenigo's biography, Monica Biffi's *Mons. Cesare Orsenigo: Nunzio Apostolico in Germania (1930–1946)* [Milan: NED, 1997], and the review of it in the *National Catholic Register*, July 5–11, 1998, p. 6.) Similarly, Morley assails the Vatican for being too "diplomatic" in requesting immigration visas for German Jews to Brazil in 1939 (p. 21), but then says that the French nuncio's protests against the Vichy regime's anti-Semitism cannot constitute "a true protest" because the language he used was too "acrimonious" (p. 68).

Second, about Morley's notion that the Vatican was only concerned with baptized Jews, Graham's review in *America* comments: "The author actually thinks that the Vatican was incapable of acting for anyone but the baptized Jews. In one document cited he finds that in January 1942 the Vatican asked the Berlin Nuncio to try to get exit visas for three Czech Jews. He writes, 'The note does not indicate that they were baptized although that must be suspected [*sic*] to warrant such attention on the part of Vatican officials.' This unfortunately is the key to this book: the author cannot or will not believe that the pope could move a finger for a Jewish family. The three were, in fact, not Catholics and theirs was only one case of innumerable papal interventions."

Third, Morley simply overlooks or dismisses a wealth of documentation and scholarship that contradicts his thesis. A particularly glaring omission is Morley's failure to examine the pope's involvement with the German resistance, including plots to overthrow Hitler, as well as vital intelligence information the pope passed along to the Allies. Had Morley done so, he might not have criticized the Vatican for maintaining diplomatic relations with Germany during the war—for it was by such means that the lines of communication between Pius and the resistance remained open.

Father Morley does acknowledge that Pius XII and his diplomats saved and protected many innocent people during the war, and so he is not nearly as extreme as some anti-Pius polemicists. Morley has shown further signs of moderation in his more recent scholarship. See, for instance, his essay, "Pope Pius XII, Roman Catholic Policy, and the Holocaust in Hungary: An Analysis of *Le Saint Siège et les victimes de la guerre, janvier 1944–juillet 1945*" in *Pope Pius XII and the Holocaust*, edited by Carroll Rittner and John Roth (New York: Continuum, 2002), pp. 154–174. In this article, Morley reviews volume 10 of *Actes et Documents* and finds considerable evidence that the Vatican and its apostolic nuncio in Hungary during the war—Monsignor Angelo Rotta—took decisive steps to thwart Nazi persecution of the Jews in Hungary.

4. Recent Opponents of Pius XII

The *Deputy* myth reached a crescendo in the 1960s and fell into relative obscurity in the 1970s and 1980s, save for Morley's *Vatican Diplomacy* and a few anti-Catholic outbursts (on this issue, see Michael Schwartz's *The Persistent Prejudice* [Huntington: Our Sunday Visitor, 1984], pp. 235–251). But in 1997, James Carroll published a long anti-Pius (and antipapal) article, "The Silence," in the *New Yorker*, April 7, 1997, pp. 52–68. (For a forceful rebuttal, see "Judging Pope Pius XII," *Inside the Vatican*, June 1997, pp. 12–26.)

There followed a stream of articles and books which attempted to reformulate and revive Hochhuth's thesis in a modern guise. These include:

a. James Carroll, Constantine's Sword: The Church and the Jews—
A History *(Boston: Houghton Mifflin, 2001).*

Novelist and National Book Award–winner James Carroll uses *Constantine's Sword* to insist upon the guilt the Catholic Church (and especially Eugenio Pacelli) bear for the Holocaust. It was uncritically endorsed by many: See Andrew Sullivan's "Christianity's Original Sin," *New York Times* book review section, January 14, 2001, pp. 5–6; David Kertzer's "The Church, at its Core, Is as Sinful as Any Other Institution," *Forward*, December 29, 2000; Robert Wistrich's "Original Sin?" *Commentary*, April 2001, p. 53; and Charles Morris's "The Worst Thing About My Church," *Atlantic Monthly*, January 2001, pp. 80–84.

But *Constantine's Sword* has not fared well among reputable scholars. Robert Louis Wilken of the University of Virginia, one of the nation's leading authorities on Christian history, wrote the best review: "Dismantling the Cross" (*Commonweal*, January 26, 2001, pp. 22–28), where he commented: "This is a book driven by theological animus and padded with irrelevant, disconcerting material from Carroll's own obsessively chronicled life."

Other valuable critiques of the book include "A Deadly Misunderstanding" by Eamon Duffy, *New York Review of Books*, July 5, 2001, pp. 24–27; "Sins of the Fathers" by Daniel Maloney, *National Review*, March 5, 2001, pp. 50–52; "Two Millennia of Catholic-Jewish Relations" by Eugene Fisher, *America*, March 5, 2001, p. 24; "A Tendentious Telling" by Thomas F.X. Noble, *First Things*, May 2001, pp. 59–63; John Silber's caustic rebuttal, "Crossed Swords," *Bostonia* (Boston University alumni magazine), Summer 2001, letters to the editor; and Ronald J. Rychlak's review for the *Washington Post*, February 12, 2001, p. C3, which dryly comments: "Carroll . . . makes a point of Pope Pius XII's refusal to announce publicly Hitler's excommunication. In writing about his own excommunication in his memoir, *An American Requiem*, however, Carroll made clear that this punishment had virtually no meaning to him. Would it have mattered more to Hitler?"

b. John Cornwell, Hitler's Pope: The Secret History of Pius XII
(New York: Viking, 1999).

A sensational polemic that attempts to prove "Eugenio Pacelli, Pope Pius XII, was instrumental in negotiating an accord that helped the Nazis rise to unhindered power—and sealed the fate of the Jews in Europe." When the book first appeared, it received a number of glowing reviews. See especially V.R. Berghan's "A Deafening Silence," *New York Times* book review section,

September 26, 1999, pp. 11–12; Saul Friedlander's "Silence is Consent," *Los Angeles Times*, October 10, 1999; and Peter Stanford's "The Wicked Pope," *Times* of London, September 19, 1999, which called Pius XII "a war criminal."

Such reviews did not last long. In the international edition of *Newsweek*, September 27, 1999, Kenneth Woodward wrote that *Hitler's Pope* was "a classic example of what happens when an ill-equipped journalist assumes the air of sober scholarship. . . . Most of his sources are secondary and written by Pacelli's harshest critics. Errors of fact and ignorance of context appear on almost every page. . . . This is bogus scholarship, filled with nonexistent secrets, aimed to shock." Peter Steinfels wrote a subtle but effective critique in his religion column for the *New York Times* ("Was Pope Pius XII a Saint, or Hitler's Pawn?" October 2, 1999). John S. Conway stated that *Hitler's Pope* was "cavalier in its use of documentary sources" and that Cornwell "searches his sources for arguments to prove his predetermined conclusion. . . . It is sad to see a writer, with the advantage of 60 years hindsight, concocting this misleading and fallacious portrait" (*Historian*, Spring 2001, pp. 671–672).

For comprehensive rebuttals to *Hitler's Pope*, see the epilogue to Ronald J. Rychlak's *Hitler, the War, and the Pope*, pp. 281–312; as well as Rychlak's exposé of how the popular news program *60 Minutes* (broadcast of March 19, 2000) whitewashed Cornwell's serious errors: "*60 Minutes* on Pius XII," *Catalyst*, May 2000. Also helpful is Peter Gumpel's "Cornwell's Cheap Shot at Pius XII," *Crisis*, December 1999, pp. 19–25, and his "Cornwell's Pope: A Nasty Caricature of a Noble and Saintly Man," Zenit News Agency, September 16, 1999.

See also William D. Rubinstein's "The Devil's Advocate" in *First Things*, January 2000, pp. 39–43, as well as the subsequent letters to the editor and Rubinstein's reply in the April 2000 issue. For longer refutations, see William Doino Jr.'s trilogy of essays in the *Wanderer*, August 10 (pp. 6–7), August 17 (p. 7), and September 7, 2000 (pp. 6–7); "The Fuzzy Picture of *Hitler's Pope*" by Ian A.T. McLean, *Political Science Reviewer* 32 (2003), pp. 159–220; as well as the international symposium of scholars featured in the French journal, *Histoire du Christianisme*, May 2001, pp. 34–104.

On October 13, 1999, shortly after the publication of *Hitler's Pope*, the Vatican's *L'Osservatore Romano* published a brief critique that took up three points: "First, that Cornwell claims to be the first and only person to have had access to the archives, but this is 'completely false,' and his researches were only confined to two series of documents (1913–1915 and 1918–1921). He never saw documents relating to the period after 1922, which are not yet open to the public. [They have since been opened.] Secondly, Cornwell claimed to have worked 'for months on end' in the archive. But the logs of the archive reveal that he worked there from 12 May to 2 June 1997, a period of just three weeks, and he did not come every day. Thirdly, Cornwell claimed that the documents he found, particularly a letter of 18 April 1919 that he described as 'like a time bomb,' had been secret until he made his re-search. But this letter had already been published in 1992 in a book by E. Fat-torini, published in Bologna" (summarized in the *Tablet*, November 20, 1999; for Cornwell's defensive reply, see the *Tablet*, November 27, 1999).

Similarly, aspects of Cornwell's earlier book, *A Thief in the Night: The Mys-terious Death of Pope John Paul I* (New York: Simon and Schuster, 1989), have also been challenged by a Vatican official. See "A Small Correction from Rome" by Archbishop John P. Foley, president of the Pontifical Council for Social Communications, letters to the editor, *Crisis*, October 2003.

Two reviews of *Hitler's Pope* in German merit special notice: Rainer Decker's "John Cornwell, Pius XII. Der Papst, der geschwiegen hat," *H-Soz-u-Kult* on *H-Net* online reviews, February 2000, and Heinz Hürten's "Pius XII—Hitler's Papst?" in *Stimmen der Zeit*, March 2000, pp. 205–208. Hürten is the author of the definitive study on German Catholicism during the Nazi era: *Deutsche Katholiken, 1918–1945* (Paderborn: Ferdinand Schöningh, 1992).

The cover of *Hitler's Pope* carries a blurred picture an unsuspecting person might think was a picture of Pacelli visiting Nazi headquarters; in fact, Pacelli never met Hitler, and never set foot in Germany during Hitler's rule (1933–1945), having left the country in 1929 to become Pius XI's Cardinal Sec-retary of State. The cover photograph is actually a picture of Nuncio Pacelli in 1927 leaving a reception for President Hindenburg in Berlin during the Weimar Republic. Equally objectionable is the truncated quotation with which Cornwell begins his book, a passage from Thomas Merton apparently lamenting the "si-lence" of Pius XII. No citation is given. The story behind the full quotation was revealed by Robert Gorman at the October 2001 meeting of the Society of Catholic Social Scientists. The full quotation comes from Merton's journal, *Dancing in the Water of Life* (San Francisco: Harper, 1997), p. 84, where the Trappist monk complains about not being allowed to publish his essay on nu-clear war. The silence about which he wrote had nothing to do with Pius XII.

c. Daniel Jonah Goldhagen, A Moral Reckoning: The Role of the Catholic Church in the Holocaust and Its Unfulfilled Duty of Repair *(New York: Knopf, 2002).*

In January 2002, the *New Republic* published a 25,000-word attack against the Roman Catholic Church. Written by Daniel Jonah Goldhagen (best known for his controversial book, *Hitler's Willing Executioners* [New York: Knopf, 1996]), the article was entitled "What Would Jesus Have Done?" (*New Republic*, January 21, 2002, pp. 21–45), and it forms the bulk of his later book, *A Moral Reckoning.*

A profoundly anti-Christian polemic, the article and book focus on Pius XII as the symbol of Catholic evil and repeat almost every accusation ever launched against the Catholic Church and the New Testament. This is hardly new. John Weiss wrote a similar diatribe against the Church in 1996 entitled, *Ideology of Death: Why the Holocaust Happened in Germany* (Chicago: Ivan R. Dee, 1996), which asserted that "Pius XII was pro-Nazi to the end" (p. 354), and theologian Hyam Maccoby has long claimed that the Gospel's teachings led inexorably to the Holocaust. On Maccoby, see Ron Rosenbaum's *Explaining Hitler: The Search for the Origins of His Evil* (New York: Random House, 1998), pp. 319–336.

After Goldhagen's essay appeared, there were a number of short rebuttals to it, not least of which was one by Andrew Sullivan in the pages of the *New Republic* itself, entitled "Mortal Sin," January 28, 2002, p. 38—although Leon Wieseltier responded with a defense of Goldhagen in the next issue, February 4, 2002, p. 42.

For a sampling of the negative reaction to Goldhagen's outburst, see: "Catholics, Jews Unite to Attack Scholar's Latest," *Forward*, January 18, 2002; Sam Schulman's "Goldhagen to Christianity: Whatever You're Doing, Stop It!" *Jewish World Review* online, January 22, 2002; and Michael Novak's "Bigotry's New Low," *National Review* online, January 28, 2002.

"The Church and the Holocaust" by Paul Gottfried in the *Spectator* of London, February 16, 2002, is a sharp reply to Goldhagen by an iconoclastic writer. In a letter to the editors of the *New Republic*, Michael Marrus, who is not uncritical of the Church, described Goldhagen's polemic as a "rant" and judged it "an unrelieved, bitter attack on his subject, a sneering disparagement of other analysts for moral equivocation, a dismissal of most contemporary scholarship, and a hunger for the black and white, the simplest of historical explanations. Unfortunately, this is a subject in which tunnel vision and a highly selective use of evidence is becoming rampant" (*New Republic*, March 18, 2002, p. 4).

The definitive response, however, is Ronald J. Rychlak's eighteen-page refutation, "Goldhagen vs. Pius XII," in *First Things*, June–July 2002, pp. 37–54. For a favorable reaction to Rychlak's article, see "Hyping the Church and the Holocaust," *National Post* online, June 4, 2002. Cardinal Christoph Schönborn, the archbishop of Vienna, also recommended Rychlak's exhaustive rebuttal to Goldhagen: see "Controversy Looms Once More Over Pius XII and the Jews," *Tablet*, October 5, 2002. As Rychlak demonstrates, Goldhagen's anti-Catholic polemic relies almost exclusively on secondary sources, makes serious and frequent errors of fact, mistranslates crucial texts, and omits exculpatory evidence.

After the book version, Goldhagen's *A Moral Reckoning*, appeared, leading historians panned it. Michael Burleigh, a renowned British authority on Nazi Germany, dismissed it as a "cartoon strip view of history" ("Vile Tales of the Vatican," *Times*, October 6, 2002, p. 8). Christopher Clark denounced the book's "venomous ranting" and dismissed its central thesis ("Doctrine of Death?" *Times Literary Supplement*, November 1, 2002, p. 14). Heinz Hürten, one of Germany's leading authorities on German Catholicism, said that he "was absolutely unimpressed by the book. . . . It is not scholarship and totally ignores the fact that most of his theories have already been disproved" ("Controversial Author Triggers Furor with Book," Reuters News Service, October 28, 2002).

The book first appeared in Germany, where a court in Munich issued a temporary restraining order against it because the book included a photograph it claimed was of Cardinal Michael Faulhaber, the anti-Nazi archbishop of Munich, at a "Nazi rally in Munich." The photograph was actually of Papal Nuncio Cesare Orsenigo, who attended, not a Nazi rally, but a 1934 Labor Day affair in Berlin, which all accredited diplomats were obligated to attend. (The photographic blunder is described in full by Karl-Joseph Hummel, head of the Commission for Contemporary History in Bonn, in "Ein Kardinal marschiert nicht. Der Vertrieb von Daniel Goldhagens neuem Buch ist zu Recht verboten worden," *Frankfurter Allgemeine Zeitung*, October 12, 2002.) The paperback edition of *A Moral Reckoning* (New York: Vintage, 2003) carries a new caption for the photograph: "Papal Nuncio Cesare Orsenigo parades in front of SA men at Berlin May Day celebration." This is still misleading: Orsenigo is not marching in any Nazi parade, but simply walking with other accredited diplomats.

Subsequent reviews against Goldhagen's book (and lecture tour) in Germany were devastating. See, in particular, Konrad Repgen's "Dostojewski nahm es mit Schuld und Suehne genauer," *Frankfurter Allgemeine Zeitung*, October 8, 2002, p. L31; Michael Feldkamp's "Anleitung zur Hetzjagd," *Rheinischer Merkur*, October 14, 2002; "Ein Prophet auf Tournee: Daniel Jonah Goldhagens Lesereise" by Patrick Bahners, *Frankfurter Allgemeine Zeitung*, October 18, 2002; and "Im Furor des Rechthabens" by Jan Ross in the October 2002 Sonderbeilage to *Die Zeit*, pp. 61–62.

The best book-length refutation of Goldhagen's thesis is Michael Feldkamp's *Goldhagens Unwillige Kirche: Alte und neue Fälschungen über Kirche und Papst während der NS-Herrschaft* (Munich: Olzog, 2003). Even left-leaning historian Georg Denzler, a well-known critic of the Church, wrote a scathing rebuttal to Goldhagen: *Widerstand ist nicht das richtige Wort. Priester, Bischöfe und Theologen im Dritten Reich* (Zürich: Pendo, 2003). For a strong French critique, see Edouard Husson's comments in "Goldhagen: l'Eglise responsable de la Shoah," *Histoire du Christianisme*, January 2003, pp. 6–9 (Husson's earlier book, *Une culpabilité ordinaire? Hitler, les Allemands et la Shoah* [Paris: François-Xavier de Guibert, 1997], refutes Goldhagen's views about Germans and the Holocaust).

Faced with this European reaction, a handful of Goldhagen apologists in the English-speaking world tried to rescue his book from obscurity. See, for example, Gerard Noel's "A Failure of Papal Nerve," *Spectator*, November 2, 2002, pp. 60–61; John K. Roth's "What the Church Owes Jews, and Itself," *Los Angeles Times*, November 3, 2002; and David Kertzer's "Sins of the Fathers,"

Washington Post, November 17, 2002, p. B10, which was embarrassingly self-serving, as one of Goldhagen's chief sources is none other than Kertzer himself.

But such pieces were the exception. Both the *Boston Globe* and the *New York Times,* usually hostile to things Catholic, rejected Goldhagen's thesis ("Calling to Account" by Jonathan Dorfman, *Boston Globe,* November 24, 2002, p. D8, and "Sins of the Fathers" by Geoffrey Wheatcroft, *New York Times* book-review section, November 24, 2002, p. 10). Commenting on Goldhagen's attempt to link the Church with the crimes of Nazi Germany, the *Times* was especially blunt: "Catholic Italy was not the Third Reich: Hitler didn't baptize Jewish children, he murdered them." (See also Goldhagen's letter protesting this review and Wheatcroft's response, *New York Times* book review section, letters to the editor, December 15, 2002.)

Istvan Deak, while repeating certain errors about Pius XII, nonetheless panned Goldhagen's work in a highly negative review ("Jews and Catholics," *New York Review of Books,* December 19, 2002, pp. 40–44; see also the letters in response to Deak, especially A.F. Crispin's, in "Jews and Catholics: An Exchange," *New York Review of Books,* March 13, 2003).

America's two leading liberal Catholic weeklies, which are not averse to criticizing the Church, categorically rejected Goldhagen's arguments; see "Goldhagen at it Again" by James J. Sheehan, *Commonweal,* November 8, 2002, pp. 28–30; and Justus George Lawler's "History Lite: Goldhagen, the Holocaust and the Truth," *Commonweal,* May 9, 2003, pp. 17–19. "Holy Collaborators?" by Marc Saperstein, *America,* December 2, 2002, pp. 23–25, is an excellent and forceful critique by a prominent scholar of Catholic-Jewish relations. See also "Anti-Semitism, Anti-Catholicism and Truth" by Donald Demarco, *National Catholic Register,* November 24–30, 2002; John S. Conway's review in the *American Jewish Congress Monthly,* November–December 2002, pp. 19–20; and Vincent Lapomarda's "Reckoning with Daniel J. Goldhagen's Views on the Roman Catholic Church, the Holocaust and Pope Pius XII," *Journal of the Historical Society,* Summer/Fall 2003, pp. 493–502.

But the best American reviews of Goldhagen's tract appeared in the conservative press, which subjected every element of Goldhagen's assertions to withering analysis. For a sampling, see Joseph Bottum's sardonic "The Usefulness of Daniel Goldhagen," *Weekly Standard* online edition, October 23, 2002; David Dalin's thorough rebuttal in the *Weekly Standard*'s print edition, "History as Bigotry: Daniel Goldhagen Slanders the Catholic Church," February 10, 2003, pp. 38–41; Mark Riebling's "Jesus, Jews and the Shoah" in *National Review,* January 27, 2003, pp. 43–45; and Dimitri Cavalli's penetrating critique, "Pope Pius XII and the Holocaust: A Reply to Daniel Goldhagen," *Modern Age,* Summer 2003, pp. 278–284. See also Ronald Rychlak's two follow-up reviews to his original *First Things* critique: "Another Reckoning," *Crisis,* January 2003, pp. 12–18, and "Dean of Catholic-Bashers," *American Conservative,* February 10, 2003, pp. 12–15.

Such reviews resonated well beyond America. See, for example, "Throwing the Book at the Church" by Tibor Krausz, *Jerusalem Report*, July 14, 2003, p. 38, which wrote that Goldhagen's thesis "won't wash: The Nazis despised Christianity, regarding it an effeminate creed of compromise, and recruits to the SS (including the Holocaust's architects and perpetrators) were required to renounce their Christian faith."

In reaction to this avalanche of criticism, Goldhagen acknowledged that he was a social scientist, conceding that "I am not a historian" and that perhaps "my historical account is not right in its every detail" (*Atlantic Unbound*, the online edition of the *Atlantic Monthly*, January 31, 2003). For those aware of the serious shortcomings of *Hitler's Willing Executioners*, effectively exposed in *Hyping the Holocaust: Scholars Answer Goldhagen*, edited by Franklin H. Littell (East Rockaway: Cummings and Hathaway, 1997), the flaws of Goldhagen's second book come as no surprise.

d. David I. Kertzer, The Popes Against the Jews: The Vatican's Role in the Rise of Modern Anti-Semitism *(New York: Knopf, 2001).*

According to a jacket blurb, *The Popes Against the Jews* "is a book filled with shocking revelations. It traces the Vatican's role in the development of modern anti-Semitism from the nineteenth century up to the outbreak of the Second World War."

Most of the issues Kertzer touches upon have already been dealt with by Catholic scholars. The writings of Jacques Maritain, Monsignor John Oesterreicher, Father Edward Flannery, Cardinal Augustin Bea, Cardinal Johannes Willebrands, Cardinal Edward Cassidy, and Cardinal Walter Kasper invalidate Kertzer's claim that the Catholic Church has failed to take an honest look at anti-Semitism within its own ranks. Kertzer's criticisms against the Vatican's statement on the Holocaust, *We Remember: A Reflection on the Shoah* (1998), are not new and have been ably answered by Cardinals Avery Dulles and Edward Cassidy (see their essays in *The Holocaust, Never to be Forgotten: Reflections on the Holy See's Document "We Remember"* [Mahwah: Paulist, 2001]). *La Civiltà Cattolica*, which Kertzer accuses of having fostered anti-Semitism in the past, also published a major refutation of Kertzer's thesis: "Antigiudaismo o Antisemitismo? Le Accuse contro La Chiesa e La 'Civiltà Cattolica'" by Giovanni Sale, S.J., *Civiltà Cattolica* 2002, volume 2, pp. 419–431; see also Sale's interview with Vatican Radio, reported on in "*The Popes Against the Jews* Misses the Mark, Says Historian," Zenit News Agency, February 13, 2002. Also of note is Owen Chadwick's critique of Kertzer for the *New York Review of Books*, March 28, 2002, p. 14.

For two extensive rebuttals to Kertzer, see Russell Hittinger's review, "Desperately Seeking Culprits," in the *Journal of the Historical Society*, Spring 2002, pp. 215–227, and Thomas Brechenmacher's review in the *Frankfurter*

Allgemeine Zeitung, November 6, 2001, summarized in English by John Jay Hughes for *Inside the Vatican,* February 2002, pp. 83–84. Brechenmacher, an eminent German scholar, has also published a long essay on papal-Jewish relations, critiquing various aspects of Kertzer's thesis (*Historisches Jahrbuch* 122 [2002], pp. 195–234), which has since been expanded into a book: *Das Ende der doppelten Schutzherrschaft. Der Heilige Stuhl und die Juden am Übergang zur Moderne 1775–1870* (Stuttgart: Hiersemann, 2004).

One of Kertzer's major assertions is that the modern popes have sanctioned lurid myths about Jewish "Ritual Murder" and promoted the notorious "Protocols of the Elders of Zion" in the years leading up to the Holocaust. In fact, the papacy was the one major force that repeatedly condemned these virulent anti-Semitic fabrications. See "Popes and Jewish 'Ritual Murder'" by W.F.T. Stockley, *Catholic World,* July 1934, pp. 450–460, and "The Credulity of Anti-Semitism" in the *Month,* December 1938, which condemned the Protocols as an absolute "fraud," containing "obvious insanities" and representing "incredible absurdity."

In his bibliography, Kertzer makes mention of the book, *The Ritual Murder Libel and the Jew: The Report by Cardinal Lorenzo Ganganelli (Pope Clement XIV),* edited by the Jewish historian Cecil Roth (London: Woburn, 1935). This book reprinted the famous and courageous condemnation of the ritual-murder libel by Cardinal Ganganelli in 1758. But Kertzer makes no mention of Roth's private audience with Pius XI, at which the pontiff was presented with the new edition of the book. Nor does Kertzer mention Roth's tribute to Pius XI, after the latter's death, in which Roth spoke of the significance of that meeting: "It was not, of course, a mere matter of presentation; by receiving in this formal fashion the new edition of this document, the pope, in effect, associated himself with the repudiation of the foul libel, which had not long before been repeated in particularly loathsome form in Germany. And he insisted, during the few moments of conversation how the protection of the Jews had not been confined to a single pope but had been the invariable policy of the papacy" ("A Memorable Interview: Condemning the Blood Libel," *Jewish Chronicle,* February 17, 1939, p. 16).

Four distinguished Jewish scholars have also refuted many of Kertzer's assertions. See Marc Saperstein's "An Indictment: Half Right," *Commonweal,* September 28, 2001, pp. 19–21; David Dalin's "Popes and Jews," *Weekly Standard,* October 29, 2001, pp. 36–38; William D. Rubinstein's "Case for the Prosecution," *First Things,* February 2002, pp. 54–58; and Michael Marrus in the *New Leader,* September/October 2001, pp. 18–19. Dalin calls the Kertzer book "both false and unpersuasive"; Rubinstein declares "it was an ultra-nationalistic ideology that lay at the heart of Hitler's anti-Semitism. Religion had nothing whatever to do with his uniquely evil brand of racial superiority and hate." Marrus, who is not uncritical of the Vatican, nevertheless concludes: "What Kertzer does not do, at least to my satisfaction, is to mobilize his evidence to elucidate our understanding of the Nazis' murder of the European Jews. Focusing as he does on the Catholic press, he does not persuade me that 'traditional' Catholic forms of dealing with the Jews became transformed into modern anti-Semitism. . . . Indeed, the closer Kertzer comes to the Holocaust, the less sure his conclusions become, and the less remarkable his contentions."

e. The Works of Michael Marrus.

Dean of graduate studies and the Chancellor Rose and Ray Wolfe Professor of Holocaust Studies at the University of Toronto, Michael Marrus's books include *Vichy France and the Jews*, coauthored with Robert O. Paxton (New York: Basic, 1981) and *The Holocaust in History* (Hanover: University Press of New England, 1987).

Among critics of Pius XII, Marrus's criticism is usually nuanced, and he has shown a willingness to check other critics of Pius XII who make unwarranted attacks. Interested in the outcast and oppressed, Marrus has also authored several studies about anti-Semitism and racism: *The Politics of Assimilation: The French Jewish Community at the Time of the Dreyfus Affair* (Oxford: Clarendon, 1981) and *The Unwanted: European Refugees in the Twentieth Century* (Oxford: Oxford University, 1985). His book on *The Nuremberg War Crimes, 1945–46* (Boston: Bedford, 1997) is valuable, as are his many articles and reviews. Especially recommended are Marrus's critique of David Kertzer's *The Popes Against the Jews* for the *New Leader*, September/October 2001, pp. 18–19, and his essay for the Toronto *Globe and Mail*, July 24, 2001, on why it is in the Vatican's own interests to release all its wartime archives as soon as possible.

An expert on Holocaust-related literature, Marrus has written an important essay on "Historiography" in *The Holocaust Encyclopedia*, edited by Walter Laqueur (New Haven: Yale University, 2001), pp. 279–285, in which he says, "Balance is the most important continuing challenge for Holocaust historians." Indeed, Marrus has chided unbalanced historians for making "unwarranted moral judgments that apply our standards, our appreciations, our sensibilities, our knowledge, and our hindsight to the events of half a century ago" (*American Scholar*, Winter 1997, p. 563).

In a review of Michael Phayer's *The Catholic Church and the Holocaust 1930–1965* and Susan Zuccotti's *Under His Very Windows* for the *Los Angeles Times*, March 4, 2001, Marrus noted how both authors make sweeping allegations against the Vatican's wartime conduct but base much of their case upon speculation about what *might* have happened had Pius XII acted another way. Calling such speculation "pointless," Marrus cautioned that there "is simply no way of knowing" what would have happened had Pius acted differently than he did—and he added his belief in the good faith of Pius.

In his many writings (particularly *The Holocaust in History*), Marrus has frequently raised questions about Pius XII's wartime conduct, and he has criticized the campaign to canonize the pope ("Elevating Pius XII Would Debase Sainthood," *Montreal Gazette*, August 2, 2002, p. B3). Marrus is by no means immune to error; he accepts as valid the dubious "Bérard Report" (written by the untrustworthy and self-serving Vichy ambassador Léon Bérard) suggesting the Vatican tolerated anti-Semitic legislation in Vichy France. His grasp of Catholic theology is weak, and he often underemploys information exonerating Pius XII (such as the pope's use of Vatican Radio).

For the most part, however, Marrus keeps an even keel and appears capable of changing his mind as new evidence emerges. His scorching critique of Daniel Goldhagen's *A Moral Reckoning*, published in the Toronto *Globe and Mail* of November 3, 2002 ("Goldhagen's argument strikes this reviewer as grossly one-sided, what the famous Swiss historian Jacob Burkhardt meant by the work of *terribles simplificateurs*—writers who, while popular, coarsened debate and thereby damaged the cause of historical truth") is particularly worth noting.

f. Michael Phayer, The Catholic Church and the Holocaust, 1930–1965 *(Bloomington: Indiana University, 2000).*

In this book, Michael Phayer, a widely published Holocaust historian, attacks most of Catholic leadership from 1930 to 1965. Covering the crucial period from Hitler's rise to the Second Vatican Council, Phayer depicts a Church attracted to power and privilege, placing diplomacy over justice; a Church infected with anti-Semitism and obsessed with communism.

While some of the points Phayer makes should cause Catholics of good conscience to pause, his sweeping allegations and grotesque portrait of Pius XII (especially regarding the pope's reaction to the Nazi roundup of Rome's Jews) is refuted by the best contemporary scholarship. Phayer accuses Pius XII of downplaying, if not whitewashing, the responsibility of certain German Catholics for their conduct during the Third Reich, but he ignores evidence to the contrary (see, for example, "Pope Says Germans Should be Humble," *New York Times*, December 28, 1945, p. 5). Phayer's refusal to consider alternatives and heavy reliance on discredited sources—including Mark Aarons and John Loftus's notorious tract *Unholy Trinity: The Vatican, the Nazis and Soviet Intelligence* (New York: St. Martin's, 1992; updated in 1998 as *The Vatican, the Nazis, and the Swiss Banks*)—makes his book one-sided and unreliable.

Phayer's work has not garnered as much attention as other books in this genre, but it has received some undeserved plaudits, notably by Richard Cohen in a cover story for *Commonweal* ("Pius XII: Not Vindicated," March 9, 2001, pp. 29–31). The admirers of Phayer's book would do well to read Konrad Repgen's expert criticism in "Connecting the Church and the Shoah," *Catholic Historical Review*, July 2002, pp. 546–553. Repgen finds Phayer's book fraught with errors, large and small, and points to Phayer's failure to use such crucial scholarship as the writings of Pierre Blet and Robert Graham, as well as the three volumes of correspondence between the Holy See and the Nazi government edited by Dieter Albrecht.

Repgen, an authority on the concordat, is particularly severe in refuting Phayer's claim that the concordat set the stage for the Nazi Holocaust. The charge, says Repgen, is without documentation, contradicts all the available evidence, and amounts to "pure fantasy." Similarly, John Jay Hughes's reply to Phayer, "Something Shameful," *Inside the Vatican*, December 2000, pp. 48–52, exposes Phayer's inadequacies as a historian. Hughes may be the only reviewer to have drawn attention to one of the worst aspects of Phayer's book: its dust jacket, which "portrays a uniformed Nazi guard holding a whip and next to him a faceless Catholic prelate, both standing on the corpse of an emaciated victim wearing the Jewish Star of David." Commenting on this cover, Hughes notes: "Clearly designed to enrage and inflame, it vividly portrays an historical falsehood. The concordat was never an alliance with Hitler. On the contrary, it was a treaty guaranteeing Church freedom and rights. . . . Without it neither the Holy See nor the German bishops would have had any legal basis for the countless protests against Nazi policies which so enraged Hitler that he promised, in his *Table Talk*, to scrap the treaty at war's conclusion. By choosing this mendacious drawing to introduce his book, Phayer has placed his work on the level of the viciously anti-Semitic nineteenth-century forgery, *Protocols of the Elders of Zion*. Is it not clear that something deeply shameful is going on?" (p. 52).

Phayer's article, "Canonizing Pius XII: Why Did the Pope Help Nazis Escape?" *Commonweal*, May 9, 2003, pp. 22–23, predictably attacks the cause of Pius XII, regurgitating discredited allegations against the wartime pontiff (who gave the postwar Nuremberg Tribunal documents to help prosecute Nazi war criminals). On this issue, see the letters by Justus George Lawler and Dimitri Cavalli rebutting Phayer in *Commonweal*, June 6, 2003, p. 2. For support of the case for Pius XII's canonization, see "A Strong Leader, a Holy Man" by Bishop Raymond Lucker (a notably liberal prelate), *National Catholic Reporter*, March 31, 2000, and "German Jesuit nears End of Campaign for Beatifying Pope Pius XII" by Nicole Winfield, Associated Press, May 14, 2003.

g. *Garry Wills,* Papal Sin: Structures of Deceit *(New York: Doubleday, 2000).*

In this polemic, the talented and popular Garry Wills tries to reveal the moral and historical falsehoods on which he believes the modern papacy rests. Throughout his book, Wills insists that all he is trying to do is reform the Catholic Church for its own good, but Wills attacks and mocks Catholic doctrine and repeats all the usual errors about Pius XII. Indeed, Wills exploits

The Deputy myth as a springboard from which to assault the essence of Roman Catholicism.

Wills goes so far that even non-Catholics have questioned him about it. In a review for the *New York Times*, left-wing philosopher Richard Rorty agreed with Wills's recommendation to "overthrow papal tyranny"—but, taking this reasoning to its logical conclusion, he opined that if what Wills says is true, "then it is not clear why we need a church of Christ" at all ("Acting Fallible," *New York Times* book review section, June 11, 2000, p. 10). *Papal Sin* is subjected to withering criticisms in Robert Lockwood's long "*Papal Sin* is Palpable Nonsense" (Catholic League for Religious and Civil Rights online, June 2000). See also James Pereiro's review, "Misinterpretations and Half-Truths," *Modern Age*, Winter 2002, pp. 87–90 and Russell Hittinger's comments in *First Things*, August–September 2000, p. 66.

In a sharp review for *Commonweal*, July 14, 2000, pp. 24–26, Eamon Duffy wrote: "There is something repellently illiberal about Wills's angry liberal certainties, his wholesale and unqualified conviction that every right-thinking Catholic must agree with him, and that the positions he rejects can be held together by nothing except rank tyranny and the intellectual equivalent of chewing gum. Every issue he discusses is open and shut, and he finds in the standard works of biblical commentary or popular history on his shelves unchallengeable proofs of his own views. The arguments made by the Church are not *prima facie* ridiculous in the way Wills characterizes them. He does little to present the arguments and reasoning offered by the Catholic Church and instead spends his time railing against the conclusions." The best critique of Wills's antipapal tract, written on a very high level and amounting to a full-scale demolition, appears in Justus George Lawler's *Popes and Politics*, pp. 72–103 and 139–187.

b. Susan Zuccotti, Under His Very Windows: The Vatican and the Holocaust in Italy *(New Haven: Yale University, 2000).*

A book that claims that although 85 percent of Italian Jews survived the Holocaust, the primate of Italy had little or nothing to do with it. Moreover, argues Zuccotti, all the praise Pius XII received during and after the war from prominent Jewish leaders was based upon "benevolent ignorance" or intellectual dishonesty designed to foster Vatican support for Israel or reduce anti-Semitism. Even the testimonials on behalf of Pius from Jewish survivors of wartime Italy, such as Michael Tagliocozzo and Eugenio Zolli, are minimized or disparaged by Zuccotti.

Among scholars in the field, the book has not fared well. They point out that Zuccotti's basic charges are not new but simply elaborate accusations already made by other anti-Pius polemicists, notably Sam Waagenaar in *The Pope's Jews*. Moreover, Zuccotti makes little use of important German sources and omits evidence that contradicts her. So, for instance, she fails to mention the pope's rescue measures at Castel Gandolfo and fails to document Cardinal Paolo Dezza's written testimony (*Osservatore della Domenica*, June 28, 1964, pp. 68–69) that Pius XII verbally told him to assist "persecuted Jews" during the German occupation.

In her analysis of the Vatican's modern attitude toward Jews, she makes no mention of Pope Benedict XV's explicit condemnation of anti-Semitism in 1916, even though it was published in *La Civiltà Cattolica* (1916, volume 2, pp. 358–359), to which Zuccotti repeatedly refers. (This papal statement was also reported in the *New York Times*, April 17, 1916, under the headline "Papal Bull Urges Equality for Jews," and in the *Tablet* of April 29, 1916.)

Nor does Zuccotti mention the Holy See's early intervention against Nazi anti-Semitism (on April 4, 1933—just two months after Hitler obtained power), even though it was recorded by Father Robert Leiber (in the German Jesuit periodical *Stimmen der Zeit*, March 1962, p. 420) forty years before Zuccotti published her book. In her examination of Pius XII's reaction to Nazi atrocities, she fails to emphasize Vatican Radio's prominent role in explicitly condemning them (*Under His Very Windows* has only one reference to the station) and fails to mention Pius's confrontational meeting with German Foreign Minister Joachim von Ribbentrop, on March 11, 1940, during which the pope "came to the defense of the Jews in Germany and Poland" (*New York Times*, March 14, 1940, p. 8). Even worse is Zuccotti's sloppiness regarding easily verifiable facts. On page 63, she claims that Pius XII's first encyclical, *Summi Pontificatus*, "never mentioned Jews." In fact, the encyclical does explicitly mention Jews (paragraph 48) and does so in the context of quoting St. Paul's belief in the unity of Christians and Jews ("where there is neither Gentile nor Jew").

In a chapter entitled, "What the Pope Knew About the Holocaust," Zuccotti deems it "likely" that Josef Müller, an anti-Nazi German lawyer, passed information about the Holocaust to Leiber, Pius XII's chief assistant, "in August or September 1943" (p. 108). Leiber presumably gave this information to the pope, who supposedly sat on this knowledge and did nothing. "The problem with Zuccotti's account," notes Mark Riebling (author of a forthcoming work on Pius XII's involvement with the anti-Nazi German Resistance), "is that Müller could not have met Leiber in August or September of 1943, when 'the ongoing murders of the Jews' [to quote Zuccotti] were increasingly known, *because Müller had been arrested on April 9 of that year.* That such an error should have been made at all, and on such a crucial point, is troubling enough. That it should have gone unprotested by academic reviewers and by Holocaust scholars—who awarded Zuccotti's work the National Jewish Book Award—suggests a more systematic problem" (private communication; see also the preface to Riebling's forthcoming book).

In reaction to her critics, Zuccotti has attempted to defend her thesis in the *Journal of Modern Italian Studies*, Summer 2002, pp. 240–261. But in the same issue, Ronald Rychlak has a crushing and heavily documented refutation of Zuccotti's views, pp. 218–240, including 109 endnotes. Many others have found Zuccotti's accusations to be "not history but guesswork" (Owen Chadwick, "Pius XII's Terrifying Dilemma: Put Yourself in His Shoes," *Tablet*, June 30, 2001, pp. 950–951). See Vincent Lapomarda's review in *Catholic Historical Review*, April 2001, pp. 343–345; Kevin Doyle's "The Case for the Prosecution," *First Things*, April 2001, pp. 52–55; William Doino Jr.'s "A Distorted History of Pius XII," *Inside the Vatican*, February 2001, pp. 54–59; Christopher Duggan's "The Silence," *New York Times* book-review section, February 4, 2001, p. 34; and "Historian off the Mark" by Dimitri Cavalli, *Journal News* (Westchester), June 23, 2003, p. 4B. Giovanni Sale's article, "Roma 1943: occupazione nazista e deportazione degli ebrei romani" (*Civiltà Cattolica* 2003, volume 4, pp. 417–429), though not a direct response to Zuccotti, reveals new archival evidence that undermines her book's thesis.

In *Popes and Politics*, Justus George Lawler demonstrates how *Under His Very Windows* is replete with egregious mistakes and contradicts Zuccotti's earlier work (particularly her *The Holocaust, the French and the Jews* [1993; reprinted Lincoln: University of Nebraska, 1999]), which displayed far more balance. A case in point: In her book on the French reaction to the Holocaust, she approvingly notes how Pius XI's 1928 condemnation of anti-Semitism inspired the French Catholic resistance to assist Jews (*The Holocaust, the French and the Jews*, p. 141); but in *Under His Very Windows*, Zuccotti disparages the 1928 statement (pp. 8–11) and claims it was "soon forgotten" (p. 9). Lawler has continued his critique of Zuccotti in a revealing exchange in the *U.S. Catholic Historian*, Spring 2002, pp. 79–117.

One of the Catholic rescuers who plays a part in Zuccotti's book has now spoken out. Don Aldo Brunacci, a Catholic priest-rescuer from Assisi and a man honored by Yad Vashem as a righteous gentile, recently gave an interview rejecting Zuccotti's suggestion (*Under His Very Windows*, pp. 260–264) that his bishop, Giuseppe Nicolini, lied to him about Pius XII. When Nicolini read to Brunacci a letter from the Holy See that instructed the bishop and his priests to rescue persecuted Jews, Zuccotti wrote, "Nicolini may have considered it useful to make his assistants believe that they were doing the pope's work" (p. 264). This is, according to Brunacci, "Impossible, impossible. . . . It is not possible that Bishop Nicolini was deceiving me. I am certain of that. . . . Zuccotti doubts that Pius XII could have issued such an order. . . . But the letter was sent out. I saw it with my own eyes, in my bishop's hands, as he read it to me. It was a letter from the Vatican asking the bishop to take measures to help protect the Jews. And we took those measures" ("The Secret Letter," *Inside the Vatican*, January 2004, pp. 74–76).

Antonio Gaspari, whose *Gli ebrei salvati da Pio XII* (Rome: Logos, 2001) is based on interviews with Italian survivors of the Nazi terror, said of Zuccotti's claim that Catholic rescue activity took place in Italy without papal support: "This is a thesis which is impossible to defend" ("New Revelations on Jews Saved by Pius XII," Zenit News Agency, February 16, 2001). The 1990 *Encyclopedia of the Holocaust* makes a sensible point that *Under His Very Windows* cannot: "In many monasteries, churches and ecclesiastical buildings in Italy, Jews were saved during the Nazi occupation, and the simultaneous opening of so many Catholic institutions could have taken place only under clear instructions by Pius XII" ("Pius XII" by Sergio I. Minerbi, volume 3, pp. 1135–1139).

i. Other Sources.

One can find less-publicized examples in this modern wave of attacks. See, for instance, *Pope Pius XII and the Holocaust*, edited by Carol Rittner and John K. Roth (New York: Leicester University, 2001), which contains an essay by Richard L. Rubenstein, "Pope Pius XII and the Shoah," that asks, "Could it be that Pius regarded the demographic elimination of Europe's Jews as a benefit for European Christendom? Put differently, did the pope recognize any moral obligation whatsoever to rescue Jews? It is my conviction that the pontiff recognized no such obligation and that he did regard the demographic removal of Europe's Jews as a benefit for European Christendom" (p. 177). Rubenstein seems to have fully embraced this view. In another essay, "A Twentieth-Century Journey" in *From the Unthinkable to the Unavoidable*, also edited by Carol Rittner and John K. Roth (Westport: Greenwood, 1997), he writes: "over time I have become convinced that during World War II Pope Pius XII and the vast majority of European Christian leaders regarded the elimination of the Jews as no less beneficial than the destruction of Bolshevism" (p. 167).

A recent essay in a similar mold is "A Question of Race: Pope Pius XII and the 'Coloured Troops' in Italy" by Robert G. Weisbord and Michael W. Honhart, *Historian*, December 2002, pp. 403–417, a polemic that depicts Pius XII as racially insensitive, if not racist—despite a lifetime of actions and papal statements against racism and discrimination. See in particular, Pius XII's condemnations of racism in his first two encyclicals: *Summi Pontificatus* (in which he announced the appointment of minority bishops) and *Sertum Laetitae* in which he explicitly praised African Americans at a time when segregation was rampant. See also "Pope Pius XII and the Negro," *Interracial Review*, December 1939, p. 179, and especially Pius XII's address (May 27, 1946) on interracial justice and brotherhood to the American Negro Publishers Association, published in *L'Osservatore Romano*, May 27–28, 1946, p. 1. Pius XII was known for quickly removing clerics who preached racial intolerance: "Not long after World War II, in what news reports described as a rare display of public racism, a pastor [in Indianapolis] of the mostly white parish assured a nervous congregation that 'no Negro will ever come to Holy Angels.' (The priest was immediately removed by Pope Pius XII)" (Dan McFeely in the *Indianapolis Star*, June 2, 2003, p. 1B).

Although the recent anti-Pius campaign has been recognized for what it is by competent scholars, scholars working in other aspects of Holocaust studies have accepted it to varying degrees. This has become apparent in otherwise valuable Holocaust reference books, collections, and encyclopedias. Even renowned authorities such as Gerald Reitlinger, Léon Poliakov, Raul Hilberg, Lucy Dawidowicz, Eli Wiesel, and Leni Yahill have demonstrated superficial knowledge of Pius XII's wartime record.

Examples include *The World Reacts to the Holocaust*, edited by David S. Wyman (Baltimore: Johns Hopkins University, 1996); *The Holocaust and History: The Known, the Unknown, the Disputed, and the Reexamined*, edited by Michael Berenbaum and Abraham J. Peck (Washington: United States Holocaust Museum, 1998); *Holocaust Scholars Write to the Vatican*, edited by Harry James Cargas (Westport: Greenwood, 1998); *The Holocaust and the Christian World: Reflections on the Past, Challenges for the Future*, edited by Carol Rittner, Stephen D. Smith, and Irena Steinfeldt (New York: Continuum, 2000); *The Vatican and the Holocaust*, edited by Randolph L. Braham (New York: Columbia University, 2000); *The Columbia Guide to the Holocaust* by Donald Niewyk and Francis Nicosia (New York: Columbia University, 2000); *Remembering for the Future: The Holocaust in an Age of Genocide*, 3 volumes, edited by Elisabeth Maxwell and John K. Roth (New York: Palgrave, 2001); *Hitler and the Holocaust* by Robert Wistrich (New York: Modern Library, 2001); *Essays on Hitler's Europe* by Istvan Deak (Lincoln: University of Nebraska, 2001); *Ethics in the Shadow of the Holocaust*, edited by Judith Banki and John Pawlikowski (Kansas City: Sheed and Ward, 2002); and *Christian Responses to the Holocaust: Moral and Ethical Issues*, edited by Donald Dietrich (Syracuse: Syracuse University, 2003).

Even the highly acclaimed *Holocaust Encyclopedia* (New Haven: Yale, 2001), edited by Walter Laqueur, repeats several anti-Pius XII myths. Worse yet, in its recommended reading list, the *Encyclopedia* lists Rolf Hochhuth's *The Deputy*, Saul Friedlander's *Pius XII and the Third Reich*, John Morley's *Vatican Diplomacy and the Jews During the Holocaust, 1939–1943*, and John Cornwell's *Hitler's Pope.*

Though European scholars have usually avoided extremism, they have their share of antipapalism as well. Among them are *Les silences de Pie XII* by Léon Papeleux (Brussels: Vokaer, 1980); George Denzler's two books, *Die Kirchen im Dritten Reich: Christen und Nazis Hand in Hand?* (Frankfurt am Main: Fischer Taschenbuch, 1984) and *Widerstand oder Anpassung?: Katholische Kirche und Drittes Reich* (Munich: Piper, 1984); and *L'Eglise catholique face au fascisme et au nazisme: les outrages à la vérité* by Henri Fabre (Brussels: Espaces et liberties, 1994).

For critiques of the mentality which drives the antipapal phenomena—especially as it relates to Pius XII—see "Nazis and Christians" by Beate Ruhm von Oppen, *World Politics* 21 (1969), pp. 392–424; "In Defense of Pius XII" by Kenneth L. Woodward, *Newsweek*, March 30, 1998, p. 35; Michael Novak's "Pius XII as Scapegoat," *First Things*, August–September 2000, pp. 20–22; "The Defamation of Pius XII" by James Kurth, *Modern Age*, Spring 2002, pp. 283–287; and especially "The Pope Pius XII Controversy" by Kenneth D. Whitehead, *Political Science Reviewer* 31 (2002), pp. 283–287—one of the finest essays ever to appear on the subject.

Philip Jenkins's *The New Anti-Catholicism: The Last Acceptable Prejudice* (New York: Oxford University, 2003) contains a chapter on "Black Legends" (pp. 177–206) in which he analyzes the scurrilous campaign against Pius XII. On this issue, see also *Christianity on Trial: Arguments Against Anti-Religious Bigotry* by Vincent Carroll and David Shiflett (San Francisco: Encounter, 2002), pp. 112–138. "Italian Newspaper Misleading in Accusing Church of Complicity with Nazism," Zenit News Agency, March 23, 2003, reveals how certain writers have blatantly misrepresented the latest revelations from the Vatican archives—a tactic characteristic of anti-Catholic polemicists.

j. The Jewish-Catholic Study Group, 1999–2002.

In the fall of 1999, the Vatican agreed to sponsor a six-member study group, consisting of three Jewish and three Catholic scholars, who were to review the eleven-volume *Actes et Documents* and report on their findings, particularly in regard to Pius XII's conduct during the Holocaust.

Unfortunately, two years later, the group collapsed without completing the project. At the time the panel disbanded in late 2001, several of its members were caught making antipapal comments and making imperious demands to examine more Vatican archives. The mandate of the panel was never to gain premature access to the Vatican's archives—which take years to catalogue—but to review the abundance of wartime material the Holy See has already made available and issue a final report on their findings. Instead of doing so, the panel issued a "preliminary" report with forty-seven questions that revealed they had never actually studied the primary documents made available to them. Worse, the panel leaked the forty-seven questions to the media before the Vatican could respond to them.

For a description of the rise and fall of the panel, including statements written by its members (some of which are quite self-serving), see *Catholic International: The Documentary Window on the World*, May 2002, pp. 1–99; but also note the response of Sister Margherita Marchione, "Pope Pius XII and the Media," *Catholic International*, November 2002, pp. 107–108. The panel's forty-seven questions can be found in *Origins*, November 9, 2000, pp. 342–351. For scholarly critiques of the panel by two of Germany's leading historians, see Konrad Repgen's "Im Haus des Geheimarchivs sind viele Wohnungen. Neue Hintergründe eines Zerwürfnisses: Zum Scheitern der jüdisch-katholischen Historikerkommission über die Rolle von Papst Pius

XII," *Frankfurter Allgemeine Zeitung*, September 27, 2001, and Walter Brandmüller's "Ein neuer Streit um Pius XII," *Die Neue Ordnung*, October 2001, pp. 371–381.

The Vatican's official reply appeared in *L'Osservatore Romano*, August 8, 2001, p. 5; see also the earlier English version, "Declaration by Pius XII Relator on Historians' Panel 'Not Completed the Task Entrusted to Them,'" and the related "Pius XII Postulator Assails 'Distorted' News Leaks; Jesuit Cites 'Irresponsible Behavior' by Some Historians," both published by the Zenit News Agency on July 26, 2001. See as well "Cardinal Says Mistrust, Polemics Doomed Holocaust Commission," Zenit News Agency, August 24, 2001, and "Historian's Accusations Against Wartime Holy See Are Refuted: Relator of Pius XII's Cause Answers Professor Michael Marrus," Zenit News Agency, November 21, 2002.

The most complete coverage of the panel appeared in *Inside the Vatican*. See especially: "Pius XII's Jury," January 2000, pp. 47–51; "Judging Pius XII," February 2000, pp. 5 and 61–67; "We Have Just a Few Questions—47, to be Precise," November 2000, pp. 20–23; "Catholic-Jewish Panel Folds: What Next?" October 2001, pp. 28–39; "A Difficult Winter," February 2002, pp. 53–55; "The Search for Real Dialogue," March 2002, pp. 33–37; and "The Pius Debate—The Big American Shootout," May 2002, pp. 34–49. See also Dimitri Cavalli's analysis, "The Commission that Couldn't Shoot Straight," *New Oxford Review*, July–August 2002, pp. 33–39, and John S. Conway's "How Not to Deal with History," *American Jewish Congress Monthly*, November/December 2001, pp. 9–13.

PART 5: MAJOR DEFENDERS

1. Edgar Alexander, *Hitler and the Pope: Pius XII and the Jews* (New York: Thomas Nelson and Sons, 1964).

One of the earliest and most committed opponents of the Nazis, Edgar Alexander, was a German Catholic émigré who published this book in the wake of the controversy aroused by Rolf Hochhuth's play *The Deputy*. In 1933, when Hitler first came to power, Alexander came into conflict with the Nazi regime by openly and vigorously assailing it in the Catholic press. A close collaborator and confidant of Father Friedrich Muckermann, the famed Jesuit anti-Nazi polemicist, Alexander was soon forced into exile. In 1937, he published *Der Mythus Hitler* (Zürich: Europa, 1937), which became a European bestseller.

Alexander was one of the first to challenge Hochhuth, writing a rebuttal in *America*, October 12, 1963, pp. 416–423. After it appeared, the producer of Hochhuth's play on Broadway reacted by calling Alexander an "ex-Nazi."

(Aside from being untrue—Alexander never joined the Nazi Party and was one of the first Germans to oppose Hitler openly—the charge was especially ironic given that Hochhuth himself was a former member of the Hitler Youth.) "Those better informed of the true situation," wrote Father Robert Graham, "such as the late Dr. Franz L. Neumann, author of [the anti-Nazi classic] *Behemoth*, gave a more correct estimate of his worth. His praise of Alexander's essay on 'Church and Society in Germany' [in *Church and Society*, edited by Joseph N. Moody (New York: Arts, 1953)] reflects his esteem and admiration for a fellow anti-Nazi" (*America*, June 27, 1964).

2. Father Pierre Blet, S.J., *Pius XII and the Second World War According to the Archives of the Vatican* (Mahwah: Paulist, 1999).

When John Paul II was asked why he believed Pius XII was "a great pope," he replied: "One must read Fr. Blet" (Catholic World News Service, March 23, 1998). Blet is the last surviving member of the four Jesuits who edited the *Actes et Documents*. In 1997, realizing the necessity of summarizing this exhaustive collection of source material for a general audience, Blet published in French the book since translated into English as *Pius XII and the Second World War*.

A longtime professor of modern history at Rome's Jesuit-run Gregorian University, Blet has also published a number of outstanding essays on Pius XII, of which the most important are his decisive refutation of Saul Friedlander's *Pius XII and the Third Reich* in *La Civiltà Cattolica* 1965, volume 2, pp. 251–258; and his more recent article, "La leggenda alla prova degli archivi. Le riccorenti accuse contro Pio XII," *Civiltà Cattolica* 1998, volume 1, pp. 531–541, translated as "Was there a Culpable Silence with Regard to the Holocaust?" in *Inside the Vatican*, May 1998, pp. 52–57. (The latter is particularly important as it answers the often-heard complaint that the Vatican is hiding incriminating documents in its archives.)

After John Cornwell's *Hitler's Pope* appeared in the fall of 1999, Blet held a news conference at which he argued that the book was "without historical value" (*Catholic World News*, October 8, 1999). In an interview a month earlier, he had already referred to *Hitler's Pope* as "science fiction" (Zenit News Agency, September 7, 1999). For additional insights into Blet's thinking, see "Pius XI is Victim of Calumny, Scholar Says," *Catholic World News Service*, October 31, 1997, and the extensive interview "Read Father Blet's Book on Pius XII" in *30 Days*, April 1998, pp. 38–43.

Blet's article "Pio XII, il Terzo 'Reich' e gli ebrei" (*Civiltà Cattolica* 2002, volume 3, pp. 117–131) deals with the recent historical scholarship on Pius XII and the Jews. On March 5, 2001, the *Frankfurter Allgemeine Zeitung* published an appreciation of Blet's contribution to Pius XII studies by Konrad Repgen, which has been translated by *L'Osservatore Romano*, weekly English edition, August 29, 2001, p. 10.

Having examined the Vatican's wartime archives, Blet is convinced that their eventual release will vindicate Pius XII ("Archives Will Show that Church Helped the Jews, Says Historian," Zenit News Agency, October 31, 2001). Central to Blet's scholarship is the firm belief that the diplomatic strategy of Pius XII, together with his principled wartime pronouncements, succeeded at reducing the number of the war's victims and alleviating their sufferings. "To affirm that the pope himself or some other person in his place might have been able to do more," concludes Blet, "is to depart from the field of history in order to venture into the undergrowth of suppositions and dreams" (*Pius XII and the Second World War*, p. 289).

3. The Works of Michael Burleigh

Burleigh is emerging as one of the finest contemporary historians of the Third Reich. On the key subject of Pope Pius XII, Burleigh is unequivocal in his support. In "Hitler's Pope Was Really a Friend of the Jews" (*Times* of London, July 28, 2002, p. 7), he refutes John Cornwell, whose *Hitler's Pope* had been serialized in the same paper three years earlier. He later added "Pius XII: The Defense," *BBC History*, October, 2002, pp. 42–45, and "Vile Tales of the Vatican," *Times*, October 6, 2002, p. 8, a rebuttal of Daniel Goldhagen's *A Moral Reckoning*.

Burleigh's full-length study, *The Third Reich: A New History* (New York: Hill and Wang, 2000), is a fine modern work on Hitler's dictatorship. An authority on the Nazi euthanasia campaign, Burleigh has also written *Death and Deliverance: 'Euthanasia' in Germany, 1900–1945* (Cambridge: Cambridge University, 1994). See also Burleigh's *Ethics and Extermination: Reflections on Nazi Genocide* (Cambridge: Cambridge University, 1997), and two works he edited: *The Racial State: Germany, 1933–1945* (Cambridge: Cambridge University, 1991), and *Confronting the Nazi Past: New Debates on Modern German History* (New York: St. Martin's, 1996).

4. The Works of Owen Chadwick

The longtime Regius Professor of Modern History at Cambridge, Chadwick is a prolific author on nearly all aspects of Church history. His essay "Weizsäcker, the Vatican and the Jews of Rome," published in the *Journal of Ecclesiastical History*, April 1977, pp. 179–199, is the definitive analysis of the Nazi roundup of Rome's Jews and the Vatican's reaction. His acclaimed *Britain and the Vatican During the Second World War* (Cambridge: Cambridge University, 1986) is an expert examination of Vatican policy during World War II from British diplomatic sources.

Chadwick has also published many essays and reviews on Pius XII for the *Tablet*, among the best of which are: "Pius XII: The Legends and the Truth" (March 28, 1998, pp. 400–401), a defense of the pope's rescue strategy during the seizure of Rome's Jews; "Was Pius XII 'Hitler's Pope'?" (September 25, 1999, pp. 1284–1285), an effective rebuttal to John Cornwell; and "Pius XII's Terrifying Dilemma: Put Yourself in His Shoes" (June 30, 2001, pp. 950–951), a devastating critique of Susan Zuccotti's *Under His Very Windows*. See also "Moral Judgement in the Historian: British Documents on Pope Pius XII during the War 1940–1944," *Römische Quartalsschrift* 80 (1985), pp. 141–147.

For an astute survey, one should read Chadwick's *A History of Christianity* (New York: St. Martin's, 1995). Also essential is his *A History of the Popes, 1830–1914* (Oxford: Clarendon, 1998). *The Secularization of the European Mind in the 19th Century* (Cambridge: Cambridge University, 1975) is Chadwick's Gifford Lectures on the anti-Christian cultural forces that led to the outbreak of totalitarianism. *The Christian Church in the Cold War* (London: Allen Lane, 1992) relates the struggle between Christianity and communism, and *Catholicism and History: The Opening of the Vatican Archives* (Cambridge: Cambridge University, 1978) explains the much-maligned Vatican archival policy.

Though not uncritical of certain aspects of Vatican diplomacy, Chadwick holds a generally supportive opinion of Pius XII. In explaining the persistence of the anti-Pacelli canards, Chadwick writes, "In this case legends grew unaided because there was a real failure on the part of many churchmen, because something horribly wrong really happened; and they also grew because propaganda fostered them—propaganda in the first instance by Stalin's men in the Cold War, when the Vatican appeared to be part of the American anti-Communist alliance and Stalin wished to shatter the pope's reputation. . . . Stalin had a political need to make this pope contemptible. So the fables came. It is still believed by many people that Pope Pius XII was a friend of the Nazis, or that he said nothing at all against racial murder during the war, or that he was so frightened for his own skin or his own palace that he was too timid to say anything whatever, or that he arranged Vatican money to help monsters like Eichmann to escape to South America. . . . [But] you do not correct the legends. You cannot even try. So no one will believe you if you do. History is much too complex to be painted with a brush that daubs a few crude red or purple lines. The legends are a daub, you cannot refute them with a different daub, they cannot be covered up by shovelling on whitewash. The only thing that corrects them is more history, and history takes time, too long a time for people's comfort, but it is the nature of history that it is only little by little that the truth about the past is found" ("Pius XII: The Legends and the Truth," *Tablet*, March 28, 1998, pp. 400–401).

5. The Works of John S. Conway

Considered one of the deans of Church historians, John S. Conway taught history for many years at the University of British Columbia. His interest in the German churches was aroused by meeting with survivors of the church struggle (*Kirchenkampf*) against the Nazis and by reading the works of Dietrich Bonhoeffer. This led to an examination of the Catholic Church and the Vatican during these years and to the study of Christian-Jewish relations and modern theology. After Rolf Hochhuth's notorious play *The Deputy* appeared in 1963, Conway was among the first historians to demolish its thesis (*Review of Politics*, January 1965, pp. 105–131; reprinted in *The Papacy and Totalitarianism Between the Two World Wars*, pp. 79–108).

In 1966, he published a series of important articles, "How Many Divisions? The Pope and the Second World War" in the *Times Literary Supplement*, reprinted in *Essays and Reviews from the Times Literary Supplement* (London: TLS, 1966), pp. 217–230. Conway's subsequent book was *The Nazi Persecution of the Churches* (New York: Basic, 1968), which was reissued in 1997 by Regent College in Vancouver.

Important essays by Conway include: "Pope Pius XII and the German Church—an Unpublished Gestapo Report" in the *Canadian Journal of History* 1 (1966), pp. 72–83, on the pontiff's efforts to coordinate a unified episcopal response to Nazi aggression; "An Unsuccessful Encounter: The Meeting Between Pope Pius XII and Ribbentrop" in *Canadian Historical Association Report for 1968*, pp. 103–116, on the pontiff's confrontational meeting with the Nazi foreign minister; "The Vatican, Great Britain and Relations with Germany, 1938–40" in *Historical Journal* 16 (1973), pp. 147–167; "Myron Taylor's Mission to the Vatican, 1940–1950" in *Church History*, March 1975, pp. 1–15; and "A German National Reich Church and American War Propaganda," *Catholic Historical Review*, July 1976, pp. 469–470.

Also see Conway's "The Churches, the Slovak State and the Jews 1939–1945" in *Slavonic and East European Review*, January 1974, pp. 85–112; and especially "Catholicism and the Jews during the Nazi Period and After" in *Judaism and Christianity Under the Impact of National Socialism*, edited by Otto Dov Kulka and Paul R. Mendes-Flohr (Jerusalem: Historical Society of Israel and Zalman Zhazar Center for Jewish History, 1987), pp. 435–451. Also significant are Conway's "Records and Documents of the Holy See Relating to the Second World War," *Yad Vashem Studies* 15 (1983), pp. 327–345; "The Vatican, Germany and the Holocaust" in *Papal Diplomacy in the Modern Age*, edited by Peter C. Kent and John F. Pollard (Westport: Praeger, 1994), pp. 105–120; and "The Vatican and the Holocaust—a Reappraisal" in *Miscellenea Historiae Ecclesiasticae* 9 (1984), pp. 475–489.

Conway has also contributed a major essay on the Catholic Church during the Nazi era to *The Holocaust Encyclopedia*, pp. 111–114. His essay, "How

Not to Deal with History," *American Jewish Congress Monthly*, November/December 2001, pp. 9–13, is an incisive critique of historians who put agendas in front of scholarly objectivity.

Finally, for Conway's critiques of major works on Pius XII, see his reviews of Carlo Falconi's *The Silence of Pius XII* (*Times Literary Supplement*, October 1970, pp. 1017–1018); Anthony Rhodes's *The Vatican in the Age of the Dictators* (*Times Literary Supplement*, June 1973, p. 693); John Morley's *Vatican Diplomacy and the Jews During the Holocaust* (*Catholic Historical Review*, January 1983, pp. 75–77); Owen Chadwick's *Britain and the Vatican During the Second World War* (*Journal of Modern History*, June 1989, pp. 372–374); John Cornwell's *Hitler's Pope* (*Historian*, Spring 2001, pp. 446–447); R.A. Braham's *The Vatican and the Holocaust* (*Church History*, March 2002, p. 210); Michael Feldkamp's *Pius XII. und Deutschland* (*Catholic Historical Review*, July 2002, pp. 611–614); and Daniel Goldhagen's *A Moral Reckoning* (*American Jewish Congress Monthly*, November–December 2002, pp. 19–20).

6. The Writings of Victor Conzemius

Longtime professor of history at the University of Lucerne Victor Conzemius is one of the most accomplished historians of the Second World War. A principled and exacting supporter of Pius XII, his articles and books are among the finest extant on the Catholic Church, Germany, and the Holocaust.

From the beginning of the attack on Pius, Conzemius rejected the campaign as spurious. Among his best writings are: "Pius XII and Nazi Germany in Historical Perspective," published in *Historical Studies: Papers Read before the Irish Conference of Historians, VII* (London: Routledge, 1969), pp. 97–124; "German Catholics and the Nazi Regime," *Irish Ecclesiastical Record* 103 (1967), pp. 326–335; "Eglises chrétiennes et totalitarianisme national-socialiste," *Revue d'histoire ecclésiastique* 63 (1968), pp. 447–503 and 868–948.

Also see his "Le Concordat du 20 Juilliet 1933 entre le Saint Siège et l'Allemagne. Esquisse d'un bilan de la recherche historique" in *Archivum Histoiriae Pontificiae* 15 (1977), pp. 333–362; "L'antisémitisme autrichien au XIXème et au XXème siècle" in *De l'antijudaisme antique à l'antisémitisme contemporain* (Lille: V. Nildprowetsky, 1979), pp. 189–208; and "Zwischen Anpassung und Widerstand. Die Christen und der Nationalsozialismus" in *Communio* 23 (1994), pp. 483–502. When *Hitler's Pope* appeared, Conzemius refuted it in the French journal *Histoire du Christianisme*, May 2001, pp. 72–77. He has also edited a major work on Swiss Catholicism during the Nazi era, *Schweizer Katholizismus 1933–1945* (Zürich: NZZ, 2001), which includes an important essay on Filippo Bernardini, the apostolic nuncio in Berne during the war: "Die Berner Nuntiatur" by U. Fink, pp. 553–597.

7. David G. Dalin, "Pius XII and the Jews," *Weekly Standard*, February 26, 2001, pp. 31–39.

Every so often an essay or book on a controversial issue changes the nature of the way people approach it. Rabbi and historian David Dalin accomplished that feat when he published this 5,000-word essay in the *Weekly Standard*. After it appeared, it became one of the most talked-about statements ever published on Pius XII: widely praised, challenged, and reprinted throughout the world.

Time and again, Dalin found that the anti-Pius polemicists were historically uninformed, engaged in speculation, and omitted key facts. This was especially true of the disgruntled Catholics whom Dalin rightly criticized for exploiting the tragedy of the Jewish people to foster their own antipapal agenda: "Almost none of the recent books about Pius XII and the Holocaust is actually about Pius XII and the Holocaust. Their real topic proves to be an intra-Catholic argument about the direction of the Church today, with the Holocaust simply the biggest club available for liberal Catholics to use against traditionalists."

Consequently, Dalin offered some heartfelt advice to his own Jewish community: "A theological debate about the future of the papacy is obviously something in which non-Catholics should not involve themselves too deeply. But Jews, whatever their feelings about the Catholic Church, have a duty to reject any attempt to usurp the Holocaust and use it for partisan purposes in such a debate—particularly when the attempt disparages the testimony of Holocaust survivors and thins out, by spreading to inappropriate figures, the condemnation that belongs to Hitler and the Nazis." Dalin insisted: "A true account of Pius XII would arrive, I believe, at exactly the opposite to Cornwell's conclusion: Pius XII was not Hitler's pope, but the closest Jews had come to having a papal supporter—and at the moment when it mattered most." And he concluded that Pius XII was "genuinely and profoundly, a righteous gentile."

Reaction to Dalin's piece was widespread and intense. Kevin Madigan replied bitterly with two attacks: "Judging Pius XII," *Christian Century*, March 14, 2001, pp. 6–7, and "What the Vatican Knew About the Holocaust, and When," *Commentary*, October 2001, pp. 43–52. Carol Rittner and John K. Roth also assailed Dalin in the introduction to *Pope Pius XII and the Holocaust* (New York: Continuum, pp. 1–13), especially pages 4–7.

But Judith Shulevitz of the *New York Times* wrote a fascinating piece, "The Case of Pius XII," which, though repeating some of the usual errors about Pius, inched her paper away from the anti-Pius campaign and acknowledged Dalin's principal point—namely, that Pius XII and his Catholic followers "did more than most to shelter Jews" (*New York Times* book review section, April 8, 2001, p. 31).

More favorable reaction followed, with many pointing to Dalin's piece as a landmark essay. See "Defenders of Pope Pius XII Becoming More Vocal" by Russell Shaw, *Our Sunday Visitor*, April 29, 2001, p. 3; "Hitler's Pope or the Good Samaritan?" by David Reinhard in *Oregonian*, June 28, 2001; *Triumph: The Power and Glory of the Catholic Church* by H.W. Crocker III (Roseville: Forum, 2001), pp. 401–405; "Pius the Hero" by John Laughland, *Spectator*, July 20, 2002, pp. 16–17; and "Hitler's Pope was Really a Friend of the Jews" by Michael Burleigh, *Times* of London, July 28, 2002, p. 7.

Rabbi Dalin is currently at work on a book comparing Jewish-Catholic relations under Pius XII and John Paul II. For further examples of Dalin's historical views, see his lecture, "A Righteous Gentile: Pope Pius XII and the Jews," available on the Catholic League's website, www.catholicleague.org; his review, "A Friend of the Jews," *First Things*, August–September 2002, pp. 66–71; and his refutations of David Kertzer ("Popes and Jews: Truths and Falsehoods in the History of Catholic-Jewish Relations," *Weekly Standard*, November 5, 2001, pp. 36–38) and Daniel Goldhagen ("History as Bigotry: Daniel Goldhagen Slanders the Catholic Church," *Weekly Standard*, February 10, 2003, pp. 38–41).

8. Michael Feldkamp, *Pius XII. und Deutschland* (Göttingen: Vandenhoeck und Ruprecht, 2000).

Feldkamp is part of the new wave of European scholars who are building an impressive body of evidence in favor of the wartime pontiff. Before writing this biography of Pius XII, Feldkamp had already produced numerous works evaluating the Vatican archives and had also authored a number of books on postwar German history, based on his research in the archives of the German Bundestag and Foreign Office. *Pius XII und Deutschland* differs from other studies on Pius XII in that it is not limited to the Nazi-era years 1933 to 1945, but deals with Pacelli's entire life, until his death in 1958. Feldkamp presents much fresh material drawn from French, German, and Italian archives, especially regarding Pacelli's activity in Munich and Berlin when he served as papal nuncio from 1917 to 1929. Pacelli's better-known years as Vatican secretary of state (1930–1939) and pope (1939–1958) are treated in great detail.

From Feldkamp's replies to critics of Pacelli, what emerges is a portrait of Pius XII as a dedicated Christian, principled man of peace, and humane pontiff who fought the evils of his age as much as any world leader, and certainly better than most. For a summary of Feldkamp's views in English, see his address "Eugenio Pacelli: The German Years," *Inside the Vatican*, May 2002, pp. 40–45.

9. The Works of Sir Martin Gilbert

In addition to being the official biographer of Winston Churchill, Martin Gilbert is the author of a three-volume *History of the Twentieth Century* (New York: William Morrow, 1997–1999), as well as separate studies on *The*

First World War (New York: Henry Holt, 1994) and *The Second World War* (New York: Henry Holt, 1991). His works on the Holocaust are indispensable: *The Holocaust: A History of the Jews of Europe During the Second World War* (New York: Henry Holt, 1985); *Auschwitz and the Allies* (New York: Henry Holt, 1981); and *Atlas of the Holocaust* (New York: Macmillan, 1982).

Gilbert documents how Pius XII was one of the first explicitly to condemn Nazi atrocities via Vatican Radio (*The Second World War*, pp. 39–40) and shows the pope's actions on behalf of Jews in both *The Holocaust* (pp. 622–623) and *Never Again* (New York: Universe, 2000, pp. 106–107). His book *The Righteous: The Unsung Heroes of the Holocaust* (New York: Henry Holt, 2003) also honors extraordinary Catholics, under the leadership of Pius XII, who rescued Jews at great peril to themselves and to the Church, throughout Nazi-occupied Europe. The book runs over 500 pages and is massively documented, as even the very secular *Guardian* acknowledged in a highly favorable review of the book ("Heroes of The Holocaust," November 23, 2002).

Overall, Gilbert estimates that the Christian churches may have saved up to half a million Jewish lives during the Holocaust, and that the majority of these were saved by the clergy and laity of the Catholic Church—the dominant religion of Nazi-occupied lands—with the backing of the pope: "Hundreds of thousands of Jews saved by the entire Catholic Church, under the leadership and with the support of Pope Pius XII, would, to my mind, be absolutely correct" (Gilbert, in an interview, "The Untold Story: Catholic Rescuers of Jews," *Inside the Vatican*, August 2003, p. 31).

After the publication of *The Righteous*, Gilbert continued his defense of Pius XII and urged other historians to do the same (see "Historian Sir Martin Gilbert Defends Pius XII," Zenit News Agency, February 20, 2003). One of Gilbert's central points is that Pius XII not only provided guidelines and inspiration to Catholic diplomats and lay rescuers but engaged in rescue efforts himself. In a major address on Christians and the Holocaust delivered at Church House in London, Gilbert declared: "The pope himself . . . gave his personal order on the eve of the German deportation of Jews from Rome to open the sanctuaries of the Vatican City to all Jews who could reach it. . . . As a result of the pope's order and of the Catholic clergy's rapid response in Rome, of Rome's 6,700 Jews, only 1,015 were actually deported. . . . The papal action, which I do not find mentioned in the current 'J'Accuse'-style debates, saved more than 4,000 lives" (quoted in *Common Ground* 1998, number 2, pp. 3–6).

10. The Works of Robert A. Graham, S.J.

Recognized before his death in 1997 as the leading Catholic expert on Vatican diplomacy during the Second World War, Father Graham—a Jesuit who earned a doctorate in political science from the University of Geneva in

1952—first achieved prominence with the publication of his award-winning *Vatican Diplomacy: A Study of Church and State on the International Plane* (Princeton: Princeton University, 1959). Five years later, when Rolf Hochhuth's play *The Deputy* appeared, it was Graham, then an editor at *America* magazine, who took the lead in exposing the play as an exercise in defamation and historical fabrication. From then on, he wrote countless articles and reviews for *America* and *La Civiltà Cattolica* on every aspect of the papacy, the war, and the Holocaust.

All the while he found time to serve as one of the team of four Jesuit scholars who edited *Actes et Documents* of the Holy See relating to the Second World War. Among his most salient articles are:

1. His 1962 review of Gordon Zahn's *German Catholics and Hitler's Wars* (London: Sheed and Ward, 1962) in *America*, April 28, 1962, pp. 145–146.
2. "A Return to Theocracy," a point-by-point refutation of Guenter Lewy's *The Catholic Church and Nazi Germany* in *America*, July 18, 1964, pp. 70–72.
3. "Pius XII and the Nazis: An Analysis of the Latest Charges that the Pope was a 'Friend' of the Axis," *America*, December 5, 1964, pp. 742–743.
4. "The Latest Charges Against Pius XII," his critique of Saul Friedlander's *Pius XII and the Third Reich* in *America*, May 21, 1966, pp. 733–736.
5. "Author Questions Pope Pius XII's Vatican Diplomacy," a review of Carlo Falconi's *The Silence of Pius XII* in the *Pilot* (of Boston), October 31, 1970.
6. "La Strana condotta di E. von Weizsäcker ambasciatore del Reich in Vaticano" in *La Civiltà Cattolica* 1970, volume 2, pp. 455–71, a description of the Nazi roundup of Rome's Jews and the Holy See's forceful opposition to it.
7. "La rappresaglia nazista alle Fosse Ardeatine: p. Pfeiffer, messaggero della carità di Pio XII" in *La Civiltà Cattolica* 1973, volume 4, pp. 467–474, the definitive article on Pius XII's innocence regarding the Ardeatine Caves massacre of over 300 Italian citizens in 1944 (a necessary rebuttal, as Pius XII was falsely accused of being involved in this massacre by Robert Katz in his 1967 book, *Death in Rome*, as well as a film based on the book).
8. "Il vaticanista falsario: L'incredibile successo di Virgilio Scattolini" in *La Civiltà Cattolica* 1973, volume 3, pp. 467–478, an exposé of the fabrications of Virgilio Scattolini, who made up stories about the Vatican's supposed assistance to Nazi agents, fooling American intelligence agents at the time and misleading the following generation of historians.
9. "La Radio Vaticana tra Londra e Berlino: Un Dossier della Guerra delle Onde, 1940–1941" in *La Civiltà Cattolica* 1976, volume 1, pp. 132–150,

on Vatican Radio's outspoken condemnations of Nazi atrocities at the beginning of the war and the reprisals they provoked.

10. "The Right to Kill in the Third Reich," *Catholic Historical Review*, January 1976, pp. 56–76, a survey of the Nazi euthanasia program, showing how Pope Pius XII was the first to condemn it and how his condemnation inspired Germany's bishops to strongly oppose it.

11. "L'enciclica Summi Pontificatus e i belligeranti nel 1939," *Civiltà Cattolica* 1984, volume 4, pp. 137–151, on the dramatic impact of Pius XII's anti-Nazi encyclical, *Summi Pontificatus.*

12. "Spie naziste attorno al Vaticano durante la seconda guerra mondiale," *Civiltà Cattolica* 1970, volume 1, pp. 21–31, on Nazi espionage against the Holy See.

13. "Voleva Hitler allontanare da Roma Pio XII?" *Civiltà Cattolica* 1972, volume 1, pp. 319–327 and pp. 454–461, and "I Progetti di Hitler per la Chiesa et l'Atteggiamento di Pio XII," *Civiltà Cattolica* 1987, volume 3, pp. 209–221—two essays on the intense hostilities between the pope and Hitler.

14. "Il Vaticano e gli ebrei profughi in Italia durante la guerra," *Civiltà Cattolica* 1987, volume 1, pp. 429–443, on the Vatican's intervention for Jews in wartime Italy.

15. "La Santa Sede e la difesa degli ebrei durante la seconda guerra mondiale," *Civiltà Cattolica* 1990, volume 3, pp. 209–226, on the Holy See's concern and protection of persecuted Jews throughout Nazi-occupied Europe.

16. Of special importance are Graham's two critiques of John Morley's *Vatican Diplomacy and the Jews During the Holocaust: 1939–1943*, published in *America* (August 9, 1980) and the *Long Island Catholic* (August 14, 1980), and his two letters in the *Tablet*, February 4 and March 11, 1995, refuting an egregious BBC documentary on Pius XII.

17. Also indispensable are Graham's refutations of the claim that Pius XII knowingly assisted the "ratline" escape of Nazi war criminals. See especially, "Did the Vatican Help Nazi War Criminals to Escape?" *30 Days*, July–August 1989, pp. 67–71, and Graham's critique of Mark Aarons and John Loftus's lurid *Unholy Trinity*: "Historian Says Book on Nazi Smuggling Based on False Reports" by Agostino Bono, *Catholic News Service*, January 30, 1992.

Of related interest is the earlier article, "U.S. Blessed with OSS Spy in Vatican; Our Spy in the Vatican," *Washington Post*, August 3, 1980, p. A1, where Graham exposes the wholesale fabrications used to "prove" a secret German-Vatican link during the war. Graham's fellow Jesuit, Father Vincent Lapomarda, dismissed *Unholy Trinity* in the *Catholic Historical Review*, October 1992, pp. 675–677, and Matteo Sanfilippo wrote a comprehensive rebuttal of such conspiracy-minded books, "Ratlines and Unholy Trinities: A Review-Essay on Recent Literature Concerning Nazi Collaborators Smuggling Operations out of Italy," available at www.vaticanfiles.net/sanfilippo_ratlines.htm.

On February 14, 1992, the Vatican published a statement, "Declaration on Nazi Refugees After World War II," which used many of Graham's findings to rebut the accusations of Vatican "assistance" to Nazi war criminals. The recent book by Uki Goni, *The Real Odessa* (London: Granta, 2002), which is even more lurid than the Aarons and Loftus book in its claims about Pius XII and the "ratline," would surely have drawn a sharp rebuke from Graham, were he alive to refute it. (See the critical review of Goni's book by Austen Ivereigh in the *Tablet*, April 6, 2002, p. 13; and the comments by Argentine Church historian Nestor Auza in the *Tablet*, March 29, 2003, stating that supposed documents "proving" Goni's allegations "simply do not exist.") For an excellent article on this subject that uses many of Graham's insights, see "Fuite des criminels nazis: le dossier noir du Vatican?" by Jean-Yves Riou, *Histoire du Christianisme*, July 2002, pp. 12–17.

In 1975, many of Graham's best essays in Italian appeared as *Il Vaticano e il Nazismo* (Rome: Cinque Lune, 1975). His works in English include *The Pope and Poland in World War Two* (London: Veritas, 1968); "Pius XII's Defense of Jews and Others" in *Pius XII and the Holocaust* (Milwaukee: Catholic League for Religious and Civil Rights, 1988); *The Vatican and Communism During World War II* (San Francisco: Ignatius, 1996); and *Nothing Sacred: Nazi Espionage Against the Vatican, 1939–1945* (London: Frank Cass, 1997), coauthored with David Alvarez. On this issue, also see Graham's article, "Foreign Intelligence and the Vatican," *Catholic World Report*, March 1992, pp. 48–53.

Graham's lectures on Pius XII, "The Good Samaritan in World War II" and "Pius XII: Years of Praise, Years of Blame" were reprinted in supplements to the *Catholic League Newsletter*, May and December 1989. On the same theme, see Graham's essays, "The Holy See and the Victims of the War," *Osservatore Romano*, June 13, 1974, pp. 6–9, and "The Human Being in the Tragic Tornado of War Necessities," *Osservatore Romano*, February 12, 1976, pp. 6–9. Graham's "Relations of Pius XII and the Catholic Community with Jewish Organizations" (*The Italian Refuge: Rescue of Jews During the Holocaust*, edited by Ivo Herzer [Washington: Catholic University, 1989], pp. 231–253), is the best essay on the subject.

Father Graham also wrote a regular column for *Columbia* magazine. Highly recommended are: "Will the Real Sister Pascalina Please Step Forward" (November 1983, p. 9), a corrective to the myths circulating about Pius XII's lifelong housekeeper; "A Valiant Lady's Struggle on a Matter of Honor" (December 1983, p. 6) on Elena Rossignani, the niece of Pius XII who brought a successful lawsuit against the film *Massacre in Rome*; "Another Phony Chapter on 'Pius and the Nazis'" (May 1984, p. 4), exposing the spurious charge that Pius XII assisted Nazi war criminals; and "Again, Potshots at a Former Pope" (March 1987, p. 3), critiquing an antipapal Italian documentary. At his death, Graham left behind an important manuscript, "Church, Shoah, and Anti-Semitism," which was eventually published in Margherita Marchione's *Pope Pius XII: Architect for Peace* (Mahwah: Paulist, 2000), pp. 157-177.

Many tributes to Graham appeared after his death, of which the best are "Robert A. Graham, S.J." by Thomas J. Reese in *Catholic Historical Review*, April 1977, pp. 361-363; "Robert Graham," *Economist*, February 22, 1997; "Robert Graham, 84, Priest Defended Wartime Pope," *New York Times*, February 17, 1997; "Gatekeeper of the Vatican's War Records" by Eugene Fisher in *National Catholic Register*, March 16-22, 1997; and "Robert Graham, S.J." by Kevin M. Doyle in *First Things*, June/July 1997, pp. 16-17.

11. The Works of Peter Hoffmann

Peter Hoffmann is the leading authority on the German resistance against Hitler. His classic work on the subject is *The History of the German Resistance 1933–1945* (third edition Montreal: McGill-Queen's University, 1996). The churches, according to Hoffmann, "were not entirely immune" to the conformism of the rest of the society in the early days of Hitler's government, but they were "the only organizations to produce some form of a popular movement against the Nazi regime." In other words, there could and should have been more anti-Nazi resistance within the Third Reich, but what resistance existed came primarily from the churches, both Catholic and Evangelical.

Hoffmann's *Stauffenberg: A Family History, 1905–1944* (Cambridge: Cambridge University, 1995) is a look at the lives and personalities of the three Stauffenberg brothers, Berthold, Alexander, and especially Claus. According to Hoffmann, Claus von Stauffenberg's crucial role in the unsuccessful plot to overthrow Hitler on July 20, 1944—for which he was arrested and executed—was directly attributable to his Catholic faith. Indeed, there is evidence in Stauffenberg's private papers that his anti-Nazi convictions were strengthened and crystallized by Pius XI's 1937 encyclical, *Mit brennender Sorge*.

Hoffmann has written extensively on Pius XII's involvement in the plots to overthrow Hitler and has published an essay on how Angelo Roncalli (the future John XXIII) carried out rescue efforts on behalf of Jews while serving as a papal diplomat. See "Peace through Coup d'Etat: The Foreign Contacts of the German Resistance 1933–1944," *Central European History* 19 (1986), pp. 3–44; "The Question of Western Allied Cooperation with the German Anti-Nazi Conspiracy, 1938–1944," *Historical Journal* 34 (1991), pp. 437–464; and "Roncalli in the Second World War: Peace Initiatives, the Greek Famine and the Persecution of the Jews," *Journal of Ecclesiastical History* 40 (1989), pp. 74–99.

12. The Works of Father John Jay Hughes

A Church historian, John Jay Hughes has become a leading American authority on Pius XII, German Catholicism, and the Holocaust. Though by no means uncritical of the Church, Hughes has little toleration for those who engage in ahistorical or defamatory attacks. Of Pius XII, he has written: "I regard the view, widely accepted in this country, that he was co-responsible for the Holocaust as one of the major falsifications of post-WWII historiography." Essays and reviews by Hughes that counter this myth include:

1. "The Pope's 'Pact with Hitler': Betrayal or Self-Defense?" *Journal of Church and State* 17 (1975), pp. 63–80, the best modern analysis, based on primary sources, of the reasons and justification for the 1933 concordat, refuting critics of it.
2. "The Silence of Pius XII," *Jewish Quarterly Review*, July 1972, pp. 80–85, Hughes's evisceration of Carlo Falconi's book of the same name.
3. Hughes's negative judgment of Klaus Scholder's influential *The Churches and the Third Reich* (Philadelphia: Fortress, 1988) in *American Historical Review*, December 1978, pp. 286–287.
4. Reviews of books by Owen Chadwick (*Britain and the Vatican During the Second World War*) and Pierre Blet (*Pius XII and the Second World War*) in *Catholic Historical Review*, January 1988, pp. 97–98, and April 1999, pp. 268–270, respectively.
5. "Pope Pius XII is Unfairly Criticized" and a critique of Garry Wills's *Papal Sin*, both appearing on the op-ed page of the St. Louis *Post-Dispatch*, March 25, 1998, and August 27, 2000.
6. "Hitler's Pope?" a highly favorable review of Ronald J. Rychlak's *Hitler, the War, and the Pope* for *First Things*, October 2000, pp. 66–71.
7. "Something Shameful," *Inside the Vatican*, December 2000, pp. 48–52, a strong rebuttal to Michael Phayer's *The Catholic Church and the Holocaust, 1930–1965*.
8. "The Vatican Archives: What's the Problem?" *Inside the Vatican*, May 2002, pp. 46–49, refuting charges of a Vatican cover-up.
9. "Papaphobia," *America*, July 15, 2002, p. 23, Hughes's review of Justus George Lawler's *Popes and Politics: Reform, Resentment, and the Holocaust*.
10. Hughes's devastating analysis of Beth A. Griech-Polelle's biography, *Bishop von Galen: German Catholicism and National Socialism* (New Haven: Yale University, 2002), which attempts to disparage the record of the great anti-Nazi bishop. See "Seriously Deficient," *Inside the Vatican*, February 2003, pp. 46–48, and the slightly different version published in *Catholic Historical Review*, April 2003, pp. 321–325.

Also worth mentioning are Hughes's analysis of Michael Feldkamp's *Pius XII. und Deutschland* for the *Catholic Historical Review*, October 2001, pp. 761ff., and, in the same issue, his study of Anton Rauscher's *Wider den Rassismus* (pp. 710–712). Father Hughes's open letter to James Carroll in *Our Sunday Visitor*, March 11, 2001, p. 10, is the heartfelt plea of a priest (Hughes) to a resigned priest (Carroll) about Christianity's fundamental opposition to anti-Semitism, as well as an eloquent refutation to Carroll's *Constantine's Sword*.

See also Hughes's essay in the *Catholic Historical Review*, July 1986, pp. 468–469, on Ulrich von Hehl's *Priester unter Hitlers Terror* (Mainz: Matthias-Grünewald, 1984), which reveals the brutal consequences that befell the Catholic clergy for speaking out against Hitler, and Hughes's review in the *Catholic Historical Review*, January 2001, pp. 116–119, of *Zeugen für Christus: Das deutsche Martyrologium des 20. Jahrhunderts*, edited by Helmut Moll (Paderborn: Ferdinand Schöningh, 1990), on Catholic martyrs under Nazism and communism.

13. Hans Jansen, *De zwijgende paus?: Protest van Pius XII en zijn medewerkers tegen de jodenvervolging in Europa* (Kampen: Kok, 2000).

This extraordinary book, over 850 pages long, has an extraordinary story behind it. Jansen, who teaches at the Free University in Brussels, is a former priest known for his many works on Christianity and anti-Semitism, including highly critical studies on the Church's historical attitude and relationship with the Jewish community.

His research revealed a noticeable change beginning in the twentieth century, which modern academics have steadfastly ignored. In fact, so disturbed was Jansen by the transparent falsehoods written about the papacy in the modern period, particularly the accusations launched against Eugenio Pacelli, that he wrote this important work to answer them. As Jansen demonstrates, the notions about Eugenio Pacelli which have become so embedded in the popular mind—that he was silent about anti-Semitism, Nazism, and the Final Solution; that he did extremely little if anything to assist the persecuted Jews, and that he was a very weak and lamentable Christian leader—are not only untrue; they are canards of the worst sort, amounting to a modern-day "Black Legend."

Jansen writes with great passion, and a number of his arguments are debatable; on the whole, however, he makes intelligent and strong arguments in defense of Pacelli, and his book has been well received and deserves translation. (It includes a summary of its findings in English, pp. 701–718.) In response to claims about the Church's "silence," Jansen summarizes "forty protests of Pius XII and his collaborators against anti-Semitism and the murder of the Jews," and remembers "how at that time his father, when the [pope's] Christmas address of 1942 was broadcast on the radio, expressed his agreement spontaneously and loudly because at last the deportation of the Jews was openly denounced" (see *Catholic Historical Review*, July 2002, p. 551). Jansen's related work, *Pius XII: Chronologie van een onophoudelijk protest* (Kampen: Kok, 2003) is a valuable collection of evidence in favor of Pius XII and the wartime Catholic Church.

14. Pinchas Lapide, *Three Popes and the Jews* (New York: Hawthorn, 1967).

In the 1960s, when the wave of attacks against Pius XII had reached a crescendo after *The Deputy*, Israeli diplomat and scholar Lapide published this work to present what he believed was a necessary Jewish defense of the pope. In a country-by-country analysis of wartime Europe, Lapide argued that Pius XII played an exceptional role in instructing his diplomats and leading the Catholic faithful to resist Nazism and protect persecuted Jews.

In his conclusion, which has since been quoted many times, Lapide wrote: "The area of Europe seized by the Nazis during the last war contained some 8,300,000 Jews. Of these, over two million escaped Hitler's clutches. Half of these survived by flight, emigration, or evacuation into the free world. But at least one million Jews lived on in the very crucible of the Nazi hell. . . . To which we may add, in the light of the preceding chapters that the Catholic Church, under the pontificate of Pius XII was instrumental in saving at least 700,000 but probably as many as 860,000 Jews from certain death at Nazi hands" (pp. 212–215).

Because Lapide did not provide comprehensive details on how he arrived at his estimate, his numbers continue to be challenged. However, at a 1975 Holocaust conference in Hamburg, Lapide stated that his estimate "was based on six months of research in the Yad Vashem, the Holocaust archive in Jerusalem" (quoted in *Catholic Historical Review*, April 1999, pp. 269–270). Yad Vashem itself thinks well enough of Lapide's scholarship to recommend his book in its "Basic Bibliography of the Holocaust" on its official web page: www.yad-vashem.org.il.

Many distinguished scholars have come to Lapide's defense. Writing in *Yad Vashem Studies* 15 (1983), pp. 327–345, John S. Conway reports that the primary archival material available "confirms the picture already drawn by such Jewish authors as Livia Rothkirchen and Pinchas Lapide. Where the Nuncios were alert, and the government susceptible to papal remonstrances, then the interventions succeeded in delaying or reducing, though not preventing, the deportations and other acts of persecution against the Jews" (p. 343). Vincent Lapomarda comments: "Susan Zuccotti, in her work *Under His Very Windows*, sought to disprove Lapide but failed to do so. Unwittingly, she lent at least partial support to his view when she showed how helpful were the nuns, monks, priests, bishops, and archbishops in saving the Jews in Italy's major cities, especially since these rescuers were, according to her, convinced that they were really doing what the pope wanted" (*America*, February 25, 2002, p. 38).

Joseph Bottum's prize-winning essay, "Pius XII and the Nazis," *Crisis*, November 2000, pp. 13–17, maintains that supporters of Pius XII like Lapide have the stronger case. In its 1998 document on the Holocaust, *We Remember: A Reflection on the Shoah*, the Holy See spoke of "what Pope Pius XII did personally or through his representatives to save hundreds of thousands of Jewish lives" (section 4; also footnote 16). These numbers, reflective of Lapide's estimate, have been challenged. However, Sir Martin Gilbert, one of the most respected Holocaust historians of our time, declared the claim that "hundreds of thousands of Jews, saved by the entire Catholic Church, under the leadership and with the support of Pope Pius XII, would, to my mind, be absolutely correct" (*Inside the Vatican*, August 2003, p. 31).

Contrary to his critics—who claim, without evidence, that he exaggerated the Church's assistance to Jews because he wanted to foster ecumenism—Lapide was by no means uncritical of the Holy See. Indeed, much of *Three Popes and the Jews* (as well as his other writings) is devoted to what Lapide regards as the Church's historical responsibility for fostering intolerance toward Jews. It is all the more remarkable, then, that Lapide refused to adopt *The Deputy* myth, precisely when it was most fashionable to do so. In 1966, after Hochhuth's play was being embraced, Lapide said, "If fairness and historical justice are keystones of Jewish morality, then keeping silent in view of slanderous attacks on a benefactor is an injustice" (*Die Welt*, July 7, 1966).

By the time he died in 1997, Lapide had established himself as much more than a Jewish supporter of Pius XII. Having obtained a doctorate in Jewish-Christian relations, he and his wife Ruth toured the globe bringing Jews and Christians together. A moving obituary commented: "Lapide spoke on numberless platforms, both alone and in dialogical sessions. From the latter he produced a dozen dialogue books with the foremost Christian theologians of the latter part of the twentieth century. . . . Without a doubt, Lapide was the outstanding Jewish champion of dialogue on the European scene for the last third of the twentieth century" (*Journal of Ecumenical Studies*, Fall 1997, p. 550).

15. Father Vincent Lapomarda, *S.J.*, *The Jesuits and the Third Reich* (Lewiston: Edwin Mellen, 1989).

A great deal has been written about Adolf Hitler's virulent opposition to all things Jewish; much less has been published about his hatred of Roman Catholicism, from which he was apostate. Nowhere was Hitler's animus against the Catholic Church more apparent than in the Nazis' war against the Society of Jesus. In *The Jesuits and the Third Reich*, Lapomarda, coordinator of the Hiatt Collection of Holocaust Materials at Holy Cross College, documents that war, which took the lives of many Jesuits. Drawing on materials of the *Kommission für Zeitgeschichte* of the Catholic Academy in Bavaria as well as Jesuit archives of various countries, Lapomarda examines the extraordinary resistance the Jesuits exhibited throughout Nazi-occupied Europe.

This resistance, he makes clear, was directly attributable to the inspiration, leadership, and instructions of Pius XII, to whom all the Jesuits took a special oath of loyalty. Two of the pontiff's closest advisors—Father Robert Leiber, his private aide, and Cardinal Augustin Bea, his confessor—were Jesuits and vigorous opponents of anti-Semitism and the Nazi regime. Leiber collaborated with the pope on secret efforts to overthrow Hitler, while Bea later became the architect of Vatican II's much-praised declaration on non-Christian religions, *Nostra Aetate*, which strongly denounced anti-Semitism. "As [Bea] stated in an interview in Spring, 1960, the pope [John XXIII] took this step [of making Bea a cardinal] mainly as a mark of respect for his predecessor, Pius XII, whose confessor Bea had been for the last 13 years of his pontificate" (*Augustin Cardinal Bea: Spiritual Profile; Notes from the Cardinal's Diary*, with a commentary by Stjepan Schmidt, S.J. [London: Geoffrey Chapman, 1971], p. 296). Through Bea's work on *Nostra Aetate*—which emphasized Catholicism's "common heritage with Jews" and reiterated that the Church "deplores all hatreds, persecutions, displays of anti-Semitism leveled at any time or from any source"—there is a connection between Pius XII and Vatican II (indeed, other than sacred scripture, no source is quoted as often in the documents of Vatican II as Pius XII). See also *Augustin Bea, the Cardinal of Unity* by Stjepan Schmidt, S.J. (New Rochelle: New City, 1992).

Lapomarda's book was written to reply in part to those who make sweeping generalizations about "Catholic indifference and inaction" during the Holocaust. As he demonstrates, anti-Nazi resistance in the Church was deep and wide, particularly among the religious orders closest to Pius XII, and he concludes his important book by calling for additional studies on the activities of other orders and congregations during the Holocaust. Lapomarda's work extends far beyond the Jesuits; his website contains links to countless articles and books on every aspect of the Catholic Church during the Nazi era (see the Hiatt Collection at www.holycross.edu/departments/history/vlapomar/hiatt/index.html).

16. Justus George Lawler, *Popes and Politics: Reform, Resentment, and the Holocaust* (New York: Continuum, 2002).

Lawler is one of the most brilliant and innovative commentators writing today. *Popes and Politics* is an intellectual tour de force, examining the charges of Pius XII's most vehement critics, whom Lawler brands "ideological denigrators."

Lawler's mastery of the moral, historical, theological, and philosophical issues surrounding the Holocaust—and in particular, the papacy's relationship
to it—is unsurpassed. Better yet, he writes with great panache. As historian
John Jay Hughes noted: "In great detail, and with biting sarcasm reminiscent
of Jonathan Swift, Lawler analyzes the anti-papal books of John Cornwell,
James Carroll, Michael Phayer, and Susan Zuccotti. He finds in their books an
'omnipresent papaphobia.' What emerges is the 'startling phenomenon of
slanted and bogus scholarship where one might least expect it: . . . among
the acknowledged professional exponents of candor, honesty, and recti-
tude'" ("Papaphobia," *America*, July 15, 2002, p. 23).

A prominent Catholic writer, Lawler is by no means uncritical of the
Church, nor does he endorse every author who writes in defense of Pius XII.
But his burning intellectual honesty provoked him to write this book and
castigate authors whom he admits he once admired. In the spring of 2002,
the *U.S. Catholic Historian* published a symposium on Lawler's book (pp.
53–117), carrying exchanges between Lawler and anti-Pius writers John
Roth, Michael Phayer, and Susan Zuccotti. The exchange both confirms
Lawler's belief that Pius XII has been wronged and brings out the shallow-
ness of the wartime pontiff's "ideological denigrators." Also of note is "History Lite: Goldhagen, the Holocaust and the Truth," *Commonweal*, May 9,
2003, pp. 17–19, Lawler's equally effective critique of Daniel Goldhagen's
antipapal polemics.

17. Jenö Lévai, *Hungarian Jewry and the Papacy: Pius XII Did Not Remain Silent* (London: Sands, 1968).

As a young man in Hungary, Jenö Lévai was able to see Eugenio Pacelli in
1938, when the then secretary of state delivered a number of searing addresses against Nazism and communism in Budapest. Years later, when the
charges against Pacelli first surfaced, Lévai, who had become one of the leading Holocaust historians, leapt to Pacelli's defense, writing *Geheime Re-
ichssache. Papst Pius XII hat nicht geschwiegen* (Cologne: Wort and Werk,
1966), subsequently translated into English as *Hungarian Jewry and the Papacy: Pius XII Did Not Remain Silent*. Using Church and state archives in
Hungary, Lévai showed how the papal nuncio and bishops "intervened again
and again on the instructions of the pope" and that because of these directives "in the autumn and winter of 1944 there was practically no Catholic
Church institution in Budapest where persecuted Jews did not find refuge."

Lévai's *Hungarian Jewry and the Papacy* also contains an outstanding
foreword and epilogue by Robert M.W. Kempner. As deputy chief U.S. prosecutor at Nuremberg, Kempner had great access to documents, and he did
not hesitate to compare those who defame Pius XII with revisionists who
deny the full reality of the Holocaust: "In the last few years there has been

no lack of farfetched or malicious attempts to obscure or interpret perversely this historical fact. . . . We are concerned here with another deliberate method which aims at reducing the guilt of those who were really responsible. This is done by focusing the guilt for the Holocaust not on Hitler as the central figure for the liquidation system but on Pope Pius XII; by propagating in print and in the theater a new theory which runs as follows: Pope Pius XII never made an energetic protest against Hitler's 'Final Solution of the Jewish Problem,' and that is how the catastrophe came to reach the proportions it did. Both the premise and the conclusion drawn from it are equally untenable. The archives of the Vatican, of the diocesan authorities and of Ribbentrop's Foreign Ministry contain a whole series of protests—direct and indirect, diplomatic and public, secret and open" (pp. ix–x).

In the book's epilogue, Kempner concluded: "I myself am thoroughly familiar with . . . the important role of the Catholic Church in the struggle against the 'Final Solution in Hungary' and have always emphasized it—among other places in my book 'Eichmann and his Accomplices' ('Eichmann und Komplizen'). Neither Rolf Hochhuth's play . . . nor the books by Guenter Lewy and Saul Friedlander provide any reason for changing this standpoint. The Church documents published for the first time in this book by Lévai . . . strengthen my favorable view of the Vatican's attitude at that time and of Pope Pius XII, for whom I have had the greatest respect ever since the time he spent in Berlin." Kempner's memoirs were published in 1983; he died a decade later. For his obituary, see "Robert Kempner, 93, a Prosecutor at Nuremberg," *New York Times*, August 17, 1993, p. B6.

18. Joseph L. Lichten, *A Question of Judgment: Pius XII and the Jews* (Washington: National Catholic Welfare Conference, 1963).

After Rolf Hochhuth's *The Deputy* appeared in 1963, one of the first Jewish supporters of Pius XII was Joseph Lichten, who was then serving as director of the international-affairs department of the Anti-Defamation League of B'nai B'rith.

He had written before of the pope for Jewish publications. See, for instance, his "Pope Pius XII and the Jews," *ADL Bulletin*, October 1958. And he wrote *A Question of Judgment* in 1963 not only to rebut Hochhuth but also to confirm the high opinion Jewish leaders had of Pius XII during and immediately after World War II. Among the facts Lichten unearthed was a little-known directive Pius XII sent out on behalf of the persecuted Jews: "It is known that in 1940 Pius XII sent out a secret instruction to the Catholic bishops of Europe entitled *Opere et caritate* (By Work and Love). The letter began with a quotation from Pius XI's encyclical excoriating Nazi doctrine, *Mit brennender Sorge* (With Burning Sorrow), and ordered that all people suffering from racial discrimination at the hands of the Nazis be given adequate help. The letter was to be read in churches with the comment that racism was incompatible with the teachings of the Catholic faith."

In 1987, after much new information had been published, Lichten pointed to the evidence in *Actes et Documents*: "A watchful student of the mounting literature on this subject, will undoubtedly notice that in studies critical of the Holy See's behavior, these facts are somewhat bashfully shunned; they seem to upset some writers' applecarts" (from *Pius XII and the Holocaust: A Reader* [Milwaukee: Catholic League for Religious and Civil Rights, 1987], p. 34).

19. The Works of John Lukacs

The Hungarian-born Lukacs is one of the most admired of contemporary historians, the author of over twenty books and countless essays and reviews. *The Hitler of History* (New York: Knopf, 1997), a fascinating survey of Hitler's biographers and their respective views, concludes that Hitler was not a product of traditional Catholic culture but an antireligious revolutionary who wanted to obliterate the Judeo-Christian heritage. *The Last European War, September 1939–December 1941* (1976; reprinted New Haven: Yale University, 2001) is a panoramic study of the origins and beginning of World War II, containing an excellent chapter on the role of religion. It is especially strong on Pius XII.

Lukacs's appraisal of Pius XII is based upon a careful study of original sources. Lukacs is one of the few multilingual scholars who has actually read and critiqued the Vatican's collection of wartime documents in *Actes et Documents*. See his four comprehensive reviews in *Catholic Historical Review*: July 1974, pp. 271–278; October 1976, pp. 667–668; January 1979, pp. 92–94; and July 1983, pp. 414–419.

When John Cornwell's *Hitler's Pope* appeared in 1999, Lukacs dismissed the book as the work of an amateur: "Cornwell's book is full of mistakes of judgment. . . . Mistakes of fact, too, abound." He calmly reminded those who uncritically endorsed it to read "the extraordinary volumes of Vatican documents about World War II published by the Holy See, which the author of *Hitler's Pope* does not seem to have done" (*National Review*, November 22, 1999, pp. 59–61).

Mention must also be made of Lukacs's classic *Historical Consciousness* (New York: Harper and Row, 1968); his works on Winston Churchill (who, like Pius XII, has often been attacked unjustly), particularly *Churchill: Visionary, Statesman, Historian* (New Haven: Yale University, 2002); and his haunting autobiography, *Confessions of an Original Sinner* (New York: Ticknor and Fields, 1990), in which he reflects upon the central theme of his many books: the overwhelming danger of nationalism.

20. The Works of Sister Margherita Marchione

Among the most passionate supporters of Pius XII is Sister Margherita Marchione, a member of the Religious Teachers Filippini. Holding a Ph.D. from Columbia University, a Fulbright scholar, and the author of almost forty books, Marchione has produced five books in defense of Pius XII: *Yours Is a Precious Witness: Memoirs of Jews and Catholics in Wartime Italy* (Mahwah: Paulist, 1997), *Pius XII: Architect for Peace* (Mahwah: Paulist, 2000), *Pope Pius XII: Consensus and Controversy* (Mahwah: Paulist, 2002), *Shepherd of Souls: A Pictorial Life of Pius XII* (Mahwah: Paulist, 2002), and *Pope Pius XII* (Milan: Ancora, 2003) on the impressive spirituality of Pius XII in the face of war.

None of these is primarily a work of scholarship. Her purpose has been rather to provide "definitive, conclusive and inspirational proof of Pius XII's efforts to protect the victims of Nazism." She was among the first to answer the modern critics of Pius XII and deserves much credit for provoking other scholars into reassessing the papacy's role during the Second World War. In a field filled with biased historians who hide behind the facade of objectivity, Marchione is refreshingly honest in declaring her unambiguous support for Pius at the outset of all her books. In her judgment, not only has the wartime pontiff been defamed, but there is more than enough evidence to prove that he was a genuine saint. For more on Sister Marchione's efforts, see "New Jersey Nun Keeps up Pressure for Beatification of Pius XII" by John Thavis, *Catholic News Service*, December 2, 2003.

21. Ralph McInerny, *The Defamation of Pope Pius XII* (South Bend: St. Augustine's, 2001).

Written by well-known philosopher and novelist Ralph McInerny, this is a no-holds-barred blast against Pius XII's enemies. The book draws heavily on previous defenders of Pius XII, and so doesn't break any new ground, but it is well written and makes a forceful case on behalf of Pius.

Hardly shy of controversy, McInerny does not hesitate to question the motivations of Pius XII's critics. He asserts that the root of the attack on Pius is hatred for the Catholic Church—in particular, hatred for Catholic teachings against the "culture of death" as represented, above all, by abortion-on-demand, which many of Pius XII's critics openly support. The irony of Pius's detractors attacking Pius for allegedly not doing more to oppose Hitler's "Final Solution"—and yet simultaneously supporting what many consider the "Final Solution" for today's unwanted pregnancies—is not lost on McInerny, and he ruthlessly exposes the moral inconsistency.

22. Matteo Luigi Napolitano, *Pio XII tra guerra e pace. Profezia e diplomazia di un papa, 1939–1945* (Rome: Città Nuova, 2002).

Napolitano, an expert in diplomatic history, is one of the outstanding historians now writing on Pius XII. His book, based upon primary sources, allows the evidence in favor of Pius XII to speak for itself. Napolitano is devoid of any ideological agenda, and thus does not manipulate the facts. He has also published many essays and reviews addressing frequently raised subjects regarding the papacy and the Holocaust. Among his most important contributions:

1. "La Chiesa di fronte alla tragedia polacca" in *Letture Urbinati di Politica e Storia*, Winter 1998, pp. 22–25, a review-essay on Allessandro Duce's book, *Pio XII e la Polonia nella seconda guerra mondiale*.

2. "Ma Pio XII non tacque: la Santa Sede nella seconda guerra mondiale" in *Letture Urbinati di Politica e Storia*, Winter 2000, pp. 33–50, a review-essay on Pierre Blet's book, *Pius XII and the Second World War*. The related, "Pio XII e il Nazismo. Il 'silenzio apparente e l'azione segreta' del Pontefice" in *Nuova Storia Contemporanea*, May–June 2001, pp. 149–156, is an interview-essay with Blet on his work and experience defending Pius XII.

3. "La Santa Sede e la seconda guerra mondiale. Memoria e ricerca storica nelle pagine della *Civiltà Cattolica*" in *Studi Urbanati di Scienze giuridiche, politiche ed economiche*," 67 (1999–2000), pp. 171–243, an analysis of the Jesuit journal *La Civiltà Cattolica* during the pontificate of Pius XII, concentrating on the war years.

4. "La Santa Sede e la Germania nazista. Note su 'lavori in corso' nelle carte dell'Archivio Segreto Vaticano" in *Letture Urbinati di politica e Storia*, Winter 2003, pp. 83–96, an essay on the (recently released) exchange of dispatches between Cardinal Pacelli and the nuncio in Berlin, Cesare Orsenigo, in which the critical approach of the future Pius XII toward the Nazis is made clear. Documentary evidence establishes how Pacelli (in coordination with Pius XI) corrected Orsenigo whenever he was perceived as appeasing the German dictatorship.

5. "Pio XII e le 'verità nascoste' della Storia. Vaticano e Shoah nel rapporto della Commissione mista ebraico-cristiana" in *Stato, Chiesa e relazioni internazionali*, edited by Marco Mugnaini (Milan: Franco Angeli, 2003), pp. 316–345, a highly critical essay on the work of the joint Jewish-Catholic commission that was commissioned to provide an assessment of the wartime conduct of Pius XII, only to implode due to unprofessional behavior and bitter polemics.

Napolitano has been in the forefront of analyzing the primary documents—both old and new—relating to the Vatican in the twentieth century, particularly with regard to fascist Italy and Nazi Germany. His expertise with primary sources has enabled him to challenge works (e.g., Uki Goni's *The Real Odessa* and Peter Godman's *Hitler and the Vatican*) that have misused or misrepresented particular archives to present a dubious thesis. His latest work is a volume cowritten with Andrea Tornielli, *Il Papa che salvò gli Ebrei. Dagli Archivi segreti del Vaticano tutta la verità su Pio XII* (Casale Monferrato: Piemme, 2004). Napolitano has established two important websites carrying many articles and links on these subjects, and containing vital information and interpretation: www.vaticanfiles.net and www. diplomatichistory.com.

23. Father Michael O'Carroll, *Pius XII: Greatness Dishonored— A Documented Study* (Dublin: Laetare, 1980).

An examination of the Vatican archives, the transcripts of the Nuremberg trials, and a plethora of other primary literature to construct an unanswerable defense of the wartime pontiff. But Father O'Carroll's book is much more than a defense; it is a serious analysis of Pius's spirituality, theology, and, above all, his contribution to the Second Vatican Council. Published the same year as John Morley's *Vatican Diplomacy and the Jews During the Holocaust*, O'Carroll's book has been generally overlooked by North American historians. O'Carroll's views carry particular authority because he spoke to many of the principals involved (including Pius XII and Chief Rabbi Isaac Herzog of Jerusalem); because he consulted the leading Jewish scholars of the Holocaust; and because O'Carroll himself was a pioneer in ecumenical relations and has impeccable credentials in fighting anti-Semitism.

Reflecting on Pius XII, O'Carroll laments the hostile propaganda but believes it will eventually collapse: "Historiography is itself part of history. The phenomenon I am briefly describing, the wholesale departure from truth by those claiming to write history, will itself one day repay examination. Such a study will not only note the reprehensible misuse of documents, but the defiant disregard of important witnesses" (pp. 20–21). In light of the evidence now available, he concludes, "the criticism of the pope is, to borrow Father Graham's phrase, 'a fabricated scandal'; Pius XII is the greatest benefactor of the Jewish race in modern times" (p. 109). In "The Triumph of Pius XII," *Catholic Herald*, March 15, 2002, O'Carroll argued that, judging by the work of a new generation of scholars, the historical tide in favor of Pius XII is well under way. See, as well, "Trenchant Catholic Writer and Ecumenist," the obituary for Father O'Carroll in the *Irish Times*, January 17, 2004, p. 12, and *A Priest in Changing Times: Memories and Opinions of Michael O'Carroll, CSSP* (Dublin: Columba, 2003).

**24.Anthony Rhodes, *The Vatican in the Age of the Dictators, 1922–1945*
(New York: Holt, Rinehart and Winston, 1973).**

   Rhodes, a distinguished British scholar, was one of the first historians to
make use of the Vatican's wartime archives, as well as the largely unexam-
ined state papers of the warring countries. It was Rhodes who discovered
(in the German archives) the Nazi reaction to Pius XII's 1942 Christmas address that condemned the pope as "a mouthpiece of the Jewish war criminals" (pp. 272–273). Rhodes's study concentrates on the Vatican's activity
during the fascist and Nazi years, and does so sympathetically but not without criticism. Pius XII's conduct toward the Jews is examined in light of Rolf
Hochhuth's allegations, and the pope is cleared of all serious charges. The
author understands, as many others do not, the overriding *pastoral* concerns that Pius XII had during the war and how these guided his actions and
statements.

**25. Ronald J. Rychlak, *Hitler, the War, and the Pope* (Columbus:
Genesis, 2000).**

   A professor of law, Rychlak has emerged as one of the most important
supporters of Pius XII in the English-speaking world. After John Cornwell's
Hitler's Pope appeared, Rychlak declared the book deeply flawed. (See
Rychlak's exchange with Cornwell, "Vatican Chronicles," *Brill's Content*,
April 2000, pp. 60–61, 120.) Soon afterwards, Rychlak published his full-
length study, *Hitler, the War, and the Pope*. Marshalling an enormous
amount of evidence, the book seeks to rescue Pius XII from the quicksands
of myth, superstition, and innuendo—and thereby to restore the wartime
pontiff to his honorable place in history. Particularly valuable is Rychlak's
epilogue, which offers a point-by-point refutation of Cornwell's allegations.
   José Sánchez, a very restrained commentator in the Pius XII debate, declares that Rychlak "effectively demolishes his interpretations, revealing
Cornwell's inadequacy as a historian" (*Pius XII and the Holocaust*, p. 5).
Writing in *Theological Studies*, December 2001, p. 869, Patrick Carey commented that Rychlak's book "is a credible interpretation of the evidence that
challenges those interpretations . . . that expected more from the pope than
the evidence and historical circumstances warranted. . . . [H]is interpretations
deserve serious consideration. The moral situation of the Holocaust is much
clearer for us today than it was in the 1940s for the pope who had to make
prudential decisions on how best to respond to the evils of his day."
   There is information in Rychlak's book available nowhere else, such as his
exposé of the canard that Pius XII was hostile to black soldiers during the
war (in fact, Pius XII was a great supporter of blacks in all affairs and at a
time of rampant discrimination; see pp. 219 and 396). For incisive reviews of

Rychlak's pivotal book, see Ian A.T. McLean's "A Review of *Hitler, the War, and the Pope*" in the 2001 *Digest* of the National Italian American Bar Association, pp. 49–57; Wayne Allen's "Pius XII and the Culture Wars," *Culture Wars*, October 2001, pp. 42–44; and Michael O'Carroll's analysis in the *Catholic Historical Review*, April 2001, pp. 522–524, which commented: "The book is a landmark . . . every major event in the life of Pius XII is dealt with; every question about him is answered and answered satisfactorily to the total confusion of critics."

Since Rychlak's critique appeared, no historian has taken Cornwell's book seriously. (For Cornwell's effort to rehabilitate his reputation, see the interview with him in *Crisis*, March 2002, pp. 26–29, and Rychlak's stinging letter to the editor, *Crisis*, April 2002.) Rychlak has provided a similar service to the scholarly world by subjecting Susan Zuccotti's *Under His Very Windows* to a bracing critique in the *Journal of Modern Italian Studies*, Summer 2002, pp. 218–240. Rychlak's attack on Constantin Costa-Gravas's film, *Amen* (based on Hochhuth's play, *The Deputy*), appeared in the March 28, 2002, European edition of the *Wall Street Journal*.

Rychlak has also written an excellent essay, "The 1933 Concordat Between Germany and the Holy See: A Reflection of Tense Relations," in the 2001 *Digest* of the National Italian American Bar Association, pp. 23–47. And to Daniel Goldhagen's virulent anti-Catholic work, Rychlak wrote four responses: an eighteen-page historical refutation in *First Things*, June–July 2002, pp. 37–54; a shorter review for *Crisis*, "Another Reckoning," January 2003, pp. 12–18; a more theological critique in the *American Conservative*, "Dean of Catholic-Bashers," February 10, 2003, pp. 12–15; and a final review in *Catholic Historical Review*, April 2003, pp. 327–333.

See also Rychlak's long letter, "Pius XII and the Holocaust," *Times Literary Supplement*, March 15, 2002, rebutting Robert Wistrich's allegations against Pius. For more on Rychlak, see the interview he granted the Zenit News Agency on April 1, 2001, and his numerous responses to Pius XII's detractors on the Catholic League for Religious and Civil Rights website (www.catholic-league.org).

26. José Sánchez, *Pope Pius XII and the Holocaust: Understanding the Controversy* (Washington: Catholic University, 2002).

This book, the outgrowth of an earlier article that generated much discussion ("The Enigma of Pius XII," *America*, September 14, 1996, pp. 18–21), was written to provide an overall survey of current scholarship on Pope Pius XII and the Holocaust, without necessarily taking a stand for or against him. But Sánchez's book amounts to a subtle but highly effective defense of Pius XII, with its conclusion that "the pope's critics tend to extremism, while defenders tend toward moderation."

At a major symposium on Pius XII in 2002, Sánchez delivered an address in which he took a more forthright position on Pius. He "asked the essential questions that have dominated Pius studies for nearly 40 years: Did the pope speak out? Did he instruct his subordinates to rescue Jews? Did he always act honorably and conscientiously? In answering these questions, Sánchez came to find himself 'on the side of the defenders.' . . . He called on the scholars not to engage in spurious accusations but to listen to what Pius XII told his closest aides about his opposition to Nazism and concern for all its victims, especially Jews. 'Why not accept him at his word?' he asked. 'He was, after all, the pope, and he prayed daily, examined his conscience often (according to his Jesuit confessor, Cardinal Bea), and he knew that he had to answer to his Creator for what he did.' His conclusion: 'With Pius, it is context, context, context. It is easy to find something to justify any position if the words are taken out of context, and the temptation is there even for historians who should know better.' As if disbelieving what he had just heard, a member of the audience asked if the talk meant 'we should all become supporters of Pius XII?' Sánchez paused, then answered, 'Yes.' He added that he had reached that conclusion after long study and reflection" ("The Pius Debate— The Big American Shoot-Out," *Inside the Vatican*, May 2002, pp. 34–39).

27. Ralph Stewart, *Pius XII and the Jews* (New Hope: St. Martin de Porres Dominican Community, 1990).

This book by a distinguished Canadian diplomat is one of the least-known monographs on Pius XII. It summarizes the issues more accurately than most and is especially good on Pius XII's reaction to the roundup of Jews in Rome and Italy, a subject that has been grossly misrepresented by countless authors. While serving as a member of the Canadian Parliament, Stewart was elected chairman of a special European committee, allowing him to conduct extensive research in Rome. Drawing upon archival and firsthand testimony, he produced this book, which is a "tribute to the most outstanding pope of this [the twentieth] century."

28. Andrea Tornielli, *Pio XII: Il Papa degli Ebrei* (Casale Monferrato: Piemme, 2001).

This work by bestselling Italian author Tornielli, Vatican correspondent for the Milanese newspaper *Il Giornale*, brings together all the latest scholarship, deconstructs the myths and canards surrounding Pius, and demonstrates why the pope acted the way he did during the war and why his critics are mistaken in their assumptions and accusations.

Tornielli has won considerable praise from European critics. For two English-language articles on the impact of his *Pio XII*, see Tornielli's interview with Vatican Radio, reprinted by the Zenit News Agency, May 29, 2001, and "Not a Few Can Be Proud of What Pius XII's Church Did," Zenit News Agency, June 23, 2001. Also of interest is Tornielli's article, "Le tirate d'orecchie di Pacelli al nunzio morbido con Hitler," in the Milan daily newspaper *Il Giornale*, April 10, 2003, p. 36, which notes that newly released Vatican archives show that Pacelli, before he became Pius XII, delivered anti-Nazi instructions to the German nuncio, Cesare Orsenigo, during the 1930s. Tornielli has recently cowritten a volume with Matteo Luigi Napolitano, *Il Papa che salvò gli Ebrei. Dagli Archivi segreti del Vaticano tutta la verità su Pio XII* (Casale Monferrato: Piemme, 2004).

PART 6: THE DEFENSE OF PIUS XII

There are six areas on which Pius XII's detractors and supporters focus: (1) the words of Eugenio Pacelli both before and after he became Pius XII, (2) the place of the 1933 concordat, (3) the role of the anti-Nazi resistance, (4) the question of communism, (5) the history of Jewish-Christian relations, and (6) the contrast to John Paul II.

1. The Words of Eugenio Pacelli

As early as 1916, Pacelli, working in the office of the secretary of state under Cardinal Pietro Gasparri, helped craft a Vatican statement explicitly condemning anti-Semitism. "The Catholic Church," reads the statement, "faithful to its divine doctrine . . . considers all men as brothers and teaches them to love one another . . . [and] never ceases to inculcate among individuals, as well as among peoples, the observance of the principles of natural law and to condemn everything which violates them. This law must be observed and respected in the case of the children of Israel, as well as of all others, because it would not be conformable to justice or to religion itself to derogate from it solely on account of religious confessions" (*Principles for Peace*, pp. 198–199).

The year after this declaration, Pacelli became an archbishop and spent twelve years as a papal nuncio in Germany (1917–1929), then another nine as the Vatican's secretary of state (1930–1939), during which he assailed every aspect of Nazism. As Pinchas Lapide notes: "Of the 44 speeches which the Nuncio Pacelli had made on German soil between 1917 and 1929, at least 40 contained attacks on Nazism or condemnations of Hitler's doctrines. 'Germanism,' said Hitler; Pacelli who never met the Fuehrer, called it 'neo-Paganism' and countered with 'humanism;' 'Racial struggle' thundered the Austrian house-painter; but the archbishop from Rome preached 'fraternal love;' to 'master race' he responded with the 'universal kinship of mankind' and against 'the combatant spirit' he stressed time and again 'peace and always peace'" (*Three Popes and the Jews*, p. 118). Many of the early speeches by Pacelli were published in *Eugenio Pacelli, Erster Apostolischer Nuntius beim Deutschen Reich: Gesammelte Reden*, edited by Monsignor Ludwig Kaas (Berlin: Germania, 1930).

On this period, see also Pacelli's letters to the Vatican's secretary of state, Pietro Gasparri, in *Germania e Santa Sede: Le nunziature di Pacelli tra la Grande guerra e la Repubblica di Weimar* by Emma Fattorini (Bologna: Il Mulino, 1992). Fattorini's book contains the 1919 letter Nuncio Pacelli sent to Gasparri (pp. 322–325) about Jewish revolutionaries in Munich—the letter that was seized upon in *Hitler's Pope* by John Cornwell, who failed to give Fattorini credit for publishing it first, suggested it was his own discovery (*Times*, September 12, 1999), and mistranslated it as an "anti-Semitic" document. For two English reviews of the Fattorini book, which find no offensive writings by Pacelli in them, see John S. Conway's critique in *Catholic Historical Review*, July 1993, pp. 555–557, and Lawrence Nemer's in *Church History*, March 1997, pp. 160–161.

On November 14, 1923, Nuncio Pacelli wrote another letter to Cardinal Gasparri. "The letter refers to Adolf Hitler's failed attempt to take over the local government in Munich in the National Socialist Party's putsch of Nov. 9, 1923—just five days before the day this letter was written. In his letter, Archbishop Pacelli—contrary to the allegations of a number of recent authors such as John Cornwell (author of *Hitler's Pope*) on the relations between Pius XII and the Nazis—denounces the National Socialist movement as an anti-Catholic threat and at the same time notes that the Cardinal of Munich [Archbishop Michael Faulhaber] had already condemned acts of persecution against Bavaria's Jews" ("1923 Letter Shows the Future Pius XII Opposed to Hitler," Zenit News Agency, March 5, 2003). For an English translation of the letter see "Pacelli Denounces the Nazis," *Inside the Vatican*, March 2003, pp. 30–31.

On June 30, 1934, a little over a year after coming to power, Hitler ordered the mass execution of his political opponents during the notorious "Night of the Long Knives." One of the many victims executed in this Nazi purge was Erich Klausener, the anti-Nazi leader of Catholic Action. Both before and after the Nazis came to power, Klausener had fought Hitlerism, and his son has testified to the support his father received from Pacelli and the Church: "The solidarity of the Catholic Church was apparent from the very beginning. Not one person backed off from us or pretended they didn't want to have anything to do with us. Everyone knew that the [Nazi] reports pertaining to my father's death were all stinking lies. We knew for a fact that the bishop supported my father 100 percent. The papal nuncio, Eugenio Pacelli, who later became Pope Pius XII, did too" (Monsignor Erich Klausener, *Voices From the Third Reich: An Oral History* [New York: Da Capo, 1994], edited by Johannes Steinhoff, et al., pp. 29–31).

Cardinal Pacelli's speeches as secretary of state appeared in *Discorsi e Panegirici* (Milan: Società, 1939). On April 28, 1935, he spoke to a quarter of a million people at Lourdes where he denounced those "inspired by a false conception of the world and life. Whether they are possessed by the superstition of race and blood, their philosophy, as that of others, rests upon principles essentially opposed to those of the Christian faith. And on such principles the Church does not consent to form a compact with them at any price" (see "Nazis Warned at Lourdes," *New York Times*, April 29, 1935, p. 8).

Two years later, Pacelli again denounced the Nazi cult of race, drawing a sharp reaction from the German Ministry of Ecclesiastical Affairs, which said: "The Statement of the Cardinal Secretary of State that his visit to France had no political purpose is contradicted by his speech in Lisieux on 11 July. With clear reference to Germany, he spoke about 'a nation led astray by bad leaders into glorification of a single race'—words which were clearly understood by the French National Front and by Germany's enemies in the world" (*Documents on German Foreign Policy 1918–1945*, Series D, 1937–1945, 1:627).

And on May 25, 1938, at the International Eucharistic Congress in Budapest, Cardinal Pacelli delivered a searing and prophetic address: "Face to face with us is drawn up the lugubrious array of the militant godless, shaking the clenched fist of the Anti-Christ against everything that we hold most sacred. . . . Has the world ever known such exasperated hatred, divisions, and deep discords as those among which it is hopelessly involved today? . . . Are we surprised, in a world in which the idea of the fear of God is lost and the teachings of Christ are not applied to the practice of real life, to see suspicion rule between class and class, between man and man, between nation and nation, between people and people, suspicion which has arrived at such a degree that its brutal force threatens every moment to cause a catastrophe, and that in any case it covers with dark clouds the horizons of today and the near future?"

Three volumes of the Vatican's protests to the Nazi government (many penned by Pacelli) exist, edited by Dieter Albrecht as *Der Notenwechsel zwischen dem Heiligen Stuhl und der Deutschen Reichsregierung* (Mainz: Matthias-Grünewald, 1965–1980). Many other protests were made orally. According to Father Robert Leiber, the German Jesuit who was Pacelli's confidant from the 1930s onward, "The *first* initiative of the Holy See toward the government in Berlin concerned the Jews. As early as April 4, 1933, 10 days after the Enabling Act, the Apostolic Nuncio in Berlin was ordered [by Cardinal Pacelli, acting on behalf of Pius XI] to intervene with the government of the Reich on behalf of the Jews and point out all the dangers of an anti-Semitic policy" (*Stimmen der Zeit*, March 1962, pp. 417–426; see also *Tablet*, March 16, 1963).

This order has now been found and released by the Vatican. See "New Proofs of Pius XII's Efforts to Assist Jews; 1933 Letter Targets 'Anti-Semitic Excesses' in Germany," Zenit News Agency, February 17, 2003, and especially Thomas Brechenmacher's commentary, "Aber er hat Hitler weder unterstützt noch unterschätzt: Kardinal Pacellis Spielräume im Frühjahr 1933," *Frank-furter Allgemeine Zeitung*, April 24, 2003, p. 42.

The Church is often accused of only having concerned itself with internal affairs, or only having spoken up for baptized Jews. But this intervention, issued explicitly on behalf of Jews as a people and as a race, refutes that. Similarly, in a protest delivered to Hitler on June 6, 1934, Pacelli wrote: "Human norms are unthinkable without embodiment in the divine. This embodiment cannot rest in an arbitrary 'divine' of the race, not in making the nation absolute. Such a 'God' of the race or the blood would be nothing more than the self-created counterpart of one's own blindness and narrowness" (see "German Catholicism and the Jews" by Konrad Repgen in *Judaism and Christianity Under the Impact of National Socialism*, p. 218).

Swiss historian Victor Conzemius comments: "The attitude of Cardinal Pacelli, as reflected in these documents, is strong and firm from the beginning; one could hardly imagine a more forceful defender of violated rights. . . . In the note of July 10, 1935—it precedes the Nuremberg Laws against the Jews of September 1935 by a few months—Pacelli states: 'There is no stipulation of the concordat which could oblige the Church to consider laws as binding in conscience for its subjects, which lack the elementary conditions of morally bindings laws.'"

"There is no doubt," concludes Conzemius, "that Pacelli used his position as a channel to reiterate the principles of natural law and human rights to a totalitarian state, which had created a new scale of sights and values. That his partner was deaf to his entreaties [only one-fifth of the protests received an answer] did not discourage him. Again and again he came back to the charge and it did not shrink from criticizing the intolerable grip of the totalitarian state on German community life at large" ("Pius XII and Nazi Germany in Historical Perspective" in *Historical Studies: Papers Read Before the Irish Conference of Historians*, edited by J.C. Beckett [London: Routledge and Kegan Paul, 1969], pp. 112–113).

One of the most remarkable of Cardinal Pacelli's protests during this time was his defense of Cardinal Mundelein after the latter's anti-Nazi sermons in America were protested by the German ambassador to the Vatican, Diego von Bergen. Pacelli answered his complaint with a striking question: "What steps has the German government taken, what steps does it intend to take in the future, against the ignoble wrongs, the slanders, the despicable calumnies which are every day renewed in the daily and weekly press of Germany, as well as in the speeches of distinguished personages, against the Church, ecclesiastical institutions, the pope, the cardinals, the bishops, the clergy and so on? To make Your Excellency's task more easy, I will myself reply. . . . The German Government, *despite all our remonstrations*, has done nothing. On the contrary, it is responsible for these things. The Government, the party, and the Ministry of Propaganda in particular, are behind this attitude in the press and in public speeches; at least they do all they can to encourage it." No reply came from von Bergen, and both Pacelli and Mundelein continued to speak their minds (for details, see Nazareno Padellaro's *Portrait of Pius XII*, p. 96; see also "L'explosion de Chicago" in Louis Chaigne's *Portrait et Vie de Pie XII* [Paris: St-Augustin, 1966], pp. 82–85).

Under interrogation at Nuremberg, deposed Nazi Foreign Minister Joachim von Ribbentrop conceded that "we had a whole desk full of protests from the Vatican. . . . There were very many we did not reply to—quite a number" (*Trials of the Major War Criminals Before the International Military Tribunal* [Nuremberg: International Military Tribunal, 1947], volume 10, pp. 140–141). See also Ribbentrop's many other comments documented in the multivolume collection *Nazi Conspiracy and Aggression, Office of United States Chief of Counsel for the Prosecution of Axis Criminality* (Washington: U.S.G.P.O., 1946). When Pacelli met with private rebuffs, he took his case public. In a letter to Cardinal Schulte of Cologne, Pacelli condemned the Nazis as "false prophets with the pride of Lucifer" and as "bearers of a new Faith and new Evangile" who were attempting to create "a mendacious antimony between faithfulness to the Church and to the Fatherland" (Pacelli to Schulte, Vatican City, March 12, 1935, cited in *Akten deutscher Bischöfe*, edited by Ludwig Volk [Mainz: Matthias-Grünewald, 1981], volume 2, pp. 113–117).

Following Pope Pius XI's death on February 10, 1939, the College of Cardinals elevated Pacelli to the papacy on March 2, 1939, provoking the *Berlin Morgenpost* to declare the next day: "The election of Cardinal Pacelli is not accepted with favor in Germany because he was always opposed to Nazism and practically determined the policies of the Vatican under his predecessor."

From the beginning of his pontificate to the outbreak of World War II on September 1, 1939, Pius XII did everything in his power to prevent the war. As Church historian Philip Hughes comments, "Pius XII made as many as six public appeals to the peoples of the world, reasoned, impassioned, . . . the appeals of an experienced statesman and man of affairs, of a mind and heart filled with pity at the thought of what horrors lay before millions of innocent people" (*A Popular History of the Catholic Church* [New York: Macmillan, 1949], p. 268). Even Donald Cameron Watt, author of the influential *How War Came: The Immediate Origins of the Second World War* (New York: Pantheon, 1989), which repeats certain errors about Eugenio Pacelli, nevertheless records Pius XII's unending efforts to prevent the war, and acknowledges that the Vatican "loathed and feared Nazism. Moreover, the pope regarded Hitler, as did Chamberlain and Halifax, as impossible to trust" (p. 558).

The pope's efforts were cited at the Nuremberg war crimes tribunal. On December 6, 1945, a member of the British Delegation addressed the tribunal: "But my Lord, Germany would not accept . . . the appeals of the pope. . . . On August 31 [1939] the pope wrote: 'The pope is unwilling to abandon hope that pending negotiations may lead to a just, pacific solution such as the whole world continues to pray for.' But the appeals were to no avail. Hitler had decided the war had to come in his lifetime. While Hitler, Ribbentrop, and Göring kept up a farce of pretending to negotiate, the Wehrmacht struck" (quoted in Gustave M. Gilbert's *Nuremberg Diary* [1947; reprinted New York: Da Capo, 1995], p. 58).

After the Nazi invasion of Poland, the pope addressed the war in three separate speeches the same month: to the new Belgian ambassador (September 14), to a group of German pilgrims (September 26), and to Cardinal Hlond and a group of Polish pilgrims (September 30). The first described the Nazi invasion as "an immeasurable catastrophe" and declared "of this new war, which already shakes the soil of Europe, and particularly that of a Catholic nation, no human prevision can calculate the frightful carnage which it bears within itself, nor what its extension and its successive complications will be." He also condemned weapons of mass destruction, including "the use of asphyxiating and poison gasses," which had been used during World War I.

The second speech called the war "a terrible scourge of God" and directly warned the German clergy not to celebrate German militarism but to repent: "The priest must now, more than ever before, be above all political and national feelings. He must console, comfort, help, exhort to prayer and penance, and must himself do penance."

The third speech made unmistakable reference to the Nazis as "the enemies of God," and spoke directly to the suffering Poles, whose country was under attack: "Before our eyes pass as a vision frightened crowds and, in black desperation, a multitude of refugees and wanderers—all those who no longer have a country or a home. There rise toward Us the agonized sobs of mothers and wives." (For excerpts from all three speeches, see *Principles for Peace*, p. 587–588; 588–589; 589–590.)

These speeches set the stage for the 1939 Christmas address in which the pontiff cried out against "atrocities . . . and the unlawful use of destructive weapons against non-combatants and refugees, against old men and women and children; a disregard for the dignity, liberty, and life of man, showing itself in actions which cry to heaven for vengeance: 'The voice of thy brother's blood crieth to me from the earth'" (address to the College of Cardinals on December 24, 1939, published in *Acta Apostolicae Sedis* 32, pp. 5–13, and *Osservatore Romano*, December 26–27, 1939, pp. 1–2; an English translation of the complete text appears in *Selected Letters and Addresses of Pius XII* [London: Catholic Truth Society, 1949], pp. 251–262).

Contrary to allegations that the pope spoke only in generalities, José Sánchez makes the point that this address explicitly mentioned "the blood-stained lands of Poland and Finland"—which had been invaded by Germany and the Soviet Union—hence: "It is difficult not to see Germany and the Soviets as the pope's chief targets in this address, as the Western Allies had not yet launched any offensive action, and certainly neither was involved in Poland or Finland" (*Pius XII and the Holocaust*, p. 52).

Among Pius XII's five principles of peace in his address was this declaration: "If a better European settlement is to be reached, there is one point in particular which should receive special attention: it is the real needs and the just demands of nations and populations and of racial minorities" (*Selected Letters and Addresses of Pius XII*, p. 260). In response, President Roosevelt praised the Vatican, urging other churches to "synchronize their peace efforts . . . to the outline of Pope Pius XII of his conception of a just peace" ("Roosevelt Aims at Sound Peace," *Christian Science Monitor*, December 27, 1939). In contrast, Nazi propagandist Joseph Goebbels railed in his diary: "The pope has made a Christmas speech. Full of bitter, covert attacks against us, against the Reich and National Socialism. All the forces of internationalism are against us. We must break them" (entry for December 27, 1939, *The Goebbels Diaries 1939–1941*, translated and edited by Fred Taylor [New York: Putnam, 1983], p. 75).

Even earlier, on September 26, 1939, less than a month after the Nazi invasion of Poland, while many Germans, including some clergymen, were celebrating German militarism, Pius XII said, "We can see and say only this: the war which has just broken out is, for all peoples who will be drawn into it, a terrible scourge of God. The priest must now, more than ever before, be above all politics and national feelings." The pope, it should be noted, made these statements to an audience of German pilgrims, and he spoke in German. (See *Discorsi e Radiomessaggi di Sua Santita Pio XII* [Cittàdel Vaticano: Tipografia Poliglotta Vaticana, 1953], volume 1, pp. 319–321.)

One of the pontiff's most important interventions—rarely mentioned by his detractors—occurred on March 11, 1940, during a meeting with Joachim von Ribbentrop, Germany's Foreign Minister. "It was an extraordinary interview, in the course of which the Nazi, following the example of his master, thought it wise to deliver a long oration about the strength of Germany and her inevitable victory. . . . Finally he came to the end of his speech." At that point, Pius XII, in a forceful and very personal way, confronted Ribbentrop with the crimes of his government: "The pope opened a great register before him, and began with cold severity the enumeration of all the facts, places, dates and detailed circumstances, duly attested by ecclesiastical authority, regarding the tortures which the invader had already begun to inflict upon the Polish people" (Charles Pichon, *The Vatican and its Role in World Affairs*, p. 158). According to news reports at the time, among those Pius most strongly defended were "the Jews in Germany and Poland." (See "Pope is Emphatic About Just Peace: Jews Rights Defended," *New York Times*, March 14, 1940, p.8; for an analysis of the primary documents relating to the meeting, see "The Meeting between Pope Pius XII and Ribbentrop" by John S. Conway, *Canadian Historical Association Report for 1968*, pp. 103–116.)

Pius XII's most famous statement was his 1942 Christmas address, which spoke out for those "hundreds of thousands who, without any fault of their own, sometimes only by reason of their nationality or race, are marked down for death or gradual extinction" (*Selected Letters and Addresses of Pius XII*, pp. 275–297; official text of the full address appears in the *Acta Apostolicae Sedis* 35, pp. 9–24).

Claims that this address was not explicit enough, because it did not name the Nazis as the perpetrators and the Jews as victims, are tantamount to claiming that because Pius XII never explicitly condemned Joseph Stalin by name during his major addresses, the Vatican therefore turned a blind eye to the Stalinist Gulag. Anyone who understood the pontiff's precarious position in 1942, the ever-present danger of reprisals, and who read and heard his addresses honestly knew exactly what the pope was saying. (On this issue, see Giovanni Sale's "Ordine interno delle nazioni e guerra mondiale nel Radiomessaggio natalizio di Pio XII del 1942" and "La tragedia degli ebrei nel Radiomessaggio natalizio di Pio XII," *Civiltà Cattolica* 2002, volume 4, pp. 343–355 and 540–553.)

Moreover, Pius XII's first encyclical, *Summi Pontificatus* (October 20, 1939), a condemnation of racism and totalitarianism issued soon after World War II began, had already defended Jews by name in paragraph 48 and expressed solidarity with them. The reaction to *Summi Pontificatus* was immense, and the Allies considered it so important that their planes dropped thousands of copies of it on German territory.

The Nazis, in contrast, despised it and either perverted or suppressed its text. (See Owen Chadwick's analysis in *Britain and the Vatican During the Second World War*, pp. 83–85. For an extensive bibliography on reaction to the encyclical from around the world, see *Guide to the Documents of Pius XII*, pp. 16–19.) Heinrich Müller, chief of the Gestapo, signed a letter on November 10, 1939, to Hans Lammers, head of the Reich chancellery, that reads: "The Encyclical is directed exclusively against Germany, both in ideology and in regard to the German-Polish dispute. How dangerous it is for our foreign relations as well as our domestic affairs is beyond discussion" (quoted in *Pius XII and the Third Reich*, pp. 36–37).

Other documents reveal this Nazi reaction to the pope's 1942 Christmas address: "In a manner never known before the pope has repudiated the National Socialist European Order. His radio allocution was a masterpiece of clerical falsification of the National Socialist *Weltanschauung*. It is true, the pope does not refer to the National Socialists in Germany by name, but his speech is one long attack on everything we stand for. . . . God, he says, regards all peoples and races as worthy of the same consideration. Here he is clearly speaking on behalf of the Jews. . . . That this speech is directed exclusively against the New Order in Europe as seen in National Socialism is clear in the papal statement that mankind owes a debt to 'all who during the war have lost their Fatherland and who, although personally blameless have, simply on account of their nationality and origin, been killed or reduced to utter destitution.' Here he is virtually accusing the German people of injustice towards the Jews and makes himself the mouthpiece of the Jewish war criminals" (report of the Nazi Reich Central Security Office to the German Foreign Office, sent on January 15, 1943; received on January 19; official German citation: Politisches Archiv des Auswärtigen Amts, Inland I D/Kirche 17/9 [R 98833]). In *The Vatican in the Age of the Dictators*, pp. 272–273, Anthony Rhodes translates and gives the date as January 22, 1943; this is incorrect. There is, however, a second Nazi report, from the Central Security Office to the Foreign Office, dated January 22, 1943, which is also hostile to the pope's Christmas speech.

Some authors have disparaged the 1942 Christmas address. Robert Wistrich (*Commentary*, April 1999, p. 27) writes: "With all due allowance for the compressed, abstract style of papal pronouncements, this is a protest that lasted for the duration of a breath." In fact, as Anthony Rhodes points out, "So important did the *Osservatore Romano* consider it that the paper was still publishing interpretative articles on it in May 1943" (*The Vatican in the Age of the Dictators*, p. 273).

John Cornwell portrays the address as practically meaningless, and quotes Mussolini's comments about it—"This is a speech of platitudes which might better be made by the parish priest"—to prove how trivial it was (*Hitler's Pope*, p. 293). In fact, as Owen Chadwick points out, the speech was "not trivial" and Mussolini was angered by it (*Britain and the Vatican During the Second World War*, p. 218). Wartime correspondent Charles Pichon is even more emphatic, asserting that Mussolini was "exasperated" by Pius XII's 1942 Christmas address, precisely because it was understood as having "condemned most strongly the anti-Semitic persecutions, the oppression of invaded lands, the inhuman conduct of the war, and also the deification of earthly things which were made into idols: the Land and the Race, the State and the Class" (*The Vatican and its Role in World Affairs*, p. 167).

Gitta Sereny contends that the pope's statement against the Nazi persecution of Jews was "one oblique reference to the fact, almost at the end of a Christmas message more than 5,000 words long" (*Into That Darkness* [New York: Vintage, 1974], p. 331). But those 5,000 words were a comprehensive refutation of everything the Nazis stood for, and thus his speech culminated with his declaration against racial murder. Ronald Rychlak writes, "The pope considered his statement to have been 'clear and comprehensive in its condemnation of the heartrending treatment of the Poles [and] Jews in occupied countries.' Others shared this view. The Polish ambassador thanked the pontiff, who 'in his last Christmas address implicitly condemned all the injustices and cruelties suffered by the Polish people at the hands of the Germans. Poland acclaims this condemnation; it thanks the Holy Father for his words. . . . ' British records reflect the opinion that 'the pope's condemnation of the treatment of the Jews and the Poles is quite unmistakable, and the message is perhaps more forceful in tone than any of his recent statements.' A Christmas Day editorial in the *New York Times* praised Pius XII for his moral leadership" (*Hitler, the War, and the Pope*, pp. 177–178; see also Rychlak's citations of the relevant primary sources concerning the 1942 address, pp. 378–379, nn. 68–88).

Pinchas Lapide points out that in their pastoral letter of February 21, 1943—issued explicitly on behalf of Jews—the Dutch bishops specifically cited Pius XII's 1942 Christmas address as their inspiration for speaking out: "We would fail in our duty if we did not publicly raise our voice against the injustice to which such a large part of our people is being subjected. In this we are following the path indicated by our Holy Father the Pope, who in his latest Christmas message declared: 'The Church would be untrue to herself . . . if she turned a deaf ear to her children's anguished cries which reach her from every class of the human family. . . . ' The churches have denounced before the increasing lack of justice; the persecution and execution of our fellow Jewish citizens. . . . In the midst of all the injustice and anguish, our sympathy goes out in a very special manner . . . to the Jews, and to our brethren in the Catholic faith who are of Jewish descent" (*Three Popes and the Jews*, p. 201).

In 2002, some remarkable new testimony emerged concerning Pius XII's Christmas address. "Protestant pastor François de Beaulieu revealed to the French weekly 'Réforme' the experience he endured in 1942 as a radio operator secretly spreading Pius XII's famous Christmas radio message against Nazism. . . . Beaulieu was arrested as he left the Wehrmacht headquarters with a German translation of Pius XII's 1942 radio Christmas message, a document that was to be destroyed, not preserved. Beaulieu said that before his arrest, he succeeded in copying and dispersing the message in Berlin, leaving an impression on his friends. In the message, Pius XII mentions the extermination of innocents because of their race or nationality. Beaulieu appeared before a military tribunal on April 16 [1943]. Thanks to the testimonies of his immediate superiors, he was spared the death penalty, but he was sentenced to prison for spreading a 'subversive and demoralizing document.' He was also accused of having a critical view of the war, and of being 'spiritually attracted to Jewish environments and sympathetic toward Jews.' Pastor Beaulieu wished to publish these facts explaining that Pius XII was not silent [and] that he spoke clearly in his Christmas Message, although the latter only reached Berlin in a few clandestine copies" ("For Berlin, Pius XII was a Subversive," Zenit News Agency, May 14, 2002).

Throughout the war, the pope frequently invoked the "wrath of God" or "the curse of God" or "God's vengeance" against the persecutors. See, in particular, his Easter address of April 13, 1941, printed in *Acta Apostolicae Sedis* 33, pp. 112–117, *Osservatore Romano*, April 14–15, 1941, p. 1, and, in English, *Catholic Mind*, April 22, 1941, pp. 1–8. The American historian Charles

Beard considered this address so important that he selected it for his wartime collection of outstanding speeches, *Voices of History: Great Speeches and Papers of the Year 1941* (New York: Franklin Watts, 1942), pp. 167–172. Also of note is Pius's June 26, 1941, address sent to an American audience, condemning the "dark paganism" that had overtaken the world. See *Acta Apostolicae Sedis* 33, pp. 351–354, and for an English translation, *New York Times*, June 27, 1941, p. 11. America had not yet entered the war, but Pius's prophetic declaration was a portent of things to come.

The pope's language was frequently trenchant and always solemn, and he made forceful public protests against the Nazi deportations and slaughters, both before and after his 1942 Christmas address. As Justus George Lawler observes: "In June, 1941, speaking of 'sin as being exalted, excused, and the master of human life,' he gave this illustration: ' . . . individuals and families are *deported, transported, separated, torn from their homes,* wandering in misery without support.' Six months after the Christmas address of 1942, in an allocution to the College of Cardinals that was published in *L'Osservatore Romano* (June 3, 1943) and in *La Civiltà Cattolica,* Pius mentioned specifically his concern for 'those who have turned an anxious and imploring eye to us, those who are tormented because of their nationality or race by major miseries and by more acute and grievous suffering, and who are sometimes even fated, without guilt on their part, to extermination.' If these are not condemnations of 'the persecution' inspired by anti-Semitism, then we need to revise our dictionaries" (*Popes and Politics,* p. 113).

Indeed, both the Nazis and the fascists censored Pius's June 2, 1943, allocution, deleting the section which condemned the "extermination" of people based upon their race. Vatican Radio, however, broadcast the entire speech (see *Tablet,* June 12, 1943, p. 282). Speaking of Pius's 1942 Christmas address and his allocution of June 2, 1943, historian Michael Walsh affirms: "Pius twice unequivocally condemned the extermination of the Jews. It must be remembered that complaints about the pope's 'silence' came only long after the war. In its immediate aftermath people remembered his assistance to the victims of persecution, his pleas for peace, and his championing of human rights" (*An Illustrated History of the Popes* [New York: St. Martin's, 1980]).

Pius XII's encyclical, *Mystici Corpus Christi* (June 29, 1943), explained the Church's universalism: "The Catholic Church . . . is confined by no boundaries or race or territory. Christ, by His blood, made the Jews and Gentiles one, 'breaking down the middle wall of partition . . . in His flesh' by which the two peoples were divided." The encyclical also reaffirmed the Holy See's December 2, 1940, condemnation of euthanasia: "Conscious of the obligations of Our high office We deem it necessary to reiterate this grave statement today, when to Our profound grief We see at times the deformed, the insane, and those suffering from hereditary disease deprived of their lives, as though they were a useless burden to society; and this procedure is hailed by some as a manifestation of human progress, and as something that is entirely in accordance with the common good. Yet who that is possessed of sound judgement does not recognize that this not only violates the natural and the divine law written in the heart of every man, but that it outrages the noblest instincts of humanity? The blood of these unfortunate victims who are all the dearer to our Redeemer because they are deserving of greater pity 'cries to God from the earth.'" (Complete official text of the encyclical in the *Acta Apostolicae Sedis* 35, pp. 193–248; see also *L'Osservatore Romano*, July 4, 1943, pp. 1–4; for English translations and worldwide commentary on *Mystici Corpus Christi*, see *Guide to the Documents of Pius XII*, pp. 78–80; for the Vatican's 1940 condemnation of euthanasia, see *Acta Apostolicae Sedis* 32, p. 553.)

During the German occupation of Rome (September 1943–June 1944), "Pius XII had been fearless in his outspoken denunciation of fascist excesses," according to eyewitness Lt. Col. Samuel I. Derry, a British prisoner of war, in *The Rome Escape Line* (New York: W.W. Norton, 1960), p. 55. Contemporary documents, witnesses, newspapers, and diaries show that Pius XII was active on behalf of Rome's persecuted people, and that his assistance was publicly known at the time, setting an example for others to follow. See "Pope Acts to Save Vatican Territory: Notices of Inviolability Posted at Entrances," *New York Times*, October 14, p. 4; "Vatican Defies Nazis by Aiding Refugees: Refuses to Yield Anti-Fascists Shielded From Foes," *New York Times*, October 22, 1943, p. 9.

Upon learning of the Nazi roundup of Rome's Jews on October 16, 1943, from Princess Enza Pignatelli Aragona Cortés, Pius XII promised the princess: "I'll do all I can" (quoted from a personal interview by Dan Kurzman in *The Race for Rome* [Garden City: Doubleday, 1975], p. xxxi). See also the princess's taped interview for the 1997 A&E film documentary *History Undercover: Pope Pius XII and the Holocaust*, where she reveals how Pius reacted emotionally to news of the roundup: "When he saw me, I knelt in his chapel. He was still wearing his chasuble after finishing Mass. He came to me and said, 'What has happened?' I told him the whole story and he was furious. He grabbed me by the shoulder and said: 'Let's go make a few phone calls!'"

After the German takeover of Rome, the Nazis repeatedly tried to suppress Vatican Radio ("Drastic Curbs Halt Vatican Radio," *New York Times*, September 16, 1943, p. 1). And they issued dire warnings over their own station: "The Berlin radio, broadcasting to Italy under auspices of the Italian puppet 'Republican Fascist Government' . . . attacked the 'pacifism and anti-German sentiments' of the Vatican and warned it not to let its policy make 'radical measures' necessary. . . . 'The Vatican, the prelates, all the hierarchy of the Church, from the Pope down to the parish priests, have this choice: either with Fascist and Catholic Italy or against it,' the broadcast added" (September 20, 1943, *Facts on File, 1943* [New York: Facts on File, 1943], p. 300).

But the pope did not relent, and he continued to get his message out. Pius XII's Christmas message of 1943 was well publicized, even under the occupation, and resonated throughout the world (for the text of the address, see *Acta Apostolicae Sedis* 36, pp. 11–24; *L'Osservatore Romano*, December 25, 1943, pp. 1–2; and, in English, *Catholic Mind*, February 1944, pp. 65–76; for commentary, see "The Pope, again a Prisoner, asks Justice in Victory," by John LaFarge, *America*, January 8, 1944, pp. 369–371). On January 19, 1944, Vatican Radio broadcast Pius XII's address urging Catholics to work for the "salvation of humanity" by preserving it "from the catastrophe into which it would be guided and led by reckless adventurers and prophets with hallucinations of a vain and false future." Germany was the first country to hear the address. (See "Germans Hear Pope on False Prophets: Pontiff's Talk on 'Adventurers' Broadcast to the Reich," *New York Times*, January 20, 1944, p. 4; for the complete text of the speech, see *Osservatore Romano*, January 20, 1944, p. 1; English excerpts in *Tablet*, January 29, 1944, p. 54.)

The papal actions in favor of the Jews aroused hatred within Nazi ranks. A recently discovered document, from wartime archives in Milan, found striking evidence that Adolf Hitler had plans "to assassinate the Pope along with all the Vatican Cardinals. The document refers to the plan as 'Rabat-Fohn.' It names the unit assigned to execute the plan to be the Eighth Division of the SS Cavalry, 'Florian Geyer,' and the reason to be 'The Papal Protest in Favor of the Jews'" (*Pope Pius XII* by Margherita Marchione, p. 72–73; see also the article in the Milan newspaper, *Il Giornale*, July 5, 1998).

The Allies liberated Rome on June 4, 1944. The next day, Pius XII greeted hundreds of thousands of people who had come to cheer him as *defensor civitatis*, defender of the city, and thank him for refusing to abandon his post (unlike other prominent officials, who had fled Rome during the occupation). The crowd was delirious with excitement. "The Piazza was jammed beyond anything seen before. All the bells of Rome pealed in deafening clangor so the vibrations seemed to come up from the pavements through your toes and course joyously through your body" (*Crown of Glory*, by Alden Hatch and Seamus Walshe, p. 179). One witness, priest-rescuer Don Aldo Brunacci, who had left Assisi to assist the pope in Rome, remembers the scene: "Yes, June 4th, 1944, was the liberation of Rome and from the Relief Offices which were near the front of St. Peter's I could see the General Clark coming up the stairs of St. Peter's in his jeep. I saw St. Peter's Square and the Via della Conciliazone fill up with crowds who had come to thank Pius XII. There were many Jews among them!" (*Inside the Vatican*, January 2004, p. 76).

Even as Rome was free, the Nazis continued their war of extermination elsewhere. On June 25, 1944, Pius XII sent a telegram to Admiral Horthy of Hungary, protesting the deportations and speaking out for those who were being persecuted "on account of their national or racial origin," asking him to do "everything in [his] power to save many unfortunate people from further pain and sorrow." For the full telegram, see Jenö Lévai's *Black Book on the Marty-dom of Hungarian Jewry* (Zürich: Central European Times, 1948), p. 232.

After the liberation of Rome—according to Oscar Halecki's *Eugenio Pacelli: Pope of Peace* (p. 340)—Pius added: "For centuries, they [Jews every-where] have been most unjustly treated and despised. It is time they were treated with justice and humanity. God wills it and the Church wills it. St. Paul tells us that the Jews are our brothers. Instead of being treated as strangers they should be welcomed as friends." And in his June 2, 1945, ad-dress to the College of Cardinals, after Nazi Germany's defeat, Pius XII de-clared that Pius XI's encyclical letter *Mit brennender Sorge* (which Pacelli himself had partially written while serving as secretary of state) had shown "what National-Socialism really was—an arrogant apostasy from Jesus Christ, the denial of His doctrine and of His work of redemption, the cult of vio-lence, the idolatry of race and blood, the overthrow of human liberty and dignity." (The complete text appears in the *Acta Apostolicae Sedis* 37, pp. 159–168, and *L'Osservatore Romano*, June 3, 1945, pp. 1–2; an English trans-lation by Canon G.D. Smith appears in *The Pope and the Nazis* [London: Catholic Truth Society, 1945] and the *Tablet*, June 9, 1945, pp. 268–270).

2. The Place of the 1933 Concordat

Few documents in the history of the Church have been more debated than the concordat between the Holy See and the Third Reich signed on July 20, 1933. The official text appears in the *Acta Apostolica Sedis* 21, pp. 389–408, and an English translation in *Controversial Concordats*, pp. 205–214.

Authorized by Pius XI and negotiated by his secretary of state, Eugenio Pacelli, the concordat has become a lightning rod among Pacelli's detractors, who see in it the first indication of his alleged appeasement of Nazi Germany. According to these critics, Pacelli, by masterminding the concordat, formally aligned the Vatican with Nazism; effectively silenced the Catholic opposition to Hitler; imposed papal control (via canon law) over an unwilling German Catholic community; secretly agreed, with his German colleague Monsignor Ludwig Kaas, to destroy Germany's anti-Nazi Catholic Center Party in ex-change for the concordat; forced the Center Party to vote for the Enabling Act (March 23, 1933), which enabled Hitler to establish a dictatorship; and gave Hitler the propaganda boost he needed to begin World War II.

This criticism is often extended to German Catholics under Hitler, espe-cially to the German bishops. Guenter Lewy's *The Catholic Church and Nazi Germany* began this argument and was followed by such works as *Capitu-lation: An Analysis of Contemporary Catholicism* by Carl Amery (London: Sheed and Ward, 1967); *The German Church Struggle and the Holocaust*, ed-ited by Franklin Littell and Hubert Locke (Detroit: Wayne State University, 1974); *The German Churches Under Hitler* by Ernst C. Helmreich (Detroit:

Wayne State University, 1979); *Betrayal: German Churches and the Holocaust*, edited by Robert P. Erickson and Susannah Heschel (Minneapolis: Fortress, 1999); *Christian Responses to the Holocaust: Moral and Ethical Issues*, edited by Donald Dietrich (Syracuse: Syracuse University, 2003); and also the essay, "The Vatican Concordat With Hitler's Reich" by Robert A. Krieg, *America*, September 1, 2003, pp. 14–17. Saul Friedlander's *Nazi Germany and the Jews: The Years of Persecution, 1933–1939* (New York: HarperCollins, 1997), the first of a projected two-volume work, is well researched, but its negative depiction of the Concordat and the Church in Germany is very one-sided. Eric A. Johnson's *Nazi Terror: The Gestapo, Jews and Ordinary Germans* (New York: Basic, 2000) is somewhat more fair to the Catholic Church under a totalitarian regime but still pursues this line of attack.

Answers to these charges are meticulously documented in the leading German works on the subject: *Staatliche Akten über die Reichskonkordatsverhandlungen, 1933* by Alfons Kupper (Mainz: Matthias-Grünewald, 1969), a collection of primary documents relating to the concordat; *Das Reichskonkordat vom 20 Juli 1933* by Ludwig Volk (Mainz: Matthias-Grünewald, 1972), the finest work on the subject; and *Deutsche Katholiken, 1918–1945* by Heinz Hürten (Paderborn: Ferdinand Schöningh, 1992), the definitive history of German Catholicism during the early twentieth century.

Michael Feldkamp's *Pius XII. und Deutschland* also analyzes and defends Pacelli's role in the concordat. Edward N. Peter's work on the Code of Canon Law, *1917 Pio-Benedictine Code of Canon Law* (San Francisco: Ignatius, 2001), which Cardinal Pacelli helped craft, is essential to understanding Church law, which the concordat helped secure in Germany. Far from impeding the integrity of the Catholic faith of German Catholics, the 1917 code actually preserved it, not least because it called for the automatic excommunication of apostates (such as Hitler), a fact that many critics of the Church—who erroneously believe that Hitler and his Nazi apostates were never excommunicated—continue to ignore.

With the publication of these books (based upon previously unavailable archives), earlier works that portrayed the concordat as a Catholic pact with Hitler were decisively refuted. Nonetheless, a number of authors continue to attack it. See, for example, as well the strident "Pakt zwischen Himmel und Hölle. Trägt die katholische Kirche eine Mitschuld am Holocaust?" by Gerhard Besier and Klaus Wiegrefe in *Der Spiegel*, April 21, 2003, pp. 64–73. And John Cornwell in *Hitler's Pope*, for another example, positively demonizes it.

Cornwell's thesis—that the concordat was an unmitigated disaster, driven by Pacelli and exploited by Hitler to construct his evil empire—is a repetition, couched in popular prose, of Klaus Schoider's *Die Kirchen und das Dritte Reich* (Frankfurt: Ullstein, 1977), later translated into English as *The Churches and the Third Reich* (Philadelphia: Fortress, 1988). Scholder's interpretations of his sources is highly questionable, and his key claim—that

Hitler exchanged a promise to conclude a concordat for Cardinal Pacelli's promise to abandon the Center Party—remains undocumented and unconvincing. Even the editors of Scholder's surviving papers admit (in an introduction to a posthumous collection of Scholder's essays) that Scholder's anti-Pacelli thesis could not be supported from the available records (see Gerhard Besier in *A Requiem for Hitler* [Philadelphia: Trinity, 1989], pp. xii–xiii).

Shortly after Scholder's work appeared, it was comprehensively refuted by Konrad Repgen. See, especially, "Über die Entstehung der Reichskonkordats Offerte im Frühjahr 1933 und die Bedeutung des Reichskonkordats" in *Vierteljahrshefte für Zeitgeschichte* 26 (1978), pp. 499–534; "Zur vatikanischen Strategie beim Reichskonkordat" in *Vierteljahrshefte für Zeitgeschichte* 31 (1983), pp. 518–534; Repgen's essay in *Demokratie und Diktatur*, edited by Manfred Funke (Düsseldorf: Droste, 1987), pp. 157–177; and also the collection of articles Repgen edited, *Die Katholiken und das Dritte Reich* (Mainz: Matthias-Grünewald, 1990).

Although the best scholarship on the concordat remains in German, two studies that draw on primary sources have appeared in English: John Jay Hughes's "The Pope's 'Pact with Hitler': Betrayal or Self-Defense?" published in *Journal of Church and State* 17 (1975), pp. 63–80, and Stewart Stehlin's comprehensive *Weimar and the Vatican, 1917–1933: German-Vatican Relations in the Interwar Years* (Princeton: Princeton University, 1983). Not to be forgotten in any of this is that Cardinal Pacelli, less than a week after the concordat was signed, published two comprehensive articles in *L'Osservatore Romano* (July 26 and 27, 1933) explaining the exact terms of the concordat and rejecting the notion that it implied any philosophical agreement with Hitler's regime.

Critics who view the concordat as a stepping-stone to the Holocaust frequently quote Hitler's dictum of July 14, 1933, that the treaty "will be especially significant in the urgent struggle against international Jewry." But what they rarely mention is that Hitler later reversed himself and came to see the concordat as subversive. The supplementary protocol to article 32 states that the concordat "does not involve any sort of limitations of official and prescribed preaching and interpretation of the dogmatic and moral teachings and principles of the Church" (an article Pacelli fought hard to obtain).

Hitler's infamous *Table Talk*, transcripts of his private tirades taken down by a stenographer, provide ample proof that the Church used this provision to resist the Nazis. On February 8, 1942, he raged: "The evil that's gnawing our vitals is our priests. . . . The time will come when I'll settle my accounts with them, and I'll go straight to the point. . . . In less than ten years from now, things will have quite another look, I can promise them." On April 7, 1942: "Now, the priests' chief activity consists in undermining National-Socialist policy. The habit of exploiting the state goes back a long way. In periods of national tension, the Catholic Church always tried to occupy positions of temporal power, and always at the expense of the German community." And on July 4, 1942: "Once the war is over we will put a swift end to the concordat. It will give me the greatest personal pleasure to point out to the Church all those occasions on which it has broken the terms of it. One need only recall the close cooperation between the Church and the murderers of [Nazi leader Reinhard] Heydrich. Catholic priests not only allowed them to hide in a Church . . . but even allowed them to entrench themselves in the sanctuary of the altar. . . . Not only the history of the past, but also present times afford numberless examples of the very hard-boiled diplomats to be found in the service of the Catholic Church, and of how extremely cautious one must be in dealing with them" (*Hitler's Table Talk: 1941–1944*, edited by H.R. Trevor-Roper [third edition New York: Enigma, 2000], pp. 304, 410, and 553–554).

The anti-Catholic activities of the Ministry of Church Affairs, established by Hitler in 1935 to bring the churches into line, provides clear evidence that the concordat did not prevent the Church from fighting the Nazis on a moral, religious, and even political level. On this issue, see Heike Kreutzer's *Das Reichskirchenministerium im Gefüge der nationalsozialistischen Herrschaft* (Düsseldorf: Droste, 2000) and John Conway's comments on the book in *German History*, October 2002, pp. 400–401. S.K. Padover's "Nazi Scapegoat Number 2," on Nazi anti-Catholicism being second only to Nazi anti-Semitism (*Reader's Digest*, February 1939, pp. 1–5), is a contemporaneous report on the Third Reich's war against the Church. Padover quotes the notorious Nazi organ *Völkischer Beobachter* (October 15, 1938, Vienna edition) as declaring: "We are armed to continue the battle against Catholicism until the point of total annihilation."

More evidence of Catholic resistance can be found in *The Persecution of the Catholic Church in the Third Reich*, a 565-page volume of primary material, including salient statements from the German Catholic bishops, a mass of documents from the anti-Catholic Nazi press, testimony regarding the Catholic-Jewish alliance, and descriptions of the tortures inflicted upon German Catholics for refusing to collaborate with the Nazi regime. Originally assembled and translated into English by Father Walter Mariaux—an exiled German Jesuit, working in the Curia, to whom the German Catholic resistance smuggled this material—the publication of this book was formally encouraged by Pius XII and welcomed by the Allies, particularly the British, who helped finance its circulation. For an excellent review of the book after its original publication, see "The Anti-Christians" by Edward Quinn in the *Tablet*, January 4, 1941, p. 12. See also *Hitler Came for Niemöller: The Nazi War Against Religion* by Leo Stein, especially Appendix B (1942; reprinted Gretna: Pelican, 2003); and Johan Snoek's *The Grey Book* (New York: Humanities, 1970) which recounts the Protestant resistance.

Ulrich von Hehl's 1984 *Priester unter Hitlers Terror* is a massive biographical and statistical survey documenting how up to one-third of the German

Catholic clergy came into conflict with the Nazi regime, experiencing everything from police interrogations to imprisonment and execution. After the
racially targeted Jews and Gypsies, few segments of the German population
experienced this level of victimization. Bernhard Stasiewski and Ludwig Volk
have edited six volumes of the correspondence and statements of the German Catholic bishops during the Nazi era: *Akten Deutscher Bischöfe über die
Lage der Kirche 1933–1945* (Mainz: Matthias-Grünewald, 1968–1985). Volume 1 contains extensive material on the background of the concordat,
showing how Pius XI, Cardinal Pacelli, and the German episcopacy coordinated their efforts. Also included in these documents are the major anti-Nazi
pastoral letters of the German bishops. (For an English summary, see Lothar
Groppe's two-part article "The Church's Struggle With the Third Reich" and
"The Church and the Jews in the Third Reich" in *Fidelity*, October 1983, pp.
12–15 and 23–27, and November 1983, pp. 18–27.)

For a recent study of Catholics and Jews under the Third Reich—contend-
ing that there was far more unity and solidarity than is now claimed by anti-
Church polemicists—see *Die Schuld: Christen und Juden im Urteil der Na-
tionalsozialisten und der Gegenwart* by Konrad Löw (Gräfelfing: Resch,
2002). An article about Löw's important study comments: "The book's greatest contribution is the documentation presented in its 355 pages, including
1,063 footnotes and a 331-item bibliography. Löw uses specific historical
documents to address aspects of Nazi policy up to now little known, in particular the continuous and systematic persecution of Catholics. The Bavarian
author demonstrates, in a critical spirit, how *Zentrum*, the Catholic Party, was
supported and voted for precisely by Jews, a phenomenon that can be explained by the fact that the Catholic Church condemned the nascent racism
and nationalism with great clarity. . . . According to Nazi theory, Christianity's
roots in the Old Testament meant that whoever was against the Jews should
also be against the Catholic Church. And ample documentation, gathered by
Löw, records Catholic assistance to Jews, which angered the Nazis" ("Nazis'
Anti-Catholicism Ran Deep," Zenit News Agency, December 23, 2002).

In *The Holy Reich: Nazi Conceptions of Christianity, 1919–1945* (Cambridge: Cambridge University, 2003), Richard Steigmann-Gall shows how
Hitler and the Nazis tried to appropriate and pervert Christianity, particularly
liberal Protestantism, but failed repeatedly to penetrate the inner sanctum of
the Catholic Church, which was seen as an enemy of the Third Reich. Hitler,
writes Steigmann-Gall, "resonated Streicher's contention that the Catholic establishment was allying itself with the Jews" (p. 65).

The memoirs of Heinrich Brüning, *Memoiren, 1918–1934* (Stuttgart:
Deutsche Verlags-Anstalt, 1970), the embittered German chancellor from
1930 to 1932 and leader of the German Catholic Center Party, are often cited
by Pacelli's detractors (particularly Klaus Scholder and John Cornwell) as
proof that Cardinal Pacelli and Monsignor Kaas sacrificed the Center Party in

exchange for the concordat. But, as Heinz Hürten points out, "historians have shown that Brüning's account has little foundation in reality" (*Stimmen der Zeit*, March 2000, pp. 205–208). And Brüning's biographer William Patch agrees that Brüning "was misguided . . . to insinuate that the Vatican bore responsibility for his fall as chancellor or the dissolution of the Center Party in 1933. . . . [T]here is no evidence that the Vatican undermined Brüning's position" (*Heinrich Brüning and the Dissolution of the Weimar Republic* [Cambridge: Cambridge University, 1998], p. 327).

Newly released documents go even further to show the Vatican was not consulted in advance about negotiations between the Center Party and Hitler on the question of full powers after the elections of March 5, 1933. See "Archives Vindicate Vatican on Hitler's Appointment, Says Review," Zenit News Agency, December 19, 2003, based on Giovanni Sale's article, "La Santa Sede e il nazismo," *Civiltà Cattolica* 2003, volume 4, pp. 552–565.

For two good histories of the party, see *The German Center Party, 1879–1933* by Ellen Lovell Evans (Carbondale: Southern Illinois University, 1981) and *The Path to Christian Democracy: German Catholics and the Party System from Windthorst to Adenauer* by Noel Cary (Cambridge: Harvard University, 1996). The life of Monsignor Ludwig Kaas—the last chairman of the Catholic Center Party, who resigned after the Enabling Law, and went to Rome to work closely with Pacelli during the concordat negotiations—is covered in three volumes by biographer Georg May, *Ludwig Kaas: der Priester, der Politiker und der Gelehrte aus der Schule von Ulrich Stutz* (Amsterdam: B.R. Grüner, 1981–1982).

This new scholarship has led many historians not especially partial to the Vatican to adopt a more balanced view. See, for example, Donald Dietrich's sympathetic treatment of the concordat in his *Catholic Citizens in the Third Reich: Psycho-Social Principles and Moral Reasoning* (New Brunswick: Transaction, 1988) and various essays in Frank J. Coppa's *Controversial Concordats*. Also of note is *Pius XII and the Holocaust* by José M. Sánchez, especially chapter 6, "The Need for Protection of German Catholics," pp. 81–89. Notable, too, is the statement by the Austrian Catholic philosopher, Dietrich von Hildebrand, a famous opponent of Hitler: "The concordat itself did not contain any yielding to Nazism—and Germany at that time was still a militarily weak country. It was not yet the dangerous aggressive power that it became in 1938; Hitler was not yet at the head of a strong and powerful state. Germany was still tolerated as a member of the 'League of Nations' in Geneva; the borders of Germany were still the ones defined in the treaty at Versailles; France was still considered the main power of Europe. But as soon as Pope Pius XI saw that Hitler was not respecting the terms of the concordat . . . he raised his voice in the magnificent encyclical, *Mit brennender Sorge*" (*Satan at Work* [St. Paul: Remnant, n.d.], p. 41).

One aspect of the concordat almost never mentioned by its critics is its provision to protect Catholics of Jewish descent: "Regardless of any Nazi doctrine to the contrary, the Church would not accept the view that a person who had been duly converted to Catholicism was still a Jew. To the Church, the issue was one of faith, not race. Accordingly, as part of the concordat, German officials agreed to regard baptized Jews as Christians. This ended up being one of the most important agreements between the Vatican and the Third Reich—one that saved the lives of thousands of Jews" ("The 1933 Concordat between Germany and the Holy See" by Ronald Rychlak in the 2001 *Digest* of the National Italian American Bar Association, p. 34; see also Rychlak's *Hitler, the War, and the Pope*, p. 60).

Many German Jews took advantage of this provision. John Lukacs notes: "Between 1900 and 1932 in Germany, six times as many Jews converted to various Protestant churches than to the Roman Catholic Church. Between 1933 [the year of the concordat] and 1939 the very opposite was true: Eighty percent of Jewish converts chose Catholicism" (*The Last European War*, p. 466, n. 81). An explanation is the one given by Rychlak: The Church, thanks in large measure to the much-maligned concordat, was acting as a refuge for persecuted Jews.

But did the concordat really save "thousands," as Rychlak maintains? John Keegan in *The Second World War* (New York: Viking, 1989) reports that "by November 1938 some 150,000 of Germany's half million Jews managed to emigrate" (p. 288). How many of these were converted Jews, how many came into the Church because of the concordat, how many were assisted out of the country by Church organizations, and how many of them ultimately survived the Holocaust, is not known with precision, but Rychlak's thousands is a very conservative estimate. What is known for certain is that contemporaries of the time credited the concordat with saving many Jewish lives in spite of the Nazis' frequent violations of it. Zsolt Aradi, a Hungarian diplomat stationed in Rome during the 1930s, who had many audiences with Pius XI and was intimately acquainted with scores of Vatican officials, confirms this: "Actually, the little freedom that the concordat left for the clergy and hierarchy was widely used to save as many persecuted Jews as could be saved" (*Pius XII*, p. 222).

The concordat was not the first international treaty signed by Nazi Germany. It was preceded by over a month, for example, by the Four Power Pact—between Britain, Germany, Italy, and France—signed on June 7, 1933; two days later, Pius XI delivered an address recognizing that the international community believed it was necessary to at least *try* to negotiate with Germany, for the sake of peace: see excerpts from his address to a pilgrimage from Spain, June 9, 1933 (*Principles for Peace*, p. 475).

On this and related issues, see Dennis Barton's monograph *Hitler's Rise to Power* (Birkenhead: Church in History Information Centre, 1986) and Henry Ashby Turner's *Hitler's Thirty Days to Power* (Reading: Addison-Wesley, 1996). Turner points to January 1933 (well before the concordat) as the pivotal moment for Germany and holds three men responsible for allowing Hitler to seize power: President Paul von Hindenburg, Chancellor Kurt von Schleicher, and former Chancellor Franz von Papen. Three others—Oskar von Hindenburg, Otto Meissner, and Alfred Hugenberg—are judged to bear lesser but still significant guilt for facilitating Hitler's dictatorship. Pius XI and Cardinal Eugenio Pacelli are not blamed for anything.

3. The Role of the Anti-Nazi Resistance

Pius XII's support for the anti-Nazi resistance that tried to overthrow Hitler is amply documented in the general works of Owen Chadwick and Peter Hoffmann. But there are also a number of specialized studies. The most authoritative is Harold C. Deutsch's *The Conspiracy Against Hitler in the Twilight War* (Minneapolis: University of Minnesota, 1970). Deutsch, who served as an American intelligence official, based much of his book on personal interviews with the surviving participants of plots to overthrow Hitler, including Father Robert Leiber, Pius XII's private assistant. Deutsch writes that as soon as the pope was approached by the German resistance, in hopes of secretly contacting the British, he responded enthusiastically: "Customarily the most deliberate of men, Pius XII on this occasion made up his mind with little if any hesitation. . . . The pope responded immediately by saying, 'The German Opposition must be heard in Britain,' and declared himself prepared to be its voice" (p. 120).

Concurring is John Waller in *The Unseen War in Europe: Espionage and Conspiracy in the Second World War* (New York: Random House, 1996); see especially chapter 10, "Operation X: The Vatican Connection," pp. 95–103. A particularly good survey is John H. Dombrowski's "The Unneutral Diplomacy of the Vatican During 1939 and 1940" in *Faith and Reason*, Winter 1988, pp. 349–425. Also helpful are Giovanni Sale's essays "La Resistenza nella Germania nazista," *Civiltà Cattolica* 2003, volume 1, pp. 229–242, and "L'attentato a Hitler, la Santa Sede e i Gesuiti," *Civiltà Cattolica* 2003, volume 1, pp. 466–479. See also *Spies in the Vatican: Espionage and Intrigue From Napoleon to the Holocaust* by David Alvarez (Kansas City: University Press of Kansas, 2002) and various articles in *The Encyclopedia of German Resistance to the Nazi Movement*, edited by Wolfgang Benz and Walter H. Pehle (New York: Continuum, 1997), especially pp. 127–129.

Other important works dealing with aspects of the resistance include *They Almost Killed Hitler* by Fabian von Schlabrendorff (New York: Macmillan, 1947); *Germany's Underground* by Allen Dulles (New York: Macmillan, 1947); *To the Bitter End* by Hans Bernd Gisevius (Boston: Houghton Mifflin, 1947); *Nicht aus den Akten* by Erich Kordt (Stuttgart: Union Deutsche Verlagsgesellschaft, 1950); and *Letzte Briefe aus dem Gefängnis Tegel* by Helmuth James von Moltke (Berlin: K.H. Henssel, 1951). On von Moltke—one of the heroes of the resistance, executed by the Nazis in January 1945—see *Helmut von Moltke: A Leader Against Hitler* by Michael Balfour and Julian Frisby (London: Macmillan, 1972) and his *Letters to Freya, 1939–1945* (New York: Knopf, 1990) edited by Beate Ruhm von Oppen.

The resistance and the plot against Hitler are topics that have seen endless discussion. Worthwhile are *Holding the Stirrup* by Elizabeth von Guttenberg (New York: Duell, Sloan, and Pearce, 1952); *Hitler's Conservative Opponents in Bavaria 1930–1945: A Study of Catholic, Monarchist and Separatist Anti-Nazi Activities* by James Donahue (Leiden: E.J. Brill, 1961); *German Resistance to Hitler: Ethical and Religious Factors* by Mary Alice Gallin (Washington: Catholic University, 1961); *The German Opposition to Hitler* by Hans Rothfels (Chicago: Henry Regnery, 1963); *The Men Who Tried to Kill Hitler* by Roger Manvell and Heinrich Fraenkel (New York: Coward-McCann, 1964); Peter Ludlow's "Papst Pius XII, die britische Regierung und die deutsche Opposition im Winter 1939/40," *Vierteljahrshefte für Zeitgeschichte* 22 (1974), pp. 299–341; *Bodyguard of Lies* by Anthony Cave Brown (New York: Harper and Row, 1975); *Canaris* by Heinz Höhne (Garden City: Doubleday, 1976); *To Kill the Devil: The Attempts on the Life of Adolf Hitler* by Herbert Malloy Mason Jr. (New York: W.W. Norton, 1978); *Orchestra nera: militari, civili, preti cattolici, pastori protestanti, una rete contro Hitler: che ruolo ebbe Pio XII?* by Domenico Bernabei (Turin: ERI, 1991), especially strong on the role of Pius XII; *German Resistance Against Hitler: The Search for Allies Abroad, 1938–1945* by Klemens von Klemperer (Oxford: Clarendon, 1992); *The Unnecessary War: Whitehall and the German Resistance to Hitler* by Patricia Meehan (London: Sinclair-Stevenson, 1992); *An Honourable Defeat: A History of German Resistance to Hitler, 1933–1945* by Anton Gill (New York: Henry Holt, 1994); *Plotting Hitler's Death* by Joachim Fest (New York: Henry Holt, 1996); *The Oster Conspiracy of 1938: The Unknown Story of the Military Plot to Kill Hitler and Avert World War II* by Terry Parssinen (New York: HarperCollins, 2003); and *Alternatives to Hitler: German Resistance under the Third Reich* by Hans Mommsen (Princeton: Princeton University, 2003).

Mark Riebling's forthcoming book breaks new ground, revealing important new details on Pius's daring efforts to rid the world of Hitler. Riebling, one of the top intelligence experts in the world, has written extensively in support of Pius XII, using primary archives from around the world. He has also been in the forefront in correcting and rebuking other historians for failing to emphasize Pius's prominent role in the numerous anti-Hitler plots. (For more, with links to important articles on this subject, see Riebling's website: www.markriebling.com.)

The memoirs of two central figures in the conspiracy against Hitler—Ulrich von Hassell and Josef Müller—are indispensable for an understanding of the resistance movement and the pope's involvement. *The von Hassell Diaries: The Story of the Forces Against Hitler Inside Germany, 1938–1944* (New York: Doubleday, 1947) contains the reflections of the famous resistance leader during the years before his arrest and execution. (The German original, *Vom andern Deutschland* [Zürich: Atlantis, 1946], contains additional notes and appendices.) Von Hassell had a high regard for Pius XII. "The pope was apparently prepared to go to surprising lengths in his understanding of German interests," he writes in his entry for March 19, 1940. Three years later, von Hassell notes: "Gisevius [his fellow conspirator], who has frequent meetings with Christian circles in foreign countries, told me that I am in good repute by the pope" (March 6, 1943).

Müller, a Catholic lawyer from Munich, served as an intermediary between the pope and the German generals. Though arrested, Müller miraculously survived the war and wrote about his harrowing experiences in *Bis zur letzten Konsequenz* (Munich: Süddeutscher Verlag, 1975).

Pius XII's relations with the anti-Nazi resistance was revealed by Müller to the American diplomat Harold H. Tittmann Jr. At the end of the war, Müller told Tittmann that the resistance had been advising Pius XII throughout the war. "Dr. Mueller said that during the war his anti-Nazi organization in Germany had always been very insistent that the Pope should refrain from making any public statement singling out the Nazis and specifically condemning them and had recommended that the Pope's remarks should be confined to generalities only. Dr. Mueller said that he was obliged to give this advice, since, if the Pope had been specific, Germans would have accused him of yielding to the promptings of foreign powers and this would have made the German Catholics even more suspected than they were and would have greatly restricted their freedom of action in their work of resistance to the Nazis. Dr. Mueller said that the policy of the Catholic resistance in Germany was that the Pope should stand aside while the German hierarchy carried out the struggle against the Nazis inside Germany, without outside influence being brought to bear. Dr. Mueller said that the Pope had followed this advice throughout the war" (memo of Harold Tittmann to Ambassador Myron Taylor, June 4, 1945, quoted in Tittmann's *Inside the Vatican of Pius XII*, pp. 212–213).

This revelation of counsel from the anti-Nazi resistance, added to the others (notably the Polish bishops under Nazi occupation) urging similar restraint, seriously undermines the case of those outside Nazi occupation—as well as critics today—that Pius XII should have "spoken out" more than he did. Tittmann emphasizes that "the Pope, on a number of occasions, had already openly condemned major offenses against morality in wartime. The terms have been general but the world well knew to whom the words of condemnation were addressed" (p. 119).

Recently released archives from the Office of Strategic Services, the American wartime intelligence organization, confirm Pius XII's involvement with the anti-Nazi resistance. The O.S.S. had a confidential interview with Father Leiber after the liberation of Rome, on August 18, 1944. In a newly declassified document detailing the interview, the O.S.S. reported: "At the present time, Father Leiber's official position is simply that of professor at the Gregoriana. His friends know, however, that he is also serving as confidential secretary to the pope, whom he sees almost daily. These friends (who include Baron Froelichsthal of the Austrian Office) consider him a thorough anti-Nazi. . . . Although he has not been in Germany since 1932, Father Leiber has unusual sources of information on the history of conspiracies against the Nazi regime." A footnote adds: "Between 1939 and 1943 the Catholic lawyer Josef Müller had been Leiber's chief contact to the German opposition. Through Müller he was in touch with oppositional circles in the Abwehr [the German intelligence] including Hans Oster and Hans von Dohnanyi, but also with the theologian Dietrich Bonhoeffer. After the arrest of Müller, Bonhoeffer and Dohnanyi, Father Leiber got his information on the German resistance through Hans Bernd Gisevius" (document 65 in *American Intelligence and the German Resistance to Hitler: A Documentary History*, edited by Jürgen Heideking, Marc Frey, and Christof Mauch [Boulder: Westview, 1996]).

It is significant that Dietrich Bonhoeffer, the famed anti-Nazi martyr, also kept Pius XII informed of his activities. Bonhoeffer trusted the pope with highly sensitive information and obviously considered him an ally. For more on Bonhoeffer, see Eberhard Bethge's *Dietrich Bonhoeffer: Theologian, Christian, Contemporary* (English translation 1970; revised edition Minneapolis: Fortress, 2000), the celebrated and authoritative biography by one of Bonhoeffer's friends. For a rebuttal of the attempt to divide Bonhoeffer and Pius XII, see "Invidious Comparisons" by Richard John Neuhaus in *First Things*, January 2000, pp. 67–68.

After the war, Pius XII typed and corrected in his own hand an article for *L'Osservatore Romano* on his role in the conspiracy. The unsigned article, whose papal origins were discovered in the archives of the Vatican by Father Robert Graham, appeared on the front page of the February 11, 1946, issue, under the title, "La verità circa un asserito intervento." For further details, see "Pope Involved in Plot Against Hitler, Says Vatican Historian, Book" in the *Pilot*, May 22, 1987, p. 14; for a facsimile of Pius XII's article for *L'Osservatore*, see *Actes et Documents* 1, p. 514.

As new evidence emerges from various archives, detailing Pius XII's contacts with the anti-Nazi resistance, more and more historians are beginning to highlight Pius's efforts, which explain why the Nazis "considered the Roman Catholic Church its most dangerous ideological adversary" (Lutheran church historian Gerhard Besier, quoted in "Protestant Witness for Pius XII," United Press International, April 2, 2003).

4.The Question of Communism

During the Second World War, Pius XII faced not only Nazism and Italian fascism, but also communism. Though the Holy See tried to publicize the evils of Stalin, as well as Hitler, the mass murders committed by communists were often overshadowed by the Third Reich's atrocities. The terror-famine in the Ukraine, conducted by Joseph Stalin in 1932 and 1933, killed an estimated seven million Ukrainians. See *The Harvest of Sorrow: Soviet Collectivization and the Terror-Famine* by Robert Conquest (Oxford: Oxford University, 1986).

With few exceptions such as the journalist Malcolm Muggeridge, the Ukrainian famine went virtually unnoticed in the Western media. Indeed, Pulitzer prize-winning reporter Walter Duranty actually praised Stalin at the time he was conducting this genocide, and Duranty was by no means alone. See *Stalin's Apologist: Walter Duranty, The New York Times Man in Moscow* by S.J. Taylor (Oxford: Oxford University, 1990).

The best work on Pius XII and communism remains *The Vatican and Communism During World War II* by Robert A. Graham. As Father Graham explained, in Pius XII's view, those subscribing to the Judeo-Christian moral tradition were obligated to oppose all totalitarian ideologies, but the pope often made strategic decisions in waging the battle. Thus in 1941, after the Nazis invaded Russia, some anticommunists wanted Pius XII to bless the act as a crusade against "godless Bolshevism," but the pontiff steadfastly refused. On the contrary, in a speech on June 29, 1941, entitled, "Divine Providence in Human Events," Pius XII, though widely expected to comment, refrained from mentioning the Soviet Union at all. Pius XII's "silence" about this subject pleased the Allies greatly. (See "Pope Keeps Silent on Axis 'Crusade'" by Herbert L. Mathews, *New York Times*, June 30, 1941; for the text of Pius XII's address, see *Acta Apostolicae Sedis* 33, pp. 319–325; an English translation appears in *Catholic Mind*, August 8, 1941, pp. 1–10).

Similarly, when some American Catholics balked at supporting America's lend-lease program to Russia, Pius XII intervened to assist the Allies. As Pierre Blet explains: "The texts published in the fifth volume of *Actes et Documents* dispose entirely of the idea that the Holy See supported the Third Reich out of fear of Soviet Russia. When Roosevelt asked the Vatican to help overcome the American Catholics' opposition to his plan to extend to Russia, fighting against the Reich, the support already being given to Great Britain, he was listened to. The Secretariat of State charged the Apostolic Delegate in Washington to entrust to an American bishop the task of explaining that [Pius XI's] encyclical *Divini Redemptoris*—which ordered Catholics to refuse alliance with all the Communist parties—was not to apply to the present situation and did not forbid the U.S.A. from helping Soviet Russia in its war against the Third Reich" (*Civiltà Cattolica* 1998, volume 1, p. 541). See also Blet's analysis in *Pius XII and the Second World War*, pp. 119–127.

Richard Overy adds that in the weeks leading up to American congressional approval of Lend-Lease aid for Russia—when the president was fighting hard to overcome resistance to it—"Roosevelt was also armed with a personal assurance from the new pope, Pius XII, that the encyclical condemning communism could be sufficiently bent to allow Catholics to support aid for the suffering Russian people. American Christians of all denominations could now rally to the cause with a clear conscience" (*Why the Allies Won* [New York: W.W. Norton, 1995], p. 285). On Pius XII's diplomatic assistance to Roosevelt during this time, see William L. Langer and S. Everett Gleason's *The World Crisis and American Foreign Policy: The Undeclared War 1940–1941* (New York: Harper and Brothers, 1953) and R.H. Dawson's *The Decision to Aid Russia, 1941* (Chapel Hill: University of North Carolina, 1959).

It is significant that the Catholic-Jewish historical panel charged in 1999 with reviewing the Holy See's wartime documents found no evidence that Pius XII saw Nazism as a bulwark against the Soviet Union (as authors such as Saul Friedlander and Guenter Lewy have argued); on the contrary, the panel wrote: "The case has repeatedly been made that the Vatican's fear of communism prompted it to mute and limit its criticism of Nazi atrocities and occupation policies. We are struck by the paucity of evidence to this effect and the subject of communism in general. Indeed our reading of the volumes presents a different picture, especially with regard to the Vatican promotion of the American bishops' support for the alliance between the United States and the Soviet Union to oppose Nazism" (*The Vatican and the Holocaust: A Preliminary Report Submitted to the Holy See's Commission for Religious Relations with the Jews and the International Jewish Committee for Interreligious Consultations* by the International Catholic-Jewish Historical Commission, October 2000; see also *Actes et Documents* 5, pp. 361ff).

Also of note: "In the British Public Record Office, there is a short message dated May 10, 1943, from the British Embassy in Madrid. It reports on a message that had been forwarded by a member of the Spanish Ministry of Foreign Affairs. According to this report, 'In a recent dispatch the Spanish Ambassador reported that in conversation with the pope, the latter informed him that he now regarded Nazism and fascism, and not communism, as he used to, as the greatest menace to civilization and the Roman Catholic Church'" (Rychlak in *Hitler, the War, and the Pope*, pp. 257 and 415 n. 78, citing British Public Records Office, FO 3711 37538).

The general wartime policy of the Vatican is summarized by Oscar Halecki: "It seems obvious, from the Vatican's refusal to proclaim a holy war against communism, that the Holy See considered Nazism an even greater danger to religion and peace than communism. . . . Because of this menace, the pope was most anxious that the Nazis be defeated in the shortest possible time, so that the free forces of the world would retain enough strength to confront the inevitable challenge of communism" (*Eugenio Pacelli: Pope of Peace*, pp. 146–147). Pius XII himself confirmed this strategy in December 1942, when he told Father Paolo Dezza (then rector of the Pontifical Gregorian University of Rome): "Yes, the Communists are a danger, but at this moment, the Nazi danger is greater still" (*Osservatore della Domenica*, June 28, 1964, pp. 68–69).

After the war, in an address to the College of Cardinals and the diplomatic corps, Pius XII said: "We took special care, notwithstanding certain tendentious pressures, not to let fall from our lips or from our pen one single word, one single sign of approval or encouragement of the war against Russia in 1941" (allocution of February 25, 1946, published in the *Acta Apostolica Sedis* 38, p. 154). And in his apostolic letter to the Russian people, *Sacro Vergente Anno* (July 7, 1952), Pius was equally explicit: "Never at that time, was heard from our lips a word that could have seemed to any of the belligerents to be unjust or harsh. We certainly reproached, as was our duty, every evil and every violation of rights; but we did this in such a way as to avoid with all care whatever might become, even unjustly, an occasion for greater affliction of the oppressed peoples. Then, when pressure was brought to bear upon us to give our approval in some way, either verbally or in writing, to the war undertaken against Russia in 1941 we never consented to do so."

One interesting fact is Pius's public opposition to the execution of Julius and Ethel Rosenberg—hardly the action of an obsessed anticommunist, insensitive to the anti-Semitism aroused by the case. On this issue, see "After 50 Years, Rosenbergs' Executions Evoke Memories," *Chicago Tribune*, June 20, 2003, p. 14.

In *Stalin's Secret War* (New York: Holt, Rinehart and Winston, 1981), Nikolai Tolstoy estimates that at least half of the estimated 20 to 30 million Russians who died during World War II were killed because of Joseph Stalin's own murderous practices. For general studies on the monumental crimes of communists, see *The Black Book of Communism: Crimes, Terror, Repression*, edited by Stéphane Courtois, et al. (Cambridge: Harvard University, 1999), which estimates the number killed at 100 million during the twentieth century; *The Gulag Archipelago* by Alexander Solzhenitszyn (New York: Harper and Row, 1974–1976); *The Great Terror* by Robert Conquest (1968; revised New York: Oxford University, 1991); *A Century of Violence in Soviet Russia* by Alexander N. Yakovlev, translated by Anthony Austin (New Haven: Yale University, 2002), an excellent modern work on the subject, written by a former Soviet official, who helped his country break free of communism; *Gulag: A History* by Anne Applebaum (New York: Doubleday, 2003); and *In Denial: Historians, Communism and Espionage* by John Earl Haynes and Harvey Klehr (San Francisco: Encounter, 2003).

On the selective indignation of intellectuals who condemn Nazism but excuse communism, see Raymond Aron's *The Opium of the Intellectuals* (originally translated 1957; new edition New Brunswick: Transaction, 2001); *Political Pilgrims: Western Intellectuals in Search of the Good Society* by Paul Hollander (fourth edition New Brunswick: Transaction, 1998); and *Reflections on a Ravaged Century* by Robert Conquest (New York: W.W. Norton, 1999).

For specific studies dealing with communist crimes against religion, particularly the Catholic Church, see *The Catholic Church in Russia Today* by Martha Edith Almedingen (New York: P.J. Kennedy and Sons, 1923); *The Bolshevik Persecution of Christianity* by Francis McCullagh (London: John Murray, 1924); *The Fall of the Russian Empire* by Edmund Walsh (Boston: Little, Brown, and Company, 1928); *Catholicism, Communism and Dictatorship* by C.J. Eustace (New York: Benziger Brothers, 1938); *Descent into Darkness: The Destruction of the Roman Catholic Church in Russia, 1917–1923* by James J. Zatko (South Bend: University of Notre Dame, 1965); the *Memoirs* of Cardinal József Mindszenty (New York: Macmillan, 1974); *The Catholic Church and the Soviet Government, 1939–1949* by Dennis J. Dunn (New York: Columbia University, 1977); *Christianity Confronts Communism* by Charles J. McFadden (Chicago: Franciscan Herald, 1982); *Moscow and the Vatican* by Alexis Ulysses Floridi, S.J. (Ann Arbor: Ardis, 1986); *The Vatican in the Age of the Cold War, 1945–1980* by Anthony Rhodes (Norwich: Michael Russell, 1992); *Il Vaticano e Mosca, 1940–1990* by Andrea Riccardi (Rome: Laterza, 1992); *The Vatican and the Red Flag: The Struggle for the Soil of Eastern Europe* by Jonathan Luxmoore and Jolenta Babiuch (London: Geoffrey Chapman, 1999); *The Catholic Martyrs of the Twentieth Century: A Comprehensive World History* by Robert Royal (New York: Crossroad, 2000).

Peter C. Kent's *The Lonely Cold War of Pope Pius XII: The Roman Catholic Church and the Division of Europe, 1943–1950* (Montreal: McGill-Queen's University, 2002) is an interesting book, though not entirely sound. In a similar vein is *Religion and the Cold War*, edited by Dianne Kirby (New York: Palgrave, 2003). *Enemies of the State: Personal Stories From the Gulag*, edited by Donald T. Critchlow (Chicago: Ivan R. Dee, 2002) is a testament to the power of faith under communism's radical system of evil.

5. Catholic-Jewish Relations

The history of Catholic-Jewish relations has been marked by tension, tragedy, and darkness—but also by friendship, heroism, and light. To understand the relationship in all its depth and complexity is almost an impossible task. Countless books have been written about it, from every conceivable angle. Many recent books have grossly misrepresented its history and created needless anger and confusion. The best books on the subject are written by men and women of faith who have no political or theological agendas to grind and are intensely devoted to truth, balance, and healthy ecumenical relations.

Selecting works that meet that criteria is a difficult task, but the following books, written by distinguished historians, theologians, and ecumenicists, can be heartily recommended as a primer on the subject: *A Social and Religious History of the Jews* by Salo Baron, 18 volumes (New York: Columbia University, 1952; revised and enlarged 1983); *The Jews: A Christian View* by F.W. Foerster, with an introduction by Robert McAfee Brown (New York: Farrar, Straus and Cudahy, 1961); *Jews, God and History* by Max I. Dimont (New York: Simon and Schuster, 1962); "On Jewish History" by Christopher Dawson, *Orbis*, Winter 1967, pp. 1247–1256; *A History of the Jews: From Earliest Times Through the Six Day War* by Cecil Roth (revised edition New York: Schocken, 1970); *A History of the Jews Since the First Century A.D.* by Frederick M. Schweitzer (New York: Macmillan, 1971); *The Anguish of the Jews: Twenty-Three Centuries of Anti-Semitism* by Edward H. Flannery (revised edition Mahwah: Paulist, 1985); *Heritage* by Abba Eban (New York: Summit, 1984); *The Church and the Jewish People* by Cardinal Augustin Bea (New York: Harper and Row, 1966); *The New Encounter Between Christians and Jews* by John M. Oesterreicher (New York: Philosophical Library, 1986); *Twenty Years of Jewish-Catholic Relations*, edited by Eugene Fisher, A. James Rudin, and Marc Tannenbaum (Mahwah: Paulist, 1986); *Encountering Jesus—Encountering Judaism: A Dialogue* by Karl Rahner and Pinchas Lapide (New York: Crossroad, 1987); *Moments of Crisis in Jewish-Christian Relations* by Marc Saperstein (Philadelphia: SCM/Trinity Press International, 1989); *Church and Jewish People: New Considerations* by Cardinal Johannes Willebrands (Mahwah: Paulist, 1992); *Faith Without Prejudice* by Eugene Fisher (New York: Crossroad, 1993); *Spiritual Pilgrimage: Texts on Jews and Judaism, 1979–1995* by John Paul II, with commentary and introduction by Eugene Fisher and Leon Klenicki (New York: Crossroad, 1995); and *The Bible, the Jews and the Death of Jesus: A Collection of Catholic Documents* by the Bishops' Committee for Ecumenical and Interreligious Affairs (Washington: U.S.C.C., 2004).

Also worth reading are *A Rabbi Talks with Jesus: An Intermillennial, Interfaith Exchange* by Jacob Neusner (New York: Image, 1994); and *Catholics Remember the Holocaust* (Washington: United States Catholic Conference, 1998). Cardinal Joseph Ratzinger's "The Heritage of Abraham: The Gift of Christmas" (*Osservatore Romano*, December 29, 2000) is a moving ecumenical statement. See also Ratzinger's *Many Religions, One Covenant: Israel, the Church and the World* (San Francisco: Ignatius, 1999). "Jews and Catholics: Beyond Apologies" by David Novak in *First Things*, January 1999, pp. 20–25, is a welcome response to the Church's acknowledgements of Jewish suffering, written by a prominent Jewish thinker. And "Should the Church Repent?"

by Avery Dulles, also in *First Things*, December 1998, pp. 36–41, is a profound reflection on the Church examination of its own past by America's
leading Catholic theologian.

Christianity in Jewish Terms, edited by Tikva Frymer-Kensky, et al. (Boulder: Westview, 2002), is a major collection of essays by Jewish scholars. On
John Paul II, see George Weigel's acclaimed *Witness to Hope: The Biography
of Pope John Paul II* (New York: Cliff Street, 1999) and "With John Paul II in
the Holy Land," *First Things*, June/July 2000, pp. 27–34, Weigel's commentary on the pope's dramatic visit to Israel, including the pope's moving
speech at Yad Vashem.

For strong refutations of the view, now quite fashionable in academia, that
Christianity caused the Holocaust, see "Anti-Semitism: Boundary of Jewish-
Christian Understanding" by Dale Stover, *Christian Century*, June 26, 1974,
pp. 668–671; "Are Christians Responsible?" by Michael Schwartz in *National
Review*, August 8, 1980, pp. 956–958; "Did Christianity Cause the Holocaust?"
by the editors of *Christianity Today*, April 27, 1998, p. 12; and "Anti-Judaism
vs. Anti-Semitism: Was Christianity Itself Responsible for the Nazi Holocaust?" by Helen M. Valois, *Lay Witness*, October 1998.

Martin Rhonheimer's "The Holocaust: What Was Not Said," *First Things*,
November 2003, pp. 18–27, attempts to reopen the debate about the Church's
responsibility for anti-Judaism, anti-Semitism, and the Holocaust, within a liberal Catholic context. Though measured and well intentioned, it was seriously
challenged by those who judged it biased, limited, and misleading. See the
exchange between Rhonheimer and his critics in the February 2004 issue of
First Things, pp. 2–5, where Rhonheimer emphasizes that "my article was not
about Pius XII and the Holocaust," and insists that it should not be interpreted
as a sweeping indictment of the entire German Church, much less the papacy:
"Indeed, countless Catholics—including Pius XII—brought honor to the
Christian name and gave shining examples of Christian brotherly love."
Overly critical views of Catholic-Jewish relations during the Nazis era have
also been challenged by Konrad Löw in *Die Schuld*, which draws upon newly
released archives to highlight the solidarity and empathy between the two
communities at a time of intense persecution.

For the Catholic attitude toward the theological and political controversies
in the Middle East, see *The Vatican and Zionism: Conflict in the Holy Land,
1895–1925* by Sergio I. Minerbi (Oxford: Oxford University, 1990), and the
more balanced studies *Vatican Policy in the Palestinian-Israeli Conflict: The
Struggle for the Holy Land* by Andrej Kreutz (New York: Greenwood, 1990)
and *The Papacy and the Middle East: The Role of the Holy See in the Arab-
Israeli Conflict, 1962–1984* by George Irani (South Bend: University of Notre
Dame, 1986). Ernest Evans's "The Vatican and Israel," *World Affairs*, Fall
1995, pp. 88–92, is an important essay, as is F. Michael Perko's "Toward a
'Sound and Lasting Basis': Relations Between the Holy See, the Zionist Move-

ment, and Israel, 1896–1996," *Israel Studies*, Spring 1997, pp. 22–49. Also worth noting is *Christian Attitudes Towards the State of Israel* by Paul Charles Merkley (Montreal: McGill-Queen's University, 2002). And see Eugene Fisher's review of Merkley, "The Churches and Israel," *First Things*, February 2002, pp. 62–66, which makes the point that the Catholic world was quite pivotal in establishing the state of Israel.

Both before and after he became pope, Eugenio Pacelli revealed a notably open attitude toward the Zionist movement and indeed befriended one of its earliest leaders, Nahum Sokolow. See *Three Pope and the Jews*, pp. 83–84, 269, 273–275; also the *Jewish Chronicle*, November 25, 1949, p. 13, recounting Benedict XV's meeting with Sokolow in 1917 (which Pacelli helped arrange), which comments: "For many years after his audience with Benedict XV, Sokolow maintained regular contact with Cardinal Gasparri and his successor Cardinal Pacelli, the present Pope Pius XII." See also the discussion in the *Tablet* (October 25, 1958, pp. 370–371), upon Pius XII's death, describing Pius's discussion in 1944 with the high commissioner for Palestine, during which the pope supported "the Jewish aspiration to create a national state in Israel, saying that he was animated with great sympathy for the Jews." Four years later Israel was established.

Yossi Klein Halevi's "Catholicism Is Our Friend," *Jerusalem Post*, December 27, 2002, p. 7B, is a remarkable tribute to the Catholic Church, praising its modern efforts on behalf of Catholic-Jewish relations and calling for an end to the canard that the Catholic Church is not interested in protecting the Jewish community. On this point, see also Klein Halevi's book, *At the Entrance to the Garden of Eden: A Jew's Search for God with Christians and Muslims in the Holy Land* (New York: William Morrow, 2001). Halevi's favorable assessment of contemporary Catholic-Jewish relations is shared by John Paul II and the chief rabbi of Rome. See "Pope Appeals to Catholics and Jews to Work Together for Peace: Receives a Delegation of World Jewish Congress," Zenit News Agency, May 22, 2003, and "Rabbi Credits Pope with New Era in Jewish-Catholic Relations: Rome's Riccardo di Segni Assesses John Paul II's Pontificate," Zenit News Agency, October 31, 2003.

Organizations that foster and chronicle the Catholic-Jewish alliance include SIDIC (Service International de Documentation Judéo-Chrétienne), run by the Sisters of Our Lady of Sion in Rome, and the related Institute for the Study of Religions and Cultures at the Pontifical Gregorian University in Rome, which houses SIDIC's enormous library and also runs the Cardinal Bea Center for Judaic Studies; the Center for the Study of Jewish and Christian Relations at Boston College; the Center for Christian-Jewish Understanding at Sacred Heart University; the Institute for Judeo-Christian Studies at Seton Hall University; and the Institute for Christian and Jewish Studies in Baltimore.

Authoritative texts on Catholic-Jewish relations issued by the Vatican and its Jewish partners can be found at the Vatican's official website (www.vatican.va), at the United States Catholic Conferences website (www.nccbuscc.org), and also at www.jcrelations.net, the most comprehensive website on Christian-Jewish relations.

One of the most important documents, "Dabru Emet: A Jewish Statement on Christians and Christianity," signed by nearly 170 Jewish scholars, was published in the *New York Times*, September 10, 2000, p. 23, and *First Things*, November 2000, pp. 39–44. The document repudiated the modern effort to blame the Holocaust on Christianity and explicitly declared, "Nazism was Not a Christian Phenomenon." On this declaration, see also "Leading Jewish Scholars Extend a Hand to Christians" by Laurie Goodstein in the *New York Times*, September 8, 2000.

Yad Vashem's official website (www.yad-vashem.org.il) has a wealth of material on Catholic-Jewish relations from World War II to the present day. Also invaluable is the multivolume *Encyclopaedia Judaica*, as well as the many articles touching on Jewish and Christian history in *The New Catholic Encyclopedia*. For comprehensive scholarly analysis of every aspect of Church history, including Jewish-Catholic relations, nothing matches the authoritative ten-volume *History of the Church*, edited by Hubert Jedin and John Dolan (New York: Crossroad, 1980–1982).

6. John Paul II and Pius XII

No pope has done more to advance the cause of Catholic-Jewish relations than John Paul II. Because of that fact, many have asked how he would have reacted to the Nazi Holocaust were he to have been pope at the time. The answer has been given by John Paul himself. Since the very beginning of his pontificate, he has consistently, forcefully, and publicly praised Pius XII's wartime record and made abundantly clear that he would have followed the same course.

On March 12, 1979, John Paul told the International Liaison Committee, "I am . . . happy to evoke in your presence today the dedicated and effective work of my predecessor Pius XII on behalf of the Jewish people" (*Spiritual Pilgrimage: Texts on Jews and Judaism*, p. 5). On September 11, 1987, John Paul II told a Jewish audience in Miami: "It is also fitting to recall the strong, unequivocal efforts of the popes against anti-Semitism and Nazism at the height of the persecution against the Jews. Back in 1938, Pius XI declared that 'anti-Semitism cannot be admitted' [September 6, 1938], and he declared the total opposition between Christianity and Nazism by stating that the Nazi cross is an 'enemy of the Cross of Christ' [Christmas allocution, 1938]. And I am convinced that history will reveal ever more clearly and convincingly how deeply Pius XII felt the tragedy of the Jewish people, and how hard and effectively he worked to assist them during the Second World War" (*Spiritual Pilgrimage*, p. 107).

On June 23, 1996, John Paul delivered an official papal statement in response to the attacks against his predecessor: "Anyone who does not limit himself to cheap polemics knows very well what Pius XII thought of the Nazi regime and how much he did to help countless people persecuted by this regime" (*Daily Telegraph*, June 24, 1996; see also *Osservatore Romano*, June 24–25, 1996, pp. 8–9).

In the fall of 1997, during a conference on the origins of anti-Semitism, John Paul "recalled the encyclical *Mit brennender Sorge*, promulgated by Pope Pius XI in 1937, and also *Summi Pontificatus* by Pope Pius XII in 1939. The latter encyclical, he pointed out, invoked the law of human solidarity and charity towards all people in a clear effort to stifle the impulses toward racial hatred" ("Pope Repeats Condemnation of Anti-Semitism," Zenit News Agency, October 31, 1997).

In March of 1998, John Paul released the Vatican's document on the Holocaust, *We Remember: A Reflection on the Shoah*, which stated: "During and after the war, Jewish communities and Jewish leaders expressed their thanks for all that had been done for them, including what Pope Pius XII did personally or through his representatives to save hundreds of thousands of Jewish lives" (*Catholics Remember the Holocaust*, Secretariat for Ecumenical and Interreligious Affairs, p. 53; also the detailed footnote 16 documenting such praise, on pp. 55–56).

The same month, John Paul II "responded to questions about the record of Pius XII by characterizing his predecessor as a 'great pope.' In further response to the question—prompted by the recent renewal of controversy over the role played by Pius XII in opposition to the Nazi persecution of the Jews—[he] said that all such questions have already been adequately answered. 'One must read Father Blet,' the pontiff said," referring to the Jesuit author of *Pius XII and the Second World War* ("Pope Calls Pius XII 'Great,'" *Catholic World News*, March 23, 1998).

And in December 2002, upon the sixtieth anniversary of Pius XII's famous Christmas allocution of 1942, John Paul II recalled the allocution and lamented the "appalling" toll the war had taken. "Pius XII was wise to have called for a 'new national and international order' in 1942, and more than half a century later, his assessment has been reconfirmed, John Paul said" ("Pope Laments Continuing Terror Threat," Associated Press, December 21, 2002; also "La lungimirante saggezza di Pio XII nel Radiomessaggio del dicembre 1942," *Osservatore della Domenica*, December 22, 2002).

PART 7: PIUS XII AND THE NATIONAL CHURCHES

For an introduction to the contributions of Pius XII during the war, see Reginald F. Walker's *Pius of Peace: A Study of the Pacific Work of His Holiness Pope Pius*

XII in the World War 1939–1945 (Dublin: M.H. Gill and Son, 1946). As Walker reveals, the pope used the Pontifical Relief Commission and the Vatican Information Office—two organizations he created after the war began—to feed, clothe, shelter, and reunite families; he also ran a separate ministry for prisoners of war on both sides of the conflict. See also the anonymous monograph *Charity Abounding: The Story of Papal Relief Work During the War* (London: Burnes, Oates and Washbourne, 1945) and Igino Giordani's *Vita Contra Morte: La Santa Sede per le Vittime della Seconda Guerra Mondiale* (Rome: Arnoldo Mondadori, 1956). For background on the fierce resistance Pius XII's humanitarian efforts faced, see *Pope Pius XII and the Nazi War Against the Catholic Church* by P.J. Oudendijk (Brisbane: Martin W. Kennedy, 1944).

A good brief study on how the modern popes, including Pius XII, resisted anti-Semitism is the little-known monograph *The Pope and the Jews: The Struggle of the Catholic Church Against Anti-Semitism During the War* by A.C.F. Beales (London: Sword of the Spirit, 1945). In fewer than forty pages, Beales documents a series of statements from the Holy See (particularly from Vatican Radio) that explicitly condemned the evils of anti-Semitism, racism, and Nazism.

Irene Marinoff's *The Heresy of National Socialism* (London: Burns, Oates & Washbourne, 1941) is an outstanding study, proving that the Church of Pius XI and Pius XII *did* condemn Nazism as a grave heresy and that this was recognized at the time by faithful Catholics everywhere. Other wartime publications include *The Pope and the War* by Denis Gwynn (London: Catholic Truth Society, 1941); *The Nazi Creed and Catholicism* by Irene Marinoff (London: Catholic Truth Society, 1942); *The Pope and Fascism* by James A. Darragh (Glasgow: John S. Burns and Sons, 1944); and *The Pope and the Nazis* (London: Catholic Truth Society, 1945), an English translation of Pius XII's end-of-the-war address to the College of Cardinals on June 2, 1945. See also *Why Didn't the Pope?* by J. Murray, S.J. (London: Catholic Truth Society, 1948), an excellent explanation of why the wartime pope acted in a moral and religious but not partisan way. The 1997 volume *The Pope and the Holocaust* by John S. Rader and Kateryna Fedoryka (Alexandria: Family Apostolate, 1997) is another helpful overview.

One of the best general surveys of Pius XII's influence upon Catholics during the war is *Pie XII: Diplomate et pasteur* by the Swiss historian Philippe Chenaux (Paris: Cerf, 2003). Erik von Kuehnelt-Leddhin's *The Intelligent American's Guide to Europe* (New Rochelle: Arlington, 1979) provides historical background on the Church's record during the war years. Elizabeth Wiskemann's *Europe of the Dictators 1919–1945* (New York: Harper and Row, 1966) is a general history by a keen wartime observer. Another indispensable study is *Judaism and Christianity Under the Impact of National Socialism*, which contains excellent essays by Konrad Repgen (on German Catholicism), John S. Conway (on Catholics and Jews during the Nazi period), Meir Michaelis (on the Vatican in fascist Italy), Livia Rothkirchen (on the Church in Slovakia and Hungary), Michael Marrus (on the French Church and the persecution of Jews), and Richard Gutteridge (on the Church and the Jews in England).

Catholics, the State, and the European Radical Right, edited by Richard J. Wolff and Jorg K. Hoensch (New York: Columbia University, 1987) is an attempt to address the Church's record toward early twentieth-century authoritarian regimes in Germany, Austria, France, Hungary, Italy, Croatia, Slovakia, and Spain; informative about history and sociopolitical currents, it is inadequate on the subject of Pius XII. Xavier de Montclos's *Les chrétiens face au nazisme et au stalinisme: l'épreuve totalitaire, 1939–1945* (Paris: Plon, 1983) is a far more valuable study. For three eminent historians who praise the papacy for its moral stature and leadership, see *Judgment of the Nations* by Christopher Dawson (New York: Sheed and Ward, 1942); *A Fight for God: 1870–1939* by Henri Daniel-Rops (New York: E.P. Dutton, 1965); and *Leftism Revisited: From de Sade and Marx to Hitler and Pol Pot* by Erik von Kuehnelt-Leddhin (Washington: Regnery Gateway, 1990).

For more overviews of the papacy's role during World War II, see *The Vatican and World Peace: A Boston College Symposium*, edited by Francis Sweeney, S.J. (Montreal: Palm, 1970) and Cardinal John Wright's speech, "The Pope and the War" (delivered June 28, 1945), in *Resonare Christum, 1939–1959: A Selection From the Sermons, Addresses, Interviews, and Papers of Cardinal John J. Wright*, edited by R. Stephen Almagno (San Francisco: Ignatius, 1985), pp. 42–53.

For information on specific national churches, their relations with Pius XII, and the political situations they faced during the war, see the following regional studies.

1. Belgium

Le Cardinal van Roey et L'Occupation Allemande en Belgique by Chanoine Leclef (Brussels: Goemare, 1945) reveals the Belgian cardinal's fierce resistance to Nazism. On March 26, 1939, just weeks after Eugenio Pacelli was installed as pope, "a pastoral letter condemning National Socialism and racial theories was read today in all Catholic churches in Eastern Belgium, including Eupen and Malmedy, the areas detached from Germany after the World War. Pro-Nazi worshipers demonstrated their disapproval when the letter was read" (Associated Press, March 26, 1939).

"Belgium," an article in the *Tablet*, September 13, 1944, describes how the Nazis threatened the archbishop because the clergy resisted the German occupation. For general background, see *The German Occupation of Belgium, 1940–1944* by Werner Warmbrunn (New York: Peter Lang, 1999); *Belgium and the Holocaust: Jews, Belgians, Germans*, edited by Dan Michman (Jerusalem:

Yad Vashem, 1998); and *La Belgique sous la botte: Résistances et collaborations 1940–1945* by Jacques Willequet (Paris: Editions Universitaires, 1986).

2. Croatia and the Balkans

There is a vast literature on the Church, the Holocaust, and the Jewish community in Croatia and the Balkans. Until the breakup of communist Yugoslavia, most of this literature reflected national claims supported by state power (particularly in Serbia's case), and very little of it was reliable for historical purposes. Moreover, some of the most important material remains untranslated.

Nevertheless, enough works exist even in English to convey a general picture. The question of the Catholic Church in the Balkans really only applies to two countries: Croatia and Bosnia-Herzegovina. (Slovenia had a Catholic Church that took a very strong antifascist position but had almost no Jews. Northern Albania had a Catholic church, but Albania protected Jews within its borders. Serbia and Macedonia were Orthodox territory, as were Romania and Bulgaria. Vojvodina, or northern Serbia, had a large Catholic population but was given by the Germans to the Hungarians.)

For the Church's record in Croatia, where many criminal acts were committed during the war by the Ustashe regime of Ante Pavelić—but where many acts of heroism also took place—see *Croatia 1941–1946* by Dennis Barton (Birkenhead: Church in History Information Centre, 1998). For the fallout and aftermath, see Stella Alexander's *Church and State in Yugoslavia Since 1945* (Cambridge: Cambridge University, 1979).

Martyrdom of the Serbs: Persecutions of the Serbian Orthodox Church and Massacre of the Serbian People (Chicago: Serbian Eastern Orthodox Diocese for the United States and Canada, 1943) was an early and harsh polemic, highly critical of the Catholic record in Croatia. Branko Bokun's *Spy in the Vatican, 1941–45* (New York: Praeger, 1973), is the wartime memoir of a partisan Serb who worked in Rome during World War II. Sarcastic and combative, Bokun's book is hostile to the Catholic Church and symbolic of the age-old feud between Serbs and Croats. On the background for these continuing resentments, see *Serbs and Croats: The Struggle for Yugoslavia* by Alex N. Dragnic (New York: Harcourt Brace Jovanovich, 1992).

A new generation of historians is fortunately moving away from diatribe, providing more balanced assessments of the region's complicated history. The leading expert on wartime Croatia is Jure Kristo of the Institute of History in Zagreb, whose many works are well documented and serve as a corrective to the anti-Croat propaganda often found in the West (see in particular his book, *Sukob simbola* [Zagreb: Globus, 2001], which contains a long bibliography on the subject). Also of note is Kristo's essay on the Catholic Church during World War II, "Katolicka crkva u II svestkom ratu 1941–1945," in the Croatian journal *Casopis za suvremenu povijest* 27 (1995), pp. 461–474.

Jere Jareb's work on the Catholic Church and Croatia is also valuable, especially his book, *Zlato i Novac Nezavisne Drzave Hrvatske izneseni u Inozemstvo 1944 i 1945* (Zagreb: Hrvatski institut za provijest Dom i svijet, 1997), concerning gold and money taken abroad from the independent Croatian state during 1944 and 1945. After examining all the relevant documents, Jareb found no evidence that Croatian fascists, led by the notorious Ante Pavelić, deposited stolen gold at the Vatican, much less that Pius XII approved of Pavelić's criminal acts. (See "Croatian Catholics and Jewish Gold," *Inside the Vatican*, August–September 1998, p. 11.)

The Case of Cardinal Aloysius Stepinac by Richard Patee (Milwaukee: Bruce, 1953) is a good biography of the famous archbishop of Zagreb, appointed a cardinal after the war by Pius XII and recently beatified by the Holy See. Despite his open defiance of Nazi racism and anti-Semitism and his assistance to persecuted Jews during the war, Stepinac was defamed as a wartime collaborator and imprisoned by the postwar communist government. His innocence and persecution by show trial, as chronicled by Patee, is now recognized by all reputable scholars. For a modern collection of documents vindicating Stepinac, see *Proces Alojziju Stepiincu*, edited by Marina Stambuk-Skalic, et al. (Zagreb: Krscanska sadasnjost, 1997). For Stepinac's anti-Nazi wartime sermons, see *Propovijedi, govori, poruke*, edited by J. Batelja and C. Tomic (Zagreb: AGM, 1996), and *Three Sermons Against Racism* by Archbishop Stepinac (Birkenhead: Church in History Information Centre, 1998). Stella Alexander's biography, *The Triple Myth: A Life of Archbishop Alojzije Stepinac* (New York: Columbia University, 1987), is better known and generally fair minded but not always accurate. Historian Aleksa Benigar has written a 900-page biography, *Alojzije Stepinac, hrvatski kardinal* (Rome: Ziral, 1974; second edition Zagreb, 1993), considered to be the benchmark life.

Ivan Muzic's *Pavelić i Stepinac* (Split: Logos, 1991) describes the archbishop's struggle against Ante Pavelić, the brutal Croat leader of the fascist Ustashe, which tried to appropriate Catholicism for its own ends during the war. The Vatican has also produced a work on Stepinac by the Italian journalist Giampaolo Mattei, *Il Cardinale Alojzije Stepinac* (Vatican City: L'Osservatore Romano, 1999); see "Vatican Book Justifies Cardinal Stepinac: Example of Opposition to Fascism, Nazism and Communism," Zenit News Agency, March 10, 1999. See also Giovanni Sale's "Il Card. A. Stepinac, un sostenitore dei Diritti di Dio e dell'uomo," *Civiltà Cattolica* 1998, volume 4, pp. 496–509. *Actes et Documents* contains much material relating to Stepinac's forceful opposition to the persecutions of Jews and Serbs.

On the campaign to defame Stepinac, see "A Patriot, Not a Nationalist" and "On Trial Again" in *Catholic World Report*, August–September 1998, pp. 36–43; on the reasons for Stepinac's beatification, see "Croatia Celebrates," *Inside the Vatican*, August–September 1998, pp. 8–10, and "Il Card. Alojzije Stepinac e Edith Stein elevati agli onori degli altari" by Giovanni Marchesi, *Civiltà Cattolica*

1998, volume 4, pp. 413–422. Also of note is Alain Finkielkraut's "Msgr. Stepinac et les deux douleurs de L'Europe," *Le Monde*, October 7, 1998, rebuking critics of Stepinac for defaming a courageous and honorable man.

On Stepinac's defense of persecuted Jews, see *Tablet*, October 19, 1946, pp. 196–198, and Charles Pichon's analysis in *The Vatican and its Role in World Affairs*, pp. 334–336; also Ronald Rychlak's *Hitler, the War, and the Pope*, pp. 303–305. In assessing Pius XII's view of Croatia, it is important to focus on Stepinac, for Pius XII entrusted the archbishop of Zagreb to communicate the Vatican's opposition to fascist and Nazi atrocities to the Croatian authorities, although the pope also had his apostolic visitor in Croatia, Abbot Joseph Marcone, protest.

Jews in Yugoslavia by Ante Sorić (Zagreb: MGC, 1989) and *Jews in Croatia* by Melita Svob (Zagreb: Zidovska opcina, 1997) provide background on the Jewish community's history and its relations with Croatian Catholics. See also *The Jews of Yugoslavia: A Quest for Community* by Harriet Pass Freidenreich (Philadelphia: Jewish Publication Society, 1979). *Anti-Semitism, Holocaust, and Anti-Fascism* (Zagreb: Jewish Community, 1997) is a collection of essays touching on these themes.

Marcus Tanner's *Croatia: A Nation Forged in War* (New Haven: Yale University, 2001) is an important scholarly study, fair to the Church's complicated record in the region. Also valuable are *Yugoslavia in Crisis, 1934–1941* by J.B. Hoptner (New York: Columbia University, 1962); *Yugoslavia's Revolution of 1941* by Dragisa N. Ristic (University Park: Pennsylvania State University, 1966); Ivo Goldstein's *Croatia: A History* (London: Hurst, 1999); and Jozo Tomasevich's *War and Revolution in Yugoslavia, 1941–1945* (Stanford: Stanford University, 2001).

The bitter attacks against the Church's wartime record in Croatia, which persist to this day, have their origins in the Communist and anticlerical press. These are best represented by the work of Viktor Novak, whose *Magnum crimen: pola vijeka klerikalizma u Hrvatskoj* (1948; reprinted Beograd: Nova knjiga, 1986) forms the basis of such later antipapal works as Carlo Falconi's *The Silence of Pius XII*. The more recent *Tito and the Rise and Fall of Yugoslavia* (New York: Carroll and Graff, 1995) by Richard West is also worthwhile. For a good critique of the latter, see John Kraljic's review in the *Journal of Croatian Studies*, 34–35 (1997), pp. 235–251.

The Yugoslav Auschwitz and the Vatican by a vitriolic partisan of Tito named Vladimir Dedijer (New York: Prometheus, 1992) is a particularly anti-Catholic and anti-Croatian polemic. For decisive refutations, see Sabrina Petra Ramet's review in the *Journal of Church and State*, Fall 1993, pp. 900–902, and George J. Prpic's review in *Catholic Historical Review*, July 1993, pp. 560–562. Also essential is *Fra Tomislav Filipovic zrtva klevete* by Martin Planinić (Suica: TRN, 1993), a biography of the notorious renegade cleric and war criminal, Miroslav Filipovic-Majstorovic (a.k.a. "Brother Satan") whom critics of the Church have falsely claimed died a priest in good standing (as Planinić shows, he was defrocked and condemned by the Church during the war—as were other apostate clerics).

An interesting work is Ciril Petesic's *Katolicko svecentso u NOB-u 1941–1945* (Zagreb: Globus, 1982) on the Catholic Church's contributions against fascism and Nazism in wartime Croatia. Prepared by the parliament of the former Socialist Republic of Croatia, it was an indication that some leftists still favor intellectual truth over crude antireligious propaganda. For evidence that many Croats themselves were victims of the fascist-Nazi empire, see Ivan Kovacic's *Kampor 1942–1943: Hrvati, Slovenci i Zidovi u konkentracijskom logoru Kampor na otoku Rabu* (Rijeka: Adamic, 1998) on the sufferings of Croats, Slovenes, and Jews in a particularly brutal concentration camp. Croatian historian Ljubo Boban also provides documentary evidence of Catholic opposition to the Ustashe in *Hrvatska u Arhiva izbjeglicke vlade 1941–1943* (Zagreb: Globus, 1985).

For a good general history of Bosnia, see Noel Malcom's *Bosnia: A Short History* (New York: New York University, 1994); see also his *Books on Bosnia: A Critical Bibliography of Works Relating to Bosnia-Herzogovenia Since 1990* (London: Bosnian Institute, 1999). *Balkan Idols: Religion and Nationalism in Yugoslav States* by Vjekoslav Perica (Oxford: Oxford University, 2002) is an excellent overview of the entire region and the explosive feuds that have touched the lives of its myriad of ethnic and religious residents. Also of note are the two-volume *History of the Balkans* by Barbara Jelavich (Cambridge: Cambridge University, 1983) and Sabrina Petra Ramet's *Balkan Babel: The Disintegration of Yugoslavia from the Death of Tito to the Fall of Milosević* (Boulder: Westview, 2002).

For Pope John Paul II's efforts to heal the bitter memories and rivalries in Croatia and the Balkans, see "Hard Feelings Overshadow Pope's Plea for Healing" by John Allen, *National Catholic Reporter*, June 4, 2003, p. 9, and Allen's "Feeling Bosnia's Pain," *National Catholic Reporter* online edition, June 27, 2003.

3. Denmark, Norway, and Sweden

Because the Scandinavian countries had small Catholic populations, Church activity there was limited. Two of the first countries to receive aid from the Pontifical Relief Commission were Denmark and Norway. "Food, medicine, and clothing were passed out by Vatican relief workers to people of all creeds and nationalities. Need was the only criterion. The pope obtained resources from those areas with which he could still communicate freely, and the Catholics of the United States were particularly generous in supplying him with goods to dispense among the peoples impoverished by the European war" (*History of the Catholic Church* by Thomas P. Neill [Milwaukee: Bruce, 1957], p. 644).

The Danes, in particular, have received considerable praise for their resistance to the Nazis' anti-Semitic campaign; see *The Danish Resistance* by David Lampe (New York: Ballantine, 1957); *The Rescue of Danish Jewry* by Leni Yahill (Philadelphia: Jewish Publication Society, 1969); *The Rescue of the Danish Jews: Moral Courage Under Stress*, edited by Leo Goldberger (New York: New York University, 1987).

Because of this, certain authors (for instance, Daniel Goldhagen, *A Moral Reckoning*, pp. 50–51) have attempted to contrast Danish heroism with Vatican diplomacy. Without dishonoring the Danish resistance, it must be emphasized that Denmark was not under the same kind of pressure as other occupied countries: "It is not historically legitimate to compare the Vatican's position [toward Poland and elsewhere] with that of Denmark. . . . [T]he Danes' courageous resistance to German racial policies . . . was possible because of Denmark's uniquely *privileged* status in Nazi Europe (Denmark, for instance, had free elections in 1943). The Nazis, who were determined to annihilate the Poles, wanted to assimilate the Danes" (James J. Sheehan, "Goldhagen at it Again," *Commonweal*, November 8, 2002, pp. 28–30 at 29). Istvan Deak, noting that Denmark was "of enormous economic importance to Germany," and was therefore "treated by the Nazis with great consideration," adds: "In fact, under Pius XII's pontificate, many Catholic clergymen and nuns took greater risks and suffered far more on behalf of the Jews than did King Christian of Denmark" (*New York Review of Books*, March 23, 2000).

For further information, see *The Holocaust Encyclopedia*, pp. 145–148 (on Denmark), pp. 446–451 (on Norway), and pp. 614–618 (on Sweden); *The Bitter Years: The Invasion and Occupation of Denmark and Norway, April 1940–May 1945* by Richard Petrow (New York: William Morrow, 1974); *The Stones Cry Out: Sweden's Response to the Persecution of the Jews, 1933–1945* by Steven Koblik (New York: Holocaust Library, 1988); *From Indifference to Activism: Swedish Diplomacy and the Holocaust, 1938–1944* by Paul Levine (Uppsala: Acta Universitatis Upsaliensis, 1998); and *Return to the Future* by Sigrid Undset (New York: Knopf, 1942), where the Nobel Prize–winning Norwegian Catholic author writes about the Nazi invasion and destruction of her country—resisted by committed Christians like herself.

4. France

Christian Resistance to Anti-Semitism: Memories from 1940–1944 by Henri de Lubac is particularly forceful about Pius XII's moral leadership. The French bishops are famous for having issued anti-Nazi, pro-Jewish pastoral letters in the summer and fall of 1942. De Lubac writes: "Several episcopal letters from France were reported in *L'Osservatore Romano*, in *La Civiltà Cattolica*, and on Vatican Radio; according to Jean Toulat, it was even 'at the express request of Pius XII' that Vatican Radio broadcast Saliège's letter twice and made comments on it for six consecutive days" (p. 162).

Saliège's letter explicitly condemned the deportations and proclaimed: "Jews are men, Jews are women, . . . they are part of mankind. They are our brothers. A Christian cannot forget that." For Saliège's wartime messages, which explicitly cite Pius XII's teachings, see *Un Évêque Français sous L'Occupation, Extraits des Messages de S. Ex. Mgr. Saliège, Archevêque de Toulouse* (Paris: Ouvrières, 1945) and *Who Shall Bear the Flame?* (South Bend: Fides, 1949).

Saliège was not alone. At the beginning of 1940, when the Nazi-Soviet destruction of Poland was in full swing—and shortly before his own country would be invaded by the Nazis—Cardinal Liénart, Bishop of Lille, wrote a Lenten pastoral in which he spoke of the "monstrous theories rising against the immutable principles of morality; of pernicious errors that are being used to justify crimes against international law. . . . We all remember, in the present collusion between bolshevism and racialism, how Pius XI associated the two errors in the same condemnation; and we all have read in the messages and letters of Pius XII his urgent appeal for a peace, not bought at the cost of free nations' independence, but founded on the mutual respect of the sacred moral rights of the person, the family and the nation" (*Tablet*, March 2, 1940, p. 201).

More evidence of French assistance to persecuted Jews, including assistance from the pope, can be found in the *Tablet*: September 5, 1942, p. 114; September 12, 1942, pp. 127–128; September 19, 1942, p. 140; October 17, 1942, p. 190; October 24, 1942, p. 202 (which reveals the rage this aid provoked within Nazi ranks, especially against Pius XII who was publicly condemned by Goebbels for his "pro-Jewish" stance); June 26, 1943, p. 306; July 10, 1943, p. 18; and September 29, 1945, pp. 152–153.

The writings of Abbé Charles Molette, the longtime director of the archives of the Church of France, are of special importance in understanding French Catholicism's resistance to Nazism. See, in particular, his *Prêtres, religieux, et religieuses dans la résistance au nazisme, 1940–1945* (Paris: Fayard, 1995) and *Résistances chrétiennes à la nazification des espirits* (Paris: F.-X. de Guibert, 1998).

For general background on wartime France, see the thorough but somewhat flawed *Politics, Society and Christianity in Vichy France* by W.D. Halls (Oxford: Berg, 1995); *France: The Dark Years, 1940–1944* by Julian Jackson (Oxford: Oxford University, 2001); and Alexander Werth's earlier, *France, 1940–1955* (London: Robert Hale, 1956). The literature on the collaboration policies of Vichy France is immense; representative of mainstream scholarship on this subject are *France Under the Germans: Collaboration and Compromise* by Philippe Burrin (New York: New Press, 1996) and *Verdict on Vichy: Power and Prejudice in the Vichy France Regime* by Michael Curtis (New York: Arcade, 2002).

These books are generally reliable, except when discussing the Church. Even though 75 percent of Jews living in France survived the Holocaust, the idea of mass French Catholic collaboration with Nazism persists. This theme is on display in the 2003 film *The Statement* (directed by Norman Jewison and based on Brian Moore's novel of the same name) about a French Catholic official, convicted of terrifying war crimes, who nonetheless finds refuge in the Church. "While the story is loosely based on factual events [the Paul Touvier case], Jewison jettisons objectivity in favor of broad-brushstroke anticlericalism, painting the Catholic hierarchy for the most part as a den of duplicitous vipers willing to cover up atrocities for the greater good (read 'public image') of the Church" (David DiCerto's review for the Catholic News Service, December 2003).

For French works dealing explicitly with Pius XII and the Catholic resistance, see *Le Pape Pie XII devant la guerre* by Gabriel-Louis Jaray (Montreal: Fides, 1946); *Sa Sainteté Pie XII et la paix du monde* by Pierre Fernessole (Paris: Beauchesne, 1947), especially pp. 74–90, which presents a long list of words and actions of Pius XII against Nazism; *Le Vatican et la seconde guerre mondiale—Action doctrinale et diplomatique en faveur de la paix* by Paul Duclos (Paris: Pedone, 1955); *Le vicaire et l'histoire* by Jacques Nobécourt (Paris: du Seuil, 1964), one of the better works in response to Hochhuth's *The Deputy*; *Portrait et vie de Pie XII* by Louis Chaigne (Paris: St-Augustin, 1966); *Pie face aux nazis* by Charles Klein (Paris: S.O.S., 1975), exceptionally important for its use of primary documents revealing the Nazis' war against the Church; and *L'Église sous Pie XII: la tourmente (1939–1945)* by Jean Chelini (Paris: Fayard, 1983), an important if uneven work by a distinguished scholar. See also Ulrich Reusch's "Le Saint-Siège, la France et l'idée de l'équilibre européen 1939–1945," in *Francia* 18/3 (1991), pp. 55–72.

Renée Bedarida has published many acclaimed studies on the French Resistance, of which two merit special attention: *Les catholiques dans la guerre, 1939–1945: entre Vichy et la Résistance* (Paris: Hachette, 1998), and *La résistance spirituelle, 1941–1944: les cahiers clandestines du Témoignage chrétien* (Paris: Albin Michel, 2001). John Sweet's *Choices in Vichy France: The French Under the Nazi Occupation* (New York: Oxford University, 1986) gives credit to French Catholics who rescued Jews. Similarly, Susan Zuccotti's *The Holocaust, the French and the Jews* is a generally sound work, sympathetic to the Church and vastly superior to her later work on Pius XII and wartime Italy. For an analysis of the French bishops' 1997 statement on the Church's role in Vichy France during the Holocaust, see "Letter From Paris" by Jean Duchesne, *First Things*, February 1998, pp. 12–14. *L'Église catholique et le peuple juif: Un autre regard* by Jean Dujardin (Paris: Calmann-Levy, 2003) is an outstanding work on the Church and the Jewish people by a noted French Catholic theologian.

5. Germany and Austria

Die Briefe Pius XII. an die Deutschen Bischöfe 1939–1944, edited by Burkhart Schneider (Mainz: Matthias-Grünewald, 1966), contains Pius XII's exhortations and encouragements to the German bishops. The most important document is Pius XII's letter of April 30, 1943, to his friend and confidant, Bishop Konrad von Preysing of Berlin (a fearless anti-Nazi), where Pius XII stated: "Regarding pronouncements by the bishops, we leave it to local senior clergymen to decide if, and to what degree, the danger of reprisals and oppression, as well as, perhaps, other circumstances caused by the length and psychological climate of the war may make restraint advisable—despite the reasons for intervention—in order to avoid greater evils. This is one of the reasons we limit ourselves in our proclamations."

To his credit, Saul Friedlander translates and publishes the letter in *Pius XII and the Third Reich*, pp. 135–143; the letter also appears in its original German in *Actes et Documents* 2, pp. 318–327. Pius XII's earlier letter to the German bishops (September 8, 1941) in which he encourages their opposition to Nazi rule, appears in English translation in *Catholic Mind*, December 1945, pp. 755–759, and was mentioned in the *New York Times*, October 20, 1945, p. C4.

Mons. Cesare Orsenigo: nunzio apostolico in Germania (1930–1946) by Monica Biffi (Milan: NED, 1997), is an important study of the controversial papal nuncio to Germany (appointed to his post before Pius XII assumed office) who was considered weak by many, but whom Pius XII prevailed upon to protest Nazi atrocities, including anti-Semitic ones.

Most scholars believe that had Orsenigo been recalled, as some in the Church requested, the Nazis would have prevented *any* nuncio from remaining in Germany, just as they banned one in Poland. Pius XII decided to retain him, believing that some influence through a German nuncio was better than none at all. Biffi concurs with this judgment and praises Pius XII's diplomacy with Hitler, which she aptly describes as a "cold war." For more on Biffi's work, see the review in the June 25, 1998, issue of *L'Osservatore Romano*. Noting Biffi's finding that Orsenigo, under the instructions of Pius XII, personally confronted Adolf Hitler about his savage persecution of the Jews, provoking the Nazi dictator to hurl a glass to the floor in anger, the Vatican newspaper commented: "In order to speak in defense of the Jews, a representative of the pope was not afraid to face Hitler directly. This episode speaks for itself." See also "Book Claims Vatican Official Confronted Hitler on Persecution," *National Catholic Register*, July 5–11, 1998, p. 6.

For an astute analysis of the Vatican's instructions to Orsenigo after the Nazis obtained power, see Thomas Brechenmacher's "Aber er hat Hitler weder unterstützt noch unterschätzt: Kardinal Pacellis Spielräume im Frühjahr 1933" (*Frankfurter Allgemeine Zeitung*, April 24, 2003, p. 42) and the remarks of Matteo Luigi Napolitano in "Le tirate d'orecchie di Pacelli al nunzio morbido con Hitler" by Andrea Tornielli in *Il Giornale*, April 10, 2003, p. 36. ("The Vatican Told Nuncio to Forgo Praise of Hitler: Professor Sees Signs of Opposition to Nazism in 1930s Archives," Zenit News Agency, May 1, 2003, is an English-language summary.) Both Brechenmacher and Napolitano cite newly released Vatican archives as documentary proof of the Vatican's early and consistent opposition to Hitler, Nazism, and anti-Semitism.

The most important work emanating from Germany on the Church's role during the Nazi era is produced by the *Kommission für Zeitgeschichte* (www.kfzg.de). Established in 1962 by the German Catholic Church to explore the history and meaning of German Catholicism, the commission now works in conjunction with the Catholic Academy in Bavaria (www.kath-akademie-bayern.de). In the last forty years, the commission has produced dozens of books on the Vatican's relations with the German Church, Nazism and the German Catholic bishops, relations between German Catholics and Jews, the Church's reaction to anti-Semitism and the Holocaust, and the Nazi war against the Church—especially the priesthood. For a survey of their most recent output, see Karl-Josef Hummel's note in *Herderkorrespondenz* 57 (2003), number 8, translated as "Facts-Interpretations-Questions: Where is Research in Catholicism Heading?" *Association of Contemporary Church Historians*, December 2003 and January 2004.

Eminent German scholars Ludwig Volk, Konrad Repgen, Dieter Albrecht, Ulrich von Hehl, Heinz Hürten, and others have contributed to this enterprise. English-speaking scholars would benefit greatly from a translation of the commission's major works. For a rare example of such scholarship in English, see Konrad Repgen's "German Catholicism and the Jews: 1933–1945" in *Judaism and Christianity Under the Impact of National Socialism*, pp. 197–226, which comments: "It is wrong to assert, as has been done repeatedly in the last twenty years, that they [Germany's wartime Catholic bishops] remained 'silent.' It could not be denied then—nor can it now—that the German bishops made mistakes and incorrect decisions in the *Kirchenkampf.* But the implication of the catchword 'silence,' namely, that the bishops lacked moral integrity, is clearly unjust" (p. 211).

Indeed, evidence of the German hierarchy's opposition to Nazism came early and was well publicized during the war. See, for example, the excerpts from anti-Nazi statements of four leading German Catholic bishops in "Germany," *Tablet*, March 2, 1940, p. 202, and especially the excerpts from Cardinal Michael Faulhaber's outspoken pastoral (provoked by Pius XII's first encyclical, *Summi Pontificatus*) in "Cardinal Faulhaber Indicts Hitlerism," *Tablet*, April 27, 1940, p. 398: "For in all its complexities mankind forms one family with a common origin, a common habitat and a common mediator with the Father. . . . [N]o patriotism may close its eyes to the universality of Christian charity." Excerpts of this pastoral also appeared in the Vatican newspaper, "La figura e l'opera di Pio XII," *Osservatore Romano*, April 14,

1940, p. 1. See also the salient excerpts from the pastoral letters of the German bishops, translated and published in the *Tablet*, May 27, 1944.

Ulrich Reusch's essay, "Motive, Ziele und Grenzen vatikanischer Friedenspolitik im 2. Weltkrieg" in *Deutschland-Italien, 1943–1945: Aspekte einer Entzweiung*, pp. 74–94, edited by Rudolf Lill (Tübingen: M. Niemeyer, 1992), is part of an important collection of essays analyzing the relationship between Germany and Italy during the war. See also Reusch's "Der Vatikan und die deutsche Kaptitulation" in *Die Kapitulation von 1945 und der Neubeginn in Deutschland*, edited by Winfried Becker (Koln: Bohlau, 1987), pp. 211–244. Wolfgang's Schieder's earlier article, "Pius XII. im Zweiten Weltkrieg, " in *Historische Zeitschrift* 207 (1968), pp. 346–356 is also helpful.

Austria, the birthplace of Hitler, has been portrayed as the most intensely anti-Semitic of the European countries in, for instance, *From Prejudice to Persecution: A History of Austrian Anti-Semitism* by Bruce Pauley (Chapel Hill: University of North Carolina, 1992); *Hitler's Austria: Popular Sentiment in the Nazi Era 1938–1945* by Evan Burr Buckey (Chapel Hill: University of North Carolina, 2000); and especially *Grüss Gott und Heil Hitler: Katholische Kirche und Nationalsozialismus in Österreich* by Stefan Moritz (Vienna: Picus, 2002), a sensationalist account that depicts the Austrian clergy in the worst possible light.

But there were Austrian Catholics who strongly opposed racism and anti-Semitism. One of the most famous was Dietrich von Hildebrand, who edited the anti-Nazi *Der Christliche Ständestaat*, until he was marked for death by Hitler and forced into exile. For von Hildebrand's story, see *The Soul of a Lion* by Alice von Hildebrand.

Gordon Zahn's *In Solitary Witness: The Life and Death of Franz Jägerstätter* (1964; revised edition Springfield: Templegate, 1986) tells the moving story of one of Austria's great anti-Nazi martyrs—a devout Catholic motivated by papal teachings. See also *The Resistance in Austria, 1938–1945* by Radomir V. Luza (Minneapolis: University of Minnesota, 1984); *Country Without a Name: Austria Under Nazi Rule, 1938–1945* by Walter B. Maas (New York: Frederick Ungar, 1979); and *Zeugen des Widerstandes* by Johann Holzner (Innsbruck: Tyrolia, 1977). For the story of Cardinal Theodor Innitzer, the archbishop of Vienna who first tried to appease the Germans but soon firmly opposed Hitler and became a rescuer, see *Innitzer: Kardinal zwischen Hitler und Rom* by Victor Reimann (Vienna: Amalthea, 1988). See also the declarations of the Austrian bishops against anti-Semitism, as found in the *Tablet*, February 11, 1938, pp. 182–184.

Any study of the Church's response to the Holocaust in Germany and Austria must examine the life and legacy of Adolf Hitler. The definitive biography is Ian Kershaw's highly acclaimed two-volume *Hitler: 1889–1936: Hubris* (New York: W.W. Norton, 1998) and *Hitler: 1936–1945: Nemesis* (New York: W.W. Norton, 2000). Kershaw is brilliant on every aspect of

Hitler's life, but only briefly (and, alas, inaccurately) comments on Pius XII's reaction to the Nazi roundup of Rome's Jews and the role of the Christian churches. For a critique of Kershaw's massive biography, see "The Meaning of Hitler" by Walter Sundberg, *First Things*, March 2001, pp. 47–51.

For a penetrating cultural analysis of the anti-Christian forces that gave birth to Nazism, published during the war, see *Europe and the German Question* by F.W. Foerster (New York: Sheed and Ward, 1940). Foerster argues that the roots of Hitlerism were paganism, nationalism, and nihilism, and thus profoundly anti-Christian. Underscoring the pagan character of Nazism is the fact that the Final Solution originated out of the notorious euthanasia or "mercy killing" campaign, which was driven by antireligious rationalists and scientists.

For more on the secular roots of Nazism, see *The Scientific Origins of National Socialism* by Daniel Gasman (New York: American Elsevier, 1971); *The Origins of Nazi Genocide: From Euthanasia to the Final Solution* by Henry Friedlander (Chapel Hill: University of North Carolina, 1995); and *Life Unworthy of Life: Racial Phobia and Mass Murder in Hitler's Germany* by James M. Glass (New York: Basic, 1997), which quotes Rudolph Hoess, commandant of Auschwitz, declaring: "National Socialism is nothing but applied biology" (p. 29).

Three Sermons in Defiance of the Nazis Preached During 1941 by Bishop von Galen (Birkenhead: Church in History Information Centre, 1986), reprints the antieuthanasia sermons of the famous anti-Nazi prelate (appointed a cardinal by Pius XII in 1946). The best biography of von Galen in German is Max Bierbaum's *Nicht Lob, nicht Furcht: das Leben des Kardinals von Galen nach unveröffentlichten. Briefen u. Dokumenten* (Munster: Regensberg, 1974); the best biography in English is *Cardinal von Galen* by Heinrich Portmann (von Galen's personal chaplain), adapted and with an introduction by R.L. Sedgwick (London: Jarrolds, 1957, from the 1953 original in German). Both these books are vastly superior to Beth Griech-Polelle's hostile and inaccurate 2002 *Bishop von Galen*. A growing body of scholars now recognize von Galen as a model bishop in the face of antireligious persecution; see "Anti-Nazi Bishop a Step Closer to Beatification," Zenit News Agency, December 21, 2003.

Interesting are the memoirs of a Catholic chaplain forced to serve in the German army: *The Shadow of His Wings: The True Story of Fr. Gereon Goldmann* (translated 1964; reprinted San Francisco: Ignatius, 2000). Solid historical background on Austrian and German culture, so crucial to understanding events in the twentieth century, can be found in *Liberty or Equality: The Challenge of Our Time* by Erik von Kuehnelt-Leddihn (Front Royal: Christendom, 1993) and *Dreams and Delusions: The Drama of German History* by Fritz Stern (New Haven: Yale University, 1999)—both particularly valuable for highlighting Catholic opposition to Hitler. Similarly, the voting patterns of German Catholics, which were overwhelmingly anti-Nazi, are analyzed in *Who Voted for Hitler?* by Richard F. Hamilton (Princeton: Princeton University, 1982) and *The Nazi Voter* by Thomas Childers (Chapel Hill: University of North Carolina, 1983).

Comprehensive histories include *Germany: 2000 Years* by Kurt F. Reinhardt, Gerhart Hoffmeister, and Frederic C. Tubach, 3 volumes (New York: Ungar, 1989 and 1992); *Germany: 1866–1945* by Gordon Craig (Oxford: Clarendon, 1978); *A History of Modern Germany* by Hajo Holborn, 3 volumes (Princeton: Princeton University, 1982); *A Concise History of Germany* by Mary Fulbrook (Cambridge: Cambridge University, 1990); and *Modern Germany: An Encyclopedia of History, People and Culture, 1871–1990,* edited by Dieter Buse and Juergen Doerr (New York: Garland, 1998).

Of the enormous literature available in English concentrating specifically on the Third Reich, three works can be highly recommended: *Modern Germany: Its History and Civilization* by Koppel S. Pinson (New York: Macmillan, 1954); *The German Dictatorship* by Karl Dietrich Bracher (New York: Praeger, 1970); and especially *The Third Reich: A New History* by Michael Burleigh (New York: Hill and Wang, 2000). See also the translated collection of essays by German scholars entitled *The Path to Dictatorship, 1918–1933* (Garden City: Doubleday, 1966), explaining the complicated events that led to Hitler's rise, with a particularly good chapter on the Church's resistance to Nazism.

6. Great Britain and Ireland

Westminster, Whitehall and the Vatican: The Role of Cardinal Hinsley 1935–43 by Thomas Moloney (Kent: Burnes and Oates, 1985) is particularly good on how the archbishop of Westminster—an outspoken opponent of the Nazis and champion of European Jews—paid credit to both Pius XI and Pius XII for their leadership. The Catholic leaders of Britain were among the earliest and most vociferous opponents of the Third Reich. On March 31, 1933, the *Jewish Chronicle* reported: "Dr. Downey, Roman Catholic archbishop of Liverpool, referred, when addressing the Liverpool University Jewish Society, to the situation which has arisen in Germany. 'I deplore that situation,' declared His Grace, 'and I for one shall do everything in my power to protest against such exaggerated and pseudo-Nationalism. It is not real Nationalism. The present Pope has, time and again, condemned this form of Nationalism'" (p. 36).

In 1938, Hinsley, in conjunction with the Vatican, set up a committee to assist German Jews (see *Tablet,* April 30, 1938, p. 638, and January 21, 1939, p. 77). In *The Pope Speaks: The Words of Pius XII* (New York: Harcourt, Brace, 1940), Charles Rankin quotes Cardinal Hinsley's condemnations of Nazism (pp. 114–120), which explicitly cited Pius XII's teachings as justification for his view that "the creed of Nazism must be denounced as the enemy of mankind" (p. 115).

On May 26, 1940, Hinsley delivered a remarkable broadcast against Hitlerism: "Peace has been murdered between nations because the party in power in Germany has avowedly canceled truth from its program and has declared that our traditional Christian civilization is to be shattered by the might of the immortal Nordic race. . . . Certainly no Catholic can have the remotest leaning towards the Nazi creed after the Encyclical of Pius XI [*Mit brennender Sorge*] in which its guile and violence were unmasked."

On July 8, 1942, Cardinal Hinsley went on the BBC "to say the truth about the crimes committed in Poland: 700,000 Jews have been killed since the beginning of the war. Of this we have clear and repeated evidence. Their innocent blood cries out to Heaven for vengeance" (quoted in *Three Popes and the Jews* by Pinchas Lapide, p. 255, who adds that these statements "could hardly have been made" without the pope's approval; indeed, shortly before this address, Pius XII had sent a letter to Cardinal Hinsley and the English bishops, on June 29, 1942, thanking them for having highly prized and taken to heart "any admonitions and recommendations which are sent forth from this Apostolic See" (*Principles for Peace*, pp. 780–781). Toward the end of the same year, Hinsley declared that the Nazis were turning Poland into a vast cemetery of Jews (*Tablet*, December 12, 1942, p. 287).

For important diplomatic documents leading up to the war, see *Anglo-Vatican Relations 1914–1939: Confidential Reports of the British Minister to the Holy See* (Boston: G.K. Hall, 1972). The series of *Documents on British Foreign Policy* and the Foreign Office papers at the Public Record Office in London have a wealth of primary documents bearing on Great Britain's wartime relations with the Vatican (expertly covered by Owen Chadwick in his *Britain and the Vatican During the Second World War*).

Also important, with numerous documents pertaining to Pius XII and other Catholic officials, are the Churchill papers stored at Churchill College in Cambridge. The finest book on Nazi Germany to come out of Great Britain is Walter Alfred Peter Phillips's *The Tragedy of Nazi Germany* (New York: Praeger, 1969). Phillips, a former British prisoner of war who suffered immensely under the Nazis, provides a remarkably fair-minded portrait of war-torn Germany and has a superb section on the Church's relations with Hitler. Graham Greene, the famed British Catholic novelist, wrote a keen appreciation of Pius XII in which he described "a Pope whom so many of us believe will rank among the greatest" (*Inside the Vatican*, April–May 2003, pp. 50–55; a reprint of the original article published in the *Month*, December 1951).

On Britain's involvement with Pius XII and the German resistance, see Peter Ludlow, "Papst Pius XII. die britische Regierung und die deutsche Opposition im Winter 1939/40," *Vierteljahrshefte für Zeitgeschichte* 22 (1974) 299–341.

On Ireland, see *Ireland and the Vatican: The Politics and Diplomacy of Church-State Relations* by Dermot Keough (Cork: Cork University, 1995) and *In Time of War: Ireland, Ulster, and the Price of Neutrality, 1939–1945* by

Robert Fisk (Philadelphia: University of Pennsylvania, 1983). T.J. Kiernan's *Pope Pius XII* is a tribute by Ireland's wartime ambassador to the Vatican.

7. Holland

See *Resistance of the Churches in the Netherlands* (New York: Netherlands Information Bureau, 1944); *The Dutch Under German Occupation, 1940–1945* by Werner Warmbrunn (Oxford: Oxford University, 1963); *The Destruction of the Dutch Jews* by Jacob Presser (New York: E.P. Dutton, 1969); *The Netherlands and Nazi Germany* by Louis de Jong (Cambridge: Harvard University, 1990); and *Victims and Survivors: The Nazi Persecution of the Jews in the Netherlands, 1940–1945* by Bob Moore (London: Arnold, 1997).

The anti-Nazi resistance among Catholics in the Netherlands was particularly strong "and in its front line," wrote L. Bleys, an anti-Nazi priest who escaped from the Netherlands but kept in contact with the resistance, in a remarkable statement in the *Tablet*, October 14, 1944. Yet although the pope supported the Dutch Church for its principled stand, he was also deeply concerned about the reprisals the Nazis inflicted upon Dutch Catholics and Jews, and these reprisals were a factor in his own developing response to the Nazis as the war unfolded.

The famous case of Edith Stein, the Catholic convert who later became Sister Teresa Benedicta of the Cross, need only be cited. "The oft-quoted public protest of the Dutch episcopate in Summer 1942—carried out in agreement with the Vatican—against the deportation of the Dutch Jews . . . was certainly a sign of lofty confessional courage, but it was a failure. Only a fortnight after the statements were read out from the pulpit the 'Reichprotektor,' [*sic*; meaning the Reichskommissar] Seyss-Inquart, in reply and in revenge, had more than 600 Catholic 'Non-Aryans' deported by the SS for extermination at Auschwitz. Among them were the saintly Carmelite Edith Stein, . . . all of them members of religious orders" (Robert M.W. Kempner, deputy United States chief prosecutor at Nuremberg, in the prologue to *Hungarian Jewry and the Papacy: Pius XII Did Not Remain Silent* by Jenö Lévai, p. xi).

Seyss-Inquart's deputy, a Nazi named Schmidt, gave an explanation for the action in a speech on August 2, 1942: "The representatives of Protestant and Roman Catholic Churches sent a protest [to the German authorities in Holland] requesting better treatment of the Jews. The Jews are Germany's most dangerous enemies. Dutchmen cannot defend themselves actively against them without considering the question through spectacles of silly humanitarian sentiment. Owing to the passive attitude of the Dutch we Germans have taken over the solution to the Jewish question, and have begun sending Jews to the East. . . . Everyone crossing the path which we consider right and necessary, or hindering us in the execution of our tasks, must, whatever his nationality, expect the same fate. In Catholic churches a document was read criticizing the anti-

Jewish measures taken to safeguard our struggle. It was apparently also read in Protestant churches in spite of the fact that the Protestant churches had announced that it was not intended to read it everywhere in public. Owing to these events, the Germans must consider the Roman Catholic Jews their worst enemies and arrange for their quickest possible transport to the East. This has already taken place" (*Tablet*, August 29, 1942, p. 103).

Edith Stein, Sister Teresa Benedicta of the Cross, wrote a letter to Pius XI in 1933 that is sometimes depicted as an indictment of the Church (see, for example, James Carroll's *Constantine's Sword*, pp. 536–543). But her actual letter, with accompanying supportive correspondence from the Vatican, has now been released, and these charges have been disproved. See "Edith Stein's Letter" by William Doino Jr. and the related articles that follow, *Inside the Vatican*, March 2003, pp. 22–31. None of Stein's writings ever attacked the Church in the way we see today; she loved the Church and wholly supported it and, in fact, united herself with Pius XII in one of her wartime letters (letter of November 17, 1940, *Collected Works*, translated by Josephine Koeppel [Washington: ICS, 1993], volume 5, p. 327).

8. Hungary

A magyar katolikus egyhaz es az emberi jogok vedelme, edited by Antal Meszlenyi (Budapest: Szent, 1947), contains the rare testimony of the papal nuncio in Budapest, Angelo Rotta (on pp. 21–30), who, assisted by his aide Tibor Baranski, rescued countless Jews and who, like Baranski, was later honored as a righteous gentile by the state of Israel. (See "Nuncio in Budapest Saved Thousands of Jews During the War: Archbishop Rotta Declared 'Righteous Among Nations'" [Zenit News Agency, February 4, 2002].) See also the important commentary on Pius XII's rescue measures in Hungary—accomplished in union with the Swedish hero Raul Wallenberg—in Harvey Rosenfeld's biography, *Raul Wallenberg: Angel of Rescue* (Buffalo: Prometheus, 1982), pp. 72–81. The book contains Baranski's powerful testimony on behalf of Pius XII.

The foremost authority on the Holocaust in Hungary is Jenö Lévai, who wrote two indispensable works: *The Black Book on the Martyrdom of Hungarian Jewry* and *Hungarian Jewry and the Papacy: Pope Pius XII Did Not Remain Silent*. Lévai is to be preferred to the many works on Hungary by Randolph Braham (particularly *The Politics of Genocide: The Holocaust in Hungary* [New York: Columbia University, 1981]), which are inaccurate and hostile to the Catholic Church. See also "The Role of the Christian Churches in the Rescue of the Budapest Jews" by Leslie Laszlo, *Hungarian Studies Review*, Spring 1984, pp. 23–42; *The Persecution of Jews in Hungary and the Catholic Church* by András Zakar (London: Hungarian Roman Catholic Chaplaincy Team, 1991); and "Transcending Boundaries: Hungarian Roman

Catholic Religious Women and the 'Persecuted Ones,'" in *In God's Name: Genocide and Religion in the Twentieth Century*, edited by Omer Bartov and Phyllis Mack (Oxford: Berghan, 1998), pp. 222–242.

Among the most courageous of Hungarian Catholic leaders is the famed Cardinal Mindszenty. See *Four Years Struggle of the Church in Hungary* by József Mindszenty (London: Longmans, Green, 1949), especially pp. 1–22, which corrects communist misrepresentations of the Church's record in Hungary; also, Mindszenty's *Memoirs* (New York: Macmillan, 1974).

Other Hungarian Catholic leaders include Vilmos Apor, appointed bishop of Györ on January 21, 1941. A fearless opponent of both Nazism and communism, and a dedicated protector of those who suffered under them, Apor survived the Nazis but was murdered by a Communist official in 1945 after refusing to hand over one hundred women hiding in his residence. On November 9, 1997, Pope John Paul II beatified Apor, emphasizing, "He was not fearful about raising his voice, in accord with evangelical principles, to denounce injustice and abuse against minorities, especially against the Jewish community." (For more on this remarkable man, see the tribute in *L'Osservatore Romano*, November 12, 1997.)

9. Italy

Antonio Gaspari has written *Nascosti in convento by* (Milan: Ancora, 1999) and *Gli ebrei salvati da Pio XII* (Rome: Logos, 2001), two books that demolish the notion that Pius XII did little or nothing to save Italian Jews. Gaspari demonstrates that Pius was directly and continually involved in their protection. On this issue, see also Gaspari's "Hidden in the Convent," *Inside the Vatican*, December 2002, pp. 24–25, which contains the story of over a hundred Jews saved at the Monastery of Santa Maria dei Sette Dolori, and the testimony of Sister Giuliana, who, as a young novice at the monastery at that time, helped protect them: "The order to accommodate the victims of Nazi persecution came from the pope." Pius XII's charitable assistance to those in need was remembered long after the war ended (see "Stone Honors Pius for Actions in War," *New York Times*, June 28, 1948, p. 3).

A key Vatican figure of the fascist-Nazi era is Monsignor (later Cardinal) Franceso Borgongini-Duca, the papal nuncio to Italy, who, acting on behalf of Pius XII, assisted persecuted Jews in Italy in a variety of ways (for example, he visited Jews held in internment camps, and brought them papal supplies; many of his actions are documented in the Holy See's *Actes et Documents*). One example of the nuncio's aid comes from Bernard Grosser, secretary of the Genoa chapter of DELASEM (a Jewish relief group) during the war Grosser told an interviewer: "We needed someone to intercede with the Interior Ministry on behalf of a person, and then I was advised to turn to Cardinal Borgoncini [*sic*] Duca, and I went to Rome, and . . . when I entered the waiting room, I announced myself, . . . and when Borgoncini Duca heard my name while stepping outside his office, he called me instantly and didn't make me wait. There were about twenty people waiting in the antechamber, he took me in quickly. . . . Then I explained the entire case to him, and so on, and when I finished the cardinal took a piece of blank paper with his letterhead, signed it, and said, 'Mr. Grosser, by all means write what it is you need and take it with you'" (quoted in *Uncertain Refuge* by Nicola Caracciolo, pp. 17–18).

Another important papal official was Father Pietro Tacchi-Venturi, the Jesuit intermediary between the Vatican and the Italian government. A number of authors (particularly Daniel Goldhagen, *A Moral Reckoning*, pp. 149–151) have accused the Jesuit of condoning anti-Semitism. But according to Vincent Lapomarda, "Venturi's efforts were so notoriously pro-Jewish that Domenico Tardini, then an official in the Vatican's diplomatic bureaucracy and later papal secretary of state for Blessed Pope John XXIII, regarded the priest as a zealot on behalf of Jews" (*Journal of the Historical Society*, Summer/Fall 2003, p. 499). See also Lapomarda's description of Tacchi-Venturi's activity (and that of other Italian Jesuits) in his *Jesuits and the Third Reich*, pp. 215–243. In his authoritative work, *The Jews in Fascist Italy: A History* (revised edition New York: Enigma, 2001), Renzo de Felice documents Tacchi-Venturi's meetings with Aldo R. Ascoli, a prominent Italian Jewish leader, during which Ascoli expressed "'the emotional feeling' of the Jewish community for the words of understanding pronounced by Pope Pius XI during his speech [against Italy's emerging racism] to the students of Propaganda Fide and, in general, for what had been done by the Holy See afterwards" (p. 411).

In his book, *Odyssey: The Last Great Escape From Nazi-Dominated Europe—The Story of Those Jews who Gambled their Lives for Freedom . . . and Won* (New York: Simon and Schuster, 1984), John Bierman describes how Borgongini-Duca, acting on "the instructions of Pius XII," told a group of Jews at the Ferramonti internment camp that the pope would "vigorously oppose" any attempt to hand them over to Germany. Borgongini-Duca "concluded by quoting the 137th Psalm—'By the waters of Babylon, we sat down and wept when we remembered thee, O Zion'—and predicting 'God willing, you will return to the Promised Land one day'" (p. 198).

On Italian clergymen, see "Rescue Italian Style" by Mae Briskin in *Jewish Monthly*, May 1986, pp. 20–25, important for the testimony offered by Don Aldo Brunacci, a priest-rescuer from Assisi: "[In 1943] I had already been charged by Bishop Nicolini with the assignment of resettling these thousands of refugees. Then one day, after our regular monthly meeting of clergy at the seminary, the bishop called me aside. He had in his hand a letter from the Secretary of State at the Vatican that said the situation of the Jews was becomingly increasingly perilous, and called upon all bishops to help them" (p. 22).

Il Clero e l'occupazione tedesca di Roma by Cardinal Pietro Palazzini (Rome: Apes, 1995), the memoirs of a priest-rescuer (honored as a righteous gentile by Yad Vashem), expressly notes that "in the last analysis, it was Pius XII himself who allowed this great work of charity," and that "the guidelines provided by Pius XII were to save human lives, on whatever side they may be" (pp. 29 and 35). On the assistance Catholic nuns provided the persecuted, see *La Resistenza in convento* by Enzo Forcella (Turin: Einaudi, 1999); also "Righteous of the Nations Among the Sisters of Sion," *Common Ground* 2 (1999), pp. 12–14.

For the historical background of the papacy's role in Italian politics, including the war years, see *Italy* by Elizabeth Wiskemann (Oxford: Oxford University, 1947); *The United States and Italy* by Henry Stuart Hughes (Cambridge: Harvard University, 1979); and *A Concise History of Italy* by Christopher Duggan (Cambridge: Cambridge University, 1984).

Among books by Italian authors on the Vatican during the war, one must include: *Il Vaticano e la guerra (1939–1940)* (Vatican City: Libreria Editrice Vaticana, 1960) and *Roma città aperta* (Ancora: Milan, 1962), both by Alberto Giovannetti; *La resistenza in Roma* by R.P. Capano (Naples: Gaetano Macchiaroli, 1963); *Pio XII e il nazismo* (Turin: Borla, 1965) by Luigi Castiglione; and *Pio XII, Hitler e Mussolini. Il Vaticano fra le dittature* (Milan: Mursia, 1988) and *Il Vaticano nella seconda guerra mondiale* (Milan: Mursia, 1992), both by G. Gariboldi Angelozzi.

The Archivio del Centro di Documentazione Ebraica Contemporanea in Milan (ACDEC) has published numerous studies on Italian Jewry, including *L'Occupazione tedesca e gli ebrei di Roma: Documenti e fatti* (Rome: Carucci, 1979), edited by Liliana Picciotto Fargion, a collection of important (if uneven) essays and documents on Rome's Jews during the German occupation; see also Fargion's *Il libro della memoria: Gli Ebrei deportati dall'Italia (1943–1945)* (Milan: Mursia, 2002).

For a guide to the immense archival resources detailing every aspect of the Italian antifascist resistance, see *Roma e Lazio: 1930–1950: guida per le ricerche: fascismo, antifascismo, guerra, resistenza, dopoguerra*, edited by Antonio Parisella, et al. (Milan: Franco Angeli, 1994). The historical society known as "Irsifar" (Istituto Romano per la Storia d'Italia dal Fascismo alla Resistenza) has been gathering documentary material pertaining to the nine months of the German occupation. It is an immense task, and it will take many years to catalogue and publish the entire archive (known as the "Archivio Dorer"); but the project is being supported by the city of Rome, and a selection has been put out on CD-ROM, along with a book of related essays, *Documenti della Resistenza a Roma e nel Lazio* (Rome: Biblink, 2001).

Any study of wartime Italy should include the memoirs of two prominent Italian statesmen of the time: Ivanoe Bonomi, a former prime minister who took refuge in Catholic churches during the German occupation of Rome, and Pietro Badoglio, the temporary head of the Italian government after Mussolini's removal from power in July 1943. See Bonomi's *Diario di un anno: 2 giugno 1943–10 guigno 1944* (Milan: Garzanti, 1947) and Badoglio's *Italy in the Second World War: Memories and Documents*, translated by Muriel Currey (Oxford: Oxford University, 1948).

Giacomo Debenedetti, an Italian Jewish scholar who survived the war years, wrote two important monographs, which have since become classics: *October 16, 1943* (on the Nazi roundup of Rome's Jews) and *Eight Jews* (on the Ardeatine Cave Massacre). Though neither deals with the Church at any length, they do provide gripping accounts of the terror encompassing Italians at that time. They have been republished under one cover: *October 16, 1943 / Eight Jews*, with a preface by Alberto Moravia (South Bend: University of Notre Dame, 2001).

The many writings of Giovanni Miccoli on Italian fascism, anti-Semitism, the Holocaust, and the Vatican—particularly his *I dilemmi e i silenzi di Pio XII* (Milan: Rizzoli, 2000)—have been praised for their balance and intelligence, but readers nevertheless should be aware of the author's omissions and erroneous assumptions, particularly in regard to Nazism. *First Words: A Childhood in Fascist Italy* by Rosetta Loy (New York: Metropolitan, 2000) is a popular autobiographical work by one of Italy's leading novelists and journalists; unfortunately, Loy's memoir is actually a left-wing polemic against the Church, derived from very shoddy history and intellectual rebellion.

Similarly, two works that have received praise are *The Italians and the Holocaust: Persecution, Rescue and Survival* by Susan Zuccotti, and Daniel Carpi's *Between Mussolini and Hitler: The Jews and the Italian Authorities in France and Tunisia* (Hanover: University Press of New England, 1994). Both authors are noted Holocaust scholars but are unreliable on anything relating to Pius XII or the Vatican. Sam Waagenaar's *The Pope's Jews* and Dan Kurzman's *The Race for Rome* are two popular accounts dealing with the German occupation of Rome, but are profoundly inaccurate in many respects, especially regarding Pius XII.

In contrast, Jonathan Steinberg, author of *All or Nothing: The Axis and the Holocaust: 1941–1943* (New York: Routledge, 1990) commends the Holy See: "The Vatican acted consistently and intensively to save Jews. As a sign of solidarity, the Papal nuncio to the Italian state, Monsignor Borgongini, paid not one but two visits to the largest concentration camp for foreign Jews in mainland Italy at Ferramonti-Tarsia in Calabria. He interceded . . . to save the Jews of Split in mid-February 1943, and the following month to prevent the Jews of the Italian zone of France being consigned to the Germans" (p. 80). *Jews Under the Italian Occupation* by Leon Poliakov and Jacques Sabille (New York: Howard Fertig, 1983), shows how the Italians acted to thwart Nazi efforts against the Jews. A valuable work of primary documents is *Il Nazionalsocialismo e la Santa Sede* by Michele Maccarone (Rome: Studium, 1947); Maccarone, an Italian priest and eyewitness to the events he describes, documents the deadly struggle between the Holy See and Hitler throughout the Third Reich.

War in Italy 1943–1945: A Brutal Story by Richard Lamb (New York: St. Martin's, 1993) is an exceptional military study by a World War II veteran, which calls Pius XII's record against the Nazi regime "impressive" and credits him with saving many lives. *Rome '44: The Battle for the Eternal City* by Raleigh Trevelyan is an engaging work with an excellent bibliography. *The Jews in Fascist Italy: A History* by Renzo de Felice is a revised English translation of de Felice's classic history. Also valuable is Cecil Roth's *The History of the Jews of Italy* (Philadelphia: Jewish Publication Society, 1946).

Italo Garzia's *Pio XII e l'Italia nella seconda guerra mondiale* (Brescia: Morcelliana, 1988) relates Pius XII's efforts to restrain Italy from entering the war and then prevent it from emulating the worst aspects of the Nazi regime. A leading Russian historian, Evghenija Tokareva, has also written an acclaimed book on fascism, Nazism, and the Catholic Church in Italy that praises Pius XII: *Fashizm, tserkov' i katolicheskoe dvizhenie v Italii: 1922–1943 gg.* (Moscow: In-t vseobshchei istorii RAN, 1999). For an English language summary, see "New Studies Document Pius XII's Opposition to Nazism," Zenit News Agency, March 15, 2000.

Two collections that can be recommended with only minor reservations are *The Italian Refuge: Rescue of Jews During the Holocaust*, edited by Ivo Herzer (Washington: Catholic University, 1989—containing an exceptional bibliography), and *Uncertain Refuge* by Nicola Caracciolo. Alexander Stille's *Benevolence and Betrayal: Five Italian Jewish Families Under Fascism* (New York: Simon and Schuster, 1991) shows how the Italian clergy typically assisted persecuted Jews, but is uninformed about Pius XII's record in this regard (it does, however, have an excellent select bibliography).

Alexander Ramati's popular *The Assisi Underground* (New York: Stein and Day, 1978) recounts events in wartime Italy from the perspective of Father Rufino Niccacci, a Catholic priest-rescuer from Assisi, honored by Yad Vashem. The book is rather ambivalent about Pius XII—possibly because Niccacci died before the book's publication and the final product was left to (the somewhat biased) Ramati (who also wrote and directed the 1985 film of the same name). But in one key passage, Niccacci quotes Cardinal Elia Dalla Costa, the archbishop of Florence, whom he visited during the war, as crediting Pius for the rescue measures undertaken in Italy: "I've been in Rome long enough to understand the pope's position. Instead of making meaningless declarations that would only antagonize the Germans, perhaps even make them occupy the Vatican itself, he issued orders—to save Jewish lives. . . . We received his message loud and clear" (p. 50).

In Arturo Sbicca's film documentary, *Assisi in Silence* (2002), numerous survivors describe how a hidden network operated—"under secret orders by Pope Pius XII"—to save endangered Jews. The film also reveals how Father Niccacci, after the war, wanted to create an ecumenical house of prayer, called "Pius XII House of Recognition," that would symbolize how Jews and

Christians could coexist, and would honor the "fatherly work of Pius XII" exhibited during the Holocaust.

More information on Pius XII's humanitarian efforts in conjunction with those of Italy's wartime bishops—particularly Cardinal Dalla Costa (of Florence), Cardinal Pietro Boetto (of Genoa), Bishop Giuseppe Placido Nicolini (of Assisi), Cardinal Ildefonso Schuster (of Milan), and Bishop Antonio Santin (of Trieste)—can be found in their various biographies and writings.

For recent documentation—including evidence of Pius XII's personal involvement in these rescue measures—see "Jewish Refugees in Rome: I Was There" by Father Vincent Zarlanga, *Vocations and Prayer Today*, April–June 2000, p. 15; "Nun's Past a Slice of WWII History" by Ashley Parrish, *Tulsa World*, February 4, 2001 (recounting the extraordinary testimony of Sister Mathilda Spielmann on how she and a group of German nuns in Rome helped 800 persecuted Jews out of Nazi-occupied Europe with a letter of authorization from Pius XII; her testimony is archived at the University of Tulsa library); "The Evidence is There" by Sister Margherita Marchione, *Inside the Vatican*, July 2001, p. 24; Sister Domenica Mitaritonna's sworn declaration asserting that the Vatican explicitly commissioned her convent during the war to rescue persecuted Jews, in *Consensus and Controversy* by Sister Marchione, p. 55; "Italian Officer Saved 300 Jews From Extermination in 1943: Priest Commissioned by Pius XII Had a Key Role," Zenit News Agency, November 12, 2001; "Israelis Honor Religious for Helping Jews During the Holocaust: Brother Stablum Saved 51 From the Nazis," Zenit News Agency, November 27, 2001; "Israel Proclaims Ursuline 'Righteous Among the Nations': Pius XII Helped Nun who Saved 103 Jews During Nazi Occupation," Zenit News Agency, December 22, 2002; "Nissim, il ragioniere che salvò 800 ebrei: E Bartali portava in bici i documenti falsi" by Francesco Alberti in *Corriere della Sera*, April 3, 2003, p. 20; and an English summary of the latter article, "Pius XII's Directive Helped Save 800 Jews in 3 Cities, Papers Reveal: Pope Told Catholic Groups to Assist Those Fleeing Nazis," Zenit News Agency, April 8, 2003.

See also "Film Financed by Vatican Saved Jews During War: Planned Delays Helped Spare 300 From the Nazis," Zenit News Agency, August 20, 2003; "Roman Parishes Helped to Save Jews During War," Zenit News Agency, September 26, 2003; "Israel to Honor Cloistered Nun for Wartime Aid," Zenit News Agency, October 31, 2003; and especially "Jesuit Journal Cites New Evidence that Pius XII Helped Save Jews" by John Thavis, Catholic News Service, December 4, 2003—a summary of Giovanni Sale's "Roma 1943: occupazione nazista e deportazione degli ebrei romani," *Civiltà Cattolica* 2003, volume 4, pp. 417–429. The latter article, based on newly released diaries and letters, shows how Pope Pius XII worked with Father Giacomo Martegani (Jesuit director of *La Civiltà Cattolica*) and Monsignor Alfredo Ottaviani (later a cardinal and head of the Vatican's doctrinal congregation) to rescue persecuted Jews.

In 2002, two previously unknown letters, written on the official letterhead of the Vatican's secretariat of state, were discovered, offering further evidence that Pius XII explicitly ordered his subordinates to assist Jews. Written to the wartime bishop of Campagna, Giuseppe Palatucci, the first letter, dated October 2, 1940, is signed by the then-Cardinal Secretary of State Luigi Maglione, who states that he is enclosing 3,000 lire; in so doing, Maglione explains that he is acting on the explicit orders ("*ordinato*") of Pius XII, who desires the money be given to assist all those being persecuted on account of their race ("*razza*").

In the second letter, signed by Maglione's assistant, Giovanni Battista Montini (the future Pope Paul VI), another check is sent to Bishop Palatucci, this time for 10,000 lire, and Montini, like Maglione, makes clear that he is acting on the order ("*venerato ordine*") of Pius XII, who is sending the money for the suffering Jews in the diocese. Montini mentions Jews by name ("*ebrei*"), and without regard to whether or not they were baptized. For more on these remarkable letters, see "Two New Documents Prove Pius XII Helped Persecuted Jews" by Antonio Gaspari, online edition of *Inside the Vatican*, January 23, 2003, and the more extensive commentary in the February 2003 edition of *Inside the Vatican*, "Uncovered: Correspondence of Pius XII," pp. 14–16. See also "Pius XII Gave Instructions Specifically to Save and Protect Jews," Zenit News Agency, January 29, 2003, and "'Hitler's Pope' tried to help Jews, say documents: Pius XII is accused of ignoring the Holocaust, but two newly printed letters suggest otherwise," *Sunday Telegraph*, February 16, 2003, p. 31.

The texts of both letters first appeared in the book *Giovanni Palatucci—Il poliziotto che salvò migliaia di ebrei*, published and edited by Italy's Department of Public Security (Rome: Laurus Robuffo, 2002), pp. 130–133. The reason the book was published by the Department of Public Security was that Giovanni Palatucci was an Italian policeman who died in Dachau in 1945 (having been sent there by the Nazis in 1944 for protecting Jews). Giovanni was the nephew of Bishop Giuseppe Palatucci of Campagna. For more on Giovanni Palatucci, who is now under consideration for sainthood, see "La Shoah e Giovanni Palatucci: L'avvio della Causa di beatificazione" by Piersandro Vanzan, S.J., *Civiltà Cattolica* 2003, volume 1, pp. 149–158, and "Cause Under Way for Policeman who Saved Jews," Zenit News Agency, October 14, 2002.

For the Vatican's assistance to escaped prisoners of war in Italy, spearheaded by Monsignor Hugh O'Flaherty, see *Be Not Fearful* by Lieutenant-Colonel John Furman (London: Anthony Blond, 1959); *Rome Escape Line* by Samuel I. Derry (London: Harrup, 1960); and *A Vatican Lifeline* by Major William Simpson (New York: Sarpedon, 1995), who comments: "Diplomatic circles in the Vatican had long known that the possibility of Hitler ordering General Wolff's Waffen SS in Italy to invade the Vatican and abduct Pope Pius XII to Liechtenstein or Germany was very real. For months the Gestapo and the SS Command in Rome had been accumulating evidence of activities which would be construed as breaches of Vatican neutrality. One vivid example was Monsignor O'Flaherty's organization" (p. 186). For O'Flaherty's own biography, see *The Scarlet Pimpernel* by J.P. Gallagher (New York: Cow-ard-McCann, 1967). See also "Vatican Aided Britons: 3 Escaped Prisoners, Now in London, Tell of Adventure," *New York Times*, June 10, 1943, p. 3. *A Spy in Rome* by Peter Tompkins (New York: Simon and Schuster, 1962) is of related interest, recounting the true story of an American agent smuggled into Rome at the dangerous climax of the German occupation. Patrick Gallo's *For Love and Country: The Italian Resistance* (Lanham: University Press of America, 2003) is a comprehensive and outstanding account of the resistance movement, which Gallo clearly shows included Pius XII and the Vatican.

10. Poland

The most important wartime study is *Pope Pius and Poland*, published by the Jesuits at America Press in New York City in 1942. An excellent early article, published during the war, is "The Pope Is a True Holy Father to Poland's Stricken People," *America*, September 12, 1943, pp. 622–623. Also worth reading are "Silenzi e parole di Pio XII per la Polonia durante la seconda guerra mondiale" by Angelo Martini, *Civiltà Cattolica* 1962, volume 2, pp. 237–249, and Robert Graham's *The Pope and Poland in World War Two*.

See also "Polish Charges Against Pius Rebutted," *New York Times*, June 1, 1967, p. 8, on the evidence from the Vatican's archives demonstrating how the pope supported persecuted Poles. For historical background on the events leading up to the war, see "Poland and the Holy See, 1918–1939" by Neal Pease, *Slavic Review*, Fall 1991, pp. 521–530. For a modern commentary on the beginning of the war, see David Alvarez's "The Vatican and the Fall of Poland" in *The Opening of the Second World War*, edited by David Pike (New York: Peter Lang, 1991). See also Manfred Clauss, *Die Beziehungen des Vatikans zu Polen während des 2. Weltkrieges* (Köln: Böhlau, 1979).

During the war, some Poles criticized the Vatican. But as Giuseppe Warszawski convincingly argued, this criticism was uninformed and unfair and directly attributable to antipapal propaganda. See his "Una prima tappa della lotta contro Pio XII nella Polonia durante la seconda guerra mondiale," *Civiltà Cattolica* 1965, volume 2, pp. 435–446; "Una tappa imprevista nella lotta contro Pio XII in Polonia durante la seconda guerra mondiale," *Civiltà Cattolica* 1965, volume 3, pp. 313–324; and "I veri autori dell'azione antipapale in Polonia durante la seconda guerra mondiale," *Civiltà Cattolica* 1965, volume 3, pp. 540–551.

In her memoirs *Il Destino passa per Varsavia* (Bologna: Cappelli, 1949), Signora Luciana Frassati Gawronska, an Italian married to a prominent Polish diplomat, mentions how she was personally received by Pius XII in private audience and describes the pope's deep concern for the Poles. Indeed,

Vatican officials made constant efforts to assist the persecuted in Poland, but were continually rebuffed by the Nazis: "The Vatican has informed the Polish government in London that repeated approaches have been made to the German Government concerning the terrible ill-treatment of the Poles in prison and concentration camps. The Vatican's demand that Polish Bishops and priests now interned should be released has been refused once more by Hitler" (*Tablet*, July 25, 1942, p. 43; see also the earlier report, "Vatican Lends Aid to Poland's Cause," *New York Times*, February 4, 1940, p. 66).

Richard Lukas's *The Forgotten Holocaust: The Poles Under German Occupation, 1939–1945* (revised edition New York: Hippocrene, 1997) is excellent on the suffering of Catholic Poles, but limited on Pius XII. Alexander B. Rossino's *Hitler Strikes Poland: Blitzkrieg, Ideology, and Atrocity* (Lawrence: University Press of Kansas, 2003) is also an important work, detailing Nazi atrocities against Catholics as well as Jews. Bedrich Hoffman's *And Who Will Kill You?* (Poznan: Pallottinum, 1994) provides an exhaustive list of Polish clergymen who suffered—and often died—under the Nazis; it is a powerful antidote to those who accuse the Polish Church of mass collaboration with the Nazis.

More attention is now being paid to the enormous sacrifice of Poland's Catholics during the war. Shortly after a ceremony honoring the countless Jews slaughtered by the Nazis in Poland, Jach Fuchs, a survivor of the Auschwitz concentration camp, said: "In Poland, Catholics were also the object of hate and persecution from the Nazis. . . . Another memorial to remember so many Catholics murdered for opposing the barbaric Nazi regime should also be built. . . . In Poland, Nazism not only targeted Judaism, but also Russians and, of course, militant Catholics" ("Catholics, Jews Both Victims of Nazis Says Jewish Leader," *Catholic World News*, May 29, 1998).

David Engel has studied the Polish government-in-exile—which occasionally made inaccurate comments about the Vatican's attitude toward Poland—in two books: *In the Shadow of Auschwitz: The Polish Government-in-Exile and the Jews, 1939–1942* (Chapel Hill: University of North Carolina, 1987) and *Facing a Holocaust: The Polish Government-in-Exile and the Jews, 1943–1945* (Chapel Hill: University of North Carolina, 1993). While these works are debatable interpretations of the Polish experience, they should be read for the wealth of information they provide.

A recent study of the wartime pope and Poland is Alesandro Duce's *Pio XII e la Polonia (1939–1945)* (Rome: Studium, 1997); it has been well received, and can be read in conjunction with more general works, such as *Poland, 1939–1947* by John Coutouvidis and Jaime Reynolds (New York: Holmes and Meier, 1986). Ronald Modras's *The Catholic Church and Anti-Semitism in Poland, 1933–1939* (London: Routledge, 1999) is an important work, and Norman Davies has written an excellent popular history in his two-volume *God's Playground: A History of Poland* (New York: Columbia University, 1984).

The controversial *Neighbors* by Jan Gross (Princeton: Princeton University, 2001), has attempted to blacken the reputation of Catholic Poland, based upon a 1941 massacre of Jews, allegedly engineered by Polish Catholics along with Nazis in the town of Jedwabne. Recent scholarship has shown the book's accusations against Poles (as distinct from the guilty Nazis) to be seriously flawed (see "The Jedwabne Massacre" by Wlodzimierz Redzioch and Richard Lukas, *Inside the Vatican*, November 2001, pp. 62–65).

11. Romania

In many respects, Romania represents a textbook example of the Vatican's concern for the persecuted during the Holocaust. The Holy See was quite active on behalf of the Jews of Romania, particularly through its heroic representative, Archbishop Andrea Cassulo, who has been proposed as a "Righteous Among the Gentiles," to Yad Vashem for his life-saving activities. As soon as Romania's brutal dictatorial regime, led by Marshal Ion Antonescu, allied itself with Nazi Germany and began employing Nazi racial measures, Cassulo objected with dramatic force. He protested Romania's decision to deport Jews, welcomed Jewish converts into the fold as a legal means of defending them under the terms of the Holy See's concordat with Romania, visited interned Jews and brought them assistance, intervened for orphaned Romanian Jewish children, and worked tirelessly with Romania's Jewish leaders for the reduction of anti-Semitic measures.

As *Actes et Documents* reveals, Cassulo's activities were carried out with the closest collaboration of Vatican officials, including Pius XII, with whom Cassulo met in the fall of 1942 and who gave him financial aid. Even John Morley, who is quick to find fault with any Church official, says of Cassulo, "the Jewish community . . . considered him their greatest ally in time of peril, and it was to him that they gave the credit for the safety of the majority of Romanian Jews" (*Vatican Diplomacy and the Jews During the Holocaust*, p. 47).

Indeed, both during and after the war, Romania's Jewish leaders, particularly Alexander Safran, the chief rabbi of Bucharest, were effusive in their praise of Cassulo and the Church; see Safran's *Resisting the Storm, Romania, 1940–1947. Memoirs*, edited by Jean Ancel (Jerusalem: Yad Vashem, 1987). For additional documentation, see Angelo Martini's "La Santa Sede e gli Ebrei della Romania durante la Seconda Guerra Mondiale," *Civiltà Cattolica* 1961, volume 3, pp. 446–463; "The Vatican's Endeavors on Behalf of Rumanian Jewry During World War II" by Theodore Lavi, *Yad Vashem Studies*, 5 (1963), pp. 405–441; *Three Popes and the Jews* by Pinchas Lapide, pp. 162–169; David Herstig's extraordinary tribute to the Church in *Die Rettung* (Stuttgart: Seewald, 1967); and *La Romania Nella Diplomazia Vaticana 1939–1944* by Ion Dumitriu-Snagov (Rome: Pontificia Università Gregoriana, 1987). For background, see *Romania: A Profile* by Ian M. Matley (New

York: Praeger, 1970) and *The Holocaust in Romania* by Radu Ioanid (Chicago: Ivan R. Dee, 2000).

12. Slovakia

For the historical background, written from a modern Slovakian perspective, see *A History of Slovakia: The Struggle for Survival* by Stanislav J. Kirschbaum (New York: St. Martin's, 1995), and three earlier works: *A History of the Czechoslovak Republic, 1918–1948* by Radomir Luza and Victor S. Mamatey (Princeton: Princeton University, 1973); *Slovakia: A Political History, 1918–1950* by Joseph A. Mikus (Milwaukee: Marquette University, 1963); and *History of Modern Slovakia* by Jozef Lettrich (New York: Praeger, 1955).

The Vatican has been accused of tacitly supporting the notorious priest-politician Jozef Tiso, who collaborated with the Germans during the Holocaust. But the available evidence demonstrates just the reverse. On the day Tiso was chosen as the first president of the Slovak Republic (September 26, 1939) the Vatican released a statement opposing the move. Expressing its "grave misgivings" and warning it would corrupt the relationship between Church and state, the Holy See pointed to the Nazi connection: "Owing to Slovakia's subservience to Germany it is not doubted that President Tiso will have to visit Berlin and most likely be seen and even photographed with Chancellor Hitler, whom the Vatican regards as a persecutor of Catholics. . . . It was recalled in this connection that the Vatican, prompted by a similar consideration, refused to sanction the appointment some months ago of a priest as Ambassador to the Holy See from a South American Republic, and the candidate had to be withdrawn" ("Tiso Chosen as First President of Slovakia; Vatican Frowns on Priest as Head of State," *New York Times*, October 27, 1939, p. 1). The very next day, the pope issued his first encyclical letter, *Summi Pontificatus*, which excoriated racism, totalitarianism, and extreme nationalism. See *New York Times*, October 28, 1939, pp. 1, 9. Of note is that the encyclical was seized at the Czech border by the Nazis; see the *Tablet*, December 16, 1939, p. 693.

George Creel says of Tiso's Slovakia: "What followed was strictly according to the Nazi pattern. Persecution of the Jews and imprisonment of every democratic voice; the creation of an Iron Guard to shoot down strikers and saboteurs; the Germanization of the school system; the expropriation of property, the confiscation of grain and foodstuffs; and the dispatch of Slovak youth to the Russian front. From Rome came the thunders of the Holy Father, denouncing these outrages, but Tiso paid no heed" (*War Criminals and Punishment* [New York: Robert M. McBride, 1944], p. 113). For more, see *Dr. Josef Tiso and Modern Slovakia* by Anthony X. Sutherland (Cleveland: First Catholic Slovak Union, 1978).

Not all Catholics in Slovakia were so blind. During the war, Jacques Maritain commented, "Recently, the Catholic prelate Paval Machàcek, vice-president of the Czecho-Slovak State Council, said in a broadcast to the Slovak people: 'It is impossible to serve simultaneously God and the devil, and it is equally impossible to be at the same time a good Christian and an anti-Semite.' Therein he echoed a more solemn voice, the voice of Pope Pius XI, saying: 'Anti-Semitism is unacceptable. Spiritually, we are Semites'" ("Atonement for All," *Commonweal*, September 18, 1942, p. 509).

The first authoritative—and still best—article on Slovakia, citing all the primary documents, was published by Father Fiorello Cavalli, "La Santa Sede contro le deportazioni degli ebrei dalla Slovacchia durante la seconda guerra mondiale," *Civiltà Cattolica* 1961, volume 3, pp. 3–18. Livia Rothkirchen's earlier *The Destruction of Slovak Jewry* (Jerusalem: Yad Vashem, 1961) is also an important work, as are her subsequent essays: "Vatican Policy and the 'Jewish Problem,'" *Yad Vashem Studies* 4 (1967), pp. 27–53; and "The Churches and the 'Final Solution,' in Slovakia" in *Judaism and Christianity Under the Impact of National Socialism*, edited by Otto Dov Kulka and Paul R. Mendes-Flohr, pp. 413–422.

Both Cavalli and Rothkirchen compliment Pius XII and his representative Giuseppe Burzio for opposing the deportation of Slovakian Jews. In a letter to the Slovak government on May 5, 1943, Pius XII explicitly condemned "the forcible removal of persons belonging to the Jewish race. . . . The Holy See would fail in its Divine Mandate if it did not deplore these measures, which gravely damage man in his natural right, merely for the reason that these people belong to a certain race" (translated by Anthony Rhodes, *The Vatican in the Age of the Dictators*, p. 347; for the original protest, see *Actes et Documents* 9, pp. 275–277).

Yeshayahu Jelinak has written an important article on the subject, "The Vatican, the Catholic Church, the Catholics, and the Persecution of the Jews During World War II," pp. 221–255, in *Jews and Non-Jews in Eastern Europe, 1918–1945*, edited by Bela Vago and George L. Mosse (New York: John Wiley & Sons, 1974). Jelinak's article, "Dr. Josef Tiso and His Biographers," *East Central Europe* 6 (1979), pp. 76–84, also merits attention.

Denis Barton's monograph, *Fr. Tiso, Slovakia and Hitler* (Birkenhead: Church in History Information Centre, 1990), refutes many accusations about the Catholic hierarchy in wartime Slovakia. Similarly, clear evidence of the Slovak bishops' appeals for Jews is found in the *Tablet*, June 12, 1943, p. 283, and July 3, 1943, p. 8. Soon after the war, the *Tablet* reaffirmed that the Slovak bishops "did in fact, in accordance with the desire of the Holy See, make most emphatic public denunciation of the persecution of the Jews" (February 15, 1947, p. 108). But the definitive work on wartime Slovakia and the Catholic Church is *Holocaust in der Slowakei und Katholische Kirche* by Walter Brandmüller (Neustadt: C.W. Schmidt, 2003), a brilliant work, reproducing many archival documents in support of the Church never before published.

13.The Soviet Union and Baltic Republics

During World War II, over one million Jews perished in the Soviet Union and the Baltic states Lithuania, Latvia, and Estonia. Because the Soviet communists had already persecuted and suppressed Christians before the Germans invaded and began slaughtering Jews, the ability of the Churches to prevent or fight these atrocities was limited. As in all countries occupied by German forces, collaboration and betrayal did occur within portions of the local populace.

But considerable resistance and rescue efforts on behalf of Jews also took place, particularly among Jesuit priests. See, in particular, Vincent Lapomarda's *The Jesuits and the Third Reich*, especially chapter 5, "The Baltic States" (pp. 153–166), and chapter 6, "Russia" (pp. 167–178).

Morality and Reality: The Life and Times of Andre Sheptyts'kyi, edited by Paul Robert Magocsi (Edmonton: Canadian Institute of Ukrainian Studies, 1989), tells the story of the heroic head of the Ukrainian Catholic Church who protected many Jews during the most horrific of German slaughters. In *A Question of Judgment*, p. 16, Joseph Lichten comments: "A Dr. Frederic, a young German Foreign Office agent, was sent on a tour through various Nazi-occupied and satellite countries to feel out their reaction to the Germans. As Frederic wrote in his confidential report to the German Foreign Office datelined Berlin, September 19, 1943, his meeting in Lwow with the Ukrainian leaders and Metropolitan Sheptysky [*sic*] was far from heartening; the Metropolitan remained adamant in saying that the killing of Jews was 'an inadmissable act,' and Frederic comments, 'In this issue the Metropolitan made the same statements and even used the same phrasing as the French, Belgian, and Dutch bishops, as if all of them were receiving the same instructions from the Vatican." (Document CXLV, a-60, archives of the Centre de Documentation Juive, translated in Philip Friedman's *Their Brothers' Keepers* [New York: Crown] 1957, p. 212).

For general background, see *The Holocaust in the Soviet Union*, edited by Jeffrey Gurock and Lucjan Dobroszycki (Armonk: M.E. Sharpe, 1993); *The Black Book of Soviet Jewry*, edited by Vasily Grossman and Ilya Ehrenburg (New York: Schocken, 1981); and *The Jews in the Soviet Union since 1917* by Nora Levin (New York: New York University, 1988).

It should be noted that Stalin's record toward Jews was scarcely more humane than Hitler's. See *The Jews in the Soviet Union* by Solomon Schwartz (Syracuse: Syracuse University, 1951); *Stalin's War Against the Jews* by Louis Rapoport (New York: Free Press, 1990); and *Stalin's Last Crime: The Plot Against the Jewish Doctors 1948–1953* by Jonathan Brent and Vladimir P. Naumov (New York: HarperCollins, 2003).

14. Spain and Portugal

Franco, Spain and the Jews by Chaim Lipschitz (New York: KTAV, 1984) is a rabbi-historian's remarkable account of Spain's rescue of thousands of endangered Jews. Without excusing Franco's regime, Lipschitz estimates that the authoritarian leader helped rescue over 40,000 persecuted Jews during the war and believes that the Vatican exercised some influence on Franco. See also Richard Patee's *This Is Spain* (Milwaukee: Bruce, 1957), pp. 395–404, and Erik von Kuehnelt-Leddihn's account of Spain and the Jewish community in *Catholic World*, October 1956, both of which give details on Catholic Spain's protection of Jews during the Holocaust.

Spain, the Jews and Franco by Haim Avni (Philadelphia: Jewish Publication Society, 1982) is less reliable but has some favorable comments on Spanish rescue efforts. Also revealing is José Sánchez's "The Popes and Nazi Germany: The View from Madrid," *Journal of Church and State*, Spring 1996, pp. 365ff. The eminent Spanish scholar Vincente Carcel Ortí has, with Juan Shenk Sanchis, published an excellent work supporting Pius XII, *Pio XII: Defensor de los judios* (Valencia: Edicep, 2002); see also the Zenit News Agency story about the book, January 14, 2003, Spanish edition.

For general background on the complicated history of Catholic-Jewish relations in Spain, see William Callahan's magisterial two-volume work, *Church, Politics and Society in Spain, 1750–1874* (Cambridge: Harvard University, 1984) and *The Catholic Church in Spain, 1875–1998* (Washington: Catholic University, 2002). For background on Franco, see *Franco* by Brian Crozier (Boston: Little Brown, 1967); *Franco: A Biography* by J.P. Fusi (New York: Harper and Row, 1987); and the somewhat less balanced *Franco: A Biography* by Paul Preston (New York: Basic, 1994).

The Spanish Civil War by Hugh Thomas (1961; revised edition New York: Modern Library, 2001) is a classic work, fairly evenhanded. *Spain and the Great Powers in the Twentieth Century*, edited by Sebastian Balfour and Paul Preston (London: Routledge, 1999) is also worthwhile, as is *Spain Betrayed: The Soviet Union in the Spanish Civil War*, edited by Ronald Radosh, et al. (New Haven: Yale University, 2001). Wayne Bowen's *Spaniards and Nazi Germany* (Columbia: University of Missouri, 2000) is hostile to Franco's Spain, but Burt Boyar's remarkable work, *Hitler Stopped by Franco* (Los Angeles: Marbella, 2001), based upon a wealth of new evidence, unequivocally credits Franco with obstructing Hitler and rescuing many Jews.

An important book, correcting many errors on the Spanish Civil War, the Church, and Franco's relationship with Hitler, is *The Last Crusade* by Walter Carroll (Front Royal: Christendom, 1996). Two earlier works along the same lines are *Spanish Rehearsal* by Arnold Lunn (London: Sheed and Ward, 1937) and *A Catholic in Republican Spain* by Prince Hubertus Friedrich of Loewenstein (London: Gollancz, 1937). See also Peter C. Kent's "The Vatican and the

Spanish Civil War," *European History Quarterly* 16 (1986), pp. 441–464, and Vincente Carcel Ortí's comprehensive account of the terrifying anti-Catholic persecutions before the Second World War: *La persecución religiosa en España durante la Segunda República, 1931–1939* (Madrid: Rialp, 1990).

The British and American ambassadors to wartime Spain both wrote memoirs: *Complacent Dictator* by Sir Samuel Hoare (New York: Knopf, 1947), and *Wartime Mission in Spain 1942–1945* by Carlton J.H. Hayes (New York: Macmillan, 1946). Hayes, the American diplomat, describes Spain's support for persecuted Jews and other refugees, makes clear how the Allies supported these relief efforts (pp. 111–115), and states that whenever "we had to make representations at the Foreign Ministry" on behalf of the refugees, "we were notably seconded by the Papal Nuncio" (p. 115).

For an analysis of how neutral counties like Spain and Portugal reacted to Jewish refugees fleeing Nazi persecution, see *Neither Friend nor Foe: The European Neutrals in World War II* by Jerrold Packard (New York: Scribner, 1992). Among the most famous Portuguese rescuers of Jews was Aristides de Sousa Mendes, a devout Catholic who, as the Portuguese consul-general at Bordeaux, issued countless Portuguese visas to those fleeing Nazi invasions—including some 10,000 persecuted Jews. For more on this great man, who was intensely loyal to the papacy, see "International Jewish Group Honors Portuguese Catholic," *Pilot*, May 15, 1987; also *Never Again* by Martin Gilbert, pp. 48–49.

15. The United States

Pope Pius XII always had warm relations with the United States, as seen in *Pius XII and the American People* by Vincent A. Yzermans (Baltimore: Helicon, 1958), a collection of the pontiff's addresses to the United States.

During the war, the Vatican kept in touch with the American Catholic Church as well as the United States government; many of these exchanges are revealed in the correspondence between the Holy See and its apostolic delegate in Washington during the war in *Actes et Documents*. The apostolic delegate in Washington during the war was Amleto Cicognani (see the obituary "Amleto Cardinal Cicognani, 90, Dean of Sacred College, Dead: Ex-Apostolic Delegate to U.S. Was World War II Liaison to Roosevelt and Truman Plea for Rome's Safety," *New York Times*, December 18, 1973, p. 44).

Other major primary documents can be found in the State Department's series, *Foreign Relations of the United States* [FRUS]. As an example, see "U.S. Document Cites Stand of Pope Pius XII on Nazis," Religious News Service, June 18, 1964, reporting on U.S. diplomat Harold Tittmann's description of Pius XII's famous 1942 Christmas address: "Taken as a whole he thought his message should be welcomed by the American people and I agreed."

Other pertinent wartime material can be found in the United States National Archives and Records Administration in College Park, Maryland, but its documents should be read with a great degree of caution—and in light of other primary sources—as they were sometimes based upon inaccurate information. Many of the stories heard today about the Holy See's alleged involvement with Nazi war criminals are based upon proven forgeries—from bad American intelligence and money-making wartime propagandists—but still housed in the National Archives, misleading researchers who think they have come upon dramatic finds.

On the other hand, newly released declassified documents from the Office of Strategic Services have confirmed primary sources revealing Hitler's intense opposition to Pius XII. See "Pius XII Rehabilitated," Zenit News Agency, July 7, 2000, citing the remarks of intelligence expert Richard Breitman, who declared "Hitler distrusted the Holy See because it hid Jews" and because "the Vatican was on the side of the Allies."

Breitman's article "New Sources on the Holocaust in Italy," *Holocaust and Genocide Studies*, Winter 2002, pp. 404–414, comments on SS Chief Herbert Kappler's attitude toward the pope during the German occupation: "on October 27 [1943] Kappler retransmitted an earlier assessment [to his superiors in Berlin]: for a long time the Vatican had been assisting Jews to escape, and the population of Rome was turning increasingly anti-German. . . . Kappler would hardly have agreed with one recent author that Pius XII was 'Hitler's Pope.' As far as Kappler was concerned, the Vatican represented a hostile influence. This was undoubtedly what his superiors felt too." See also the extensive evidence, released under the Nuremberg Project at Rutgers University, relating to the Nuremberg war crimes trial ("The Case Against the Nazis," *New York Times*, January 13, 2002, p. D-7). One chilling document, "The Persecution of the Christian Churches," establishes the Nazi hatred for Christianity and its plan to subvert and destroy the papacy.

The activities of Monsignor Walter Carroll, an American priest from Pittsburgh assigned to the Vatican secretariat of state during the war, should not be overlooked. Among other things, Carroll served as Vatican liaison to the Allied forces during the conflict, traveling in areas of grave danger, and he is mentioned numerous times in *Actes et Documents*. It is said that he kept a diary and left behind other documents shedding light on the Vatican's efforts to defeat the Nazis and help the persecuted, but most of these private papers have not been located (or organized) yet. For the limited information we have about this courageous priest, see "Monsignor Walter S. Carroll, 1908–1950," a eulogy in *Resonare Christum: Volume 1, 1939–1959, A Selection from the Sermons, Addresses, Interviews, and Papers of Cardinal John J. Wright* (San Francisco: Ignatius, 1985), pp. 125–129, with related notes on pp. 395–396.

For a summary of the Vatican's relations with the American Catholic bishops during the war years, see "The National Catholic Welfare Conference: An Experience in Episcopal Leadership, 1935–1945," an unpublished 1987 doctoral dissertation at the Catholic University of America by Earl Boyea that describes the interaction of Pius XII and the American episcopacy during the war in their fight against totalitarianism.

America's Bishop: The Life and Times of Fulton J. Sheen by Thomas C. Reeves (San Francisco: Encounter, 2001) shows the close relations between Pius XII and America's most gifted Catholic speaker and teacher during the war. Sheen was a deadly enemy of anti-Semitism and racism who consulted the pope during the war for his anti-Nazi speeches. See especially Sheen's collections of these sermons: *War and Guilt* (Huntington: Our Sunday Visitor, 1941), *Peace* (Huntington: Our Sunday Visitor, 1942), and *A Declaration of Independence* (Milwaukee: Bruce, 1941)—all of which explicitly denounce Hitler, Mussolini, and Stalin, condemn anti-Semitism, and repeatedly invoke the teachings of Pius XII. See also the biography of Sheen's predecessor on American radio, Father James Gillis, who was also an outspoken enemy of racism, anti-Semitism, and Hitlerism: *James Gillis, Paulist* by James Finley (New York: Hanover, 1958).

The Cardinal Spellman Story by Robert Gannon (Garden City: Doubleday, 1962) is an indispensable work relating the life and legacy of one of Pius XII's closest American friends, who became the military vicar of the Armed Forces of the United States. It has a wealth of information not available elsewhere, including details on how Pacelli helped muffle the notorious anti-Semitic priest Charles Coughlin during his 1936 trip to America. Pacelli, both as cardinal secretary of state and as pope, was never close to Coughlin and refused to meet him. After Pacelli became pope, he worked with Father James M. Drought, vicar-general of the Maryknoll Fathers, in keeping Coughlin at bay. On this issue, see the gratitude of Admiral Lewis L. Strauss, a distinguished American Jewish leader, in his memoirs *Men and Decisions* (New York: Doubleday, 1962), p. 121.

The wartime archives of the various American Catholic dioceses are also a treasure trove of information. Pius XII's influence on the American episcopacy during the Holocaust was demonstrated at their annual meeting in November 1942, when the United States bishops released a statement declaring: "We feel a deep sense of revulsion against the cruel indignities heaped upon Jews in conquered countries and upon defenseless peoples not of our faith. . . . Deeply moved by the arrest and maltreatment of the Jews, we cannot stifle the cry of conscience. In the name of humanity and Christian principles, our voice is raised" (reprinted in *Catholics Remember the Holocaust* [Washington: United States Catholic Conference, 1998], p. 17; see also, *Our Bishops Speak: National Pastoral and Annual Statements of the Hierarchy of the United Sates*, edited by Raphael M. Huber [Milwaukee: Bruce, 1952] p. 113).

Ronald Rychlak comments that "the statement was made in cooperation with Pius XII, whom the bishops cited three times. In a letter to the bishops and archbishops, written at this time, Pius expressed his satisfaction with their 'constant and understanding collaboration'" ("A Lawyer Looks at History," paper delivered by Ronald Rychlak at Millersville, Pennsylvania, April 15, 2002). Rychlak discovered Pius XII's involvement in the papers of Cardinal Francis Spellman and cites in particular "Victory and Peace," the American bishops' pastoral letter of November 1942, published in the December 1942 issue of *Catholic Action*, pp. 8–10, and "Holy Father Extends Thanks to American Catholics for Aid," *Catholic News*, November 21, 1942.

The importance of Spellman's relationship with Pius XII for the Allies during the war is highlighted in "Cardinal Spellman" by Roger Butterfield, *Reader's Digest*, April 1946, pp. 30–36. In contrast, Gershon Greenberg's essay, "American Catholics During the Holocaust," *Simon Wiesenthal Center Annual* 4 (1987), pp. 175–201, while interesting and informative in parts, fails to give sufficient credit to Spellman and other Catholic leaders during the war.

For more on the coordination between Pius XII, the Roosevelt Administration, and the American hierarchy, see "Franklin Roosevelt and the Vatican: The Myron Taylor Appointment" by George A. Flynn, *Catholic Historical Review*, July 1972, pp. 185–187; *The Vatican and the American Hierarchy from 1870 to 1965* by Gerald P. Fogarty (Collegeville: Liturgical, 1985); and *This Confident Church: Catholic Leadership and Life in Chicago, 1940–1965* by Steven M. Avella (South Bend: University of Notre Dame, 1992). As Avella reveals, one of the key players in this alliance was Cardinal Samuel Stritch, the archbishop of Chicago, who had a collection of papal documents published during the war, *Principles For Peace: Selections from Papal Documents Leo XIII to Pius XII*, for which President Roosevelt personally thanked Stritch (*This Confident Church*, pp. 57–58). Background on American's wartime cardinals can be found in *Our American Princes: The Story of the Seventeen American Cardinals* by Francis Beauchesne Thornton (New York: G.P. Putnam's Sons, 1963).

For an important (if uneven) collection of essays on American relations with both Pius XI and Pius XII, see *FDR, the Vatican, and the Roman Catholic Church in America, 1933–1945*, edited by D.B. Woolner and R.G. Kurial (New York: Palgrave Macmillan, 2003). On this issue, see also *Roosevelt and Romanism: Catholics and American Diplomacy, 1937–1945* by George Q. Flynn (Westport: Greenwood, 1976). Joseph Persico's *Roosevelt's Secret War: FDR and World War II Espionage* (New York: Random House, 2001) contains interesting material on America's undercover operations and the Vatican.

Though disagreeing on tactics and strategy—particularly the policy of "unconditional surrender"—the Vatican and the Roosevelt administration were always cordial. On September 19, 1942, Myron Taylor, Roosevelt's personal representative to the Holy See, wrote a remarkable letter to the pope: "In the just war which they are now waging, the people of the United States of America derive great spiritual strength and moral encouragement from a review of the utterances of His Holiness Pope Pius XII and of his Venerated Predecessor. Americans, Catholics and non-Catholics, have been profoundly impressed by the searing condemnation of Nazi religious persecution pronounced by Pope Pius XI in *Mit brennender Sorge*; by the elevated teaching on law and human dignity contained in the *Summi Pontificatus* of Pope Pius XII; by the famous Five Points laid down in 1939 by the same Pope as the essential postulates of a just peace; and by the forthright and heroic expressions of indignation made by Pope Pius XII when Germany invaded the Low countries. Now that we are fighting against the very things which the popes condemned, our conviction of complete victory is one with our confidence in the unwavering tenacity with which the Holy See will continue its magnificent moral leading" (*Actes et Documents* 5, pp. 684-685). That the Catholic leadership cited papal teaching to oppose anti-Semitism and totalitarianism during the war is shown in the monograph, *American Democracy vs. Racism, Communism* by Monsignor John A. Ryan (New York: Paulist, 1941).

A number of authors have accused the Allies, Great Britain and America in particular, of having failed to take appropriate action to save as many Jews as was possible. Others have defended the Allies. Examples from the debate include *While Six Million Died: A Chronicle of American Apathy* by Arthur D. Morse (1968; reprinted Woodstock: Overlook, 1983); *The Terrible Secret: Suppression of the Truth about Hitler's Final Solution* (Boston: Little Brown, 1980); *Breaking the Silence: The Germans Who Exposed the Final Solution* by Walter Laqueur and Richard Breitman (Boston: Little Brown, 1986); *The Abandonment of the Jews: America and the Holocaust, 1941–1945* by David Wyman (New York: Pantheon, 1984); *The Jews Were Expendable: Free Diplomacy and the Holocaust* by Monty Noam Penkower (1983; reprinted Detroit: Wayne State University, 1988); *FDR and the Holocaust*, edited by Verne Newton (New York: St. Martin's, 1996); *Britain and the Jews of Europe, 1939–1945* by Bernard Wasserstein (London: Leicester University, 1999); the collection of essays, *The Bombing of Auschwitz: Should the Allies Have Attempted It?* edited by Michael J. Neufeld and Michael Berenbaum (New York: St. Martins, 2000); and *The Conquerors: Roosevelt, Truman and the Destruction of Hitler's Germany, 1941–1945* by Michael R. Beschloss (New York: Simon and Schuster, 2002).

For a forceful reply to these authors that also defends Pius XII, see William Rubinstein's *The Myth of Rescue: Why the Democracies Could Not Have Saved More Jews From the Nazis* (London: Routledge, 1997). Commenting on Walter Laqueur's suggestion that the Vatican has suppressed incriminating documents, Robert Graham observes: "We [the four Jesuit editors of *Actes et Documents]* had complete and uninhibited access to the Vatican's files. It is absurd and childish to suppose that the Vatican 'betrayed' the Jews. One sample of this idiocy is the statement of such an intelligent man as Walter Laqueur who in the *Terrible Secret*, page 57, says the secret telegrams of the Vatican will someday be revealed (presumably by some government which intercepted them). He has absolutely no basis . . . for such an allegation. And I can say that we published all the telegrams he predicts will be published" (personal letter, December 5, 1987).

About the Contributors

Joseph Bottum is Books & Arts editor of the *Weekly Standard*, poetry editor of the journal *First Things*, and author of *The Fall & Other Poems*.

John S. Conway is emeritus professor of history at the University of British Columbia and author of the standard work *The Nazi Persecution of the Churches 1933–1945*, as well as numerous articles dealing with the Holocaust and the churches.

David G. Dalin, an ordained rabbi, is professor of history and political science at Ave Maria University. He is the author or coauthor of five books, most recently *The Presidents of the United States and the Jews*.

Rainer Decker is director of the Department of History at the Studienseminar Sekundarstufe II in Paderborn, Germany, and author of *Die Paepste und die Hexen: Aus den geheimen Akten der Inquisition*.

William Doino Jr. is a Catholic author and commentator. A contributing editor to *Inside the Vatican*, he has published in such journals as *National Review*, *Modern Age*, and *Crisis*, and is now researching and writing a book on the Vatican's role during the Second World War.

Kevin M. Doyle, a graduate of Fordham College and the University of Virginia Law School, defends poor people charged with capital crimes.

Russell Hittinger is the William K. Warren Professor of Catholic Studies and research professor of law at the University of Tulsa, where he is chair of the Department of Philosophy and Religion.

Father John Jay Hughes, a priest of the Catholic archdiocese of St. Louis, is the author of ten books and several hundred articles and book reviews. Born in New York City in 1928 as the son and grandson of Anglican priests, John Jay Hughes served as a priest in the Episcopal Church himself for six years before becoming a Catholic in 1960 and a Catholic priest in 1968. Doctoral studies and teaching in Germany in the 1960s kindled his interest in the German Church struggle and the Holocaust.

Justus George Lawler is editor-at-large of the Continuum International Publishing Group and author most recently of *Popes and Politics: Reform, Resentment, and the Holocaust* and *Hopkins Re-Constructed: Art, Poetry, and the Tradition.*

Michael Novak, a theologian, author, and former United States ambassador, holds the George Frederick Jewett Chair in Religion and Public Policy at the American Enterprise Institute. His many books include *The Open Church* (1964), *The Rise of the Unmeltable Ethnics* (1972), *The Spirit of Democratic Capitalism* (1982), and *On Two Wings* (2001). In 1994 he received the Templeton Prize for Progress in Religion.

Ronald J. Rychlak is Mississippi Defense Lawyers Association Professor of Law and associate dean for academic affairs at the University of Mississippi School of Law. He is the author of *Hitler, the War, and the Pope.*

Robert Louis Wilken is the William R. Kenan Jr. Professor of the History of Christianity at the University of Virginia. His books include *The Christians as the Romans Saw Them* (1984) and *The Spirit of Early Christian Thought* (2003).